# Cases on Technologies for Teaching Criminology and Victimology:
## Methodologies and Practices

Raffaella Sette
*University of Bologna, Italy*

Information Science REFERENCE
**INFORMATION SCIENCE REFERENCE**
Hershey · New York

Director of Editorial Content: Kristin Klinger
Senior Managing Editor: Jamie Snavely
Assistant Managing Editor: Michael Brehm
Publishing Assistant: Sean Woznicki
Typesetter: Michael Brehm
Cover Design: Lisa Tosheff
Printed at: Yurchak Printing Inc.

Published in the United States of America by
Information Science Reference (an imprint of IGI Global)
701 E. Chocolate Avenue
Hershey PA 17033
Tel: 717-533-8845
Fax: 717-533-8661
E-mail: cust@igi-global.com
Web site: http://www.igi-global.com/reference



Library of Congress Cataloging-in-Publication Data

Cases on technologies for teaching criminology and victimology : methodologies and practices / Raffaella Sette, editor.
p. cm.
Includes bibliographical references and index.
Summary: "This book is for those involved in the planning, development and implementation of different teaching methodologies of criminology and victimology in the academic field, in the police academies and in victim support services"--Provided by publisher.
ISBN 978-1-60566-872-7 (hardcover) -- ISBN 978-1-60566-873-4 (ebook) 1. Criminology--Study and teaching. 2. Victims of crimes. 3. Criminology--Case studies. 4. Victims of crimes--Case studies. I. Sette, Raffaella.
HV6024.C37 2010
364.071--dc22
2009026287

British Cataloguing in Publication Data
A Cataloguing in Publication record for this book is available from the British Library.

All work contributed to this book is new, previously-unpublished material. The views expressed in this book are those of the authors, but not necessarily of the publisher.

## Editorial Advisory Board

# Table of Contents

# Detailed Table of Contents



This chapter suggests a theoretical and empirical approach that makes use of an integrated methodology from a criminological, sociological, psychological and psychiatric perspective, in order to analyze the personality of the perpetrator of the crime or to examine a witness in order to assess his credibility. In particular, the Psychiatric expertise pursues the objective of ascertain the mental state of a person in the moment when he committed the fact provided by law as a crime, he is charged, therefore his level of responsibility, or in order to attempt to understand his future behavior considering the evaluation of the possible existence of social dangerousness. After a close observation of the concepts of mental competence, imputability and social dangerousness, the chapter focuses on the analysis of some expert cases, by comparing different methods related to clinical psychology (interview, level test, personality psycho-diagnostic tests that can be used even in the criminological field, defined as applied, to which are attributed practical aims pursued with scientific means. Finally, it points out the importance of providing reliable, coherent and non labeling judgments about the subject who has been submitted to psychiatric expertise. To achieve this aim, the criminologist, with psychiatric or psychological training, has many rudiments at his disposal in order to make well-founded choices, by adopting a non judging scientific behavior, wondering both about the reason of the criminal's behavior and the help that can be supplied in order to adopt a suitable conduct in future.

The field of study (and the teaching) of the criminal sociology presents multiple aspects and shows itself at various levels, the methods to implement for the exploration of the numerous research leads that it conceals are multiple and varied as well. This case, as a rough guide, proposes some modalities of approach in this domain.



The state of a discipline—or, more simply, the state of a discourse field and the related academic practices—cannot be understood outside the historical framework of its national genesis. According to Mucchielli (2004), this 'broad picture' view of France suggests a three-period split: (1) paradigmatic assertions and the impossible transdisciplinary dialogue typical of the years 1880-1940; (2) the normative context of the years 1945-1975, and the fresh associations it brought about; (3) the renewed dissociation between professional rationales and transdisciplinary dialogue from the mid-1970s onwards, alongside the considerable development of social science research. Finally, the authors question the current situation and the renewed, politically motivated attempt at establishing criminology as a full discipline in France.



Although in Greece the publication of books of criminological interest began in the last decades of the 19th century, the subject of Criminology was introduced by Professor Konstantinos Gardikas first at Athens University in 1930 and, then, at Panteios School of Social and Political Sciences in 1932. Some years later, in 1938, the chair of Criminology and Penology was established at the University of Athens. The involvement of K. Gardikas along with three other European experts in the foundation of Interpol in 1923, also resulted in the creation of an important Branch of Criminological Services with many specialized research laboratories which is evolving constantly incorporating all of modern technologies. In our days, Criminology is taught mainly at the schools of Law and of Sociology. In spite of the absence of an autonomous Department of Criminology in the Greek universities, there is a special Section of Criminology in the Department of Sociology at Panteion University. In-depth concentration is obtained in the context of the postgraduate programs as well as through those for the Ph.D. Criminological research is conducted in the universities where some criminological laboratories or centers operate as well as in the National Center of Social Research and the Center of Safety Studies of the Ministry of the Interior, to name a few. The professional domain of criminologists has extended in recent years (administration of penal justice, prisons, agencies for drug addicts or juveniles and immigrants, prevention services). In spite of this, the job market is relatively limited in comparison to the needs of society.

## Section 2
## Criminology and Victimology: Operational Tools for New Social Problems



This chapter introduces the birth of the project named P.E.N.T.A.C.R.I.M.E. based on a dynamic teaching approach. The contemporary Criminology has to face today's complexity, then the Criminologist has to apply a multidisciplinary and interdisciplinary way of thinking to deeply understand the brand-new Criminal and Deviant phenomena. During the latest years Communication has gained a main role in human life especially about the group relationships. The author shows the philosophy, methodology and technology profile of this seminar project that can be represent a new and useful way to grasp the meaning of Media processes and Media technology in the so-called new Terrorism, the Global Terrorism. Thanks to the interconnection between technology mediated teaching and learning it is possible to create an open-source Knowledge model to be used as valuable tool both in research and practice field.



The advent of the GIS technology has revolutionized the traditional field of information and cartographic production. The GIS, indeed, enables the management of much more numerous and more complex data and it is able to overcome the static and the traditional two-dimensional cartography. The Geographic Information Systems (GIS), that is used in various fields and disciplines, represent, also, in the university research, a valuable tool for investigation. In criminology, in particular, it has facilitated, regarding the city of Bologna, on the one hand, a kind of crime mapping on the nature of the so called "petty crimes" within the jurisdiction of the criminal Justice of the Peace, and the creation of a city's map on which have been identified support centers for victims operating in them. The use of GIS software is the basis in order to realize and put into practice not only operational measures designed to combat and to prevent crime, but it is also of help to social control measures, to public policy and to security. To the end of ensuring public safety, nowadays, it is essential, to have a clear, spatial and graphics representation, of the high concentrations of crime areas and of the degraded ones, in which there is a greater likelihood that some type of crime is committed.

Despite the increasing number of child psychological, physical and sexual abuse cases, and the subsequent need for interagency interventions, professional knowledge about the dynamics, nature, strengths and difficulties of the integrated response to child abuse is not universal. In addition to this, training programs for the delivery of a multidisciplinary approach to child abuse cases has always received little attention. The purpose of this chapter is to describe the postgraduate training course "Assessment and treatment approach when handling child abuse cases and paedophilia", developed by the University of Modena and Reggio Emilia (Italy), as an example of a university based and multidisciplinary training to child abuse professionals. This program is aimed at assisting graduated communities' professionals - such as child psychiatrists, psychologists, social workers, educators, law enforcement officers, judges and lawyers - to develop evidence based strategies to respond to child abuse. First the training program will be presented, describing contents and methods used to facilitate critical reflection and analysis of practice/policy: lectures, case studies, work-groups and team-building, web-based and experiential learning. Furthermore, the impact on trainee knowledge, attitudes, and behaviors will be described and discussed on the basis of the existing literature. Barriers to multidisciplinary work such as work style and communication differences among professions, attitudes and behaviors toward children, will be also critically discussed.



The focus of this paper is to describe a case concerning the key role of security technologies to observe, describe and some way record teenagers' behaviors and social action at school, at home and in the daily life as a whole. A kind of security "public eye" to protect/control them is pivotal especially according to some High School Policies in Italy aimed to cancel each "blind spot" or "black hole" from the youngsters' daily life to facilitate cross double checking among parents, relatives, social networks and teachers. In Italy the deviance of youth is increasing and the crime cases involving very young boys, like baby gangs and teenagers working for organized crime are growing rapidly. Among robberies, theft, and dang pushing the juvenile criminality in the Campania Region (an Italian Southern Region) continues to represent a critical point in this society and is unfortunately increasing. The family plays a key role and inside it often baby gangsters, whose parents are completely unaware of what is happening in their children's lives. "Between school and family" is a project that aspires at tracing a connection between the school and the family thanks to the influence of new technologies and the way in which they influence the interpersonal relationships. What will be, for example, if every school place a fingerprint reader?



This chapter shows the production of a video documentary, realized to deepen the knowledge about actual interventions to assist the victims of a particular crime of international interest, namely the trafficking of women for purposes of sexual exploitation. The video documentary has been made in Italy and especially through a restricted area in the North of the Country, Emilia-Romagna region, where particularly widespread are the phenomenon and the heterogeneity of interventions brought against. The dynamics of trafficking and exploitation are described as well as the legislation on them and the interventions brought about in order to give the victims the chance to redeem from the condition of sexual exploitation. This part is accompanied with the step-by-step explanation of how the video documentary has been made. The relevant objective is to define the modalities used to set up the video, in order to examine part of the actual interventions aimed to defend the victims, and to underline how it represents a useful effective document for teaching the dynamics associated with this particular kind of crime.



Criminology attempts to explain the causes of crime using two different approaches: the anthropological and the sociological. The anthropological approach focuses on man as the author of crime, and seeks to determine the physical, psychological, motivational, and psychosocial factors, that may have led to the criminal conduct. The sociological approach, on the other hand looks at the macro social factors influencing the insurgence of crime. The problem of social control, namely the way in which a society is able to integrate individuals around a single coherent system of customs, traditions and norms, and thus guarantee community security is connected to the concept of social disorder. The concept of social disorder is also linked to that of marginality, characteristic of the immigrant condition: the loss of cultural roots and the lack of integration in the new cultural context places immigrants in the margins of society. Instances of social problems resulting were reported news broadcasts of events occurring towards the end of 2008 in Italy which suddenly brought to light a series of similar events, evidencing ever more frequent occurrences of racism and xenophobia. These episodes spoke for themselves. Evident as the light of day, it was no longer easy to conceal their true matrix. From the homicide of a Milan boy (from http://www.rainews24.rai.it/notizia.asp?newsid=85897) who had allegedly stolen a packet of biscuits, to the homicides of Castel Volturno immigrants (Castel Volturno is a Southern Italian little city) (from http://www.corriere.it/cronache/08_settembre_19/rivolta_castelvolturno_immigrati_de6698dc-8635-11dd-bef9-00144f02aabc.shtml), the violent Parma bashings, the injuries sustained by a young man from Ghana, and to those in Rome against a Chinese citizen. But this is not the end of the story. This study will analyze the Abba's homicide. Abba was a young man, an Italian citizen, and the son of Burkina Faso immigrants with Italian citizenship; he was born and grown up in Milan. The theoretical premises on which this case is based are those reported in victimology literature, it has been chosen for it's similarity to other cases of xenophobia and because it brings new insights to present notions existing within criminology and applied victimology, (such as concepts of social disorder and social fear), and as such constitutes a significant contribution to this field of study.



This case study looks at the postgraduate program in Criminology and Police Science at the Ruhr-

University Bochum, Germany. This practice oriented course of study is designed as a distance learning course (*blended learning*) and therefore focuses on techniques of e-learning. The case study describes the history of origins and examines the educational situation before this master's program was established and how an idea became reality. It is one of the very few possibilities in Germany to receive a deeper insight into criminology and police science. Despite the fact, that the students are all professionals and thus working mostly full time, the technical premises make a discourse possible as in on-campus programs. These innovative forms of learning are the focal point of the following case study. It is our aim to provide insight into how a master's program could be set up and to promote new concepts of e-learning in the field of criminology.

**Section 3**
**Criminology and Victimology: Disciplines that Look at the Professionals (of Teaching)**

**Chapter 12**
The Present Cybercrime: Operational and Instructive Experiences .................................................. 195
*Antonio Apruzzese, Italian National Police, Italy*

The preponderant role played by the computer means, which is the more and more direct aim of the criminal action through sophisticated computer technologies, incites to reconsider the classical criminological and victimological patterns. In fact, new kinds of criminality linked to the use of sophisticated computer technologies, which are taking up the state agencies in the activities of prevention and repression, have recently assumed aspects of great and worrying importance. So, the need to formulate suitable training course of the personnel of those police branch (Postal and Communication Police of the Italian National Police), specialized in countering the high tech crime, is becoming more and more compulsory.

**Chapter 13**
The Professional Training of the Italian Surveillance Magistracy: The Useful Knowledge of Criminology and Victimology for a Working Italian Prison System .......................... 202
*Giovanna Fanci, University of Macerata, Italy*
The Italian prison system is characterized by a sort of schizophrenia (Ferrajoli, 2000) due to two opposite principles of legal framework: the certainty of sentence and the re-educative purpose of imprisonment. The action of the Surveillance Judge (*Magistrato di sorveglianza)* – a relevant authority for the enforcement of a criminal judgment – takes its place in the heart of such tension. In fact, he must ensure a right implementation of the sentence and, at the same time, he has to attend that the sentence serving is realized in accordance with penal rules and, particularly, with the re-educative aim. Therefore this study will highlight the importance of professional training for serving sentences judges whose educational programming would provide for inputs of criminology and victimology studies. They supply the Surveillance Magistracy (*Magistratura di sorveglianza)* with cognitive tools to identify the right treatment program for the convicted personality and to promote a mediation process between offenders and victims.

This article introduces the main division within the police corps in Italy and explains some historical reasons and their different task. Then it is exposed the recent change of the local police from political evolution of the State and new tasks established by law. This fast translation entailed a new training of policemen and in few years many changes occurred. While analyzing what happened in these years and which choices were made, it is argued that local police well adapted to new role with flexible cultural instruments. Main school were organized to satisfy the need of standard training, but corps independence allowed to realize single efficient projects particularly needed. Conclusion is the appreciation of free training method for police subjects.



This chapter introduces the Italian experience about university in prison. Since ten years many faculties all over the country signed cooperation agreements with penitentiary administrations to pursue and realize the prisoners right to study at the highest levels. Prison management engage itself to warrant structural possibilities to study: quietly sections where prisoners can concentrate while preparing exams, entry license to professors and didactic materials, personnel engaged in monitoring detainees programs of rehabilitation through study. University carries out academic tutorship to support study careers and individual preparations to exams and degree. A bilateral connection links the two institutions: on the one hand, university forwards a service to warrant the prisoners' right to study. Prison, on the other hand, is an important matter of study for academics (particularly to specific branches: criminology, sociology of law, sociology of deviance, penal and penitentiary law, psychology). This paper offers a national survey about these experiences and concentrate about a specific case: the University of Turin inside the local prison, where Faculties of Law and Political Sciences forward, since 1998, a didactic project, with the involvement of professors and assistants in lectures and exams inside the prison. A specific section is reserved to a certain number of prisoners determined in carrying out a study program, till the degree. The aim is to examine how academic studies may be considered as a specific opportunity to put the rehabilitation ideal into practice, as the article 27 of the Italian Constitution asserts ("punishment must aim to re-education"). Education, combined with work, religion, leisure activity, sport and family contacts, is the means to pursue such function. The university involvement into these projects makes possible a better comprehension about life in prison and an active participation into implementation of detainees people's rights.

# Foreword
## Criminology and Victimology: Are We Teaching Social "Sciences" or Not?

### SOME OPENING WORDS

In my opinion the foremost credit of the casebook masterly edited by Raffaella Sette, Cases on Technologies for Teaching Criminology and Victimology: Methodologies and Practices, is probably that of admitting a lot of postgraduate students of criminology, victimology and sociology of deviance together with some leading scholars, both academics and lay persons, in the domain of the analysis of the latest changes that, despite their critical unsettlement, have been affecting penal policies from a standpoint that is cleverly not restricted to the Italian concern.

The choice of providing such a meaningful chance to the youngest learners, most of them attending the Ph.D. course in Criminology at Bologna University, to acquaint the scientific community with their research findings seems to me all the more remarkable because of its link to the scope – unfortunately as uncommon as the former one – of widening abroad the knowledge and scholarship of the Italian culture and higher education in the realms of criminology, victimology and law. At the same time they seize on the opportunity to deal with another criminological cultures, among them the French and Greek ones, which, despite their different background, share – even if in a very puzzling way – their roots with our culture, as Mucchielli recalls in the light of the criminal anthropology narrative and its endeavour to disentangle from criminal law. As a matter of fact evidence is provided for the different array of teachings bringing back to criminological sciences in the Italian Universities: at Medical School, formerly with Criminal Anthropology, then with Legal Medicine, set also at the Law School; by now in the light of autonomous degree curricula bringing back to Political Sciences, Psychology, Sociology and Educational Sciences.

In the following accounts the proposal of a problem solving approach, explicitly turned towards the public of security managers and operators and their standing vocational training as a hallmark of the present-day higher education, fits in with a theoretical and epistemological view regarding criminology precisely oriented to security management policies. Even so this suggestion does not leave out of the more "classical" socio-anthropological foreground, on the authority of the French and Italian secular tradition that dates back to the end of the 19$^{th}$ century: above all, it endeavors to join the various facets of the criminal phenomenon up in a comprehensive prospect which would – in Bessette's own words – "take into account the general economy governing human behaviors".

## IN VIEW OF THEORETICAL CRIMINOLOGY: FROM THE SOCIO-ANTHROPOLOGICAL ACCOUNT TO THE COMPARISON METHOD

While the sociological view chews over the macro social factors bearing upon the crime and scrutinizes how a coherent system of customs, traditions and social norms can be arranged to vouch for the community security the anthropological standpoint focuses on physical, psychological, motivational, and psycho-social factors that may affect the criminal behavior, so that each society undergoes different levels of crime and "fear" arising from the cultural domain, in a socially conveyed manner.

Every report argues over a conflicting macro sociological view, as maintained by the theoretical approach of societal reaction to crime and its leading explanations.

Therefore the strategies of deviant and antisocial behaviour prevention match the convict's resocialization claim, so that the typical victimological account has to be redefined in the light of social ties gathering, with respect to which the conflict attitude appears to be strongly decreasing.

By the way I would suggest thinking about a couple of issues. The ruling point is that empirical research has shown some significant correlations: firstly between urban decay and the weakness of social ties, opposite to the communal security; then between crime rate and urbanization; and at last between antisocial behavior and sense of insecurity (either the *fear of crime* as individual character or the *concern about crime* shared among the societal group). Vice versa, no significant correlation has been found between fear of crime and the (in case repeated) victimization process previously experienced.

How would it be consistent with the second point, that is "the prospect of crime and the likelihood of becoming its victim"? Or, as Romano remarks, "a phenomenon that is becoming more and more a defining feature of contemporary society", moreover deeply affected by value judgments ruled by local and government authorities to maintain an overall social order and strengthen social ties among the community.

I think we should mull over this belief, that appears to be overstated by some stereotypes that depict a sort of irrationality arising from the emphasized risk of victimization of women and elderly persons, above all if it would be associated with *actual* victimization that, according to several social surveys, apparently gathers in these populations, as opposed to the *true* uneven distribution of this type of risk, and in spite of its change in space and time.

The empirical research findings deny the outcome foregoing: to the contrary they highlight that fear of crime is more spread than effective victimization since the feeling of insecurity basically depends on social disorder, i.e. antisocial behaviors that break shared rules and social norms concerning the common resources management.

The following pages are helpful to glimpse that theoretical concerns of issues more involved in criminology and victimology intersect the needs of the vocational training. In fact the penal policies analysis cannot be (or appear) disjoined from the survey of several courses of professionalization, nor the review of professions institutionalization processes bringing back to social security setting can be left in the background, as shown by the French experience, the Fanci's account of the markedly sociological features and Piselli's report about the Italian local police vocational training as stated by the constitutional law enacted in 2001 appointing the Regions' Authority.

First of all it is about suggesting a reconstruction of legitimacy courses of criminological sciences and their relevant methodologies, up to a point that, strictly speaking, "criminology" cannot definitely act upon a "science" but rather a domain of research and applications or, as Sellin told some seventy years ago, "a science of synthesis".

Indeed it is the proper foreground where the formative needs of security workers can find a suitable account. It is a question of frequently uneven ways, marked by a continuous switch between law and sociology experienced somewhere and that at times – for example in France – has encompassed criminology into criminal law realm, in so far the former had to become ancillary to the latter, at least before the gap between law and social sciences has been filled in.

Such detachment from social sciences deepened as the incoming psychoanalytical approach was achieving. Afterwards, as everyone knows, the dialogue between criminology and social sciences began again in 1948, with the new series of the *Année Sociologique*.

Moving from a durkheimian interpretation of the criminal phenomenon referring to the social norms and social reaction, that is any rule infringement that breaks away from collective values, Bessette's study focuses on the action which entails the social reaction named "punishment" as the object of the criminal sociology and on its shift to criminal anthropology. In the author's view the socio-anthropological approach to crime – and its most relevant method, able to discriminate amongst *gesture people* and *speech people,* an interdependence that reflects the connection between the anthropological bases of the behaviour, learning theories and social practices – best applies to the regulation systems analysis in human societies. It does to the extent that a lot of "building blocks" – the processes governing social reactions, the rule codification arising from social structures, the institutions of social control (police, courts, prison authorities) functioning, the emerging statistical regularities or clusters that help to depict a structure of criminality as well as its evolution and to map either "criminogenic" areas or "sensitive" districts – gives an account of a sociogenesis fitting the misdemeanours, their cultural underpinnings and the ways to counterbalance social influences in various societies.

In a few words we have to put the issues, technologies and tools that criminological research supplies to security managers into the globalized framework of globalization and social, political and economic change; but, in spite of their usefulness, we do not think of new technologies from the organizational standpoint as means prevailing on the investigative activities purposes: otherwise the "syndrome" reported by Goldstein in 1979 would be undoubtedly reproduced.

## THE REALM OF SECURITY WORKERS BETWEEN COMMUNICATION AND NEW TECHNOLOGIES

Close to professional training and upgrading security workers ought to be absolutely aware of the duty they perform whenever they bring into practice public policies. Actually this role is often inherent to the administrative action management since it entails an explicit choice between penal and welfare policies. For instance it occurs when they entitle social workers to take charge of cases that look like antisocial behaviours instead of rape, sex, alcohol or drug abuse, family violence, child sexual abuse or disease, etc., referred to households that formerly have been (or on the contrary did not) cared for by professional social service on the "social control failure" groundwork.

To sum up I would like to give an outline of the issues at the core of each chapter. In this view I believe that the best thing to do would be to set all sections forth, even I am entirely aware of the fact that my choice expresses a subjective standpoint.

As is to be expected the authors have been concerned with a lot of subjects. Each of them is able to depict the skills every security worker needs for, but they focus altogether on three main issues: investigation techniques – see Balloni and Bisi and Bianchini and Sicurella – transnational organized crime and terrorism – see Apruzzese and Antinori – and intelligence-led policing with the social policies support – see Ricci Lucchi and Caffo, Forresi and Lepri.

In doing so I rely upon my synopsis being an interesting assessment of the most important expertise required within the security domain.

## Investigation Techniques

In their survey Balloni and Bisi depict some diagnostic tools for the analysis of the offender's personality referring to clinical psychology. Among them, the authors noticeably point out to the use of psychiatric report to scrutinize the mental state of the offender, to "predict" his future behavior and give direction about the penitentiary treatment in view of his "rehabilitation". Beyond that they discuss the objectivity of data which eventually rise from the diagnosis and the need of exploring every condition that has affected the offender's behavior. This framework, both theory and evidence-based, well establishes the clinical criminology discipline and its practice which aim at the individualization of penitentiary treatment.

Bianchini and Sicurella frame the crime mapping as investigative inquiry technique, and especially discuss the use of GIS (Geographic Information System) in criminology referring their case study to the GIS practice in Bologna to survey the so-called "petty crimes" and outline the crime size and space-time conditions for minimizing the victimization risk. By the way the cartographic approach to data representation has operated since Guerry's Social Cartography (1833); then it has become a hallmark of the human ecology approach at Chicago School in the 1930s. Since Parks and Burgess's work localization and characterization of the urban areas – i.e. the concentric model – have been depicted as districts where a lot of researchers have set deviant phenomena and social diseases owing to the weakness of social networks and ties both in the neighborhood and the community, in the light of the town spatial structure.

As stated by this well-known theoretical approach criminal activities gather into some definite urban districts. Assuming this theory-driven belief crime mapping matches suits to the raising probability of giving or taking criminal offences due to the cluster of deviant behaviors and/or social disease into a critical area.

## Transnational Organized Crime and Terrorism

Apruzzese abridges the transnational organized crime relating to high tech and computer related crime, the so-called cyber crime, connected to the telecommunication conveyance of financial flows, whose organizational structure is undoubtedly marked by a well-defined role boundary.

The author gives a detailed account of the action of receiving stolen goods, since in this criminal domain it has been undergoing a noteworthy change. Indeed he outlines the path of human resources training between the hyper specialization and the multi subject approaches.

In this foreground the postgraduate curricula in criminology ought to provide police trainees with the skill of getting in touch with the corresponding criminal investigation police departments abroad.

For his part Antinori's essay depicts communicative strategies of terrorist organizations and looks over the relative patterns. Then the author sets them within a very shifting framework of the economic, social and political change due to globalization. To this extent his point is that the media approach to terrorism acts as an important asset for the self-legitimacy of this phenomenon in the world-wide political system.

## Intelligence-Led Policing with the Social Policies Support

The Ricci Lucchi's review points out to the analysis of actions against women trade for sexual exploitation, both as stated by law and maintained through best practices arising from European countries.

According to its historical and cultural roots, since the Middle Ages this phenomenon has been dealt with a relief account that refers both to poverty and morality. This criminal behavior is a species from a genus «trade of human beings» managed by criminal organizations which by now critically affects immigration processes and prostitution from the victim's attitude.

The author dwells on the role of road units which theoretical background is a harm decrease policy which takes into account the burdensome appraisal of these phenomena. So we can use as a substitute for their description estimation data and accounts coming from relief associations which support women who have been victimized and report on successful rehabilitation paths experienced by women themselves.

In turn Caffo, Forresi and Lepri discuss the knowledge about child abuse since the 1960s, when it had shifted to a medical problem, up to now, mainly reporting a lot of new types of victimization, such as sexual exploitation, sexual tourism, ritual abuses, child pornography and sexual offences via the Internet, according to data arising from Police databases and non profit organizations, above all the 24 hours help line *Telefono Azzurro*, and testing a connection with psychological disorders experienced during the youth or adulthood. So abused and careless children ought to be considered a real population at risk since their higher rates of substance abuse, depression, and anxiety disorders, suicide, conduct and eating disorders and, as a rule, higher incidence of health problems in the grown-up persons who had been formerly victimized children in regard to the non-abused people.

The authors contend a multidisciplinary approach stressing the educational agencies concern in the management of suspected or plain child sexual abuse or neglect cases and its various risk factors, ranging from family to community levels, which is a complex process that calls for several professionals – whose expertise can be improved through the postgraduate training programs – and agencies intervention.

## THE INMATE'S RESOCIALIZATION FUNCTION: PRISON POLICIES CONCERNING HIGHER EDUCATION AND SPECIALIZED TRAINING

Firstly we look at prison policies through the lens of Fanci's essay. She handles from a distinguished theoretical standpoint the distinctiveness of the Italian *Magistratura di Sorveglianza* (both the Judge and the Court of Surveillance) into the framework of world-wide judicial systems, above all the common law ones, where the prison management is appointed to administrative agencies. As Italian scholars recognize, the judicial feature of the *Magistratura di Sorveglianza* deeply bears upon the structural and institutional dimension of the prison: so it appears to be a compelling domain of inquiry.

This typical form of control also affects the change of the punishment view: it is as much interesting as it deals with a decision making that entails some expertise – basically from criminology and victimology, as Balloni and Bisi argue in their analysis – to handle the offender's personality.

Looking at a twin matter Ronco portrays the higher education project in prison carried on by Turin University Political Sciences unit.

This pattern has been conceived as a suitable right set between the present inmate's realm and his sight for the future by means of the rehabilitation he has experienced meanwhile. This chance looks like an inmate's private asset, but at the same time it is useful to disclose both the prison world and organization towards the whole society. According to the higher educational project achieved at Turin University (even though in Italy at the moment another fourteen programs are being carried out) the author also sketches the drop out rate, that undertakes very uncommon features as opposed to customary undergraduates, such as move to another prison, release after the sentence expiry and admittance to steps substitute for detention.

Nevertheless, when we talk about "rehabilitation" function we should carry back to the Galtung's distinguished article, *The Social Functions of a Prison*. Some fifty years ago, the Norwegian highbrow urged to mark the rehabilitation function off the resocialization one, because "resocialization implies rehabilitation, *but the converse need not be true*".

We recognize that "[P]enologically and socially the most important fact is whether a released convict commits a new crime or not. If he does not, *rehabilitation* may be said to have taken place, but this is not the same as resocialization". The former "*may result from the disappearance of the illegal acts from the action-space*", while the latter "means that he [the released convict] abstains from criminal acts when these acts are in his action-space, but are excluded because of the constrains from anticipated personal sanctions".

Moreover in Galtung's view "the presence of the resocialization function on the manifest level serves, in our cultural climate, ...to make partly latent the culturally difficult function of retribution. Thus, what happens to prisoners in Norwegian prisons is now very often referred to by the prison authorities by means of the eulogism 'treatment'". Notice that in the prison policies province we still use both the language and understandings of the Norwegian scholar.

Galtung asserted that "resocialization can take place much in the same way as it continuously takes place in all primary groups. But this presupposes that the prisoner is offered other primary relations than those he can obtain in the prisoners' community – and the only possibility seems to be primary relations with the guards, and this is proscribed". So, according to his thesis, when we deal with the higher education programs enhanced inside the prison building, as suggested by Ronco, definitely we think about the resocialization function of punishment.

I mean the educational pursuit fulfils an "escape mechanism", as Galtung maintained in 1958: something that allows the inmate to run away the prison "world", even though not the prison community.

## TEACHING METHODS IN CRIMINOLOGY

Despite unlike ways of teaching this subject that have been experienced around European countries we can notice a thread: the troublesome start up of postgraduate programs in criminology. Such awkwardness – reported by Zarafonitou – has to deal with the way "the institutional framework for higher education and scientific research was shaped as well as the conditions which criminologists are called upon to confront as professionals".

To summarize educational methodologies on the one hand arise from the commonly accepted theoretical approach, on the other hand from the formative needs of the security managers and workers.

As a matter of fact the link between the postgraduate programs and the needs and requests emerging from the professional training field would be another common feature. Nevertheless the province of trained police officers does not meet a suitable appraisal with the criminology concern neither within the educational system and its formative curricula or the education and so-called "help professions" (above all psychology and social work) professional domains.

Further issue is the pivotal setting of the criminological teachings at law schools, where they perform as subjects subsidiary to criminal law, or else within sociologically oriented curricula, in line with the current beliefs and theoretical realm pointing out to the causes of deviant behavior.

Until today criminological teachings have been usually set within three key groups of subjects: the core of penal sciences, referring to law schools as organizational milieu; the domain of sociological sciences; the area of communication sciences.

This latter realm has been becoming more and more relevant on account of the analysis of "fear of crime" awareness and the enhancement of communicative and socially inclusive networks as suitable appliances to gather up people at risk and to manage the security problem. Provided that the police science was the prevailing criminological approach, the most favored features would be the police acquaintance with societal groups, the communicative patterns and the way the police itself is beheld by citizens. For instance Ziegleder e Feldmann-Hahn explain that "[T]he students become acquainted with the institutions of social control and prosecution. Further topics are criminal geography, crime and age, gender and nationality as well as repression and prevention".

As these authors portray an appreciable attention is paid to social sciences: not only to philosophy and psychology, but mainly at learning the police office in the background of several cultures and societies, according to the legal systems comparison, in keeping with the authority – the state or private agencies – appointed to training and education.

In so far the Greek establishment is the most surprising one because, in spite of the absence of a committed criminal investigation department or whatever intelligence-led policing, educational programs in criminology have been set up both at the School for Police Officers and at School for Correctional Officers, who will enter the prison staff, whereas, quite surprisingly, there is no course in criminology to attend at National School for Judges.

As shown by professional training at Bologna Local Police Department, where the technological innovation has affected the domain of people and traffic control, the Italian evidence, as stated by Piselli, is quite dissimilar. According to some Italian statutes in the author's view the enhancement of the local police joins to the institutional change of the political system from a State-oriented to regional and local oriented Constitution. As stated by regional law 21/2007 this connection also affects the professional training of local police officers owing to the centralization of this task in accordance with a standardized curriculum that comes up to a far-reaching training activity supported at the trade union level.

At length my purpose is to briefly deal with the use of criminal research findings in the domain of policy making.

I first notice that, notwithstanding the current criminological approach as penal-welfare model, the social and educational policies seem to be regarded as social control purposes just a result of the juvenile crime rate increase.

As long as the causes of this phenomenon – among them the acceptance by peers groups, the change of ways of life, and the exacerbated individualism – have been fairly well recognized, Passaro goes over the outstanding points of a proposal of preventing from the raise of violent behaviors by means of new educational and social models that ought to be brought into practice by family, school and the whole society.

The author outlines the educational project named "Between school and family" which targets are both to further the culture of compliance with social norms in line with a multidisciplinary approach to learning and to shape an educational network which should be able to keep in touch families and schools and to spur on children, their parents and teachers to communicate using new technologies for monitoring and supervising the teenagers' daily lives. The pivotal lines of the project point out to communication improvement and institutional change that aim at engaging local authorities with the planning of integrated social policies and bringing them into practice.

My second point is that, generally speaking, we can encounter a lack of interest in pure criminological research since its findings don't matter very much to state departments and policy makers who are involved in policy planning and its achievement. This is the Greek case, but also the French situation is quite unexpected.

In fact, as reported by Mucchielli, the vocational training in the security domain copes with the State-supported research centers, that not only centralize the scientific activity in the realms of juvenile delinquency, police hearing and victimological inquiries, but also engage in a deep political control over the knowledge production. The target of this control is the validation from the scientific standpoint of the contemporary French political system security trends.

Finally, if we think about the criminologist as an expert, his leading character would be the way he meets with some regulation patterns, that is: within the penal system in step with the enforcement of criminal judgments; and within the juvenile justice system, where he acts as social worker under the Ministry of Justice.

Last of all the criminologist broadly performs as a social scientist.

*Monica Raiteri,*
*Law School, Macerata University, Italy*

## REFERENCES

Brown, A. P. (2004). Anti-Social Behaviour, Crime Control and Social Control. *Howard Journal, 43*(2), 203-211.

Galtung, J. (1958). The Social Functions of a Prison. *Social Problems, 6*(2), 127-140.

***Monica Raiteri*** *is Full Professor of Sociology of Law, Crime and Social Change at Law School, University of Macerata, Italy; Dean of Unified Graduate Courses in Social Work, Theories, Cultures and Techniques for Social Work and Policy making and Planning of Social Service for People.*

# Preface
## A Look to the Recent Past and Projection to the Future

Criminology is a relatively young, dynamic, multidisciplinary and of synthesis scientific discipline (Fattah, 2008), whose aim is the study of the human being that comes into conflict with the society. In other words, it deals with, on the one hand, the examination of the criminal actions and those who perpetrated them, on the other hand, with particularly regard to the victimology, in order to analyze the crime victim figure and the methods employed for favoring his social readaptation in his own life environment.

Starting from this definition, in order to begin the preface of this volume concerning the criminology and victimology teaching in different fields and world areas, I would like to refer briefly to a speech presented in the 12th International Congress on Criminology that took place in Seoul (Republic of Korea) from the 24th to 29th August 1998.

The goal of this report (Sherman, 1998) was to relate a dream that projected a professor of criminology in the month of August 2098 to visit a big city which appeared, ten years ago as well as today, like a milk and honey land for the Criminology and the Victimology as well.

This professor, during the dream, was going to different institutional subjects, starting from the 'District Criminologist' of the police station, followed by the 'Prosecutor's Chief Criminologist', followed by 'Mr. XX, Ph. D., Licensed School Criminologist', with the 'Medical Criminologist' of the Department of Health', and last the 'Economic Criminologist' of the 'Department of Economic Development' of that city.

Among those professionals, by explaining their daily activities to the professor, whom, I say it again, was dreaming this job journey, pointed out how the criminology and the victimology also be the theoretical base to intervene operatively, starting from different perspectives, against the deviance or criminal actions (for instance, truancy from school, bullying incident, auto theft, burglary, armed robbery, arson, assault, murder) which were implemented in such oneiric city.

For instance, the professor of criminology was filled of wonder when the "Chief Criminologist" of the Prosecutors staff showed him the graphic that recorded the data concerning the results of a trial, lasted two years, about the sentences issued by each prosecutor of that city: "For each of the ten offense types, there were two bars. One showed the recidivism rates for cases assigned to short terms in jail. The other showed recidivism rates for similar cases given long terms in jail. The results were striking. For property offenses, the recidivism rates were lower with longer average jail terms. But for violent offenses, including assault and robbery, the recidivism rates were lower with shorter average jail terms" (Sherman, 1998, p. 47).

The professor asks to the "Chief Criminologist" to tell him the reasons of such excellent results. The latter points out that the active involvement of the crime victims is the basis of the prosecution and the apparent attention of the judges at the end of the 21st century, toward the results of the criminological researches that have been carried out by his staff. Actually, the outcomes, for instance, of some surveys concerning the recidivism rate, are applied afterwards by planning and using ad hoc intervention techniques.

Other pleasant surprises were reserved to the criminology professor during his oneiric journey in this futuristic city of the year 2098, at the end he woke up and he noticed that actually any of the imagined activities had been carried out yet, even so he would continue to hope that a tenth of the activities he dreamt at least would born in the recent past where he was plunged.

It was a recent past (I remember it was the year 1998) concerning a criminology that, developing among social sciences and judicial sciences, would had to cover a tortuous and difficult path, but behind the scientific disputes, would had to prove the social usefulness of its own knowledge, studies and empiric researches. (Picca, 1998, pp. 54-55).

It was a recent past where the results of a research where I collaborated personally, whose field of the criminology teaching programs in various degree or specialization courses offered in different countries of the world were collected and analyzed (Balloni, Bisi, Sette, 1998; Sette, 1998).

The conclusion of this research pointed out, on the one hand the need to train some experts in the criminological field, which in their workplace would deal with activities of prevention, repression and control of the deviance and crime, whose training was obtained within specific university course of study, but on the other hand, warned us against the fact that "although there are in some countries many university courses and institutionalized programs for security, these latter are not given their proper due. The students attending them quickly learn that, when it is time to apply for a job at a company, candidates with backgrounds in law enforcement or investigation enjoy a privileged position" (Bisi, 1998, p. 18).

It was at last a recent past where the information, obtained through researching various curricula in criminology, has led to the creation of a three-year undergraduate course for "Security and Social Control Operators" which started during academic year 1997-1998 at the Faculty of Political Science "Roberto Ruffilli" at the University of Bologna (Italy). Its purpose was "to offer training at university diploma level for the management of modern investigation, security and control strategies" (Bisi, 1998, p. 29).

## BACK TO THE PRESENT

During the last ten years from the first journey to the unreal city of the year 2098, the professor of criminology continues more frequently to plug in fabulous oneiric adventures because the condition of the branch of learning he loves studies and teaches does not provide him any comforting signs of evolution in the imagined direction.

In fact, he is plunged in a present time where:

The difficulty that the criminology continues to face in order to win fully autonomy is tangible, even scholars of criminology do not agree about the direction to follow in order to attain that goal. Nowadays some people are pointing out that, in many countries in the world, the criminology is in expansion both from the scientific point of view and as far as its institutional autonomy in the academic field is concerned (Garland, 2008), while others, in different contexts (like Italy, for instance), maintain that it still needs to acquire prestige and to free both its undeserved reputation, of European extraction, as an auxiliary branch of the criminal law and that, of American extraction, as subset of the sociology (Fattah, 2008, p. 168).

The labor market is not still ripe enough in order to open thoroughly to the placement of the criminological professions, so, as pointed out in the previous paragraph, when the "security" and the "investigation" are concerned, the firms prefer, for instance, to employ persons who have previous experiences in the police. Otherwise, a situation where the graduates in criminology suffer the (fair or unfair?) competition of the social workers (who had obtained a further qualification in criminology) when it comes to occupy a post in fields connected to the criminology (jobs working with marginal groups: homeless, street corner work…, social work, social aid, education and teaching) (Goethals, 2007, p. 26).

Few subjects attract more attention and give rise to numerous debates than those connected to the crime and the victimization. Unfortunately, those debates are very frequently based upon the emotions rather than the information and, in this domain, the criminology has to assume the role of professionals' educator able to study scientifically the criminal behavior, the criminalization and victimization processes, the role that is assumed by the security control in order to find different methods of intervention to solve different situations and problems (http://www.socialsciences.uottawa.ca). We cannot underestimate, however, that in relation to the growing attention due to the questions connected to the "citizen's security", the teaching of the criminology has a great success, but the danger is that this discipline act as "lark-mirror" to attract a large number of students interested in this discipline, who contribute to fill the coffers of the universities, without anticipating neither a formative offer that is up to expectations nor suitable professional insertion course.

With reference to Italy, among the academic world and the professional world, there is a lack of significant interaction through the different competent Ministries, which it would be important in order to promote a scientific and professional education acknowledged institutionally for the crime professions. In fact, the dialogue between University and other Ministries stopped in 2006 later on the change of the Government. It was a course that anticipated the project of a interdepartmental decree by acting in concert with the Secretary of State for Education, the Home Secretary, the Secretary of Justice and the Secretary of Agriculture, concerning the establishment of the classes of the three year degree course and the specialist degree course in crime and security sciences, in order to set the general criteria about the definition of the different university didactic training courses of experts in criminology, that is to say those who have professional and relational competence to operate in the security sector and to be able to analyze the criminal phenomena that are implemented locally, without neglecting the international perspectives (Balloni, A., & Bisi, R. & Sette, R., 2008, p. 40).

These considerations allow us to reflect on the present and to connect to Tony Peter's assertions, President of the International Society of Criminology, during his address delivered in the opening of the 15$^{th}$ World Congress on Criminology (Barcelona Spain – 20-25 July 2008), about the state of the criminology and victimology teaching skills in universities. In particular, he quoted that: "Challenging socio-economic and political developments urge criminologists to step forward as creative independent and critical scientists who contribute to a fast growing body of theoretical knowledge and socio-empirical academic research" (Peters, 2008, p. 12).

In fact, the future of the criminology as an autonomous discipline undoubtedly depends, among other things, on promoting its teaching in universities through well-defined courses to train future professionals in the prevention and reduction of crime in various settings (Balloni, Bisi & Sette, 2008).

Universities, police academies and the victim support services in many parts all around the world teach those disciplines in order to train professionals who are able to make decisions and to plan strategies in the wide fields of the law enforcement, of the crime prevention, of the criminal justice administration, of the crime victim services and of the security management.

This is to say that the criminology and the victimology become applied sciences whose activities are set between the art and the science, where the intuition in the choice of the methods affects the result. Since the aim is to refer not only to an epistemological outline, but also to a real outline of the everyday reality in which the professionals have to work in order to represent and to solve the problems.

It stands to reason that in front of the challenge that the globalization sends to our society, for instance, the growth of the need "for advanced knowledge about new forms of crime (fraud, corporate crime, organized crime, cyber crime…) and for a 'more appropriate approach' to crime" (Goethals, 2007, pg 21). Old and new challenges require, naturally, the scientific research development in the criminological and victimological domain, which are more and more studied in detail and methodologically correct, and consequently they produce new jobs.

Concerning this, in Belgium, "the Leuven Institute of criminology has been monitoring the professional position of criminologist-alumni of the Katholieke Univestiteit Leuven since 1980" by the transmission of a survey that focused on the different topics among them the "actual job situation" (Goethals, 2007, pg. 22-28). In particular, one of the object of this research was to understand if the ex students of criminology of this University really did a "criminological job". The collected data showed that "more than half of the respondents (57%) are employed in the criminological core-sector, and another 14% in area narrowly related to the criminological area. One out of three (30%) is employed outside the criminological and related professions" (Ibidem, pp. 24-25). In particular with regard to variation occurred during those years, this study pointed out that, from 1990, "the percentage of alumni employed in the core areas has strongly increased", even if inconsistently , passing from 29,4% of the period 1978-81 to 57% of the last years 2001-2004. The areas "police, youth protection, and corrections, including community sanctions" absorb the higher percentage of ex students of criminology that are employed in the "core criminological areas", while the criminology related areas give opportunities to operators who are involved in "marginal groups (homeless; street corner work…), social work, social aid, education and teaching" (Ibidem, p. 26).

The issue of this research, undoubtedly positive, has to be connected to the deed that, in Belgium, for instance, as regards the police, the figure of the criminologist is brought out because this institution also provides the employment of employees with degrees concerning the disciplinary area of the criminology, as inferred in the recruitment page of the Belgian Police's website (http://www.jobpol.be). In this way, it is possible to achieve a close connection between the University world, which trains the future criminologists, and the work, which needs specific competences.

This does not happen very frequently, as in Italy with regard to the criminology and the victimology, even if it has been pointed out recently that the "work culture should become more and more the integral part of the university culture": University has to be able to develop the abilities of the future graduates which are needed by the nation offering "a large range of basic knowledge useful to operate in a world that changes continuously, which requires comprehension skills in order to understand the reference contexts, the ability to make "problem diagnosis" and their solution, to be able to stand comparison with different cultures and techniques" (Moratti, 2003).

However, what usually happens in different countries, with regard to the "criminological jobs", as underlined at the beginning of this paragraph, is that the "employers are not familiar with the criminology degree" and "the competition with other types of social scientists for the jobs in the criminological job market is strong" (Goethals, 2007, p. 32).

So we agree with who ascertain that the criminology development, as independent academic discipline, and the contribution that it can provide to the professional training of the future criminologists, "is a function of the close collaboration between academics and policy makers through consulting and research, and vice versa through the hiring of policy makers for academic teaching. This close relationship is of utmost importance to narrow the gap between academia and the job market, and is one of the main conditions to create criminological functions" (Ibidem, p. 33. In this sense see also: Balloni, A., & Bisi, R. & Sette, R., 1998; Balloni, A., & Bisi, R. & Sette, R., 2008; Balloni, A. & Sette, R. (Eds.), 2000; Bisi, R. (Ed.), 1998; Bisi, R., 1999).

## OBJECTIVES OF THE BOOK

It is a well-known fact that the explanation and the social reaction against the crime are influenced by the historical and cultural context. So, didactic methodologies for criminology and victimology are subjected to continuous change in relation to theories and needs strictly linked to the criminological and victimological profession.

So the aim of this work is an ambitious one, in order to contribute to a decisive and sweet awakening of the criminology professor who, after the oneiric state wherein he fell in 1998, can find himself, even if it is not a condition of complete consciousness, he could be in a drowsiness state which prelude to a situation of a renewed fervor of activities where he will find out, with the Cartesian astonishment of "am I dreaming or awake?", the existence of the concrete possibility of:

To set up dynamic didactic course for the criminology and victimology teaching in the university field through different multimedia technologies and the interaction of means that are also employed both by the different branched of the sociology, as the urban sociology, and by professionals of the social control agencies.

To insert the criminology and the victimology in the domain of the educational courses of different professionals (Magistrates, Lawyers, Medical Doctors, penitentiary workers) that plan and carry out a course of help on behalf of sentenced subjects, detained in prison or in enforcement of a judgment in a measure alternative to the imprisonment, in order to provide them means direct to the activation of profitable collaborations, both with the different institutes and services that are present on the territory and with the victims of the crime, in order to formulate treatment programs which point out and respect to the individuality of each one (Bisi, 1990, p. 64).

In short, to propose, without preconceived ideologies, the development of the criminological and victimological discipline, with regard to his difficulties and his concrete possibilities to overcome those situations.

Therefore the aim of the book, by the contribution coming from different parts of the world of the researchers, academics and experts, to know the state of the art of the research in the criminology and the victimology and their teaching in order to analyze the significant role of those disciplines in the professionals' training.

The mutual exchanges among the points of view of the Universities with the Police Academies and the victim supports services are able to promote a reciprocal enrichment and to provide important information for a better training and to identify more precisely the needs imposed from the reality to the professionals that have to face the crime and the victimization answering to the actual challenges of the globalization and the rapid social change.

The book wants to study how the interaction among the culture and the academic research and the specific professional training needs of criminology and victimology experts start a positive interaction that is able to show new solutions.

The book develops through case studies that can observe, in a holistic and dynamic way, real teaching, training and research situations.

In particular, the goals of the book are:

- to provide a judicious mix of practical experiences and research in the form of case studies;
- to observe, in an holistic and dynamic way, real teaching and research situations of the criminology and victimology;
- to analyze the for and against of different teaching methodologies of the criminology and the victimology in the academic field, in the Police Academies and in victim support services;
- to be the point of reference for those whom, for various reasons, are involved in the planning, in the development and in the implementation of didactic programs.

## ORGANIZATION OF THE BOOK

The book is organized into fifteen chapters. A brief description of each of the chapters follows:

The chapters from 1 to 4 propose theoretical and empirical approaches, by using an integrated methodology from the criminological, sociological, psychological and psychiatric point of view for the analysis of the personality of a perpetrator of a crime or for the examination of a witness in order to assess his credibility.

The chapter 5 describes the use of a dynamic didactic approach, defined P.e.N.T.A.C.R.I.M.E. (Project on Electronic 'Ntensive Advanced Teaching for Criminological Research & Intelligence Era in Media) for the study of cases related to some terrorist organizations.

The chapter 6 shows the use of the GIS (Geographic Information System) in the domain of an academic research, for the implementation, with regard to the Italian city of Bologna, on the one hand, of a kind of crime mapping concerning the crimes defined petty offences pertaining to the penal justice of the peace, and on the other hand, for the creation of a city map whereon the victim support services which have been identified work.

The purpose of the chapter 7 is to describe the postgraduate training course "Assessment and treatment approach when handling child abuse cases and pedophilia", developed by the University of Modena and Reggio Emilia (Italy), as an example of a university based and multidisciplinary training of graduated communities' professionals - such as child psychiatrists, psychologists, social workers, educators, law enforcement officers, judges and lawyers – in order to develop evidence based strategies to respond to child abuse.

The focus of the chapter 8 is to describe a case concerning the key role of security technologies to observe, describe and in some way record teenagers' behaviors and social action at school, at home and in the daily life as a whole.

The chapter 9 presents the production of a video documentary, carried out in order to study in detail the intervention implemented in favor of the victims of a specific crime of international importance, in this case the traffic in women for sexual exploitation.

The chapter 10 analyzes the murder of a young man, an Italian citizen, born and grown up in Milan, son of a Burkina Faso immigrant with Italian citizenship.

Nowadays, digital identity theft (also known as phishing) has become one of the most lucrative illegitimate business. Pharming and keylogging are some of the latest and utmost sophisticated data processing techniques used by computer crime fraudsters. Latest entries are the "botnets", herds of infected machines. Organized crime is becoming more and more involved in this new high-tech crime world that can easily assure huge profits. The chapter 12 shows as the Italian State Police tries to respond more effectively to this new rising challenge.

The case study of the chapter 11 looks at the postgraduate program in Criminology and Police Science at the Ruhr-University of Bochum, Germany. This practice oriented course of study is designed as a distance learning course (blended-learning) and therefore focuses on techniques of e-learning.

The chapter 13 highlights the importance of professional training for serving sentences judges whose educational programming would provide for inputs of criminology and victimology studies. In particular this training course wants to provide to the surveillance magistrate appropriate cognitive means that, in Italy, has the duty of defining suitable treatment programs for the sentenced and to encourage some process of mediation between the perpetrator of the crime and his victim.

The chapter 14 dwells upon the need of professional training, in the criminological and victimological field, of the local police workers in Italy and it analyzes some courses which are given by the Local Police Academies.

The chapter 15 analyzes a peculiar situation wherein the University came in prison: the aim is to examine how academic studies may be considered as a specific opportunity to put the rehabilitation ideal into practice, as the article 27 of the Italian constitution asserts ("Punishment must aim to re-education").

## CONCLUSION

The book will contain many contributions by authors from different part of the world. The authors are leading researchers, academicians and practitioners in the field of criminology and victimology. The contributions span the entire spectrum of the field: from the research through the didactic methodologies (traditional learning, computer applications, and e-learning) for applied criminology and victimology.

To sum up I wish that this work can represent a valid convergence point of the state of the art of the research and the teaching of the criminology and the victimology.

## REFERENCES


Balloni, A., & Bisi, R. & Sette, R. (1998). La didattica in criminologia: l'evoluzione di una disciplina e l'esigenza di una professionalità. *Rassegna Italiana di Criminologia, IX* (1), 23-53.

Balloni, A., & Bisi, R. & Sette, R. (2008). Un parcours historique et évolutif de l'enseignement de la criminologie à l'Université de Bologne. *Rivista di Criminologia, Vittimologia e Sicurezza, II* (3), 32-43, from Italian Society of Victimology Web site, http://www.vittimologia.it/rivista/articolo_balloni_bisi_sette_2008-03.pdf

Balloni, A. & Sette, R. (Eds.). (2000). *Didattica in criminologia applicata. Formazione degli operatori della sicurezza e del controllo sociale*. Bologna: Clueb.

Bisi, R. (1990). *Operatori penitenziari a confronto*. Bologna: Clueb.

Bisi, R. (Ed.). (1998). *Criminology Teachings from Theory to Professional Training.* Bologna, Italy: Clueb.

Bisi, R. (1998). Criminology, Safety and Professional Training. In R. Bisi (Ed.), *Criminology Teachings from Theory to Professional Training* (pp. 15-21). Bologna, Italy: Clueb.

Bisi, R. (1999). Teaching and Professional Training in Criminology. *European Journal of Crime, Criminal Law and Criminal Justice*, *7* (2), 103-129.

Fattah, E. A. (2008). The Future of Criminology as a Social Science and Academic Discipline: Reflection on Criminology's Unholy Alliance with Criminal Policy & on Current Misguided Attempts to Divorce Victimology from Criminology. *International Annals of Criminology*, *46* (1/2), 137-170.

Garland, D. (2008). Disciplining Criminology? *International Annals of Criminology*, *46* (1/2), 19-37.

Goethals, J. (2007). The criminological profession: the development of a job market for criminologists in (Flanders) Belgium. *International Annals of Criminology*, *45* (1/2), 19-36.

Moratti, L. (2003). *Nuova università e mondo del lavoro*. Intervento del Ministro dell'Istruzione, dell'Università e della Ricerca Scientifica, Roma, Auditorium Confindustria, 29 gennaio. Retrieved from http://www.pubblica.istruzione.it/ministro/interventi/2003/universita_lavoro.shtml

Peters, T. (2008). Allocution du Président de la Société Internationale de Criminologie. *International Annals of Criminology, 46* (1/2), 11-17.

Picca, G. (1998). L'avenir de la criminologie en Asie et dans le monde. *International Annals of Criminology, 36* (1/2), 53-63.

Sette, R. (1998). Courses in Criminology in different parts of the world. In R. Bisi (Ed.), *Criminology Teachings from Theory to Professional Training* (pp. 24-29, 33-47). Bologna, Italy: Clueb.

Sette, R. (1999). *L'insegnamento della criminologia nelle Università e in altre istituzioni.* Bologna: Clueb.

Sette, R. (2004). Criminology online: an Italian Experience. *European Journal of Open and Distance Learning, II.* Retrieved from European Journal of Open and Distance Learning Web site: http://www.eurodl.org/materials/contrib/2004/Sette.html

Sette, R. (2007). Experimentation and challenge: on-line criminology at the University of Bologna (Italy). In R.C. Sharma & S. Mishra (Eds.), *Cases on Global E-Learning Practices: Successes and Pitfalls* (pp. 161-175). Hershey, PA: Idea Group Inc.

Sherman, L. W. (1998). Criminology and Crime Prevention in the 21st Century. *International Annals of Criminology, 36* (1/2), 43-52.

# Acknowledgment

The editor would like to acknowledge the help of all involved in the collation and review process of the book, without whose support the project could not have been satisfactorily completed.

Particular thanks to the members of the Editorial Advisory Board: Augusto Balloni, Bruno Bertelli, Roberta Bisi, Ernesto Caffo and Andrea Pitasi.

Most of the authors of cases included in this also served as referees for articles written by other authors. Thanks go to all those who provided comprehensive reviews.

Their critical comments, but constructive, about the chapters have been very useful and much appreciated.

Special thanks also go to the publishing team at IGI Global. In particular to Julia Mosemann, who continuously prodded via e-mail for keeping the project on schedule and to Jan Travers, whose enthusiasm motivated me to initially accept her invitation for taking on this project.

In closing, I wish to thank all of the authors for their insights and excellent contributions to this book. I also want to thank all of the people who assisted me in the reviewing process.

*Raffaella Sette*
*University of Bologna, Italy*

Section 1

# Teaching Criminology:

## Trends & Challenges

# Chapter 1
# Applied Criminology and Forensic Psychiatry:
## Cases and Practices

**Augusto Balloni**
*University of Bologna, Italy*

**Roberta Bisi**
*University of Bologna, Italy*

## EXECUTIVE SUMMARY

*This chapter suggests a theoretical and empirical approach that makes use of an integrated methodology from a criminological, sociological, psychological and psychiatric perspective, in order to analyze the personality of the perpetrator of the crime or to examine a witness in order to assess his credibility. In particular, the Psychiatric expertise pursues the objective of ascertain the mental state of a person in the moment when he committed the fact provided by law as a crime, he is charged, therefore his level of responsibility, or in order to attempt to understand his future behavior considering the evaluation of the possible existence of social dangerousness. After a close observation of the concepts of mental competence, imputability and social dangerousness, the chapter focuses on the analysis of some expert cases, by comparing different methods related to clinical psychology (interview, level test, personality psycho-diagnostic tests that can be used even in the criminological field, defined as applied, to which are attributed practical aims pursued with scientific means. Finally, it points out the importance of providing reliable, coherent and non labeling judgments about the subject who has been submitted to psychiatric expertise. To achieve this aim, the criminologist, with psychiatric or psychological training, has many rudiments at his disposal in order to make well-founded choices, by adopting a non judging scientific behavior, wondering both about the reason of the criminal's behavior and the help that can be supplied in order to adopt a suitable conduct in future.*

DOI: 10.4018/978-1-60566-872-7.ch001

## THE CRIME BETWEEN STEREOTYPES AND REALITY

In the field of criminological and psycho-sociological studies of the deviance, when we are referring to interpretative patterns or schemes of analysis, we can believe that they are linked to a particular way of defining the man, the rule, the violation and the social reaction. The different meanings, in accordance with the definition and the dealing of these terms, have different implications as far as the criminal policy is concerned, depending on the cultural-ideological orientation where they are included.

The classic school, developed in the politico-cultural milieu of the enlightenment, for instance, turns his attention to the rational assumptions of punishability and, starting from the free will principle, that is the man free in the choice of his own behavior, considers the subject accountable for his actions because the crime is a conscious and voluntary violation of the penal law. To the positive school, on the contrary, developed during the XIX century, in opposition to the rationalism of the enlightenment, the crime appears an unavoidable manifestation of determined causes and not an expression of the free and responsible choice from the subject.

In this perspective the perpetrators of crime should be subjected to social defense measures suitable to prevent further criminal manifestations, by their removal from the society and, as far as possible, their social reintegration.

Considering the man as provided of free will or, on the contrary, determined in his way to behave from several factors, implicates opposite consequences as regards the penal definitions and the judicial interventions.

Both the addresses prevent, however, the finalization of theoretical and operational means fit to consider the infringement as a process that is referred to a subject able to act actively upon the surrounding reality, but that is at the same time determined by it. The possibility of going over the dogma of the guilty as a moral being totally free in the choice of his actions or, on the contrary, the dogma of the offender as a being totally determined has been proposed again by someone in the man' s consideration as a social actor (Debuyst, 1990, pp. 21-23).

By the expression of social actor we intend to indicate a subject that doesn't represent an abstraction insofar as he is holder of personal opinions, that are directly linked both to the position in the social context he belongs to and his personal background and future plans. So it is a subject that interprets the surrounding reality and acts accordingly because it is continuously called to intervene towards a variety of social transformations, result of transitions, coming out from the action of several factors, interacting among themselves in and with the time.

In this evolution process we cannot neglect crime and delinquency phenomena that, especially in the last few years, are assuming very alarming features both for their general trend and for the manifestation of specific rises in some kind of crime. Actually, we are not only present to a quantitative but qualitative springing up of various kind of crime and deviant behavior that is supported by an even more hard definition of what is lawful and what is unlawful, even in those behavioral fields where these certitudes seemed now consolidated.

The Courts system continues, in fact, to suggest concrete problems to solve to those who, in different way, are interested in themes concerning criminality and deviance (Bisi, 2002, pp. 507-527).

## IMPUTABILITY, SOCIAL DANGEROUSNESS AND TREATMENT: PSYCHO-DIAGNOSTIC ORIENTATION

In particular, in the criminological field one of the most recurrent problems is that of establishing the mental state of the subject when the fact he was charged happened. The reference is addressed, especially, to the psychiatric expertise that, however, has a peculiar position because it never serves to prove if a fact subsists or not, but it serves to ascertain what is the mental state of the subject when the fact he was charged happened (Balloni, 1999, pp. 3899-3931). In particular the psychiatric expertise is not used to prove if a subject has committed a fact provided by law as a crime, but it serves to ascertain through which mental dynamism (with or without mental capacity or with a greatly diminished mental capacity) a subject has committed the fact to which the crime qualification is attributed. It is clear that, in the psychiatric expertise field, only the one who committed the fact provided by law as crime arouse interest; that is to say that as protagonist has got in touch with a rule of law and getting into such a relation gave rise, through signs, evidences or testimonies, such a connotation of his own behavioral style or peculiarities of the way he behaves in order to give rise to the hypothesis or conjecture of a psychopathological status or condition. These are situations that, even if they can be variously definable at the clinical level, can depict a partial or total mental disease (Semerari, 1975). Actually, the survey topic of the psychiatric expertise is an individual that has to be examined in relation to his psycho-physical state and in the field of the attributed criminal fact.

Now, it should be useful to make some concise comments on the imputability. Actually, according to the article 85 of the Italian penal code, in order that a subject can be charged and, therefore, liable to punishment, he must be in possession of "mental capacity". In the Italian penal system, in fact, the article 88 of the penal code (total mental disease) provides that "anyone who, when the fact has been committed, was, because of insanity, in a such mental state excluding the mental capacity, is not chargeable" and the article 89 of the penal code (partial mental disease) provides that "anyone who, when the fact has been committed, was, because of insanity, in a such mental state diminishing considerably, without excluding, the mental capacity, will answer for the committed crime, but the punishment will be reduced". Afterward we need, first of all, that the mental disease comes from a temporary or irreversible insanity, that it has caused such a mental state in order to exclude or to greatly diminish the mental capacity. Moreover, the total or partial, mental disease caused by the insanity, must subsist when the subject committed the crime. It stands to reason that the distinguishing criterion among the two kinds of mental disease, enforced by the above mentioned articles, appears merely quantitative and not qualitative: actually, in the hypothesis at the art.89, we use the expression "to diminish greatly ".

Then, in relation to the hypothesis contained in the provisions of the articles 88 and 89 of the penal code, we must specify that the notions of disease and insanity have to be kept separate from each other, because they do not coincide thoroughly (Balloni, 2004). The illness concept is less wide than that of insanity, and, if the first refers to a well individualized morbid state and susceptible of a determined evolution, the latter pertains to a function deviance that becomes an unsteady and aberrant function deviance from the norm. Referring to Schneider's classical concept – which the subject matter is addressed to - we identify the medico-legal notion of mental disease with the psychiatric one of psychosis, both acute and chronic in evolution (Portigliatti Barbos & Marini, 1964, p. 128-129).

From this point of view, those psychic alterations, believed originated from morbid somatic processes, known or postulated, that stop the normal continuity of the vital development, can be included in the term disease, because inside them we can find the abnormality, the dynamism, the need of diagnostic-therapeutic services and a repercussion of functional nature (general or local), peculiarities that have been attributed to those diseases, as, for instance, the encephalitis, but also the maniac-depressive psychoses and the schizophrenias.

Therefore, in the field of the causes that exclude the imputability and contribute to reduce the punishment, we have to define, that is to ascertain the mental state or to evaluate the level of the mental capacity when a crime is attributed to a person. Moreover, we also need to define the defendant's mental state when we are investigating because in presence of psychic disorders, that depict such an insanity that can influence on the mental capacity, can be the key element on the basis of a future behavioral judgment and an eventual social dangerousness should be established.

These investigations, after all, require the definition of the mental state of the subject when he became the perpetrator of the crime, sometimes even if it is not placed in recent former times, by stating precisely his mental state, in case we recognize him to be affected by a mental insanity, to deliver a judgment, that is a prognosis about the future behavior.

In order to reach such judgments, the inquiry means are those typically used in psychiatry, psychology and, in some aspects, of sociology because we have to attain a bio-psycho-social knowledge of the subject.

## METHOD AND ANALYSIS OF SOME CASES

The experience obtained through the analysis of some expert cases allow us to put in, now, an empirical approach by which it is possible and profitable to compare different operational ways to organize the subject's psycho-pathological structure. In reference to those methods (interview, level test, personality psycho-diagnostics) which are used in the clinical psychology, so methodologies that can be used even in the criminological field that we can define as applied. To the applied criminology we can attribute practical aims, pursued by scientific means, especially when we explore the personality of the perpetrator of the crime in order to evaluate his responsibility level and consequently the imputability, or in order to understand his future behavioral by evaluating the existence or not of social dangerousness, or when we are evaluating a witness to understand his credibility.

In order to provide an answer to questions pertinent to these problems, we need to collect the data and the signs and link them logically. So we can refer to different methods that, from the interview and the use of tests, are linked to the subject's handwriting personality examination having ascertained that the graphology, as branch of learning, is a mean to obtain personality knowledge (Bisi, 1992; Ceccarelli, 1998).

The possibility that the graphology can be included among the means we can use in order to focus the personality structure aptitudes and characteristics, points out the opportunity that it should be included in a " battery " test suitable to survey the subject's personality examined.

If the clinical examination is a technique, the test would often represent an inquiry moment either clinical or experimental. The whole is for the psychologists "a clinic armed with tests" (Raymond & Bornstein, 1988) in order to intervene over the problems concerning the *responsibility, the criminal etiology,* so the opportunity to outline the subject's personality features and provide an explanation of the facts and some useful suggestions about the *penitentiary treatment* in order to contribute to the rehabilitation of the guilty and his reintegration into social life and to the preventive danger measures in order to exclude the commitment of other crimes.

The possibility of operating making use of the contribution of several methods reminds, like a model, the<<circumstantial paradigm>>, that is the <<explanation model (common, for instance, to the psychoanalytic procedure and the police investigation>> that is based on the systematic research of significant signs, to find the event historical reconstruction and the identification of a guilty or a motivational source" (Bosinelli, 1982).

Within the different cases examined, using this methodology of complex technical investigation we will take the D.M.'s case into consideration, that has been charged of:

1. the crimes as set forth in art.81-575 of the penal code because he fired against S.R., R.G. and C.M., a lot of pistol shots which reached them in vital organs, inside the bar... causing their death. In.... December the 6th 1991;
2. of the penal crime as set forth in art.81cpv Penal Code 10-12 and 14 under the law issued on October 14th 1974 no.497 for being in unlawful possession and in implementation of the same criminal plan and having brought in a public place a 7,65 caliber common weapon. In... in the period before, after and next to December the 6th 1991.

On April 11th 1992, the authors of this essay have been appointed by the preliminary investigations Magistrate of the Court of Rovereto (Trento, Italy) so as to ascertain if D.M. had mental capacity or even if this capacity was, because of insanity, excluded or greatly diminished .

The prescribed time in order to respond to questions has been set within June 19th 1992. The experts, within this deadline, have examined carefully the records of the trial and they have detained the subject of the expertise giving to him the following mental tests: 1) Rorschach's test; 2) Wechlser's Adult Intelligence Scale (WAIS); 3) Handwriting personality analysis.

To pursue the aims of the handwriting personality analysis, handwriting tests collected in the trial dossier and others successively have been used. The subject of the expertise has been also examined from the somatic and neurological point of view and has been submitted, in the presence of one of the experts, to an electroencephalographic examination in the neurological clinic of the University of Bologna.

## Biography

D.M., born in ....on 1952, was detained in the District Penitentiary (*Casa Circondariale*) when the experts accepted the assignment, after the arrest of December 23rd 1991. On 04.21.1992 he was transferred successively and temporarily in the District Penitentiary of... in order to be submitted to the necessary verifications and examinations useful to complete the psychiatric expertise.

D.M. reported that at the time of the event lived in... Moreover he specified the his parents were both died: the father, farm worker, when he was 63 as a consequence of industrial accident, while his mother, diabetic, housewife and his father's assistant in agricultural activities, died in 1991, when she was 68, consequently to a fall that caused the fracture of the femur.

D.M. is the last of eight brothers, five males and three females. Among the males two death occurred: in fact, one brother who emigrated in... died when he was 44 because of an heart attack and the other died when he was 34 because a renal infection.

All the brothers are married and live in... excepting two sisters who live in... The subject of the expertise denied any neuropsychiatric defects in ascendants and collaterals. He reported he was born within the term of an eutocia and he had normal psychophysical development. He did not attend the nursery school and when he was 5, after his father's death, had been sent to a boarding school where he could not apply to study diligently, because he was homesick and "he always thought to his mother".

He lived in this boarding school till 11 years old, he was always successful student obtaining the elementary school leaving certificate. The subject attended the junior high school in...within the boarding school...where he succeeded the first two years; during the third year he escaped because he got bad, since he was hit anytime he transgressed.

When he was 14 he started working as blacksmith in the native country for few months, then he went away abroad with his eldest brother. The first time he came back in Italy, he worked as manual worker, in... in a telephonic facilities firm. He stayed until he was 16 after then he went again abroad working firstly for the railroad, then, with a brother, in a motor firm for two years and finally, as car-breaker, in a car recycling.

After a period of about six years where D.M. stayed away from Italy, he came back when he was 22 in order to do his national service. Once he was discharged, he decided to study as to obtain the driving license to drive the trailer trucks and, in order to bear the expense, he worked as farm worker.

The driving license obtained, he started working as truck driver.

The subject was single and father of a child of 12, born from the life in common with A.F., a prostitute, mother of two children, who he lived with for few years. A.F., during the family life with the subject, has never practiced the prostitution and she told to the subject that she has been forced to the prostitution by her husband. The dispute with the cohabitant started when A.F.'s daughter decided to leave the school and "to bring home" the guy that she had an affair with. If her mother agreed, D.M. objected. In this way the relationship started wasting to the point that the subject had some rage reactions, afterward he grabbed A.F.'s neck so violently that she was injured. Moreover he was charged of domestic violence and rape against the partner. Afterward she withdrew the charge and D.M. was released after less more then 40 days imprisonment. Then he begun to work again in the firm...and he was forced to live on the truck the firm entrusted him, because he did not have any domicile.

This situation protracted for three months, when he met S., the girl that run the nightclub where the trial event took place. The girl, defined as "beautiful and showy" by D.M., did not have the parents, her mother died when she was 11, while her father died one year before she met D.M.

A pensioner helped her in the running of the club; he trafficked in jewelry and he exhibited them to the customers because they offered them as a gift to S. in order to have some sex.

During 1989, D.M. started an intense affair with S., and she proposed him the opportunity to leave his job as truck driver as to devote themselves to the running of the nightclub. Nevertheless, short time later, he noticed that S. loved to be courted by all the customers and D.M., very fond of the girl, endured particularly even because any time he beard evidence of frustration and disappointment for such a situation, the pensioner, that D.M. caught petting with the girl, unfailingly reminded him that to love S. he had to tolerate her unfaithfulness two or three times per month.

The subject stated that he was forced to leave the work in the nightclub, to begin after to work as truck driver, because he had never got from S. any wages even if he worked fourteen, fifteen hours per day.

In that time the girl found herself in straitened circumstances because, after a father's car accident in which there were some injured, the insurance was willing to indemnify the damages only partially. So, S. revealed to D.M. that she feared that the club could be seized and he, again, in the face of her despair, resigned in order to begin again to work in the night.

This continuous hesitation among different occupations happened several times, since the subject stated that he changed, within two years and half, height workplaces.

During a weekend, D.M. called the girl telling to her that within a couple of days he would have joined her. When he arrived, S. introduced him her "new boy friend". The subject went away the club, continued to do transports but, fifteen days later, he passed in front of the club and saw the pensioner, S. and her new friend. In this lapse of time he remembered that there was a toy pistol of his child in the truck, he seized it and, with it, threatened the girl as to demand an explanation about the real reason that drove her to live him.

Subsequently, a night in September 1991, he called her to ask her when he could go in order to pick up his personal belongings. The girl answered the she would go personally to him as to give them back, adding, afterward, that her boyfriend, that he was present during the call, was very sorrowful and he seemed understand that S. would left him very early. In fact, that was what happened: S. accompanied D.M. in his journeys abroad promising him that they would soon get married.

The subject defined this period as particularly happy, "a real paradise" that, however, finished very soon. In fact, a night, coming back from one of his work trip, D.M. noticed that in the nightclub there was a new guy, C.M., with which S. seemed to be on familiar and confidence term.

C.M. sneered at D.M. telling him that he would soon have taken his place in S.' life, making him jealous. This situation continued for a few time, till a night, around half past one, D.M. came back in the club and caught them (C.M. and S.) behaving lovingly. On this occasion, C.M. took a stick and hit D.M., who knew that there was a pistol in the club, he took it and fired firstly to C.M. and then to R.G. (the "old man"). Concerning this, he told that he remembered a strong clouding of consciousness after the fact and that he discovered S. died in his arms.

During the two following weeks he worked as usually did, then he tried to call the night club repeatedly, and having no answer, he decided to call a friend who told him what happened and, consequently S.' death.

Now D.M. came to know from newspapers that he was wanted, he stated that he called the 'Carabiniers' who arrested him in a motorway restaurant, at the motorway exit…D.M., once he has been taken to the 'Carabiniers' Station, he told that he slept several hours because he took, before the arrest, the contents of two bottles of sleeping pills.

## Somatic Examination

The subject was, at the moment of the expert assignment, in good state of nutrition and sanguification, during the examination we did not find any organs or system trouble.

During the neurological examination lesion signs or irritations of the central or peripheral nervous system were not found.

## Psychic Examination

The subject, whose behavior was always correct and whose clothes neat, agreed willingly to the themes discussed within our different meetings. We could ascertain that he was oriented in the time, in the space and toward his own person that he did not present any sense perception troubles and that had a good attention.

Reconstructing his biography, he proved to be able to place in an orderly way, chronologically, recent and early memories. The subject seemed depressed, worried and anxious: these frames of mind do not shape pathologies of the affectivity but abnormal variations in mood, reactive to the situation and events that generate it.

In this perspective, some subject's behavior must be interpreted that are entered in psychological defense mechanisms and that are implemented whenever he tried to justify any illegal behavior and conduct.

Particularly, the subject, in the recalling of conflicts with his first partner and in the sequence of actions that brought him to events concerning the trial, he pointed out and brought out other people's behaviors by which he tried to justify his conduct. In this perspective enter, as significant examples, some episodes: he denied aggressive manifestations toward his first partner's children saying, on the contrary, that they made fun of him by referring false school success just before the vacations.

Moreover, the choice of the first partner's daughter to bring her boyfriend in their residence to live together was a fact that exasperated him to the point that he had aggressive manifestations which, to him, were not dangerous manifestations.

From this viewpoint even the events subject of the trial has to be set. Evoking them, the subject stated that he has been teased by the "old man" and the new S.' lover, this is the reason why, exasperated, he could no more restrain himself.

These behaviors, with the elements collected during the reconstruction of his clinical biography, are data which allowed us to exclude, with regard of the subject, troubles concerning the mind contents, the train of thought and the critical and judgment capacity.

Therefore we could assert that from the facts did not come out during the meetings, troubles concerning the more elevated psychic functions (perception, thought, memory, attention), but we pointed out sad determination of the mood. This variation in mood enters, without any doubt, in the reactive depression, caused directly by an external situation that, in the examined case, is realized in the detention and in the judicial event where the subject is the protagonist.

## Psychodiagnostics Examination

**Rorschach' test result:** the number and the contents of the answers point out intellective performances not much brilliant or poor (A% elevated, no M answer) with content stereotypy and poor thought fluency. The high percentage of answers with animal contents, combined with the tendency to stereotype, discloses anxiety and depression, which are factors that condition the subject to stay in the well-trodden path, making him not much pliant, barely motivated to the creativity and with an high control of his own spontaneity.

The latter aspect affects considerably the affectivity too, that seems to be inhibited, coerced and repressed (T.R.I. = 0:0,5): in fact, to the conscious hyper-control of his own spontaneity follows an affective poverty with an excessive formalism and stiffness.

Moreover we can notice, in fact, that the subject tends to withdraw into himself, reducing the reactions toward the external world, as we can notice for the depressive people. Such situation can be linked to an attempt to escape from the reality in order to shirk his problems and to overcome the anxiety.

The frequent rotation of the tables, unmethodically, can be sign of poor interest in the implementation of the test and manifestation of a well controlled anxiety.

Some interpretative behaviors (R/mutilation and shape criticism in the Table V) show insecurity, emotional trouble and fear related to aggressive impulse. Particular comments (choc in the table VI,VII,IX) came out some conflicts with female figures.

On the whole, the test does not point out any significant personality system trouble, but emphasizes anxiety signs and depression signs of mood that can orient to the so called reactive depression, in a subject with unsolved psychic conflicts.

## Psychometric Examination

The intelligence quotient score (I.Q.), according to Wechsler's adult intelligence scale (WAIS), was 94, that score is placed in the average, within the limits from 90 to 109. The scores obtained in the verbal scale (I.Q.= 98) are better than those of the nonverbal scale (I.Q.= 91). Such lack of result homogeneity reveals a better ability to deal with words and symbols rather than to handle objects and to perceive visual schemes: that can prove that the subject is able to give a better performance because his efficiency in the nonverbal test can be inhibited by emotional-affective factors and incomplete collaboration.

## Analysis of the Handwriting Personality

The author's handwriting denotes some difficulty in the process continuity, at the ideative level; he, however, is in a constant swinging situation between the doubt and the certainty that prevents him to have synthetic picture of the problems, because the analysis opposes the synthesis and the thought is lost behind the intuitions that do not complement each other, the mind judgment are sectorial and unilateral ("disconnected")[1]. All things considered, the subject, even if he has a sufficient ideative knowledge, appears insecure and undecided taking an overall of the situation.

The handwriting points out uncertainty ("hesitant")[2] forcing the writer to second thoughts and to new analysis of the situations, arousing obstacle and impotence in sensations in the attainment of his goals. These factors can drive him to a store of emotions that can tend to uncontrollable behaviors ("Sign-off-and-on Carved II")[3].

The author's handwriting examined denotes then conflictual extroversion and scarcely defined, linked to a kind of egocentrism that runs a risk to feel unreturned and unsatisfied because of the sensation of giving more than he receives. Such situation can drive him to a possessive affectivity that leads to jealousy, victimization and complaining behaviors ("leaning")[4] and "top opening of 'a' and 'o' "[5]).

## Case Remarks

Somatic, neurological and electroencephalographic examination did not point out any anomalies or troubles concerning the different organs or systems, nor lesions nor irritation of the nervous system had been found. So, from the somatic and neurological point of view, no trouble concerning the subject had been pointed out.

About the psychic examination, the psychometric one (Adult intelligence scale score) and the psycho-diagnostic one (Rorschach's test), we have to point out that similar aspects have been found within the different controls, that is to say that according to them, any significant psychic functions trouble able to explain an insanity have been come out.

From the above mentioned examination, in fact, we notice a reactive behavior concerning the subject's background situation. Particularly, the psychic examination points out sad determination of the mood that shapes a reactive depression, showed by the Rorschach's test, that concludes with the following analysis: "the test does not point out any significant personality system trouble, but emphasizes anxiety signs and depression signs of the mood which can orient to the so called reactive depression, in a subject with unsolved psychic conflicts".

Concerning the test we have to specify that the answers provided by the perpetrators of crimes, especially those imprisoned and prisoners on remand, are characterized by the reduction in the number, by the tendency to refuse some tables, by stereotipization that is not a real perseveration, but it assumes the meaning of answer repetition, even banal, linked to a kind of conventional behavior and to a poor interpretative conduct, with an accentuated spontaneity control.

Moreover, the intellectual depressive inhibition affects negatively the productivity of Rorschach's test, even if the subject's intellective performances were standard.

After we resort to the handwriting personality analysis that, as expressive behavior, reveals the subject's experiences also in relation to the ambient situations.

In the subject's case, this examination points out doubts and insecurities that place him among those persons who tend to bring out only partial aspects or details of the surrounding reality, that interfere the goals, causing store of emotion and consequently emotive reactions characterized by rage and passion.

These ways of reacting, pointed out properly by the handwriting analysis, are linked up with the egocentrism and the dissatisfaction that can rise jealousy, sense of injustice, so victimization and complaining behaviors, that is to say prone to such mournful conduct especially linked to dissatisfaction.

In the psycho-diagnostics field, the totality of the examination that have been carried out steers to the exclusion, with regard to the subject, of the existence of an alienation state of the mind, but points out disharmonies of the personality structures especially in the affective-emotional area, with some difficulty in the deep human contacts. The results of these examinations are surely affected by the situation, on account of the charge of triple murder and of the imprisonment, so certain abnormal and disharmonic aspects of the subject's personality could be more clear and accentuated, especially as far as the affective-emotional area is concerned.

These factors contributed to the exclusion, at the moment of the expertise, the existence of an alienation or mental disease with regard to the subject: because of his biography, it was possible to extend this exclusion also to the past, so when the events of the trial occurred.

## CRIMINOLOGY AND ANALYSIS MEANS: INTERACTION NEEDS

The use of different means in the psycho-diagnostic analysis, also in the criminological domain, can contribute to outline many operating levels of the psyche by providing an high number of information useful to the diagnosis that by comparing the evidences, improves and benefits from them.

Therefore, the handwriting personality examination and Rorschach's test complete each other because "the graphology very often shows that Rorschach does not mention. On the other hand the writing does not show the genius' creative aptitude instead of Rorschach that sometimes attains this aptitude (first of all from K and from the Orig.); the writing does not allow to formulate psychiatric diagnosis, what it is possible, not always but frequently, with Rorschach" (Bohm, 1969, pp. 22-23).

Furthermore Rorschach's test has in common with the graphology "the main rule of his methodology of interpretation, that is to say: intuitive perception of the whole, with the scientific control of the parties; this rule can also be formulated with Ludwig Klages' expression (Klages, 1928, p.11): We must have the whole if we want to study successfully the parties" (Klages, 1928, p. 225).

In particular, the use of Rorschach's test in the criminological field has been object of many studies (Rizzo & Ferracuti, 1958; Meloy, Hansen, & Weiner, 1997, pp. 52-62). Some hypothesis that have been considered in these studies see the criminal act like an expression of egocentrism and immaturity: in the Rorschach's test these two features can be investigate by examining, within the initialing of a protocol, the ratio among the answers FC/CF-C considering that stable affective relationship, mature and connected to the object is represented by 2-3FC,0-1 CF or: 4-6 FC, 2-3CF, 0-1C[6].

In order to recognize if within a protocol the affective expression is balanced, this ratio should be respected accordingly to the amount of answers. In fact, an affective organizational model on the grounds of the kind of Color with a marked preponderance of FC indicates an ambient adaptation that could lead to pliability, to dependence, to the passive submission. The preponderance of the answers CF provides indications of psychic restlessness that is expressed by swing mood, impulsiveness, reactivity and suggestibility while the affective organizational model on the grounds of the kind of Color dominated by the C allows indications of impulsiveness whose only aim is the prompt outburst, the absolute lack of control, the excessive use of the primary process (Giambelluca, Parisi, & Pes, 1995). In Rorschach's protocol, in order to evaluate the capacity adaptation to the ambient and that of social contact of the subject, it will be important to consider the answers FC

*Table 1.*

| **Tavola I** | **Lat. 10" Tot. 10"** | |
|---|---|---|
| [you can hold it longer…] 1) @ A moth | Yes, an insect whose life lasts one day, it is like a butterfly, the color is plain. In the whole table with the head in 5 (usual AV), it is dark like a night butterfly. | G F+ / FC'n A V[7] |
| | | |
| **Tavola II** | **Lat. 15" Tot. 15"** | |
| 1) @ Human Shade | They are shades (D1+1) because of their dark color. Human because they have a massive shape like a person. They are double, they are the same thing, that is to say like the other. | D F+- / C'nF Hs O+-→ RD[8] |
| | | |
| **Tavola III** | **Lat. 20" Tot. 20"** | |
| 1) A rite | An heathen rite around an idol. The flames because they really have the shape of the flames (D3). These are the persons (D7) that are probably priests, guardian men of the sacred, who stand around an idol, in other words who perform the cult. They are priest because they perform the rite and have the barrier of the sacred and profane. The idol (D4) is probably a spider because it has a lot of legs (Ddl 6) | G M ↑ o↗ H/Foc[9] /Sce[10] (V) (O±) |
| | | |
| **Tavola IV** | **Lat. 7" Tot. 7"** | |
| A man seen from below | In the middle there is a bar stool (D1) and the man is sitting on: it is as if there is a pain of glass, we can see through; or a man who is seen by a child and the man seems big. Location: usual HV | G F+ H V → M↓ |
| | | |
| **Tavola V** | **Lat. 6" Tot. 6"** | |
| A chimera | An animal of the medieval or pre-medieval mythology with the head of the lion (D1) and the body of the goat. | G F- A/mit[11] O- |
| | | |
| **Tavola VI** | **Lat. 30" Tot. 30"** | |
| ↓ A standard | A symbol that is brought in peace or in war in order to say: "we come from this village"; there is an handle with some feathers (D1) and here the bearing part (D2) | G F+- Obj[12] /Arald[13] |
| | | |
| **Tavola VII** | **Lat. 25" Tot. 25"** | Choc vuoto |
| [He gives me back immediately, I invite him to hold it again.] ↓ keystone | Yes, a door colonnade like you find in certain villas. This is the arch (D4) and these are the columns (D1). There are animals as if they were elephants. | G F+ Arch[14] → Refusal |
| | | |
| **Tavola VIII** | **Lat. 45" Tot. 45"** | |
| A Totem | A kind of animist idol. They are quadrupeds (D1).There are many animals: a frog (D3) and butterflies (D2) because they are colored | G FC + Arald (V) |
| | | |
| **Tavola IX** | **Lat. 10" Tot. 10"** | |

*continued on following page*

*Table 1. continued*

| Tavola I | Lat. 10" Tot. 10" | |
|---|---|---|
| A chalice with a finely decorated rim | It started from Dim3 that gives the impression of the clearness. D4 is the chalice pedestal and D2 and D1 are the irregular rim of the chalice. Irregular because nor smooth nor compact. Sometimes there are such sumptuous chalices, of medieval shape. They are men (the green ones) that hold up the witches. They are witches because they are dressed like witches. | I m G F C / F (c) + O b j → F I |
| | | |
| Tavola X | Lat. 20" Tot. 20" | |
| ↓An owl | The owl with the eyes in the 6. Sometimes the owl have a small colored feathering under the brest (D13). D3 is the muzzle; (D12) is the small beak, sharp and the different pink nuances are the edge of the face of the owl. | DDim F+- A O - |

@ = Rotation of the table

and the answers with human content (H-Hd). The latter provides many indications about the self and the object relations interiorized.

The Rorschach's protocol that has been quoted is of a minor, supposed non chargeable because of his age, when he committed the crime he was not 14 yet.

## Rorschach's Test Protocol

Therefore in the criminological field, during the expertise control, especially for the psychic examination, we have to specify that the interview marks out the main gully in order to orient into the knowledge of the other, that a psychometric examination can provide some information about the subject's intellective potential, that a projective test suggests diagnostic confirmations particularly relating to the personality structure, but we must stress that there are other aspects that can be hold in due consideration. We are referring to expressive manifestations, which include diaries or written text of various kinds that permit both the analysis of the content and the analysis of the handwriting personality. The latter, the handwriting expression, which does not get out of neglecting the ethical problems related to behavioral judgments, concerning the possibility to affect the same behavior and concerning the ability in predicting the behavior, allows us to assume how the graphology can contribute to provide information regarding any characteristics of the personality. This way of proceeding, depicted as technique of a complex investigation, can justify an increased engagement toward the data research, objective and objectifiable, as the basis for the comprehension of the mental troubles and the characteristics of personality (Balloni & Bisi, 1993, pp. 65-78).

The evaluation of an event through different methodologies can mean that the evaluation is carried out from several perspectives because the result must have the greatest utility from the diagnostic and prognostic point of view.

So, in the field of the criminological and psychiatric activity, it is necessary, sometimes, to draw up an expert- report, we ought to keep in mind an operating scheme that can be developed in several points:

1. We start from an introduction, referring to the judicial authority who provided the investigation or to the lawyer who required an expertise where indications concerning the subject in exam (name, surname, age, address) specifying the crime charges

*Figure 1. Cognitive area of Rorschach's test. Rorschach's computations according the methodology of Rorschach's Roman School*

| | | | | |
|---|---|---|---|---|
| T. racc. R: 20' | T. total 40' | | T.m. Lat: 19" | |
| R: 10 | R+: 7 | R+%:70 | R ± %: 40 | |
| Kind of comprehension: G Dim | | | | |
| Sequence: incalculable | | | | |
| F%: 70 | F+%: 64 | F±%: 43 | | |
| G+% (R): 55 | G+% (G): 73 | | G O+%: | |
| G/M: 7.50/1 | M/m:1/0 | H+A/Hd+Ad: 6/0 | | |
| H%: 20 | H% extended :30 | | A%: 30 | A% extended: 30 |
| H%: + A%: 50 | H% extended + A% extended: 60 | | | |
| N. Cont. 1°: 5 | 1°+2°: 8 | | | |
| V: 3 | | V%: 30 | V(O+)%: | (V)(O±)%: 17 |
| O: 2.50 | O %: 25 | O+: 0.75 | O+%: 30 | |
| Index of reality: 4 | | | | |

*Figure 2. Affectivity area of Rorschach's test. Rorschach's computations according the methodology of Rorschach's Roman School*

T.V.I.: 1/1

t.v.i.: 0/2

I. Affectivity:

$$\frac{RN}{RC} : \ldots 1 \ldots$$

$$\frac{RVIII + IX + X}{R} . 100 : 30$$

Quality of the affections:

↑ ……2…

↓ …………

↑↓ …………

I. impulsiveness: $\frac{II + III}{VIII + IX + X} : \ldots 0.67 \ldots$

I. Self-control: $\frac{M + FC}{CF + C} : \ldots 3/0 \ldots$

alive things / dead things: …5/5…

pleasant things./ unpleasant things.: ………

*Figure 3. Result of Rorschach's test*[15]

| |
|---|
| The data concerning the subject's examination of reality point out that the functions of the ego are unimpaired (R+% = 70; F% = 70; F+% = 64; G+% (R) = 55; G+% (G) = 73; A% = 30; A% + H% = 50), so mental organic troubles, psychotic troubles and severe personality disorders can be excluded. The subject, however, tends to exaggerate his abilities and his talent in order to draw attention on himself as "special person" (no. of R low with kind of comprehension moved on the left; G>M; T.V.I. coercive, arald contents, scene and interpretation which express "cultural exhibitionism").However he has difficulties to integrate meaningfully and personally his intellective abilities, difficulties that can be traced back to the scanty ability to be in contact with his own inner world. (N. M basso e G/M = 7.50/1).<br>The affectivity is inhibited, not stabilized and it is linked up to an organization cultural-structural of the personality characterized by mood basically depressive and by an excessive control (no. of R. low; G+ absent; T.V.I. coercive ;G/M with unbalanced value, in favor of the M).<br>There are also all the peculiarities coming from immaturity and preponderance of a psychic functioning where there was not a suitable integration between the primary process and the secondary process of the subject, that depones for an incomplete differentiation and integration of the psychic parts of the mind. The conflict among the drive parts of the mind prevails, which are certainly contrasted by some functions of the ego, but not sufficiently controlled (R+% = 70; F+% = 64; R±% = 40; F±% = 43; kind of comprehension incomplete).<br>Affections and object relationships present in their immaturity symbiotic and dependence features mixed with egocentrism and scanty knowledge of the other. (kind of comprehension incomplete; T.V.I. and t.v.i. which tend to be coercive; contents categories:2,3,6).<br>There are anxiety, adaptation difficulty (presence of answers FC'n, C'nF) and the subject uneasiness appears through the index of impulsiveness quite high (0.67) which indicates the lack of channels where address more fluently the subject's drive heritage. |

attributed to him, the time available for the inquiry, the activities and the place where they have to be carried out.

2. Then the investigation that has been carried out with its outcome. In this field we explain the clinical biography or history of the subject we have to examine, with the information extracted from documents owned by the expert or technical consultant. Moreover, in this part of the expertise- report are related the outcomes of the somatic, neurological and psico-diagnostic examinations that can be followed by the data obtained by psicodiagnostic controls (intelligence scale, projective test, handwriting personality analysis outcomes)

We can conclude this part with a conclusive diagnostic specification.

3. The observations and considerations are a crucial moment because reminding the final diagnosis, we have to start this objective and coherent examination that brings us to the formulation of a judgment of imputability and social dangerousness. Indications and observations must be very accurate because the expert or the technical consultant that are vague can not enjoy a high reputation. The data discussed and revised, in view of the final judgment or of the answer to the question formulated, have to be objective and objectifiable because they have to face the critics of the parties or of the cross examination, where the weak points and the contradictions of an expert- report or an exposition during a public audience can be pointed out. In this field we can refer to scientific works and clinical analysis, be careful to the exactitude of the quotations and their pertinence.

## CURRENT CHALLENGES

An expertise-report will always be characterized, in the final part, by a series of answers to the questions formulated or by conclusions concerning the problem to solve. This is an expressive and significant synthesis of the whole activity that has been carried out. In the operating line sketched out, the objectivity and the logic have to appear in order to make a psychiatric expertise comprehensible and in this way useful, without using equivocal or difficult expressions, keeping in mind that the expertise report can be read by other experts, but also by non expert that have to understand the message of an expert.

We have to add that the fundamental structure of a psychiatric expertise -report is not different compared to the past, while we have to notice that the methods of investigation can evolve as well as the utilization and the application of diagnostic criteria.

In the psychiatric and criminological praxis it is desirable that the researches concerning the judgments pronounced in the ambit of the deviance, considering that these judgments are connected with the methodology used and to the operator training, especially pointing out that the judgments will acquire more value and coherence if they explore all the conditions that will influence the behavior.

In fact, Di Tullio in his treatise, in the general reflections, that put before the chapter concerning the causes of the criminality, explains some observations very useful even in this field because he observes that "everything which hitherto has been explained, with regard to the clinical criminology, about the importance represented by different problems of the human being, of the personality and its characterological variations, of the social psychology and the cultural anthropology, of the psychopathic personalities, of abnormal reactions, of psychopathic developments, of neurosis, of mental diseases, in order to prepare the study to face the complex problem of the causes of the criminality.

However it is important that the scholar be conscious of the fact that any treatment of this subject can never be adequate to bring all the causes able to drive a person to do more or less serious crime actions to the light. This is because, as we have already pointed out, any crime is always the expression of casual factors which are not only non-manifold and of various natures, but absolutely original and unrepeatable" (Di Tullio, 1975, p. 155).

It is impossible to believe to attain a definite and precise interpretation of the deviant and criminal behavior, it is also important to provide reliable, coherent and non-labeling judgments, especially when the concept of individualization of the treatment is made topic, when we propose the hypothesis, conforming to the Italian penitentiary system, of a real judgment on the defendant's personality and the acquisition, in any state and stage of the trial on the merits and during the debate, of elements that consent to an accomplished knowledge of the subject, excluding the general information.

Now, we cannot conclude, but we must open and face a series of problems concerning the definition of deviance and the criminologist's role. On the basis of the collected data and considered the possible interpretations of the deviance, especially the relationship among the mental diseases and the criminal conduct, it is clear that the problem concerning the definition of the deviance become fundamental. In fact if we think about the deviant behaviors as individual pathology or as psychological maladjustment, we are tending to a restrictive and limited approach. On the other hand, if we consider the deviance as the signal that something does not work at the social level, we will favor the ambient causes. Moreover, if we define the deviance as the expression of the human variety, we have to be able to evaluate and to tolerate it without resort to labels that censure a person both from the psychiatric and the criminological point of view.

Now it is clear that the definition of the problem is closely linked to the causes, which can include biological, psychological and social factor, The criminologist, with a psychiatric or psychological training, with a lot of factors only, can do well-founded choices and will be able to bear in mind that the different kind of the individual reactions against identical situation are different, that the meaning that was attributed by the men to their conduct can change from individual to individual, so it would be incorrect to claim that the causes of the deviance or of the criminality have been found without realizing the big limits that the researches objectively have in this field.

It is an important exercise, for a criminologist, to discuss a case, because, especially when the psychiatry is concerned, the need to know the causes of the human reactions against the life stimulus comes out: strictly in the criminological-psychiatric field we do not face the normality or the abnormality only, but also actions considered despicable which concern women, men and children that the society has sentenced or declared victims. This behavior is a stimulus that influences the criminologist, the psychiatrist and the psychologist, with other factor of his acquaintance.

The blameworthy and understandable social evaluation, especially in front of case of perpetrators of serious crimes and all the other factors, are a strong stimulus the expert has a contact with. In such a complex situation the expert tries to keep a cold scientific survey attitude, without judging or sentencing, but especially by wondering about why the criminal acted in that way and how can we help him to behave less dangerously in the future. In this perspective it is hard to keep a scientific objectivity and the expert, against his will, has to judge, to evaluate, to hate and to pity as someone else.

This is the real open conclusion that proposes again the action-research pointing concretely to social practice interventions, from one hand, and pursuing an interaction of laboratory survey and a research in the field, from the other hand. In this way, theory and practice could interact profitably in order to provide answers concerning both the theoretical problems and the practical social problems.

## REFERENCES


Balloni, A. (1999). Psichiatria forense. In P. Pancheri, G.B. Cassano (Eds.), *Trattato italiano di psichiatria* (pp.3899-3931). Milano, Italy: Masson.

Balloni, A. (2004). *Criminologia e psicopatologia. Analisi di 110 perizie psichiatriche*. Bologna, Italy: Pàtron.

Balloni, A. & Bisi, R. (1993). Le tecniche complesse di indagine nelle tossicodipendenze. *Giovani realtà*, XIII(46), 65-78.

Bisi, R. (1992). *Grafologia e strutturalismo. Analisi e prospettive*. Bologna, Italy: Clueb.

Bisi, R. (2002). La psicodiagnostica in criminologia: orientamenti e prospettive. In G. Mucciarelli, R. Chattat, G. Celani (Eds.), *Teoria e pratica dei test* (pp. 507-527). Padova, Italy: Piccin.

Bohm, E. (1969). *Manuale di psicodiagnostica di Rorschach*. Firenze, Italy: Giunti-Barbèra.

Bosinelli, M. (Ed.). (1982). *Metodi in psicologia clinica*. Bologna, Italy: il Mulino.

Ceccarelli, G. (1998). *Psicologia e grafologia: quale rapporto?* Milano, Italy: Angeli.

Debuyst, C. (1990). Présentation et justification du thème. In AA.VV., *Acteur social et délinquance Hommage à Christian Debuyst* (pp. 21-23). Liège-Bruxelles, Belgium: Pierre Mardaga Editeur.

Di Tullio, B. (1975). *Principi di criminologia generale e clinica con note di psicopatologia sociale* ($5^{th}$ ed.). Roma, Italy: Lombardo Editore.

Giambelluca, F. C., Parisi, S., & Pes, P. (1995). *L'interpretazione psicoanalitica del Rorschach. Modello dinamico strutturale*. Roma: Edizioni Kappa.

Klages, L. (1928). *Die Grundlagen der Charakterkunde.* Leipzig, Germany: Johann Ambrosius Barth.

Meloy, S. R., Hansen, L. T., & Weiner, I. B. (1997). Authority of the Rorschach: Legal Citations During the Past 50 years. *Journal of Personality Assessment, 69*(1), 52–62. doi:10.1207/s15327752jpa6901_3

Palaferri, N. (2001). *Dizionario grafologico morettiano.* Urbino, Italy: Libreria "G. Moretti".

Portigliatti Barbos, M., & Marini, G. (1964). *La capacità di intendere e di volere nel sistema penale italiano.* Milano, Italy: Giuffrè.

Raymond, S. G., & Bornstein, S. J. (1988). Examen psychologique et médico-psycologique judiciaire. *Encycl. Méd. Chir. Psychiatrie, 37903*(A10), 11–19.

Rizzo, C., & Ferracuti, F. (1958). Impiego del test di Rorschach in criminologia clinica. *Comunicazione presentata al IV Congresso internazionale Rorschach.* Bruxelles, Belgium. 1st - 4th August.

Semerari, A., & Citterio, C. (1975). *Medicina criminologica e psichiatria forense.* Milano, Italy: Vallardi.

## ADDITIONAL READINGS

Arieti, S. (Ed.). (1969). *Manuale di psichiatria.* Torino, Italy: Boringhieri. Balloni, A. (1983). *Criminologia in prospettiva.* Bologna, Italy: Clueb. Balloni, A. (1985). In tema di politica del controllo sociale e della pena. In G. Zappa (Ed.), *Carcere Ente locale Opinione Pubblica* (pp. 179-189). Bologna, Italy: Clueb.

Balloni, A. (1985). In tema di trattamento e di perizia psichiatrica. Intervento all'incontro del C.S.M. con i Magistrati di Sorveglianza, Grottaferrata, Italy 11-13 November 1983. *C.S.M., Quaderni di incontro di studio,* nuova serie (2), 157-170.

Balloni, A. (1988). Le misure di sicurezza nella nuova legge. Relazione all'incontro di studio "Problemi applicativi della legge n.663/86", Frascati, Italy 26-28 June 1987. *Quaderni del C. SM, 3*(15), 113–123.

Balloni, A. (Ed.). (1989). *Vittime Crimine Difesa Sociale.* Bologna, Italy: Clueb.

Balloni, A. (1990). Colpa, crimine e spazio di vita: il caso Ludwig nella prospettiva della teoria del campo, *Atti del Primo Congresso Nazionale della Società Italiana di psichiatria Forense,* Psychopatologia, Associazione "La Ginestra". Brescia, Italy: Tipolitografia Emmebigrafica, 89-98.

Balloni, A. (1990). Nuove metodologie nell'indagine peritale con riferimento alla psicopatologia. In M.A. Lombardi (Ed.), *La Perizia e la Consulenza tecnica: stato attuale e prospettive* (pp. 195-206). Pisa, Italy: Pacini Editore.

Balloni, A. (Ed.). (1990). *Criminalità e giustizia minorile in Emilia-Romagna.* Bologna, Italy: Clueb.

Bisi, R. (1999). *Devianza e criminalità giovanile.* In G. B. Cassano, & P. Pancheri et al. (Eds.), *Trattato italiano di psichiatria (vol. III)* (pp. 3115-3121), Milano, Italy: Masson.

Bravo, A. (1998). *Variazioni naturali e artificiose della grafia.* Urbino, Italy: Libreria "Girolamo Moretti".

Burla, F., & Contreras, L. & Ferracuti S. (2000), Validità discriminante del disegno di figura umana e valutazione dei tratti compulsivi ed aggressivi in pazienti borderline. *Rassegna italiana di criminologia,* XI (2), 147-163.

Canestrari, R., Ricci-Bitti, P., & Caterina, R. (1995). *Psicodinamica dell'interazione nel colloquio clinico.* In G. Trentini (Ed.). *Manuale del colloquio e dell'intervista* (pp. 146-170), Torino, Italy: Utet.

Crisi, A. (1998). *Manuale del test di Wartegg.* Roma: Edizioni scientifiche Ma.Gi.

Ferrarotti, F. (1981). *Storia e storie di vita.* Bari, Italy: Laterza.

Giovanelli, G. C. (2001) *Corso di formazione all'uso clinico di una batteria di test.* Typescripts not published.

Oas, P. (1984). Validity of the Draw-A-Person and Bender-Gestalt tests as a measure of impulsivity with adolescents. *Journal of Consulting and Clinical Psychology, 52,* 1011–1019. doi:10.1037/0022-006X.52.6.1011

Pinkus, L. (1978). *Teoria della psicoterapia analitica breve.* Roma: Borla.

Rapaport, D. (1977). *Il modello concettuale della psicoanalisi.* Milano, Italy: Feltrinelli.

Trabucchi, A. (1991). *Istitutizioni di diritto civile.* Padova, Italy: Cedam.

Wanderer, Z. W. (1969). Validity of clinical judgements based on Human Figure Drawings. *Journal of Consulting and Clinical Psychology, 33,* 143–150. doi:10.1037/h0027181

## ENDNOTES

1. The sign "disconnected" within the graphological Italian system issued by Padre Girolamo Moretti, indicates that, within the handwritten text, the letters are not linked together, as they be indipendent each other (Palaferri, 2001, p. 266).
2. The sign "hesitant" indicates that, inside the words, any word groups of two or three letters change inclination rightward, leftward or 90° perpendicular with the base line (Palaferri, 2001, p. 281).[3] It is the sudden and intense pressure change of the writing (spasmus), especially in the upper and lower loops of the letters, so when we change the direction of the line (Palaferri, 2001, p. 157).
4. The inclination of the writing is defined "leaning" when the letters are inclined rightward.
5. The constituent element of this sign concerns the upper vertex of the small letters "o", "a" and the derived "d","g","q": in particular, they present some openings aligned with the letters, in order to be like "v" or "u" (Palaferri, 2001, p. 54).
6. Among the perceptive stimulus stimulated by Rorschach tables, the more important distinction is the chromatic component: 5 out of ten are colored. Among them, two have only the red as chromatic component, while the others have a large number of pastel colors, without the red.
   FC = are the Shape-Color interpretations. They are especially determined by the shape of the blot identified; also the color has influence on the interpretation.
   CF = are the interpretation of Color-Shape. They are interpretations which consider prevalently the color of the blot without neglecting thoroughly the shape, which is prevalently imprecise and vague;
   C = are the interpretations of Color only. They are interpretations determined by the blot color only, while the formal aspect seems inexistent.
7. Vulgar / banal.
8. Answer of Double.
9. Fire.
10. Scene.
11. Mithology.
12. Object.
13. Heraldry.
14. Architecture.

15 Formal answers are the interpretation suggested exclusively by the shape of the stain and represent the category more considerable in the majority of the protocols. They are classified in F+ (interpretations of good shape); F- (bad interpretation); F+- (vague, indefinite or imprecise interpretations). Related very closely to F+% is the evaluation of R+%. Besides the qualitative evaluation of the answers of the form only, in the R+% is included that of all the other answers, even those with different determinants from F.

G = global interpretation: the entire stain is included in the perceptive act;

M = are the interpretation of the human or anthrop-similar animal movement which are seen in humanized behavior;

A = interpretation of entire animals

H = interpretation if human figure;

T.V.I. = Kind of inner life primary. It serves to establish the quantitative ratio between the kinaesthetic answers and the chromaesthesia answers. From the psychodiagnostic point of view it compares, on the one hand, the elements prevalently introversive and interior of the subject, on the other hand, the aspects the relate him with the external world, with the object, with the ambient. Accordingly with the different ratio among the elements which compose him, the T.V.I is divided in: coerced, coercive, introversive, extroversive, ambiversive, dilated;

t.v.i. = kind of inner life minor . It is carried out from the calculation of the minor kinesthesias and of the minor chromesthesias. The difference between the T.V.I. and the t.v.i. is whether the T.V.I. indicates how the subject works and expresses himself in a determined moment of his existence, the t.v.i. indicates prevalently the basic structure of the personality.

FC'n = answers of Shape-grey-black color. For instance: table I G "moth" ;

C'nF = answers of Color grey-black Shape. For instance: table IV G "lump of coal";

Index of impulsiveness = it is obtained by the ratio among the answers provided in the tables II and III and those provided in the tables VIII,IX and X. It indicates the participation of the latent impulses in the affective behavior.

Kind of comprehension = it is an index that correlates all the kind of comprehension. The way of comprehension or localization concerns the area of the table which a particular answer is referred to.

Anyway, the kind of comprehension is considered an index that is useful to establish how the subject faces the situations.

# APPENDIX: SUPPORT MATERIALS

## Questions and Answers

1. What does it mean by imputability concerning the Italian penal code?

The concept of imputability means that a subject can be charged with a crime if we start from the assumption that he, if he wanted, could act in a different way (art.85 Italian Penal Code), therefore he has mental capacity.

2. What does (understanding) capacity mean?

To be in the frame of mind that allows the subject to know not only the outer reality but also to realize the social value, positive or negative, the events that happen outside him and the acts he carries out.

3. What does (wishing) capacity mean?

This is the subject's aptitude to decide by himself in sight of the goal.

4. What does social control mean?

The social control is a set of mechanisms, of reactive actions and sanctions that a community uses to prevent or to eliminate deviant behaviors inside.

5. What does social dangerousness mean?

The social dangerousness judgment can be divided in two parts: a) verification of the qualities where we can deduce the probable commission of new crimes. b) Judgment about the criminal future of the subject that is criminal prognosis.

## Epilogue and Lessons Learned

1. **Forensic psychiatry:** The forensic Psychiatry is the expression of the relation between the psychiatry and justice activity and participates to the justice activity when it needs correct interpretation of those rules of law that considers situations of psychiatric interest. The forensic psychiatry participates to bring, in a psychopathological perspective, to the light a subject that is in particular relation with the rule. In this field of activity, the mean prevalently used by the forensic psychiatrist is the psychiatric expertise.

2. **Psychiatric expertise:** The psychiatric expertise has a particular position because it is never used to prove if a fact exists or not, but it is used to verify the mental state of a subject when the fact (crime) he was charged happened. Particularly the psychiatric expertise is not used to prove if a subject has committed a fact provided as crime, but it is used to ascertain by which mental dynamism (with or without mental capacity or diminished considerably) a subject has committed the fact qualified as crime.

3. **Methodologies in forensic psychiatry:** Concerning those methods (interview, level test, psychodiagnostic techniques of the personality) used in clinical psychology, so to methods which can be used in the particular field of the criminology that we can define as applied. To the applied criminology, in fact, we can attribute practical aims carried out by scientific means, especially when we are exploring the crime

author's personality in order to evaluate his level of responsibility and consequently of imputability, or in order to try to understand his future behavior evaluating the existence or not of social dangerousness, or when we analyze a witness in order to evaluate his credibility.

# Chapter 2
# Teaching Criminology:
## Socio-Anthropology of Crime

**Jean-Michel Bessette**
*University of Franche-Comté, France*

## EXECUTIVE SUMMARY

*The field of study (and the teaching) of the criminal sociology presents multiple aspects and shows itself at various levels, the methods to implement for the exploration of the numerous research leads that it conceals are multiple and varied as well. This case, as a rough guide, proposes some modalities of approach in this domain.*

## BACKGROUND

Any constituted human group generates a set of values, norms, rules, and rites – whether in the form of customs or laws. Broadly speaking, this set is bound together thus contributing to the maintenance of its structure. This normative set acts on the social body as a regulation system. Of course, values, norms and rules are contingent on space and time, imprinting their particular marks on the forms of collective life which is hence diversified depending on societies.

Therefore, this is an entire field of the social which is ruled by collective norms and regulations, and which transgression, threatening the more or less precarious balance constituent of the social structure, can lead a group – through the actors/agents[1] qualified to do it – to this reaction that we name punishment. Thus, the triple articulation rules impositions – transgression – social reaction constitutes the focal point of the field of criminal sociology. This is a state of this research field, that the mediatical topicality of our societies makes central in collective preoccupations (the issues which are agitated regarding delinquency, criminality and terrorism facts have indeed become major practical, political and ideological stakes), that we propose to present here.

Sociologists are interested in the study of the criminal phenomenon in many respects. Any act of transgression is an open window on society. Because it challenges society and breaks away from collec-

DOI: 10.4018/978-1-60566-872-7.ch002

tive values, crime offers the one who observes it a particular point of view and its study opens the way to a fertile approach for sociologists. In times of crisis, crime is tell-tale sign – and a punctual crisis in itself – bringing out the cogs of society. Indicating – by exceeding them – the limits imposed to its members, not only does crime enable us to see the roots on which the life of a community is based, but through the social reactions that it elicits, it also shows how a society is reinforced or preserved, while maintaining a perspective on the issue of social change. It is a significant element allowing to grasp the degree of cohesion of collective values and solidarities, and to follow their evolution. Furthermore, through the study of the diverse actors/agents that it stages – Code authors, Code breakers, victims, or the diverse institutional actors/agents and other entrepreneurs of morality who stigmatize the authors of transgressions and contribute to attribute the qualification of criminals to them – it is the opposition inside and between the various groups and the social formations that the analysis of the criminal phenomenon emphasizes. Finally, through the study of the processes facilitating the "acting out", it is the formation and the development of the personal identities – and more particularly the ways social life imprints its mark on the individual – that it is given to observe.

French sociologist Émile Durkheim (1858-1917) can be considered as one of the inspirers of the modern criminal sociology. Demolishing the almost inevitable moral judgments on this object, he claims the application of the fundamental rule of his sociological method to the study of the criminal phenomenon: consider it as a thing. It is in The Division of Labour in Society, that we find his famous definition of crime: "...an act is criminal when it offends the strong, well-defined states of the collective consciousness..." (Durkheim, 1986). These collective feelings are "strong" because they are common to the majority of the members of a particular society. They are also "well-defined", that is specified in (penal) codified rules. On the other hand, crime is also defined by Durkheim as a punished act, that is by the social reaction that it elicits: "We can not say that an act offends the common consciousness because it is criminal, but that it is criminal because it offends the common consciousness. We do not condemn it because it is a crime, but it is a crime because we condemn it." By referring to the social norm on the one hand and to the social reaction on the other hand, Durkheim emphasizes two constituent essential features of the issues of the criminal sociology. He goes even farther. Indeed, he dares to write: "There is no society that is not confronted with the problem of criminality. Its form changes (...) but, everywhere and always, there have been men who have behaved in such a way as to draw upon themselves penal repression. There is, then, no phenomenon that represents more indisputably all the symptoms of normality, since it appears closely connected with the conditions of all collective life." Crime is a normal phenomenon (by opposition to a pathological, accidental or contingent one). Not only is it normal, but it is necessary (because it is not able to not be and the fundamental conditions of social organization imply it logically). Finally, and in order to go the whole hog, crime is also useful, because it contributes – directly or indirectly – to the evolution of the customs and the law. If we consider crime simultaneously as a normal, necessary and useful phenomenon, "the fundamental facts of criminality present themselves to us in an entirely new light. Contrary to what is commonly believed, the criminal no longer seems a totally unsociable being, a sort of parasitic element, a strange and unassimilable body, introduced into the midst of society. (...) he plays a definite role in social life."

It can be seen that Durkheim sketched – in his time – a completely original perspective of crime, and it is only more than half a century later that the sociologists took the road which he had thus marked out. Moreover, an attentive reading allows to notice that his sketch embraces simultaneously the etiological perspective (that is the study of the causes of the criminal behavior – and radically the acting out) and the social reaction perspective (the study of the constitution of the norms and of society reaction to transgression) which would later be acknowledged by researchers in the field of the criminal sociology.

Thus, from the end of the 19th century, Durkheim appointed crime as a fact ensuing from the regular functioning of society – as a normal fact, related to the society in which it occurs – and the criminality as a socially-constructed object, susceptible to methodically led investigations. The theoretical bases of the criminal sociology were cast.

## CRIME: PURPOSE AND METHODS

### Purpose

Regarding the facts of delinquency and criminality, prenotions and passions often come to burden the methodical study of the facts. It is thus advisable to well-define the object of the study to bound precisely the field of research on which the sociologist will try hard to focus his attention. In this respect, it is important to implement the methodological precept concerning the definition: "Always take for research object a group of phenomena beforehand defined by certain common characters, and include in the same research all those which answer this definition. For example, we notice the existence of a certain number of acts which all present this outside character that, once carried out, they determine on behalf of society this particular reaction – italics mine – that we name punishment. We make a group sui generis, on which we impose a common section ; we call crime any (legally) punished act and we make of the so defined crime the object of a science."

The action which entails the social reaction that we name punishment, here is thus the object of the criminal sociology, clearly appointed in its generality.

Criminological literature generally refers to three registers defining three different levels of crime: the real crime, the apparent crime and the legal crime.

*Real crime* would be constituted by all the infractions committed in a given population during a definite period of time. It is – by definition – an unknown element, since 1) many infractions are not found out, 2) any infraction is not the object of a complaint and 3) all the complaints do not necessarily correspond to infractions!

*Apparent crime* is, as for it, formed by all the infractions which are reported to the police and the public prosecutor's department. It is considered as apparent because it consists of infractions which are not judged by the courts yet. In practice, all the complaints will not be retained (dismissal, discharge...). The sociologist –who does not have to play entrepreneur's role of morality – will rely only cautiously on this precarious "reality" to carry out his research. However, at this level of criminality, it is permissible to study certain aspects of the processes of rules imposition, stigmatization and labeling which are constituent elements of the diverse phenomena of deviance and criminality.

*Legal crime*, finally, presents the very characters required by the durkheimian definition of crime – any legally punished act – and constitutes, therefore, a well-specified study base. In this frame are included all the types of infractions defined by the Code (fines, offenses and crimes), and legally sanctioned in an actual way.

The general framework of this research field being clearly bounded, we are now capable of proposing a general programmatics for a socio-anthropological approach to crime:

This one would apply to the study of the diverse aspects of collective life relative to the establishment of rules legally codified (primary criminalization) and to their transgressions, as well as to the processes governing the social reactions (secondary criminalization) which can ensue from these transgressions: stigmatization, labeling, pronouncement and sentencing. It would study the modalities of elaboration, application and evolution of the codifications in their connections with the social structures (history, penal law, legal anthropology, sociology of the law). It would analyze the functioning of the institutions of social control, police, justice, prison authority, watched education (sociology of organizations). It would examine if tendencial regularities emerge (statistics, demography, geography) allowing to give an account of a sociogenesis appropriate for certain criminal infractions. It would also try hard to bring to light the historic and social logics facilitating the production of delinquencies and criminalities. Through the study of concrete criminal "dramas" (case study, "in situation"), it would try to understand the occasional causes allowing to elaborate a typology of delinquency and criminality facts. It would finally attempt to encircle the complex processes facilitating what it is advisable to call the "acting out » (psychology, psychiatry, psychoanalysis). Vast program...

Synthetically, we can say that the general field of the criminal sociology articulates itself around two additional poles, developing from a sociology of the social reaction to an anthropology of the acting out. We shall see how the consideration of this articulation will gradually lead us from criminal sociology to criminal anthropology.

## Methods

The field of study of the criminal sociology presenting multiple aspects and showing itself at various levels, the methods to implement for the exploration of the numerous research leads that it conceals are multiple and varied as well. Here are, as a rough guide – the way always remaining opened to the sociological imagination – some modalities of approach in this domain.

In the general frame of the study of both social control and social reaction, the inventory of the establishment of the norms, of their implementation, their transgression and the diverse modalities of restoring the social balances (systems of codifications, inculcation, distribution, regulations, penalties) in the various societies – in brief a criminal ethnology in association with the legal anthropology – constitute research areas which are rich in potentialities. A comparative approach to this field of studies should eventually facilitate the possibilities of theorization relative to the question of the regulation modes of the collective sets. The variety and the types of social reactions to deviance seeming connected to the diverse social contexts (religious, economic, political, etc., in brief, historical), the systematic study of the codes, the case law (analysis of contents, thematic analysis) in a perspective of historical and sociological critique, allows to analyze the cultural foundations underlying their constitution and their implementation. Such a study can also bring elements of information interesting the general problem of the social reaction (value system, norms and ideologies). The establishment of a reasoned catalog of the multiple forms of social reaction to deviance in space and time would open the way to the elaboration of an anthropology of regulation systems in human societies.

The statistical study remains a privileged mode of approach for the research in criminal sociology. Actually, it allows to understand the crime "from the outside". Certainly, the criminal statistics do not fall from the sky ! They are a social production among the others, and it is important to adopt counter to them a critical attitude by analyzing the historic and social conditions of their production. Thus, the diverse sources supplying the criminal statistics must be considered with caution, and we precisely wondered if they did not express just as much the level of efficiency, as well as the diverse cultures of professions and the professional ideologies of the administrations and actors/agents in charge of establishing them, than they measured crime. Depending on the theoretical orientation he wants to give to his study, the researcher will refer to one source or another, with keeping in mind the limits of any "data", generally. Beyond these reserves, it remains that the statistics supplying the figures of legal crime constitute a relevant indicator of the state of the crime such as we were able to define it: the social reaction to the transgression of legally codified rules. Thus, they convey institutions' modalities of functioning (police, justice, prison, etc.) and express the state of social relations in a given society at some point. It is up to the researcher to proceed to the theoretical and methodological arbitrations (critique of the sources) necessary for the scientific conduct of his research.

The statistical analysis allows to extract a *structure of criminality* (the relative frequencies of the various categories and types of crimes), as well as its evolution. Once the structure of the global criminality is underlined, we shall try hard to study the relations between diverse sociological variables and criminality (sex, age, civil status, nationality, profession, space – urban/rural – social rhythms, economic phenomena, etc.). We can also recourse to comparative mapping to study possible specificities ("criminogenic" areas, "sensitive" districts, regional peculiarities, etc.). The study of the combinatorial between these variables (multivariate analysis, factorial analysis) reveals particular configurations which draw the main lines of crime constellation peculiar to such social universe, to such group, in such time, to such society... Thus, for France, in the second half of the 20th century, we notice that, generally speaking, crime appears as an essentially male phenomenon ; that there is a specific structure of the feminine crime (more cunning); that the structure of crime also depends on the age, the profession, the civil status, the nationality, etc. and differs as a function of the diverse modalities of combination of these various variables. In the end, the statistical analysis testify to the eminently sociological and polymorphic character of the criminal phenomenon.

The tendencial regularities emerging from the statistics authorize the formulation of hypotheses relative to likely chains of determination, emphasizing factors susceptible to account for a *sociogenesis* of the forms of criminality. The statistical analysis brings elements of answer to the following interrogation: "What are the social conditions of production of such or such crime ?" Actually, these tendancial regularities allow the constitution of *typologies*. Then, the point is to operate a synthesis, to order in a global perspective the diverse meditative elements of information. We shall define particular types of classification, depending on the methods of distribution of the various variables taken into account in such or such category of infraction. The constituted types could serve as beacons for the construction of new hypotheses whose the probation will allow to get fresh ideas feeding the theoretical reflection.

It is also important to *combine quantitative study and qualitative study*, in order to open to differentiated sources of information and perceive "the movement of the whole, the living aspect of the phenomenon" in its interrelations. Therefore, depending on the established typologies, we will be able to conduct case studies again. These can be carried out from varied documents: files of judicial archives, miscellaneous statements, survey reports, personality inquiries, handrail of commissionership, etc. The in-depth and meticulous study of typical cases, the statement and the analysis of exemplary or exceptional biographies (condemned persons, actors/agents of the judicial institution, of the police, etc.) allow to enrich the "cold" statistical apprehension, and to approach such or such crime in its specifically dramatic aspects. It is at the reconstruction of typical criminal dramas that we can then end up, taking into account "in situation" the interrelations between the multiple elements and the diverse social actors/agents forming the criminal *nexus*[2]. Hence is outlined the way to an anthropology of the relations between aggressors and assaulted in criminal matter. In this perspective, a comparative sociological approach to the condemned persons and the victims, embracing the study of their interrelations, constitutes a promising research lead.

The field of the criminal sociology also includes *the study of the social reaction*. It is to say that it is moreover necessary to take into account the role of the diverse institutional actors/agents and "entrepreneurs of morality" who participate in the elaboration of rules, codes and collective representations of deviance and crime, their implementation (representations of the norm, the crime, the justice, the criminal), and the operations of *labeling* and *stigmatization* which will lead so-and-so to be considered as a criminal. Besides the police institution, one of the privileged theaters where these constituent operations of the social reaction express themselves is the court. *The observation of the trial*, in particular the trial of assizes, allows to see at work, through the combined actions of diverse actors/agents (magistrates, witnesses, policemen, experts, members of the jury, lawyers, etc.), the multiple aspects which compose the social reaction, and contribute to stigmatize the individual qualified as criminal. These observations can be completed by biographies, *reconstructions of delinquent or criminal "careers"*, deepened interviews with the actors/agents of social control previously evoked, but also with other speakers of the criminological field (jurists, psychiatrists, medical, prison, specialized education agents) or other institutions of work and social control, without forgetting the media.

A particular chapter of the criminal sociology also owes to be dedicated to the facts of terrorism. Terrorism indeed represents a particular aspect of crime and their study puts in a crucial way the question of the specificity of the facts of individual crime and collective crime, as well as the question of the borders between *legal violence* and *illegal violence*.

Many other leads, that we can not enumerate all-comprehensive here, offer themselves to the ingenuity of the researcher in criminal sociology. Without forgetting the issue of the evolution of the customs, the law and the modes of infraction which go together with the evolution of societies (*e.g.*, the development of the infractions in informatical matter). In any case, the research field of the criminal sociology remains opened...

## THE EXPLANATORY THEORIES

Investigation work on the diverse aspects of the field of the criminal sociology, ending in the observation that *crime is a social production*, opens the way to theoretical elaboration. *Any structure of society generates its own types of criminality (and of deviance), and we can rightly speak about a sociogenesis of the facts of deviance and criminality.* If we want to grasp the processes of sociological order which underlie the criminal phenomenon in its various updating, it is then necessary to replace the information collected through the exploration of the multiple research leads (previously evoked) in the structural frame of the considered groupings and societies types. Hence were elaborated diverse schemes of analysis of the facts of crime.

We can mainly quote:

- the analysis developed by E. Durkheim advancing the notion of *anomie*;
- the theory of the *culture conflict* by T. Sellin and the theory of the *differential association* by D. Sutherland;
- the explanation of *functionalist* type by R. K. Merton;
- the analysis in terms of *class struggle* or *class conflict* by R. Dahrendorf;
- the approaches in terms of *social reaction* – stigmatization and labeling – by H. Becker.

Doubtless, the various explanatory schemes we have just evoked partially report – each at its level – the sociogenesis of certain forms of crime. However, the variety through which the criminal phenomenon appears makes vain any attempt of univocal explanation which would claim to account for "crime" in general. Indeed, it would be illusory to hope for embracing in a unitarian theory a phenomenon which becomes updated of multiple manners. That is why the main explanatory theories developed to analyze the criminal phenomenon must be considered more as additional than contradictory.

## A TRANSDISCIPLINARY DIRECTION

Should one resolve to see in what it is advisable to call "criminology" a mere artefact, the product of the coincidental conjunction of viewpoints from different disciplines on a protean phenomenon ? In short, in scientific myth ? Indeed, some people think that, strictly speaking, "criminology" does not constitute a science but rather a domain both of research and applications. The "criminologist" would be a kind of *king without a kingdom*... Already fifty years ago, Thorsten Sellin wondered if "criminology" was a science of synthesis. "Criminology is not a science in the limited meaning of the word. However, this term of "criminology" has to remain, either to simply cover the different studies more or less connate which only have a common aspect, being interested in the crimes and in the criminals, or to designate a discipline which assigns to itself as essential function the integration and the synthesis of the conclusions provided by (this) research."

Then? Multidisciplinary, interdisciplinary, transdisciplinary ? In very truth, "criminological" research and action are related to the one or the other depending on the case. Multidisciplinary when several researchers collaborate in the study of the same object, each staying within the limits of its discipline[3]. Interdisciplinary and transdisciplinary when researchers' approaches from diverse disciplines do not consist in a simple juxtaposition but, weaving footbridges, proceed to recombinations, reorganizations, hybridizations. As a bastard science, rich in these combinatorial, "criminology" shows itself sometimes centrifugal, sometimes centripetal, oscillating between unexpected swarmings, empires' arrangement and discovery of unsuspected horizons. Actually, "criminology" theater constitutes a privileged place of paradigmatic tension, convenient to scientific discovery. It facilitates the expression of this essential tension evoked by Thomas Kuhn, a dialectic mobilizing quite at once the expression of *convergent* (classical or conservative) and *divergent* (creative or formative) ways of thinking, "in the perspective of rectified errors which characterizes scientific thought".

In his article entitled *"Criminology", a discipline of synthesis*, Sellin concluded: "I am inclined to give the royal title (of king without kingdom whom would be the criminologist) to the one who makes the integration and the synthesis of the researchers' conclusions in the diverse biological, mental and social sciences". In fact, in the scientific domain as in the political domain, monarches' time is past. Doubtless, the disciplines do exist and their existence is necessary for the advancement of research. But beyond disciplinary withdrawals, cenacles or chapels, for us, researchers who investigate the domain of crime, "the knowledge line is the same, as soon as we tear ourselves away from the narcissistic sphere of our own normality". All things considered, it is up to the diverse citizens-researchers working in the domain of crime to build together the savant city of the "criminologists".

Confronted with the dislocation of criminology and the multiple partial explanatory plans which are proposed by the diverse sociological theories relative to crime, we can wonder if it is possible to elaborate an integrated theory of deviance and criminality. If we herewith understand a theory which would simply render an account of the diverse modalities through which crime shows itself, the answer is certainly negative. It is important to adjust the methodological principles, useful to make possible the theoretical synthesis required by the observation of the facts, to the complexity of reality. As well, in order to try to grasp the criminal phenomenon in its constituent pluridimensionality, it is advisable to adopt a determinedly transdisciplinary approach. Beyond formal disciplinary splits, it is thus important to open the study of the facts of deviance and criminality to the anthropological viewpoint.

## Toward an Anthropological Approach to Crime

*De facto*, the study which takes for object the criminal phenomenon brought to light in diverse landings of the anthropological reality. It is thus towards the perspective of the interrelations which animate, at various levels, these varied hierarchical landings, that henceforth turns the research. To understand a phenomenon, it is indeed necessary to embrace, as much as possible, all the processes which govern it. It is thus advisable to approach the study of the diverse constituent landings of the criminal phenomenon (psychoanalytical, biological legal, statistical, economic, linguistic, psychological aspects, etc.) on a dynamic prospect. Then, we shall see that if the social acts on us "from the outside" (field), it also acts "from the inside" (habitus). And the consideration of the constituent totality of the criminal phenomenon commands to investigate these two aspects whose the articulation (social reaction / acting out) is the heart of the criminological interrogation. It is in this theoretical and methodological prospect that are gradually outlined the features of a criminal anthropology.

Retying with a secular tradition (French and Italian pioneers of the end of the 19th century indeed met themselves, during the international congresses, under the banner of anthropology), and going beyond the bounds of a frame appearing as obsolete and henceforth suspect of a summary biological determinism (as the one into which the upholders of the "sociobiology" lock themselves), the criminal anthropology, as a science of synthesis, tries hard to combine in one global view – taking into account the general economy governing human behaviors –, the study of the diverse constituents aspects of the criminal phenomenon. The idea is thus to integrate the particular approaches aiming at the same object: crime, institutions, and the actors / agents it implies. We can indeed, from the results of the statistical analysis and the theorization of the classic sociology, prolong the analysis in an anthropological perspective, by integrating, in a synthetic way, the observations operated at diverse levels.

## Crime: A Total Social Phenomenon ?

Crime lies in the conjunction of the individual and the collective, staging actors / agents and institutions. The criminal is an individual incriminated according to his behavior. Individual / incrimination, actors-agents / institutions... There are additional, inseparable sectors, whose the study requires the implementation of all the spectrum of analysis possibilities offered by anthropological sciences. The history of crime sociology shows us the passage from an aetiological approach (mainly attached to the study of the act (of the behavior) which will be qualified as criminal), to an approach focused on social reactions, that is globally attached to the study of the processes of incrimination. Actually, here are two main aspects, (but there are many others...) of the totality to be studied. Thus, Durkheim shows that if the norms, faiths, social practices act on us from the outside (and it is to this level that we can read the processes commanding to social reactions) they also act on us from the inside (and it is at this level that we can approach the processes commanding to the acting out). It is in the same perspective that the notion of social control, "designating at first the social processes which have for object the production of behaviors conform to the norms, came to cover all the mechanisms which assure the interiorization of the social order, the regulation of the personal expression, the structuration of the Ego". The consideration of this totality constituting the criminal phenomenon thus demands to study the external regulations (institutions) in their connections with the internal regulations (the people as they are instituted through diverse modalities of socialization). To a sociological approach to the reasons and the actions of the penal, it is advisable to articulate an anthropological approach to the actors / agents and the diverse constituent elements of the criminal phenomenon (criminal, victim, entrepreneurs of morality, legislator, experts, judges, etc., but also the economic context, the groups, the classes or the social formations).

Doubtless, crime can be approached as a total social phenomenon, as one of these social facts which imply multiple landings of the reality – legal, economic, linguistic, religious etc., making us enter groups' life – and which sometimes moves the totality of society and of its institutions. Let us see, in this perspective, some results that the anthropological approach applied to crime has already allowed to obtain and, following the main thread of some current studies, let us explore the leads offered to research and reflection.

## New Research Leads

The anthropological approach allows, for instance, to clarify certain aspects of the process of violent acting out (controlled or not). We saw that the statistical studies concerning crime indicate, generally speaking, that crimes more particularly involve individuals stemming from the most disadvantaged social strata, specifically laborers. But, if the statistical analysis reveals that the social and occupational hierarchy of legal crime illustrates, in its way, the "classic" opposition between social classes – laborious classes, dangerous classes –, at a closer look, it seems that the major anthropological criterion which orders in a relevant way this hierarchy designates more exactly the opposition between manual and intellectual, between *gesture people* and *speech people*. Indeed, the social and occupational scale of criminality carries, in its two extremities, on the one hand categories whose the common characteristic is to be manuals (whose the type can be embodied in broad outline by the laborers or handworkers – exactly, those who work with the hand – who are strongly over represented among the condemned persons, with crimes as murder, compound theft or lethal knocks), and on the other hand categories whose the common characteristic is to be intellectuals (whose the type can be embodied by the professors – those who carry forward the word – who are, them, strongly sub-represented, with crimes as false entry, the qualified breach of trust or the diversion of public deniers...). Although, this antinomic bipolarisation (manual / intellectual) whom shows the criminal statistics refers to a fundamental anthropological reality: the constituent bipolarity of the "anterior field" which makes possible, in the *homo sapiens*, the relation between the hand and the face, between the gesture and the speech, and which expresses, through the joint production of tools and symbols, an essential characteristic of humanity... (Leroi-Gourhan, 1993).

This interdependence of the gesture and the speech, whose the criminal statistics denounces the caesura, reveals a fundamental perspective of research (centered on the connection between the anthropological foundations of the behavior and learning theories), whose the methodical investigation allows to grasp better the relationships between action and symbolization (Bessette, 1982).

*De facto*, the approach to the criminal phenomenon in terms both socio and psycho-linguistic brings a particular lighting on this question. Social practices interfere with linguistic practices, differentiated social practices promoting the development of different linguistic practices in manuals and intellectuals. The positions occupied by both in the social relations of production find an echo at the linguistic level which expresses symbolically these positions and the capacities which are attached to it. Linguistic practices convey and model specific sociological and psychological features – emotional, cognitive and, in the end, behavioral –. Thus, in order to replace this analysis in the criminological frame, it is worth noting that in a conflicting situation, the ones (the intellectuals) verbalize more easily, tending to resolve the conflict by the symbol, whereas the others (the manuals) use more easily the gesture, the acting out.

The sociolinguistic approach showing the influence, socially determined, of the differential speech code development on the forming of personality (Bernstein, 1971) and simultaneously on likely behavioral determinations (acting out) can also get integrated into the biologic approach. Indeed, recent findings in neurosciences allow to specify the neurological substratum and the functional modalities governing the incorporation and the expression of impulsive behaviours and thoughtful behaviours, in particular regarding the connections hand / face, gesture / speech, drives / symbols. The answers to a situation of conflict (attack, illness, frustration) are susceptible to varied modulations in mankind, depending on the sociocultural incorporated learnings (habitus). Thus, we begin to perceive more accurately the set of processes through which certain violent behaviours – mastered or not – get actualized (Laborit, 1970; Karli, 1987).

The anthropological approach, integrating the legal, economic, statistical, sociological, psycholinguistics, neurological landings, authorizes a global, dynamic, interrelational vision of the phenomena and, in this perspective, the acting out can appear as a particular mode of adaptation, making unnecessary the recourse to interpretations of pathological kind. This research orientation is directly in line with the continuation of the issue of "the total man", such as Mauss had anticipated it when he wrote in Sociology and Anthropology (third part: Real and practical relations between psychology and sociology): "in society itself, when we study a special fact, it is with the total psychophysiological complex that we are dealing". *De facto*, the sociolinguistic approach and the knowledge always more detailed of the *neuronal man* confirm the intuition of Mauss by clarifying it. The legal criminal statistics and the analyses which it elicits bring to light this distinction between "instinctive or rather *total* men that we meet in the broadest strata of our own populations and above all in the most backward strata", and "the civilized men of the higher castes of our civilizations (...) who [are] able to regulate the different spheres of [their] consciousness". The labourer, "average man is not master of himself... he is a total". The professor, on the contrary, "is not only divided into halves in himself: he is divided... he knows how to exercise, thanks to his education, to his concepts, to his deliberated choices, a control over each one of his acts". This study of "the relations between the different compartments of the mentality and those which exist between those compartments and the organism" (Mauss, 1960), as well as the study of the links existing between a sociology of the practices and a sociology of the representations, find in the anthropological approach applied to crime the way of their *realization*. To go forward in the knowledge of the criminal phenomenon, it is henceforth up to the researchers to enter the subtle game of transdisciplinarity.

## A MODEL OF TRANSDISCIPLINARITY: MASTER'S DEGREE IN SOCIOLOGY/ CRIMINOLOGY OF THE UNIVERSITY OF FRANCHE-COMTÉ (FRANCE)

The Criminology specialization that was created within the Master's Degree in Sciences of Man and Society at the University of Franche-Comté shows a high degree of interdisciplinarity – one of the principles of criminology. Its subject matter, the social fact "Crime", will be examined by researchers and by experts on norms, deviance and crime specialists from a wide array of backgrounds: lawyers, historians, psychiatrists, psychologists, sociologists, anthropologists... but also civil and police officers, attorneys, prison employees and social workers, whose different perspectives will allow the development of a truly criminological vision (that of a synthetic science). The purpose of this specialization is to give students and potential continuing education candidates both theoretical and methodological tools that can be applied to problems related to deviance, crime and criminality, in order to develop more specific skills which can, in turn, find an application in urban, social or public policies. This specialization should be of interest not only for young social workers, but also for civil officers, doctors, lawyers, psychologists, special needs educators and high-ranking local authorities or police officers. Beyond its rich socio-anthropological content (the integration of common tools of analysis, the culture of discipline, and the familiarization with various authors, categories and systems), this course will let students acquire and master the theoretical and methodological tools specific to the field of criminology. Therefore, the acquisition of knowledge in the legal, historical and aetiological (sciences of the mind) fields should enable students of this course to approach social events related to abnormal behaviors, crime and criminality with the necessary critical hindsight to take action.

This course then brings together history, law, medical science and psychology, though it is still rooted in a socio-anthropological approach of the social fact "crime". This approach implies that all social actors/agents are taken into account, not only as producers (politicians – legislators –, authorities, police officers, experts, social workers and other institutional actors), but also as products (criminals, deviants, social outcasts) of social activity. The social and historical logic of the production of values, of norms and of laws will be analyzed, as well as the conditions of their application as a regulation system of the social.

## TO CONCLUDE...

Any social life evolves between the two bornes that are the sameness and the otherness, the norm and the transgression. "So that there were no crimes (nor deviance) - wrote Durkheim - a leveling of the individual consciousnesses would be needed (...) which is neither possible, nor desirable ; But so that there was no repression (no social reaction), an absence of moral homogeneity would be needed, which is irreconcilable with the existence of a society" (Durkheim, 1983, translation mine). Consequently, in a society, the definitions of "normal" and "abnormal" behaviors are generally complementary. With the result that the today's deviance is sometimes the tomorrow's norm. And in front of the always increasing hold of the technological rationality over our societies which, in a very democratic way, invades and controls bodies and souls, the deviants's existence – those "Strangers" or "Oustiders" evoked by Camus or Marcuse – shows after all the inalienable opening of the field of the human adventure. In a world which aims at unidimensionality, a critical look leads us, by a reversal of perspective, to meditate this reflection of J. Monod: "the contempt that the overwhelming majority of men dedicates to those whom they hold for enslaved in a worse savagery than theirs, this contempt is too deep not to indicate that the condition of the so-called "civilized" results almost everywhere from a forced integration" (translation mine).

Navigating between norms and transgressions, between singularity and otherness, the problem of the deviance finally refers to the fundamental problem of anthropology which aims at unveiling the socio-historic processes presiding over the differentiation. Isn't it the ability to constantly reinvent himself the peculiarity of being human, and does not the anthropological reality consist in the production of differences (cultures), from an invariant matrix (*homo sapiens*) ? Isn't man, quite at once, a producer of standards, but also of differences ? This issue reveals the dialectic of the individual and the collective, the actor and the system... This fundamental interrogation recuts the questionings of "criminology".

In the end, the anthropological study of the facts of deviance teaches us that the deviant is always "the other"... As well, by inventing their deviants - which are the negatives on which they re-elaborate ceaselessly their own image – societies make once again nothing else than – according to the expression of Marcel Mauss – *paying themselves of the counterfeit money of their dream.*

## ACKNOWLEDGMENT

A special thank-you to Guillaume Magueijo and Renzo Bianchi, whose help has been very useful to translate this chapter.

## REFERENCES

Becker, H. S. (1963). *Outsiders*. Paris, France: A.M. Métailié.

Bernstein, B. (1971). *Class, Codes and Control.* London: Routledge & Kegan Paul.

Bessette, J. M. (1982). *Sociologie du crime.* Paris: PUF.

Durkheim, E. (1983). *Les Règles de la Méthode sociologique*. Paris: PUF.

Durkheim, E. (1985). *Le suicide.* Paris: PUF.

Durkheim, E. (1986). *De la division du travail social.* Paris: PUF.

Karli, P. (1987). *L'homme agressif.* Paris: O. Jacob.

Laborit, H. (1970). *L'agressivité détournée.* Paris: UGE.

Leroi-Gourhan, A. (1963-1964). *Le geste et la parole*. 2 tomes. Paris: Albin Michel.

Marcuse, H. (1968). *L'homme unidimensionnel.* Paris: Minuit

Mauss, M. (1966). *Sociologie et anthropologie.* Paris: PUF.

Merton, R. K. (1965). *Eléments de théorie et de méthode sociologique.* Paris: Plon.

Sutherland, E. H., & Cressey, D. R. (1966). *Principes de criminologie*. Paris: Cujas.

## ENDNOTES

1. It is advisable to overstep the false antinomy actor vs agent. In practice, depending on the occupied positions, polarizations and situations (in the regarded field), the same individuals are alternatively, or even simultaneously actor or agent.
2. Nexus: interrelational set constituted by the actors/agents and the diverse factorial and situational elements involved in a (criminal) drama. By drama, we mean here – with no link to any tragic connotation – the social precipitate, outcome of varied exchanges at diverse levels between actors/agents imbricated in an interrelational network which defines a particular social configuration: in this particular case, a crime.
3. Jailed within the limits of his own brain?

# Chapter 3
# The Misfortunes of "Criminology" in France:
## A Specific History (1880-2009)

**Laurent Mucchielli**
*CESDIP- CNRS, France*

## EXECUTIVE SUMMARY

*The state of a discipline—or, more simply, the state of a discourse field and the related academic practices—cannot be understood outside the historical framework of its national genesis. According to Mucchielli (2004), this 'broad picture' view of France suggests a three-period split: (1) paradigmatic assertions and the impossible transdisciplinary dialogue typical of the years 1880-1940; (2) the normative context of the years 1945-1975, and the fresh associations it brought about; (3) the renewed dissociation between professional rationales and transdisciplinary dialogue from the mid-1970s onwards, alongside the considerable development of social science research. Finally, the authors question the current situation and the renewed, politically motivated attempt at establishing criminology as a full discipline in France.*

## BETWEEN THE BIOLOGICAL AND THE SOCIAL: THE SEARCH FOR A CRIME PARADIGM IN FRANCE (1880-1940)

In France, in the 1880s, as crime research was in the process of being institutionalized as a new scholarly discipline—a trend that pervaded the entire Western world—, the scientific discourse was dominated by the question of the individual genesis of crime. This issue was almost exclusively addressed from a biomedical perspective, through various theories purporting to somehow identify in certain individuals the existence of "natural" predispositions for aggression, crime, or even flatly "Evil" (Pick, 1989, p.44; Renneville, 1997, p.452; Mucchielli, 2006). The novel discipline that emerged in France at the time was not called "Criminology" by its proponents yet, but "Criminal Anthropology" ("*Anthropologie criminelle*"). However, some French medical doctors—including Alexandre Lacassagne (1823-1924), Professor of Forensic Medicine at

DOI: 10.4018/978-1-60566-872-7.ch003

Lyon University School of Medicine and main promoter of the new field—frequently alluded to the "social factors of crime" and did challenge, at least *in part*, Cesare Lombroso's concept of the born criminal. The "Criminal Anthropology" designation mainly aimed at taking strategic distance from the Italian school, from which they were in fact intellectually – e.g. professionally – very close (Mucchielli, 1994a; Renneville, 1995). Only in the then budding field of social science could proper research on crime as a social phenomenon be seen emerging at the time.

## Crime as a Social Phenomenon

During the 1890s, non-medical research endeavours focussing on the social dimension of crime were scarce and did not put forward any sociological methodology. Gabriel Tarde (1843-1904), for example, offered in his extensive works a great many thoughts about crime and penalty, through a series of books of which some were internationally acclaimed, in particular *La criminalité comparée* (1886) (*Comparative Criminality*), and *La philosophie pénale* (1890) (translated into English as *Penal Philosophy*, 1968, 2nd ed. 2000). Moreover, despite occupying prominent positions from 1894 onwards (as head of the Judicial Statistics department at the Ministry of Justice, and co-director of Lacassagne's journal, *Archives d'anthropologie criminelle*), and being elected to Collège de France in 1900, Tarde never trained any scholars or launched any research programme.

Besides Tarde, several intellectuals devoted at least some effort to crime study at the time. For a while, the most active and creative among them was Henri Joly (1839-1925), who taught "criminal and penitentiary science " at Paris University School of Law, starting 1887, and published a string of noted books at the end of the 1880s (Veilt, 1994). The dominant theme running through his criminological works was moral degradation rather than biological lowliness. To him, the criminal was a "misled man", not a "survivor of primitive ages". This degradation itself partook to the rootlessness of modern man, forced to leave his family, his village, his trade, to go and seek a job in the anonymity and isolation of the big city. Joly set up to prove his theory using countless geographical maps, published in his 1889 book *La France criminelle* (*Criminal France*). Joly's works, however, rather failed to reach a broader audience.

One has to turn to the group founded in 1897 by Émile Durkheim (1858-1917) around his journal *L'Année sociologique* to first notice the emergence of a trend towards criminal sociology. This group brought together young philosophers who were convinced that sociology needed to be endowed with a proper scientific agenda based on autonomy from other sciences (Mucchielli, 1998). Among them, Gaston Richard (1860-1935) was picked by Durkheim to head the "Criminal sociology and moral statistics" section of the journal. It fell upon him to lay the foundations for a sociology of crime, in a complete turnaround to the biologization of behaviours that prevailed at the time. The work accomplished around Richard, from a critical point of view (see for example the notion of "criminogenic environment") as well as through its scholarly contribution proper (historical analysis of shifting value and work systems, and their effect on criminality), constitutes an attempt at gradually building both the object and the agenda of a criminal sociology (Mucchielli, 1994b). As compared to the influence enjoyed by Durkheimians in other scientific spheres at the time, however, their critical work in the field of criminology was a failure. There are at least three reasons for this: first, the considerable strength and autonomy of the psychiatric circles, whose discourse increasingly prevailed once the fad for criminology subsided, and whose alliance with magistrates was already institutionalised. Then, the medical world displayed remarkable cohesion around its mainly hereditarist concept of crime. Finally, sociological research almost vanished from this area at the turn of the century, after Richard left the Durkheimian group.

## From Criminal Anthropology to Psychiatry: A Shift in Medical Criminology

While the works of Italian and French criminal anthropology scholars reigned almost supreme in the years 1880-1895, the last decade of the century saw the alienists gradually regain the upper hand on the medical discourse, a supremacy that can be explained in several ways. While the sheer overall volume of publications is hardly a sufficient criterion, a closer look at international conferences on criminology, in terms of both membership of the organising committees and quality of speakers, also gives a measure of the institutional weight of the various groups. Even though the "criminal anthropology" designation stayed, academics who defined themselves as anthropologists declined steadily in numbers. As criticism against the criminal type and the relevance of anthropometrics swelled in all countries, the third International Criminal Anthropology Congress, held in Brussels in 1892, signalled a first symbolic break up, as the Italian delegation refused to attend, considering their ideas to be inadequately represented. Indeed, the Brussels Congress can be seen as an "artillery barrage" operation. The French (Debierre, Lacassagne, Manouvrier, and Tarde); the Dutch (Jelgersma, Masoin, and Van Hamel); the Belgians (Cuylits, Dallemagne, Houzé, and Struelens); Benedikt, of Austria; as well as the Germans (Näcke and Von Liszt): these scholars unanimously agreed that, although physical stigmata may frequently characterise criminals, they could not be used to define any individual as a criminal or be construed to infer general roots to criminal behaviour.

At the turn of the century, except for the rearguard of Lombroso's followers, it seems that only Lacassagne and his students still believed in the virtues of anthropometry.

## Hereditarist Theories: From Degeneration to Constitutionalism

Throughout the years 1880-1914, mental health circles largely shared the vision of inneism and hereditary determinism used by anthropologists in their constructs, albeit expressed in different ways. Their favourite model was degeneration theory. Charles Féré and Valentin Magnan were the most active French alienists at early criminal anthropology congresses. Féré was the first to get involved in criminology discussions, with his 1888 book *Dégénérescence et criminalité* (*Degeneration and Criminality*). Magnan, however, established a more authoritative reputation. A mere general practitioner at Saint-Anne Hospital in Paris, outstripped by Ball in the 1877 race for the Chair of Mental Illnesses at University of Paris School of Medicine, his diligent attendance at criminal anthropology conferences may have been mainly motivated by the will to build the international reputation he was lacking. He certainly did take a very early interest in social problems while working on alcoholism, however. Whatever the case may be, Magnan came to the criminal field intending to defend and propagate the theory of degeneration he had inherited from his first master, Prosper Lucas.

At the Brussels 1892 congress, Magnan presented a report entitled "*Morbid Criminal Obsession*", in which he distinguished between the "delusional insane" ("*aliénés délirants*") and the 'higher degenerate" ("*dégénérés lucides*"), pushed by "morbid obsessions" that the alienist should endeavour to identify and describe: homicide, theft, pyromania, or sexual perversion. Magnan's report serves as yet another illustration of the ultra-deterministic view of biology held by alienists of the time. He identified for example four different categories of sexual perverts, based on features exclusively pertaining to brain physiology: The "spinals", whose unconscious acts were motivated by elementary organic reaction mechanisms; the "posterior spinal cerebrals", for whom the mere sight of an individual of the opposite sex sparked the sexual impulse; the "anterior spinal cerebrals", who simply displayed some specific form of perversion, located in the anterior cerebral cortex, which gave an abnormal orientation to their desire – e.g. either applied it to inappropriate subjects (incest, homosexuality, zoophilia) or through inappropriate channels (exhibitionism, mutilation, etc.); and finally the "anterior or psychic cerebrals" who, on the contrary, only functioned at the frontal level, as their conscious desire failed to trigger normal physiological functions.

Physiological causality, as we can see, was hugely influential in the psychiatric theories that dominated the turn of the century. Magnan's successor, Ernest Dupré, worked from the same assumptions on concepts such as "morbid constitution" and "constitutional perversity"; and it is the very same inspiration that thoroughly guided the works of Georges Heuyer on child psychiatry, at least during the interwar period (Lefaucheur, 1994).

## The Situation during the Interwar Period

It is hard to see where exactly sociological ideas might have fit into such a paradigmatic framework.

Generally speaking, French scholarship became less fertile during the interwar period. At the international level, sociological thought emanated mainly from the U.S., the Chicago School in particular. Their research, however, remained little known in France. Maurice Halbwachs (1877-1945) who was, along with Marcel Mauss, the key man of the interwar Durkheimian system, was interested in suicide and not criminality. In addition, his vision of the Chicago School and its research on the city was rather aloof (Marcel, 1999). While "judicial and moral sociology" studies always remained central among Durkheimians (such as Louis Gernet, Paul Fauconnet, and Georges Davy), any interest for crime in modern societies disappeared almost entirely from interwar French academic sociology.

In fact, during the interwar period, the field of "criminology", as it was called – or "criminal science", or even "penitentiary science" – was dominated by jurists, along with medical practitioners appearing in court (forensic and psychiatric experts) (Kaluszynski, 1994, p.231-233). This trend actually started before WWI in academic circles, with certain law schools offering courses covering criminal law, criminology, and/or penitentiary science (Pinatel, 1957, p.417). This triggered new dynamics in legal studies, in an institutional alliance uniting doctors and jurists, with the latter calling the shots this time. On the academic front, this alliance was finally recognized in 1922 with the creation of the Paris Institute of Criminology, jointly run by the Paris Law and Medicine schools, with a four-pronged curriculum: (1) criminal law, (2) forensic medicine and criminal psychiatry, (3) scientific police, (4) penitentiary science. Ever since then, criminology, or "criminal science", has continued to feature in law schools, as a scholarly appendix to penal law.

In 1936, criminology was given a proper means of expression with the *Revue de science criminelle et de droit pénal comparé* (*Review of criminal science and comparative penal law*), headed by two Professors of the Paris Law School (Louis Hugueney and Henri Donnedieu de Vabres), with a committee comprising, besides other jurists, psychiatrist Claude, forensic scientist Balthazard, as well as Sannié, director of the Scientific Police Institute (and a Professor at Paris School of Medicine).

Finally, on a paradigmatic level, after the revival of psychiatry at the expense of criminal anthropology, the interwar in France was mainly characterised by the gradual ushering in of psychoanalysis (Mucchielli, 1994b, p.363-409). Pioneering French psychoanalysts (Hesnard, Laforgue, Marie Bonaparte, etc.), however, in keeping with a literal understanding of Freud's writings, all enhanced the criminal nature of

Man, its "aggressive instincts" and "original violence", with analyses consistently revolving around the conventional psychiatric wisdom of the times: the "constitutional factor", the "physiological foundation" of criminal conduct. Such a paradigm made any convergence toward social science fairly difficult at best. Moreover, these initial psychoanalytic attempts at criminal science were mainly based on pathological case studies (paranoid delirium, crimes of passion).

## THE ERA OF DIALOGUE AND ITS NORMATIVE CONTEXT (1945-1975)

The end of WWII signalled a new dawn for human sciences, which were increasingly involved in social and political life. In the legal sphere, this new philosophical era translated in particular into the principles of the "new social defence", developed in France by Marc Ancel (1902-1990) to the point where it offered a common ground to many jurists during the years 1950-60 (Levasseur, 1991; Enguéléguélé, 1998). In addition, the socialist ideal (in the broadest sense) had growing influence throughout Europe. In the field of penal policy, this quite naturally involved a willingness to focus on education (or re-education) and prevention, to offer psychological support to challenging teenagers, and to deeply reform the prison system (Faugeron, 1991b). Still, this movement was neither fundamentally new, no absolutely prevailing. Old trends persisted and did contradict it at times. But as we will see, the scientific sphere offers three examples of the bridge-building potential allowed by this common cultural ground: first, as jurists opened up to sociology; second, as a transdisciplinary dialogue developed around the issues of juvenile delinquency; and third, as a theoretical dialogue seemed – at least for a while – to have been sparked between sociology and psychology.

### Keeping Traditional Criminology Alive

One example of traditional criminology staying very much alive is the thought and action of Jean Pinatel (1913-1999) from 1950-1980. In his capacity of *Inspecteur général de l'administration pénitentiaire* (Inspector General of Prisons), Pinatel was a member of the Amor Commission, which was in charge of reforming the prison system in 1945. He first introduced himself as an expert in "criminal science", then in "criminology", which he taught for many years at the Paris Institute of Criminology. In the immediate aftermath of the war, and for several decades, he was one of the main contributors to the *Revue de science criminelle et de droit pénal comparé*.

Pinatel defended criminology as it was practiced during the first half of the century – starting with biology, following up with psychopathology and, *in fine*, possibly borrowing from sociology a few general frameworks/contexts that more or less favoured criminality. Such was the outline of his courses; and such was the scientific agenda that informed the International Congress of Criminology organised in Paris in 1950 by Pinatel, drawing on his membership of the International Society for Criminology, which he dominated for almost thirty years (Pirès, 1979). This is understandable, given that Pinatel had defined criminology as a study of the criminal, whose core task was to study the "criminal personality" in order to subsequently diagnose the "dangerous state", thus safeguarding society from trouble. Although Pinatel, in the 1970s, facing the rise of sociological criticism and "critical criminology" in the Western world, partially conceded to the sociological approach, these were mere "*ad hoc* changes", to borrow the words of Thomas Kuhn (1972), which never seriously challenged the theoretical core of the classical "paradigm" defended by Pinatel.

Generally speaking, post-war French law schools witnessed a strong increase in the interest for criminology. In the 1960s, specialised curricula were offered in Paris (at the Institute of Criminology as well as at the Criminal Science department of the Institute of Comparative Law, headed by Marc Ancel and Yvonne Marx), Aix-en-Provence (Penal Science and Criminology Institute, headed by Raymond Gassin), Bordeaux (Criminal Science Institute headed by Jean-Pierre Delmas Saint-Hilaire), Montpellier (Criminal Science Institute headed by J.-M. Aussel), Poitiers (Criminal Science Institute first headed by Pierre Couvrat, then by Jean Pradel), Toulouse (Criminology and Penal Science Institute headed by Roger Merle), and Lille (Institute of Criminology headed by Georges Levasseur), as well as Strasbourg (Criminal Science Institute headed by Jacques Léauté), Nancy, etc.

## The Dialogue between Jurists and Sociologists and the Revival of Criminal Sociology

That said, the sociological approach of the criminal phenomenon also found a favourable echo with many jurists-criminologists of the time, particularly in and around Durkheimian circles. *L'Année sociologique*, the twice reborn journal (it reappeared in 1948), was central to this renewed discussion, whose main supporter was Henri Lévy-Bruhl (1884-1964). In this new journal, he was in charge of the "sociology of law and moral" section, along with Georges Davy. Lévy-Bruhl put crime studies fairly high on his research agenda, considering that "a social ensemble best reveals its personality through its attitude to crime". As early as 1950-51, under the auspices of CES (Centre d'Études Sociologiques), he conducted a "criminology survey", subsequently presented at the 2nd International Congress of Criminology, entitled "Statistical survey of breach of trust". Simultaneously, a "criminal sociology research group" was born, with Lévy-Bruhl as a guardian figure – however, André Davidovitch (1912-1986) quickly became one of the most active members, before gradually taking over the leadership (Marcel, Mucchielli, 2006). This group, built from a handful of scholars and students attracted to EPHE (*École Pratique des Hautes Études*—Practical School of Advanced Studies) by the teaching of Lévy-Bruhl, quickly exceeded this framework, gradually expanding until it became what had to be called a small team. Its 1956-57 agenda shows, beyond Davidovitch's prime study ("Fraud and Bad Cheque Issuance"), that Constantin Oeconomo was researching the " Psychosociological and sociological aspects of war: special delinquency in the army"; while Dimitri Kalogeropoulos, a graduate from Paris Institute of Criminology and the Institute of Comparative Law, was working on "Blood crimes"; and René Benjamin, a supply teacher at CES, was announcing a research project exploring "resocialising delinquents: the role of the religious feeling". New scholars flocked during the following years; various studies were launched – about incest (Denis Szabo, whose doctoral thesis would later be entitled "Crimes and cities") or about criminality in Paris (Vasile Stanciu). The dynamics were triggered: a new, hybrid discipline, "criminal sociology", was born—albeit, paradoxically, thanks to a jurist who initiated the institutional blending with sociology.

This synergy, however, was stopped in its tracks when Lévy-Bruhl died in 1964. The event prompted a split, and Lévy-Bruhl's "sociological heritage" was picked up by a team built around Davidovitch. Law scholars followed Jean Carbonnier (1908-2003), who played a pivotal role, replacing Lévy-Bruhl at the board of l'*Année Sociologique*, drawing together many of his former students, and co-founding a research group with Georges Levasseur—"Research and measure of institutional and normative transformations of contemporary society"—which, in January 1968, became the Laboratory for criminal and penal sociology of Paris II University. Why did this split happen? Theoretical divergences were noticeable. Carbonnier had his own particular idea of judicial sociology: although certainly linked to an intellectual posture that approaches the judicial fact "from outside", it should only do so with an aim to help the legislator. In that sense, while he claimed some Durkheimian affiliation, in the world of jurists this intellectual lineage came "at little cost", since he somehow managed to append judicial sociology to law studies (Soubiran-Paillet, 2000). Davidovitch had other views, more faithful to the Durkheimian paradigm, which he developed within the small unit he led at CES until his retirement in 1981: the "Criminal Sociology Research Unit". There, Davidovitch carried out a string of major research works on judicial statistics, on the activity of Prosecutor's office bodies, on the mapping of criminality in the city, as well as on several specific crimes (bad cheques and traffic delinquency in particular). Over the years, he was able to refine his analysis system within the framework of a well-defined research programme, "observing the judicial machine as it copes with criminality, and analysing criminality as a product of that machine. These products, insofar as they are the outcome of selective interventions, convey in objective terms (they are indicators) the attitude – or attitudes – of magistrates, at the various levels of the judicial apparatus, as they confront the various types of crime". During many years, he was also a noted columnist for *L'Année sociologique*.

## Developing a Transdisciplinary Area: Youth Delinquency

Youth delinquency was one of the main areas of convergence and debate for academics and professionals of the field after 1945 (Tétard, 1985). In addition to the tradition of child psychiatry initiated in particular by Heuyer and his students, juvenile court judge Jean Chazal de Mauriac (1907-1991), who was quite close to Marc Ancel, played an important role in this area as early as the Vichy period, but mostly after the war. Later on, that theme developed mainly from an institutional point of view, given the opening, in 1958, within the Ministry of Justice, of the Training and Research Centre for Correctional Education (CFR-ES - *Centre de Formation et de Recherche de l'Éducation Surveillée*) in Vaucresson (in the suburbs of Paris). The creation of this centre was motivated by the reorganization of juvenile courts through the ordinance of Feb. 2, 1945 on delinquent youth: after establishing a new Office for Correctional Education at the French Ministry of Justice and implementing a string of supervisory measures for endangered and delinquent youth, a training centre was required for newly hired employees.

In 1958, the training activities were strengthened by the addition of a research unit which subsequently grew on its own and was significantly reinforced from 1964 onwards, when psychologist Jacques Sélosse was chosen to lead the research effort. Vaucresson quickly became the most important criminology research centre in France, with a transdisciplinary team (psychologists, sociologists, psycho-educationalists, statisticians, plus one neuropsychiatrist, one jurist, and one demographer), albeit slightly dominated by clinicians. In 1963, the centre finally launched its own journal: the *Annales de Vaucresson*. The following ten years were the golden age of the Vaucresson centre. At the onset of the 1970s, research developed along five lines: (1) analysing juvenile "social inadequacy" phenomena – mainly gangs and delinquency (car theft, drug use, violent crimes); (2) studying the methods of intervention of youth workers with juvenile delinquents; (3) evaluating the outcomes of this rehabilitation work; (4) researching the general roots of juvenile delinquency growth (school and economic developments in particular); (5) continuous education methods as applied to youth workers. From a "socio-criminological" perspective, the first line delivered the most in terms of new information. Some of this research helped enhance new aspects of juvenile delinquency in a consumer society. This particularly holds true of research on car and motorcycle theft, which showed that the point was often not so much appropriating goods, even in order to sell them, as fun or utility (for a night); the main danger being the fact that such a behaviour was likely to generate traffic accidents.

In the area of juvenile delinquency, the Vaucresson centre stands as the main transdisciplinary research attempt known in France. However, from the end of the 1970s onwards, this attempt gradually faded away.

### Social Sciences and Psychological Sciences: A Dialogue at Last?

The years 1945-1975 witnessed a historically unprecedented opening-up phenomenon that made it possible to start building bridges between sociology and psychology. Before WWII, irreconcilable paradigms would pitch sociology, totally impervious to individual psychology, against psychology, which appeared unable to get rid of biological determinism. This situation, however, quickly evolved after the war, as first illustrated by Daniel Lagache (1903-1972) (Mucchielli, 1994c, p.381-409). Lagache was strongly influenced by phenomenology during the 1930s (including both Jaspers and Minkowski in general psychopathology, as well as Belgian psychocriminologist Étienne De Greeff), and also felt the influence of psychosociologist Kurt Lewin. Thus it is that, during the 1950s-60s, he came to develop a theory of criminal psychology that entailed a strong social dimension. However, being at the time also highly involved in psychoanalysis, he apparently lacked a partner to build this frontier at that point in history.

Still, two other clinicians did more directly invest the field of criminology, building partnerships with social scientists (Mucchielli, 1997, p.18-22). One is Marcel Colin, bringing along with him what would come to be known, from the first French Congress of Criminology (Lyon, 1960) onwards, as the "second school of Lyon" – the team he later lead at Lyon Medical School's Institute of Forensic Medicine and Clinical Criminology. Colin—who was deeply influenced intellectually by Sartrian existentialism and who also leaned towards interactionism in many respects, in addition to being closely linked to English antipsychiatrists—strongly supported the idea that the clinic should have a fundamentally therapeutic purpose, opposing the deterministic concept of "criminal personality", a phrase that, according to him, should be "banned from psychiatric vocabulary." He became indeed a fellow traveller of both French sociologists and European critical criminologists, especially around the network that was built during the first half of the 1970s, founding in particular the journal *Déviance et société*. The same goes for De Greeff's pupil Christian Debuyst, a Professor of Criminology in Leuven (Belgium), who, in the 1960s-70s, published empirical research enhancing the scholarly potential of a convergence between phenomenology and interactionism, and who also wrote seminal texts condemning such concepts as the "criminal personality" and "dangerosity". Debuyst was himself, in the most practical sense and to this very day, a fellow traveller of deviance sociologists and critical criminologists. These towering figures of past decades' criminological clinic, however, had no worthy successors. Ever since the 1980s, the scientific field has evolved in such a way as to either not allow such convergence, or even provoke new clashes.

## INSTITUTIONAL GROWTH, THE ESTRANGEMENT OF DISCIPLINES AND THE SUPREMACY OF SOCIAL SCIENCE RESEARCH (1975-2000)

From the end of the 1960s onwards, research in criminology enjoyed a new institutional boom, owing to a purposeful research policy initiated by the French Ministry of Justice (Mucchielli, Marcel, 2002). It also received significant support from the General office for scientific and technical research (*Direction générale à la recherche scientifique et technique*). In addition to the Vaucresson centre, the *Chancellerie* created in 1964 the National Centre for Penitentiary Studies and Research (*Centre National d'Études et de Recherches Pénitentiaires* – CNERP), and then, in 1968, the Penal and Criminological Studies Service (*Service d'Études Pénales et Criminologiques* – SEPC). To supplement this segmented development and support these research centres, two coordinating and fund-raising structures were created: 1968 saw the advent of the Coordination Committee for Research in Criminology (*Comité de Coordination des Recherche Criminologiques* – CCRC), a 21-member body chaired by Paul Amor; followed the year after by the Research Coordination Service (*Service de Coordination de la Recherche* – SCR).

While CNERP never really took off as a research centre, SEPC was to usher in the third age of criminal sociology in France.

## A Sociology of Social Reaction

SEPC was initiated by Philippe Robert (a magistrate with a PhD in sociology from Bordeaux University) and born at the end of 1968, reporting to the Office of Criminal Affairs and Pardons (*Direction des affaires criminelles et des grâces*) at the Ministry of Justice. In addition to its expected research output, its other assignments were the general secretariat of CCRC, as well as managing the *Compte général de l'administration de la justice* (judicial statistics). SEPC enjoyed a quick growth, so much so that it came second only to Vaucresson among research centres, and gradually conquered partial autonomy from the Ministry, in terms of both processes and output, soon co-reporting to CNRS, the National Centre for Scientific Research (*Centre National de la Recherche Scientifique*), resulting in a peculiar positioning in the field of French criminology. It swiftly established strong network ties in Europe and North-America (e.g. French-speaking Canada), which chiefly resulted in the creation of a new journal in 1977. *Déviance et société* was born in a peculiar intellectual atmosphere marked by growing controversy surrounding the penal system, and the arrival of interactionism (the second Chicago School and its labelling theory) and "critical criminology" (Mucchielli, 1997).

Some of SEPC's initial research areas were inspired by the direct needs of criminal justice (forecasting registered criminality; maintaining administrative statistics; monitoring apparent foreigner delinquency or drug trafficking). Others rather focussed on the analysis of institutional processes (studying the costs of crime or the penal handling of business criminality; constituting collective rape as a category), and studied the image of the institution in society (studies on social representations of the criminal justice system). However, beyond those headings, which were quite commonplace in the field of criminology at the time, SEPC was actually taking a critical stance. In 1973, Philippe Robert published in l'*Année sociologique* (which he had joined thanks to Davidovitch) a text announcing the crisis of positivist criminology—in his own words "*criminologie du passage à l'acte*", literally "acting out criminology"—i.e. aetiology theories. First, he argued that these bio-psychological research studies were based on non-representative crime samples. He then proceeded to introduce labelling theory, stating that the process through which an individual steps from occasional to chronic delinquency "stems from a stigmatization of the social reaction that takes place when the public classifies as a deviant someone who merely engaged in a deviant act." From this perspective, criminology could be turned into a "science of social mechanisms of rejection", hinging on the analysis of the penal system. Robert then tried to launch a relevant research programme, based on two questions: how does society create norms; and how does it sanction them? Besides traditional empirical fields such as the analysis of penal statistics (from policing to prison) and the study of the social representations of justice, SEPC researchers gradually developed research on the mechanisms of transfer toward judicial authorities, and on the genesis of penal norms (legislative sociology) – later on even establishing ties with historians on the latter theme. Throughout the 1970s and 1980s, SEPC thus produced cutting-edge research in this area, in a well-defined paradigmatic framework which *de facto* excluded any potential collaboration with psychological sciences. Robert's position has always been that criminology should be considered a discipline without an object, whose transdisciplinarity was a mere façade, devoid of any heuristic value ; by contrast, he preferred a sociology of crime, rooted in a given paradigm and in a cumulative empirical research approach.

Without even mentioning political agendas that led some to reject any non-external perspective on research objects (such as prison, for instance), discrepancies in professional rationales were too critical among the various players for any meaningful research collaboration to take place.

## The Evolution of the Institutional Context, 1980-2000

In May 1981, left-wing leader François Mitterrand became President of the French Republic, in a dramatic upset that created the conditions for an actual reorganization of research within the Ministry of Justice – the project had been in the air for several years, but never implemented. As a result, both CNERP and SCR disappeared, and a new convention was signed between the *Chancellerie* and CNRS in 1983. Only CFR-ES and SEPC remained: the former became the Vaucresson Centre for Transdisciplinary Research (*Centre de recherches interdisciplinaires de Vaucresson* – CRIV), while the latter was called the Sociological Research Centre on Law and Penal Institutions (*Centre de recherches sociologiques sur le droit et les institutions pénales* – CESDIP). In addition to boasting a rather long-standing relationship with CNRS, CESDIP was the main recipient of the redeployment of staff from late CNERP, which added penitentiary issues to its research agenda. CRIV, however, found the situation much less favourable, challenged as it was by a structural crisis that it never really managed to overcome. Outside these two units, most scholars of the field who had been assigned to general-purpose research centres felt rather isolated, so that over the 1980s, CESDIP gradually emerged as the only crime-orientated social science research centre, which it remains to this day. Furthermore, it managed to regularly push fresh ideas, developing in particular pioneering—in France—victimisation surveys, as well as, from the 1990s onwards, research studies on the feeling of insecurity, and policing research.

The 1990s partially challenged this situation, with the institutional development of three new areas of research, once again directly spurred by State requests:

- First came research on drugs, at the beginning of the 1980s, with a dramatic decade-long growth. This phenomenon was linked to strong institutional demand motivated by the increase in drug consumption and the AIDS epidemic. An interministerial drug-fight structure was implemented in 1982, which gradually became autonomous. 1993 saw the creation of a Public interest group called French Observatory of Drugs and Drug Addictions (*Observatoire français des drogues et des toxicomanies* – OFDT), which goes to show that government funding was a lasting trend and the will to stabilise statistical indicators genuine. A research network ("*Psychotropes, Politiques, Sociétés*") was born in 1994, followed by a CNRS laboratory in 2001 (called CESAMES – *Centre de recherche Psychotropes, Santé Mentale, Société*).
- The other area that developed dramatically during the 1990s is policing research. The creation, in 1991, of the Institute for Higher Studies on Interior Security (*Institut des*

*hautes études de la sécurité intérieure* – IHESI) provided significant funding for this research. The institute, for that matter, has become quite an important player of the field as a whole, funding research and publishing a journal that boasts numerous academic contributions (the *Cahiers de la sécurité intérieure*). However, its dependence on the political power subjects it to periodical turmoil.

- Finally, the Ministry for Town Planning (created in 1990) also provided important support for research on delinquency throughout the 1990s, while the Interministerial delegation for road traffic safety also funded many studies on traffic crime.

Hence, from the mid-1990s onwards, research production was scattered among several, diverse places. These issues were extensively discussed at CLERSÉ (Lille Centre for Sociological and Economic Research and Studies of CNRS, Lille 1 University) around Dominique Duprez; at GRASS (CNRS Social and Sociability Analysis Group, Paris 8 University) around Francis Bailleau; and at CERSA (CNRS Administrative Science Study and Research Centre, Paris 2 University), headed by Jacques Chevallier. Moreover, crime research never totally deserted law schools – some jurists still define themselves as "criminologists". Most active among them is Robert Cario, in charge of the "Jean Pinatel Criminal Science Unit" at Pau University, and publishing director of the "Sciences criminelles" series at L'Harmattan publisher.

## The Main Areas of Social Science Research, 1980-2000

Despite the Vaucresson centre crisis, the development of sociological research during the 1980s prompted several authors to re-appropriate the subject of juvenile delinquency while researching the subject of working class youth. Such was the case for "*Jeunesses et Sociétés*" (Youth and Societies) network, which gradually drew together dozens of academics and researchers in a think tank mostly influenced by the work of Pierre Bourdieu – one example is sociologist Gérard Mauger and his seminal work on "youth gangs". Others include several scholars from Alain Touraine's circle of influence, who worked on collective action in working class neighbourhoods (François Dubet, Didier Lapeyronnie, Adil Jazouli).

Then, as social developments put such issues as juvenile delinquency and rioting under the spotlights of the media/political stage again and sparked fresh institutional demand (especially around the policing category of "urban violence"), scholarly output increased, in the second half of the 1990s in particular. Research studies, however, in a departure from the previous decade, focussed mainly on quantitative methods, given the ever-growing impact of statistics and "expertise" in mainstream media. Here, we should mention Hugues Lagrange and his work on victimisation and juvenile delinquency; as well as Sébastian Roché's 1999 self-reported survey on delinquency; or the emergence of "school violence" as a sub-theme – again, due to a strong demand from the political sphere (Eric Debarbieux). At the turn of the century, Laurent Mucchielli's work first queried the influence of this political and media "agenda building" around "youth violence", before starting new research on criminal behaviour (homicide, rape), juvenile delinquency, and the riot phenomenon.

*A contrario*, upper class delinquency (the so-called "white-collar crime"), either in the private or in the public sector, has never ranked too high on the French collective research agenda. Only political and administrative corruption attracted the shared attention of political scientists and sociologists at some point (at the end of the 1980s, to be precise), because this phenomenon happened to be topical in the media at the time.

These new trends notwithstanding, research during the years 1980-2000 kept focussing on the penal system (see research statements by Faugeron, 1991a ; Renouard *et alii*., 1992 ; Faget, Wyvekens, 1999 ; Mucchielli, 1999a), albeit in a somewhat patchy way, given the scarcity of research on sentencing processes. Conversely, research about criminal justice professions developed sharply. Certainly the most scrutinized area was policing—magistrates, lawyers, and social workers have been comparatively subjected to fewer studies. Finally, one should mention the emergence of research on private security agents, and more recently on ombudsmen. Then again, in the wake of Michel Foucault's though-provoking 1975 book *Discipline and punish*, and thanks to new partnerships involving historians, sociologists, and demographers, prison studies have always been a forte of French scholarship: statistical research (on prison population; on how this population's movements hinged on economic conditions; on the penal and social follow-up of cohorts); historical research (on the history of prisons and the living conditions of inmates); quantitative research on training, attitudes, and behaviours in the daily life of all prison stakeholders (officers as well as inmates); specific research on police custody.

Finally, as mentioned above, victim research became central from the mid-1980s onwards. French scholarship had fallen significantly behind North-American research and was missing out on theoretical discussions spurred by victimology. CESDIP researchers had developed their surveys with the aim of creating some form of sociology of penal control, focussing in particular on how victims dealt with police forces and the judiciary. Gradually, however, these studies came to be considered as a mere tool for improving the knowledge and statistical measure of delinquency, furthering the picture drawn by police forces (recorded crimes).

## Conclusion: The Political Return of Criminology and Dangerosity (2002-2009)

While "political demand" had strongly stimulated research during the 1980s and 1990s, one of the salient features of the years 2002-2009 in France was the growing attempts at political control of knowledge production (Mucchielli, 2008). Following the 2001-2002 election campaign – largely dominated by the theme of "insecurity" – and the 2002 change of government (when the Right was returned to power), one has to observe that IHESI (henceforth INHES – *Institut National des Hautes Etudes sur la Sécurité*) was subjected to a political and ideological "overhaul", as most of its scholars were dismissed. *Les cahiers de la sécurité*, which had become a social science journal, returned to its initial condition of governmental outlet. Nicolas Sarkozy (then Minister of Interior) subsequently implemented the long-deferred creation of a National Observatory of Delinquency (OND), which actually still reports to this Ministry today. Leadership of OND was handed over by the Minister to Alain Bauer, owner of a private security consulting firm. Finally, after N.Sarkozy was elected President of the French Republic in 2007, A.Bauer was entrusted with a "Mission on strategy training and research", whose objective was to reorganize all units of security expertise scattered among various ministries into one single, government-controlled institution, while also trying to gain better control over academic and scientific research. Hence the current discussion, in France, of a project aiming at "developing criminology at the university", which is perceived by some authors as an excuse to impose yet new general guidelines upon scholarship and garner scientific support to back the current government's securitarian agenda. These developments have sparked a hard critical debate in research circles, especially since A. Bauer was appointed directly by the government on the first chair of "Criminology" in France, at the Conservatoire

National des Arts et Métiers (February 2009). This is probably the first act of the development of a new state criminology in France.

## CURRENT CHALLENGES

If criminology is to be defined as a truly transdisciplinary, institutionalised body of knowledge on a well-defined object, then no such discipline exists in France today (does it exist in other countries, however, except as a mere, superficial juxtaposition?). From an empirical research point of view, the discipline that most consistently caters for this area has to be sociology (with a little help from its friends, statistics and demography); although history, especially during the years 1970-1990, did contribute significantly indeed. More recently, political science injected fresh ideas by raising new issues (studies on the feeling of insecurity; analysis of public policy). Social sciences, then, should be understood in the broadest sense here – in which case transdisciplinarity does indeed exist. The rift with what might be termed individual psychological sciences is, however, unmistakable. There are several explanations for this: from an intellectual perspective, dialogue is almost nonexistent between social sciences, which are resolutely empirical, and individual psychological sciences, which tend to rely unacceptably heavily on theoretical assumptions (be they biological or psychoanalytical) from an epistemological perspective (Mucchielli, 1999b). True, psychologists and psychiatrists have got rid of these theoretical constraints, but there is simply no place for them and social science scholars to start a dialogue, albeit a critical one. In many respects, knowledge objects appear to have been implicitly distributed in such a way as to almost never allow the parties to meet: sociologists got the wide-ranging surveys, everyday juvenile and elite delinquency, public policy, penal institutions, etc.; while psychologists took over blood crimes, sexual cases, and individual expertise).

In addition, it seems that social science scholars and jurists are estranged by an epistemological gap. Here, it is important to note that, contrary to what happens in other countries, collaboration between social science scholars and law professionals is not part of the latter's initial training. In France, magistrates and social workers attached to the Office for Judicial Protection of Youth, policemen and *gendarmes*, prison administration staff, lawyers—all have their own, specialised schools, which they usually join after undergraduate law studies. University "criminology" would therefore be a subject almost without students... Finally, the recent revival of the French Society of Criminology (*Association Française de Criminologie* - AFC) has very little to do with these grand discussions on crime analysis and the intellectual state of the area. It mainly enhances the topicality of criminological and penal issues in today's public arena, as well as the interest practioners of the field find in such a forum. Scholars, however, seem mildly concerned at best.

As for empirical research, it is facing yet another crucial challenge today, namely its increasing reliance on public procurement – compounded by an inversely proportional affiliation with scientific policy. The end of the "big CEO" and "big theories" era, which was in fact quite auspicious from an institutional point of view to a certain extent (as recruiting teachers and researchers was made fairly easy), is gradually ushering us into the age of theoretical uncertainty, individualistic practices et scarcity of means. As research programmes increasingly rely on public procurement, many issues arise, such as "erratic sprinkling that thwarts long-term team building; fluctuations of scientific police because of political upsets" (Faget, Wyvekens, 1999, p.148), or even, in some cases, the very independence of research from political and administrative agendas. Therefore, although this link between research and public procurement is indeed vital to both parties (laboratories often have no other way of putting nontenured researchers on the payroll), scholars should resist this trend more, by trying to reorganize around stimulating teaching and research centres strong enough to guarantee the independence, continuity, and consistency of their shared expertise.

## REFERENCES


Enguéléguélé, S. (1998). *Les politiques pénales (1958-1995).* Paris: l'Harmattan.

Faget, J., & Wyvekens, A. (1999). Bilan de la recherche sur le crime et la justice en France de 1990 à 1998. Van Outrive, L., & Robert, Ph. (Eds). *Crime et justice en Europe depuis 1990,* (pp. 147-172). Paris: L'Harmattan.

Faugeron, C. (1991a). La production de l'ordre et le contrôle pénal. Bilan de la recherche en France depuis 1980. *Déviance et Société, 15*(1), 51–91.

Faugeron, C. (1991b). De la Libération à la guerre d'Algérie: l'espoir d'une réforme pénitentiaire. Petit, J.-G. (Ed.). *Histoire des galères, bagnes, prisons.* Toulouse: Privat, 289-317.

Kaluszynski, M. (1994). Identités professionnelles, identités politiques: médecins et juristes face au crime au tournant du 19è et du 20è siècle. In L. Mucchielli, (Ed.), *Histoire de la criminologie française,* (pp. 215-235). Paris: L'Harmattan.

Kuhn, T. (1972). *La structure des révolutions scientifiques.* Paris: Flammarion.

Lefaucheur, N. (1994). Psychiatrie infantile et délinquance juvénile. L. Mucchielli, (Ed.), *Histoire de la criminologie française,* (pp. 313-332). Paris: L'Harmattan.

Levasseur, G. (1991). L'influence de Marc Ancel sur la législation répressive française contemporaine. *Revue de science criminelle et de droit pénal comparé, 1*, 9-24.

Marcel, J.-C., & Mucchielli, L. (2006). André Davidovitch ou le deuxième âge de la sociologie criminelle en France . *L'Annee Sociologique, 56*(1), 83–117. doi:10.3917/anso.061.0083

Mucchielli, L. (1994a). Hérédité et " Milieu social ": le faux antagonisme franco-italien. La place de Lacassagne dans l'histoire de la criminologie. L. Mucchielli, (Ed.), *Histoire de la criminologie française* (pp. 189-214). Paris: L'Harmattan.

Mucchielli, L. (1994b). Le sens du crime. Histoire des (r)apports de la psychanalyse à la criminologie. L. Mucchielli, (Ed.), *Histoire de la criminologie française,* (pp.351-409). Paris: L'Harmattan.

Mucchielli, L. (1997). Une sociologie militante du contrôle social. Naissance du projet et formation de l'équipe francophone, des origines au milieu des années quatre-vingt. *Déviance et Société, 21*(1), 7–45.

Mucchielli, L. (1998). *La découverte du social. Naissance de la sociologie en France (1870-1914).* Paris: La Découverte.

Mucchielli, L. (1999a). Les champs de la sociologie pénale. Vingt ans de recherches et de débats dans " Déviance et société ". *Déviance et Société, 23*(1), 3–40.

Mucchielli, L. (1999b). Quelques interrogations épistémologiques sur la psychiatrie criminologique française, *Revue internationale de criminologie et de police scientifique et technique, 4*, 461-487.

Mucchielli, L. (2004). L'impossible constitution d'une discipline criminologique en France. Cadres institutionnels, enjeux normatifs et développements de la recherche des années 1880 à nos jours. *Criminologie, 37*(1), 13–42.

Mucchielli, L. (2006). Criminology, hygienism and eugenics in France (1870-1914): the medical debates on the elimination of "incorrigible" criminals. Becker, P. & Wetzell, R. (Eds.). *Criminals and their scientists. The history of Criminology in International Perspective,*(pp. 207-230. Cambridge, UK: Cambridge University Press.

Mucchielli, L. (2008). Une " nouvelle criminologie " française ? Pourquoi ? Pour qui ?, *Revue de science criminelle et de droit pénal comparé, 4*, 795-803.

Mucchielli, L., & Marcel, J.-C. (2002). La sociologie du crime en France depuis 1945. Mucchielli, L., & Robert, Ph. (Eds.). *Crime et sécurité: l'état des savoirs*, (pp. 53-63). Paris: La Découverte.

Pick, D. (1989). *Faces of Degeneration. A European Disorder, c.1848-c.1918.* Cambridge, UK: Cambridge University Press.

Pinatel, J. (1957). Les données du problème de l'enseignement de la criminologie. *Revue de science criminelle et de droit pénal comparé*, 411-421.

Renneville, M. (1995). Alexandre Lacassagne. Un médecin-anthropologue face à la criminalité. *Gradhiva, 17*, 127–140.

Renneville, M. (1997). *La médecine du crime. Essai sur l'émergence d'un regard médical sur la criminalité en France (1785-1885).* Lille: Presses Universitaires du Septentrion.

Renouard, J.-M., Pradel, J., & Boucher, N. (1992). *La recherche française dans le champ pénal. Bilan et synthèse.* Paris: CEDAS.

Soubiran-Paillet, F. (2000). Juristes et sociologues français d'après-guerre: une rencontre sans lendemain. *Genèses*, *41*, 125–142. doi:10.3406/genes.2000.1653

Tétard, F. (1985). " Délinquance juvénile ": stratégie, concept ou discipline? Collectif. *Problèmes de la jeunesse, marginalité et délinquance juvénile* (Vol. 2, pp. 125-147). Vaucresson: CFR-ES.

Veilt, P. (1994). La géographie sociale du crime et la pratique réformatrice d'Henri Joly. In L. Mucchielli, (Ed.). *Histoire de la criminologie française,* (pp. 269-285). Paris: L'Harmattan.

# Chapter 4
# Criminology as a Discipline in Modern Greece: Teaching, Research and Profession

**Christina Zarafonitou**
*Panteion University, Greece*

## EXECUTIVE SUMMARY

*Although in Greece the publication of books of criminological interest began in the last decades of the 19th century, the subject of Criminology was introduced by Professor Konstantinos Gardikas first at Athens University in 1930 and, then, at Panteios School of Social and Political Sciences in 1932. Some years later, in 1938, the chair of Criminology and Penology was established at the University of Athens. The involvement of K. Gardikas along with three other European experts in the foundation of Interpol in 1923, also resulted in the creation of an important Branch of Criminological Services with many specialized research laboratories which is evolving constantly incorporating all of modern technologies. In our days, Criminology is taught mainly at the schools of Law and of Sociology. In spite of the absence of an autonomous Department of Criminology in the Greek universities, there is a special Section of Criminology in the Department of Sociology at Panteion University. In-depth concentration is obtained in the context of the postgraduate programs as well as through those for the Ph.D. Criminological research is conducted in the universities where some criminological laboratories or centers operate as well as in the National Center of Social Research and the Center of Safety Studies of the Ministry of the Interior, to name a few. The professional domain of criminologists has extended in recent years (administration of penal justice, prisons, agencies for drug addicts or juveniles and immigrants, prevention services). In spite of this, the job market is relatively limited in comparison to the needs of society.*

## INTRODUCTION

Although Greece was the second country in the world, after Belgium, where Criminology was taught at a University Department before the Second World War (Farsedakis, 2007, p. 72), the evolution of this science was confined to teaching and it did not have the impressive post war development which was recorded internationally. The reasons for this are

DOI: 10.4018/978-1-60566-872-7.ch004

not different from the factors that influenced the overall socio-political evolution of the country. On this basis the institutional framework for higher education and scientific research was shaped as well as the conditions which criminologists are called upon to confront as professionals.

The present chapter will try to present, through brief retrospection, the structure of Criminology in contemporary Greece which consists of three dimensions: the teaching, the research and the profession. In this context, the most important difficulties which Criminology faced will be dealt with and an attempt will be made to offer a convincing interpretation for the reservation with which the professional existence of the criminologist was encountered in modern Greek reality[1].

## THE TEACHING OF CRIMINOLOGY

Although in Greece the publication of books of criminological interest began in the last decades of the 19th century, (Spinellis, 2005, p. 32)[2], the teaching of Criminology[3] began with Professor Konstantinos Gardikas (1896-1984), first at Athens University in 1930 and, immediately after, at Panteios School of Political Sciences, in 1932 (Spinellis, 1997, p. 77) where an independent Chair of Criminology and Forensic Sciences was created. Professor Gardikas was the first Professor appointed to teach this discipline (Farsedakis, 2008b). Some years later, in 1938, the chair of Criminology and Penology was established at the University of Athens and K. Gardikas was also the first who assumed its responsibility (Courakis, 2000).

It is noteworthy that Criminology was included in the first program of Panteios School of Political Sciences (3 July 1930), which was organized in five branches: (a) Political Sciences (b) Law (c) Economic Sciences (d) Sociology, Criminology and Penology and (e) Journalism, Geography and Philosophy (Twenty five years seniority- Eikosipentaetiris, 1957:15). Teaching at an academic level evolved through different stages before reaching its present form whose major characteristics are the absence of an independent University Department of Criminology and its expansion, beyond the Schools of Law and Sociology, into different Social Sciences as well as in the Police Academy which will be noted below.

1) Panteion University

The only independent Section of Criminology is in the Department of Sociology at Panteion University, at which a post-graduate program also exists. The development of Criminology at Panteion University[4] set forth important events, examples of which are noted below, which proved to be turning points in the history of the science in modern Greece:

- The above-mentioned commencement of the teaching of Criminology from 1932 and the development of an independent Course "Criminalistics and Criminology with elements of forensic medicine" which was taught by Professor Ioannis Papazachariou[5] from 1942, who was also the vice-rector of Panteios Higher School of Political Sciences (1951-1955) (Twenty five years seniority-Eikosipentaetiris, 1957, p. 94).
- The significant contribution of Professor Alice Yotopoulos-Marangopoulos who occupied the chair of Criminology and Forensic Sciences in 1976, gave new impetus to the teaching of Criminology. Professor A. Yotopoulos-Marangopoulos brought together many new criminologists and transferred the study of Criminology to the newly created Department of Sociology which played a decisive role in the further development of the science. The Department of Sociology was established in 1983 and it constituted one of the three which were created in Panteios Higher School of Political Sciences after the legislative modification

of L.1282/1282. The other two were the Department of Political Science and International Studies and the Department of Public Administration (P.D. 462/83), (University Guide, 2003:10).

- Professor A.Yotopoulos-Marangopoulos was rector two times during the years 1979-1980 and 1983-1984 (Magganas, 2003, p. 27- 43). Her interest in Criminology was combined with her intense activity in the area of human rights since she is the permanent president of the Marangopoulos Foundation for Human Rights as well as of the Hellenic Society of Criminology (from 1978 until the present), (Magganas, 2003, p. 43).
- Professor James Farsedakis, who succeeded Professor A. Yotopoulos-Marangopoulos and directed the Section of Criminology for twenty years (1987-2007), has contributed to the enhancement of this Section especially in recent years through the selection of the teaching and research staff and the courses taught. Emeritus Professor J. Farsedakis continues to offer his knowledge in the context of postgraduate criminological studies and he remains the President of the Hellenic Center of Criminology, a Research Center that he founded at Panteion University. His contribution was decisive because of his scientific horizons and the meritocracy on which his selections were based. Thus today the Section of Criminology at Panteion University is considered scientifically pluralistic and well-grounded.
- In 1984 the Postgraduate Seminar in Criminological Studies was established by Professor A. Yotopoulos-Marangopoulos in collaboration with the late Professor and Vice-Rector Elias Daskalakis as well as with Professor J. Farsedakis. Later it evolved into the current Postgraduate Program of Studies "Contemporary criminality and its confrontation" (2003 until today), which was created and put into effect under the scientific direction of Professor J. Farsedakis. Meanwhile, the Section of Criminology participated in the Postgraduate Program of Studies "Social exclusion and minorities" (1998-2003), attached to the Department of Sociology (in collaboration with the Department of Psychology). This program resulted in three specialization: Sociology, Criminology and Psychology (University Guide, 2003:92). The Postgraduate Program of Euro-American Consortium with the participation of three American (American University Washington, Florida State University και Sam Houston-Texas University) and three European Universities (Panteion University, University of Bologna and University of Barcelona) also operated in the Section of Criminology.

The inclusion of Criminology in Sociology affected the former's curriculum. Thus, although the first studies in Criminology were equivalent to those of the Law School, the program of studies was gradually enriched and a wider range of courses were included from the science of Criminology and especially those of a sociological approach. The late Professor E. Daskalakis played a major role in this new direction along with the previously mentioned professors (A. Yotopoulos-Marangopoulos and J. Farsedakis).

E. Daskalakis (1937-1986), a jurist like the others mentioned previously, contributed -along with professor Farsedakis- decisively to the creation of the Section of Criminology and was its first director. Beyond teaching Criminology at Panteion University and at the Police Academy, he collaborated with the National Center of Social Research. Within this framework he organized and conducted the research on the Administration of Penal Justice in Greece as well as the research on the Prison institution. He also assumed the responsibility for the research on Drugs which was realized in the context of the Section of Criminology (Farsedakis, 2000:19). The combination of research with theory as well as the critical approach to the main criminological issues characterized his work. His monographies on the Criminology of social reaction (Daskalakis, 1985) and the Treatment of criminals (Daskalakis, 1985), reflect a contemporary approach to criminological thought as well as to the penal-welfare model of criminal policy.

In our days, the four-year undergraduate program of studies[6] of the section of Criminology includes a wide variety of courses in Criminology which allow students to continue at a postgraduate level in Greece or abroad. The only compulsory course, Introduction to Criminology, is taught in the first semester of studies. All the rest are optional courses which cover a wide range of theoretical and practical approaches to Criminology as well as special aspects of the criminological phenomenon, namely:

History of Criminological Theories, Criminological Theory I, General Part of Penal Law and Elements of Penal Procedure, Social Control of Crime I, Empirical Criminology I, Drugs: Legislation and Politics, Criminological Theory II, Social Control of Crime II, Empirical Criminology II, Criminological Approaches of Penal Law and of Institutions of Penal Justice, Criminality and Social Control of Minors, Comparative Criminology, Critical Criminology, Criminological Approaches of Penal Law and of Institutions of Penal Justice II, Organized Crime, Criticism of the Practice of Crime Social Control I: Interrogation and Penal Trial, Penology- The Treatment of the Offender, Sociology of Law, Stage in Criminology, Aspects of Criminality I: Computer Technology and Crime, Criminal Policy, The Criminological Contribution of International Organizations, Criminology and Literature, Criminological Aspects of European Integration, Financial Criminality, The Criminal Issue and its Scientific-Criminological Administration.

Criminological courses are also taught in the Department of Psychology, in the Department of Media and Communication as well as in the Department of Social Anthropology of Panteion University. The objective of the two-year MA program "Contemporary criminality and its confrontation" is the study of contemporary aspects of crime, its generating factors and procedures, the explanatory theoretical and empirical approaches as well as the analysis of the trends of criminal policy. In this context the following courses are included:

- Contemporary Aspects of Criminality. General approach.
- Organized Crime and Economical Criminality. Phenomenology, Aspects, Factors.
- New Technologies and Crime.
- Urban Crime, Feeling of Insecurity and Punitiveness in Contemporary Greek and European Reality.
- Contemporary International Trends of Criminal Policy, especially in the European context and Human Rights.
- Crime Prevention. Strategies, Programs, Agencies in Greece and in E.U. Victims Assistance.
- Epistemological and Methodological Issues of Criminology.
- Methodology of Criminological Research.
- Master's Dissertation.

The teaching of Criminology, mainly at the postgraduate level, is supplemented with presentations of distinguished professionals from Greece and Europe who, at the request of the professors, cover current and vital criminological issues. The section of Criminology at Panteion University is already on the way to becoming an independent University Department. A decision of the Senate of the University on this point has been taken, but its approval is still pending at the Ministry of Education.

2) Law Schools

- i.- At the Faculty of Law of the University of Athens, the instruction of Criminology is assumed by the Section of Penal Sciences of the Department of Law[7]. As was previously mentioned, Professor Gardikas [8] first started teaching Criminology in Greece at this university in 1930. Because of the pleasure he found in learning, he was able to complete his doctoral thesis "Homicide in Ancient Greece and especially in Attica" in 1918 at the age of 22 at the University of Geneva. He continued further to analyze the influence of Plato and Aristotle in penal philosophy as well as in the penal-philosophical ideas which are found in ancient Greek tragedy [9] (Courakis, 2000, p. 39) The three volumes of 2600 pages which were published between 1936 and 1955 (volume 1: Criminology: The general and the individual causes of crime, volume 2: Police Science, volume 3: Penology) became a classic and have been reprinted many times (Spinellis 1997, p. 79; Courakis, 2000, p. 42). Additionally, Professor Gardikas was the first director of the Office of Criminological Service which, from 1929, took on the scientific research of crimes, (Spinellis, 1997, p. 79). The above department followed the founding of the International Organization of Criminological Police which later developed into the International Police Committee of Prosecution which was recommended after the Conference of Vienna in 1923 by four European experts, one of which was Professor Gardikas, (Farsedakis, 1984, p. 70).

Criminology continued to be taught in the framework of the penal sciences in the Faculty of Law of Athens University. The courses taught today at the undergraduate level are:

a. Compulsory Courses: Criminal Law I: General Principles, Criminal Law II: Crimes of the Criminal Code, Criminal Procedure, Applications of Criminal Law-Criminal Procedure
b. Optional Courses (obligatory option): Criminology, Penology, Judicial Psychology and Psychiatry, Special Criminal Laws, Law of Economic Criminality, International Criminal Law (intersectional with Section of International Studies)
c. Optional Courses (Free Option): Juvenile Justice, Criminalistics, Criminal and Criminological Approach of Gender.

At the postgraduate level, a MA of Penal Studies with two specialization in Criminal Law, and Criminal Procedure and Criminology has been offered the last 15 years. In this context, the Compulsory Courses are: Criminal Law I & II: Special Issues, Criminal Procedure I & II: Special Issues and Methodology of Criminology (only for the direction of Criminology).

The Optional Courses are: Criminal Justice System, Theory of Penalties, History of Criminal Institutions, Theoretical Criminology, Crime Policy, Human Rights and Criminal Law, from classical to administrative Criminology.

At Athens University, there are also courses on Criminology in the Faculty of Communication and Media Studies (The construction of violence and crime in the media, Criminal policy, Communication and security, The "image" of the criminal), at Theological School as well as in the postgraduate program "Political Science and Sociology" of the School of Political Sciences[10].

- The Alma Mater Thessalonicensis was the second Greek University which founded in 1925 in Thessaloniki (law 3341/1925). By virtue of law 3108/1954 (art.7) it is renamed Aristotle University of Thessaloniki. The Law Department was established in 1930-1931 and the organization of studies was realized by the law 1262/1983 on the "Structure and function of Higher Education establishments". Finally, by virtue of the ministerial decree B1/809/1993, the postgraduate program of Penal and Criminological Sciences was approved[11].

The criminological courses included in the undergraduate program of the Section of Penal and Criminological Sciences at the Law School of Aristotle University of Thessaloniki are only courses of general option: Criminalistics, Penology, Criminology, Juvenile Law, Forensic Psychology, Stage in Criminology and Penal Sciences.

The postgraduate program organized by this Section grants both a master's degree and a Ph.D. in penal and criminological sciences. The courses included in the specialization of Penal and criminological Sciences are: Penal Law, Penal Procedure, Criminology-Penology, Penal Philosophy, Special Penal Laws, Financial Penal Law, International Penal Law, Juvenile Penal Law and Comparative International Penal Law.

- Criminological courses are also taught in the Law School and the Department of Social Administration of Democritus University of Thrace[12]. This University was established in July 1973 and the Department of Law Studies was founded in 1974 and started to function in the same year. The Department of Social Administration is established by the P.D. 304/1994 and its function started in the academic year 1996-97.

Among the criminological courses taught in the Section of Penal and Criminological Studies is Penology (compulsory course) as well as Criminology, Specific Criminology, Criminalistics, Victimology, Juvenile Law (optional courses). In the context of postgraduate studies, the criminological courses are classified in two unities: Criminal Policy and Special Criminological Issues.

The criminological courses taught, respectively, in the Department of Social Administration are: Criminology and Criminal Policy, Police-Policing, as well as courses on Social Exclusion, Minorities, Immigration etc.

3) Other Universities

In recent years, the number of Universities in Greece has increased and thus the teaching of criminological courses has expanded. They are now included not only in Law faculties and Sociology but also in programs of Political Science, Psychology, and Anthropology. However, as was mentioned earlier, an independent Department of Criminology does not exist, only the Section of Criminology at Panteion University.

In this context, Criminology is taught in the Departments of Sociology of the Aegean University and of the University of Crete but mainly from the viewpoint of the Sociology of crime or of deviance.

- The criminological courses taught in the Department of Sociology of Aegean University[13] are limited to Deviance Sociology and Criminal Policy, while the interest is mainly focused on the sociological approaches of immigration, minorities, gender, everyday life and so on. In contrast, the Criminological Approaches of Crime and its Confrontation is a compulsory course of the postgraduate program "Research for the local social development and cohesion". The course on the Research on Deviance, Criminality and Criminal Policy is included among the optional courses of this program.
- At the University of Crete[14], the teaching

of Criminology is included in the programs of the Departments of Sociology and of Philosophy and Social Studies. The optional course of Sociology of Law and the optional seminar of Special Issues of Criminology are taught in the context of the Department of Sociology. Respectively, Sociological Theories of Deviance, Sociology of Deviance and Social Control, Collective Youth Deviance, Subculture Theory and Cultural Processes and Deviant Behavior are included in the undergraduate program of the Department of Philosophy and Social Studies. Criminological courses are also taught in the context of the postgraduate program Culture and Human Development of this Department as well as of the joined postgraduate program on Bioethics of the Departments of Biology, Medicine, Sociology and Philosophy and Social Studies of the University of Crete.

- The teaching of Criminology is included also in the program of the Department of Social and Educational Policy of the University of Peloponnese[15]. This Department was established with the Presidential Decree 118/2003 and is part of the Faculty of Social Sciences located in Corinth. The particular undergraduate courses taught in this context are: Introduction to Criminology (the only compulsory course), Juvenile Delinquency and its Social Control, Criminal Policy, Penology, European Criminology, Theories of Social Control and Victimology. At a postgraduate level, the teaching of criminology is included in the master of "Social discriminations, immigration and citizenship" and the special criminological courses are: Immigration law: European and National Dimensions and Immigration, Integration Policies and Deviance.
- Although the above account is not complete since Criminology is part of many educational programs at various university departments, it is worth noting that it is included in the program of studies of the Institute of Social Studies at the Technological Educational Institute (TEI) of Messolonghi. Finally, various criminological courses are taught in the context of the Police Academy and especially in the School of Police Officers, which has equal status with the rest of the universities in the country. However, it is worth noting that no course of Criminology is taught at the National School for Judges. The expansion of criminological education has led also to the production of an increased number of Ph.D.'s dedicated to criminological topics, which will be dealt with below.

## CRIMINOLOGICAL RESEARCH

In contrast to the increase in the teaching of Criminology at different universities, research in this area is limited. In fact, only a few national research centers exist and they rarely deal with pure criminological research. Some research centers or laboratories have been established and function at universities. A first general assessment of criminological research in Greece suggests that it is under-funded and it lacks the interest of the State.

a. When E. Daskalakis assumed the responsibility for criminological research at the National Center of Social Research, the two important research projects mentioned previously were conducted on "Administration of Penal Justice in Greece" as well as the research on the "Prison Institution". He was also in charge of the criminological part of the research on "Drugs in Greece" which was conducted by the Section of Criminology of Panteion University (Farsedakis, 1991, p. XI). In fact, E. Daskalakis balanced the theoretical and the empirical in his professional efforts, as becomes obvious in his documents. After 1985 when the law 1514/85 for the development of scientific and technological research was passed and put into effect, the National Center of Social Research was restructured into Institutes (Lambropoulou, 2003, p. 837). Thus, the Institute of Political Sociology has taken on the research in the field of delinquency, xenophobia, and law and justice.

b. B. In the context of the Research Center for Gender Equality (KETHI), some important criminological empirical studies are carried out[16], as for example: "Women and Homicide: Research on Women's Prisons of Korydallos", "The Sexual Harassment against Women in the Workplace", "Domestic Violence against Women: First Epidemiological Research in Greece", "A Bibliographical Review regarding Violence against Women by their Partner and the Supporting Structures in Greece", "Gender and Social Exclusion" .

c. The Center of Safety Studies (KE.ME.A.), created under law 3378/12-9-2005, is a research, advisory and decision-making body which is governed by the Ministry of the Interior and undertakes issues of criminological interest too. However, its existence is very recent for it to have notable research experience.

d. Research is also conducted in the framework of university research laboratories and criminological centers.

   i. At the Law School of Athens, the Laboratory of Criminological and Penal Research was the first to be created by the late I. Daskalopoulos. It was later reestablished under the presidential decree 535/1991 (Spinelli, 2005, p. 34)[17]. At this time, the first director was Professor C. D. Spinelli and then, from 2001 until today, Professor N. Courakis[18].

   The activities of the laboratory have included: *free educational seminars* (e.g. judicial graphology) and *screenings/discussion of crime movies* (in cooperation with the Panteion University and the center of Social Studies of the Technological Educational Institute of Messolonghi), *more than ten already completed scientific surveys* on a wide range of topics, such as the condition of and the problems faced by female inmates (1994-1996), adolescent inmates from Greek prisons (1993-1995), including repeated observations of their progress (1992-2002), the delinquent behavior in adolescents and adolescent gangs in contemporary Greece (2002-2004), euthanasia (scientific coordinators Professors N. Kourakis and K.D. Spinellis, 2005-2007), domestic violence (ed. F. Milioni), the relationship between insecurity, punitiveness and criminal policy (scientific coordinators Professors Ch. Zarafonitou and N. Courakis). Furthermore, the Laboratory has organized a series of *scientific events and conferences*, among which the first Conference of Criminology for Students (in cooperation with the center of Social Studies of the Technological Educational Institute of Messolonghi), has published several criminology books in its book series*, has *evaluated drug treatment programs* applied in prisons, and has published the first Greek *on line journal of Criminology* (http://www.theartofcrime.gr/).

   ii. The Hellenic Criminological Center at Panteion University, which was founded in 1990, conducts research and trains researchers in the field of Criminology. Director of the Center and its founder is Emeritus Professor J. Farsedakis. Several research projects are included in the activities of the Center; for example, "Subcultures and Deviance in the Western Suburbs of Athens" (Astrinakis, Stylianoudi, 1996), "Petty Criminality in

Attica", (1998) under the scientific responsibility of Professor D. Kalogeropoulos and "Restructuring of the Services of the Greek Police", under the scientific responsibility of Professor J. Farsedakis (2003).

Criminological research is also carried out on a personal initiative by the teaching staff of the Section of Criminology, mainly in the post graduate program of studies or in the context of European Programs. Examples of such work are the research studies on "Social values of delinquents and non-delinquents" (Magganas, Lazos, 1997)[19], three research studies on Fear of crime among Greek and immigrant inhabitants of Athens" (Zarafonitou, 2002, 2006; 2006a), the research on "(Un) safety, punitivity and criminal policy" (Zarafonitou, Courakis, 2009) as well as the European Research Program "The cultural dimensions of corruption - The importance of attitudes about corruption for its prevention" (Lambropoulou, 2008). Numerous important criminological topics have been researched also for doctoral dissertations at the Section of Criminology at Panteion University. Here, also, distinguished criminologists from Greece and abroad have been invited to conferences and other professional activities, as in the International Congress "Contemporary criminality, its confrontation and Criminology", in honour of Professor J. Farsedakis, organized by the Section of Criminology, in June 2008.

iii. In 1974, upon the foundation of Democritus University of Komotini, the Laboratory of Criminology and Judicial Psychiatry was also established at the Section of Penal and Criminological Sciences of its Law School. The laboratory was later re-named "Laboratory of Criminology" by its director and current professor at the Department of Media Studies of the University of Athens, Yannis Panousis (Spinellli, 1985, p. 36). It has been functioning under this new name since 1986 first under the directorship of Professor Panousis and, since 1997, under Professor Ch. Dimopoulos. Its activities include research on issues such as penal reform, participation in the European program AGIS which deals with trafficking, educational seminars, lectures and conferences, and the publication of the criminological review "Chronics" under the directorship of Professor Panousis. Many of these activities are conducted in cooperation with the post-graduate program of the Section of Penal and Criminological Sciences of the University's Department of Social Administration.

iv. Significant professional meetings and conferences have been organized by the Section of Penal and Criminological Sciences of the Law School of the University of Thessaloniki. Examples of such events are the "Professional meetings of the Penal and Criminological Sciences of the Universities of Thessaloniki and Thrace", the "Greek-German conferences", and the conference in honor of Professor I. Manoledakis.

v. Correspondingly, the professional events of the Section of Social and Educational Policies of the University of the Peloponnese are of high quality as those organized by *Groupe Européen de recherches sur la justice pénale* under the professional auspices of Professor Th. Papatheodorou and the Common Studies Sessions which are organized by Professor V. Karydis. Greek and foreign criminologists attend the above-mentioned functions and their work is often published[20].

vi. vi.-Professional and research activities in the area of Criminology are also conducted by the remaining university sections of Social Sciences of the University of the Aegean, where the first Meeting of Greek Criminologist was organized in June 2006, as well as by the Technological Educational Institute (TEI) of Messolonghi where a

Laboratory of Social Studies has been founded and operates under the directorship of Professor Ch. Tsouramanis.

Generally, empirical research on Criminology is not adequately developed in Greece, both quantitatively and thematically. The funding of such research is rare and, when it does occur through European programs, the information is not distributed since it does not materialize under organized research bodies. It is noteworthy that in most cases, with few exceptions, departments of the State do not show an interest in the funding of criminological research nor in the utilization of the conclusions reached by the research which have been published in professional or scientific publications.

## CRIMINOLOGY AS PROFESSION

At the XXIX International Course of Criminology in Pamplona, which took place between the 15-22nd of June, 1980, Professor A. Yotopoulos-Marangopoulos (1981, p. 124) made the following statement in regards to Greek reality at the time:

Criminal policy is the work of practitioners, and "tough" laws are considered, generally, the most appropriate measures in dealing with criminality. Criminal policy is drawn up by high ranking civil servants of the ministries of justice and public order under the direction of the ministers and in cooperation with some "qualified" individuals, usually penologists, and judges. If criminologists do participate, it is rarely.

After 29 years, the situation has barely changed. Especially in the field of criminal policy, a "scientific culture" continues to be absent and, as a result, the selection of the ministers' advisers and of applied policies is made, in most cases, using political not scientific criteria. Indicative of such methods is the "Report on the situation in Greek prisons and the possibilities of amelioration of the penitentiary system" which was drafted in 1994 by the Parliamentary Committee on the examination of the penitentiary system and of the living conditions of the inmates (scientific collaborators: Professors J. Farsedakis and N. Courakis). According to its co-author N. Courakis (2005, p. 298), this report was submitted to Parliament four years later (Session KZ΄, 23-11-1998). The findings and proposals of the committee were widely approved and accepted. However, political interest in applying the findings was not parallel to the enthusiasm that was expressed initially (Courakis, 2005, p. 298; Alexiadis, 2004, p. 110).

However, even in the cases where the contribution of criminologists is present in the formation of legislation, as in the case of correctional legislation, it is not present at the stage of enforcement because of the lack of appropriate criminological education of the specific agencies. For example, in the case of the enforcement of criminal legislation, it is worth noting that in Greece judges are not specialized in penal justice, for they alternate posts and may undertake penal cases concurrently. In addition, apart from their university education in Criminology, the National School for Judges does not include lessons in Criminology in its curriculum. However, many judges hold a master's degree in Criminology and express a personal interest in participating and attending professional activities in Criminology.

In the case of the police force, specialization of its members is not offered despite the varied courses available because the Greek police is one body which is concerned with many different areas such as traffic control, crime prevention, repression, market inspection, and many more. Thus, a specialized body of judicial police does not exist as in other western countries with the exception of forensic sciences experts. As in the case of the judges, some police officers have undergraduate and postgraduate degrees. However, this does not mean that this education will be put into practice.

Finally, in reference to the penitentiary personnel which is divided into the administrative staff, the guards for the interior, and guards for the exterior (Alexiadis, 2001, p. 199), courses in Criminology are included only in the intensive training of the guards for the interior who attend the School for Correctional Officers in order to be made permanent employees (Courakis, 2005, p. 318). On the contrary, the guards for the exterior are selected based on their "physical and psychological suitability" (Courakis, 2005, p. 319).

According to the Internal Regulation of Operation of General Prison Establishment (Ministry of Justice, Num. of Reference 58819/7-4-2003), "Specialised Scientific Personnel" are employed like social workers, psychologists, criminologists, sociologists and teachers who are under the administrative monitoring and control of the director of the prison. According to Article 55 of the above mentioned decision:

"The criminologist examines the law and the real situation of detainees with the aim to harmonise, according to the jurisprudence of the European Court of Human Rights, the means and methods of serving of sentences, the recommendations and elementary rules of international organisations. For this purpose, he or she studies the archival data, communicates with the detainees individually, or by team, collaborates with the relevant prison services of the Ministry of Justice, the police, the judicial administrations, and any other related public services. More specifically the criminologist:

1. maintains regular collaboration with the public prosecutor-supervisor by providing legal help for the detainees, informing him or her about all institutional problems in serving sentences and in attributing penal justice.
2. watches the tendencies and the developments of theory and (case law) jurisprudence with regard to temporary detention, serving of sentences and security measures.
3. studies and evaluates the application of institutions that involve:
   i. the reduction of sentences within the prison, the beneficial calculation of work days, the conditional discharge of inmates, the detainees leaves, the incorporation of temporary detention as a part of the overall sentence, and
   ii. differentiations of the rules of incarceration, especially regarding the detainees' work and employment, their discipline, their committal in a prison establishment or in a high security ward.
4. communicates with the police, the juridical and public services, the institutions of legal help, the authorities of serving of sentences and also the other native or non- native prison establishments, for the examination of cases of detainees with regard to their legal situation.
5. communicates with institutions of higher education, governmental and non-governmental organisations, academicians, research institutes and centres in order to examine the modern tendencies and developments in the implementation of sentences and the organisation of prison establishment.
6. participates in scientific events in order to be informed constantly, utilises his experience to hand over penal justice and the execution of sentences".

The above impressive duties of the criminologist which are mentioned in the regulations of the prison establishment cannot possibly be adhered to even if all sides were in agreement because of one basic difficulty; that is, in the Greek prisons only one criminologist is employed even though the Ministry of Justice has made provisions for thirteen such positions (Coulouris, 2008, p. 144). The basic requirements are a University degree in Law, Political Science, Economics or Social Sciences, and a postgraduate degree in Criminology. It is obvious that many candidates have these standard requirements which would make it possible to choose the most appropriate ones if the positions were announced. There are many pressing *intra muros* needs, an example of which is described by the above-mentioned criminologist of Korydallos Prison (Coulouris, 2008, p. 145):

In recent years, from the year 2000 until the first half of 2007, the number of inmates on a daily basis fluctuates between 1850 to 2350, whereas the number set by the official records of the Ministry of Justice is 640. The population of the prison is made up of males over 21 years of age, some of which are awaiting trial as well as those who have been convicted. They are cramped into six wards without any further division according to their crime, sentence, or penal history.

It is worth noting, also, that the Penitentiary Code (law 2776/1999) does not explicitly allude to the participation of a criminologist in the prison staff, but mention is made of a "legal" or "specialized" professional (Coulouris, 2008, p. 150).

It is obvious that the role of a criminologist in the penal system is unacknowledged. However, it is worth noting that in recent years a series of regulations concerning the execution of sentences has been put into effect. One such case is the function of adult probation officers into whose ranks social professionals and criminologists can be included. The Probation Officers Service was established by law 1941/1991, was modified by N.2207/94 and put into effect by PD 195/2006 (FEK 199/12-9-2006), namely after 15 years (Papathanassopoulos, 2006, p. 1069; Mavris, 2008). According to Article 1 of PD 195/2006, the probation officers mission is:

a) to assist and oversee persons whose sentences have been suspended and who are under probation (art. 100A Penal Code) or whose sentences have been diverted to social service (art. 82 Penal Code),
b) to carry out social research on temporary inmates or on persons who have been given restraining orders (art. 282 Code of Penal Procedure).

One more agency was put into effect in the area of social integration of ex-detainees for which the role of the criminologist may be significant. It concerns the "Epanodos" (Return) under Article 81 par. 1 of the Penitentiary Code (Law 2776/1999) which is activated in post-penitentiary care under the supervision of the Minister of Justice. The general purpose of "Epanodos" is the "occupational training and rehabilitation, the financial support and the gradual social reinstatement of ex-prisoners". In order for this agency to be formed, it was necessary for a presidential decree to be issued which was published four years later (PD 300/2003, FEK A' 256). Neither at this time was the "Epanodos" put into effect because one more decision from the Minister of Justice was required for the formation of its board of directors. It took another four years (1.3.2007) for this to occur while a reorganization of the board took place on 29/10/2007 (Courakis, 2008). Nevertheless, the president of the board of directors is Professor of Criminology N. Courakis and its members include some criminologists.

Criminologists are also employed as probation officers for minors, a social service under the Ministry of Justice (Zagoura, 2008, p. 74). According to article 9, par. 1 of the PD 49/1979 "On the operation of the minor's probation officers service", the minor's probation officer "guides and assists the minor in his social life, making every effort to bring about a smooth social readjustment" (Zagoura, 2008, p. 75). His role is significant even after the reformation of the penal legislation for minors (law 3189/03) which refers to this service as "the main agency for the reception and treatment of the minor offender" while at the same time pointing out its role in prevention, guidance and control during all the stages of the penal process (Zagoura, 2008, p. 74).

The above reference is only indicative of the most significant services of the Ministry of Justice where criminologists are employed as social scientists. Criminologists need to be added to the administrative personnel of the above mentioned ministry as well as to those of the Ministries of the Interior and Public Order along with their role as professional advisors in other bodies and ad-hoc committees. Distinguished criminologists have, on occasion, served as presidents or members of the Central Professional Council of Prisons which formulates penitentiary policy (D.D.Spinelli, A.Magganas e.g.). Professor Y. Panoussis, who served as president of this council, reports:

*"...even in its capacity as an advisory board, it can perform a significant role since it can propose to the Minister of Justice measures of penitentiary and criminal policy and training of penitentiary personnel, set regulations for the functioning of detention centers and committees for social support, or propose the creation of new centers or new categories of detainees" (Panoussis, 2008, p. 124).*

The Central Council for the Prevention of Delinquency, which operates at the Ministry of the Interior, plays an equally important role in formulating and implementing preventive criminal policy. Under the direction of Professor of Criminology N. Courakis, it coordinates the function of the Local Councils for the Prevention of Delinquency (art. 13 of the law 3387/2005), (Courakis, 2006, p. 11).

## REFERENCES


Alexiadis, St. (2001). *Penology*. Athens-Thessaloniki: Sakkoulas Publ. S.A., (in Greek).

Alexiadis, St. (2004). *Criminology*. Athens-Thessaloniki: Sakkoulas Publ. S.A., (in Greek).

Alexiadis, St. (2008). The Criminology from yesterday to tomorrow. In *Essays in honour of Anna Benaki-Psarouda, Penal Sciences-Theory and practice* (pp. 1169-1184). Athens-Komotini: A.Sakkoulas Publ. (in Greek).

Anagnostakis, S. (1964). *Bibliography of criminological and penal studies in Greece* (1830-1964). Athens: Center of Criminological Research (in Greek).

Astrinakis, A., & Stylianoudi, L. (Eds.). (1996). Heavy metal, rockabilly fanatic fans. *Juvenile cultures and subcultures in western Attica*. Athens: Ellinika Grammata, (in Greek).

Coulouris, N. (2008). The role of the criminologist in the prison: known secrets and true lies. In S. Vidali & P. Zagoura (Eds.). *Consultative and prison.* (pp.141-168). Athens-Komotini: A.Sakkoulas Publ. (in Greek).

Courakis, N. (2000). The K. Gardikas' contribution in criminological science. In C.D. Spinellis (Ed.), *K. Gardikas the founder of Criminology in Greece* (pp.37-45). Athens-Komotini: A.Sakkoulas Publ. (in Greek).

Courakis, N. (2005). *Penal repression*. Athens-Komotini: A.Sakkoulas Publ. (in Greek).

Courakis, N. (2006). *In order to feel safe in a society with active citizen.* Athens-Komotini: A.Sakkoulas Publ. (in Greek).

Courakis, N. (2008). After prison care: The main condition for the decrease of the recidivism as well as for a humanitarian criminal policy. [Penal Speech]. *Poenikos Logos*, *2*, 253–257.

Courakis, N. (2008). Crime and Criminology through the perspective of 2020. *Youths, crime and society*, *1*, 20-23 (in Greek).

Courakis, N. (n.d.). *The Laboratory of penal and criminological research of the Athens University*. Retrieved from http://www.law.uoa.gr/crime-research/ergastirio.htm (in Greek).

Daskalakis, E. (1985). *The Criminology of social reaction*. Athens-Komotini: A.Sakkoulas Publ. (in Greek).

Daskalakis, E. (1985). *The treatment of the offender*. Athens-Komotini: A.Sakkoulas Publ. (in Greek).

Daskalakis, E., et al. (Eds.). (1983). *The administration of penal justice in Greece*. Athens: National Centers of Social Research (in Greek).

Farsedakis, J. (1984). *Criminal investigation, human rights and criminogenesis*. Athens: Nomiki Vivliothiki (in Greek).

Farsedakis, J. (1990). *The criminological thought. From the antiquity until our days*. Vol A'. Athens: Nomiki Vivliothiki (in Greek).

Farsedakis, J. (1991). Introductory note. In *Offering in memory to Elias Daskalakis*. Athens: Panteion University, (in Greek).

Farsedakis, J. (1996). *Elements of Criminology*. Athens: Nomiki Vivliothiki (in Greek).

Farsedakis, J. (2000). Introduction. In I. Daskalaki et al. (Eds.). *Offenders and victims in the threshold of 21th century*. Athens: National Centers of Social Research (in Greek).

Farsedakis, J. (2003). For advancement of Criminology, Prerequisities and demands. In *Essays in Honour of Alice Yotopoulos-Marangopoulos. Human rights-Crime-Criminal Policy* (357-366). Athens-Brussels: Nomiki Vivliothiki-Bruylant.

Farsedakis, J. (2007). The state of penal justice in Greece. In Str. Georgoulas (Ed.), *Criminology in Greece today, Volume in honor of Professor St. Alexiadis* (pp.72-76). Athens: Center of military unit's distraction (in Greek).

Farsedakis, J. (2008a). Criminology and human rights. In *Essays in honor of Anna Benaki-Psarouda, Penal Sciences-Theory and practice* (pp.1141-1148). Athens-Komotini: A.Sakkoulas Publ. (in Greek).

FarsedakisJ. (2008b): www.theartofcrime.gr, v.8.

Lambropoulou, E. (2003). The teaching of Criminology in Greece and the contemporary criminological research. *Poeniki Dikaiosyni (Penal Justice)*, vo. 7, 833-839 (in Greek).

Lambropoulou, E. (2005). Crime, Criminal Justice and Criminology in Greece. *European Journal of Criminology*, *2*(2), 211–247. doi:10.1177/1477370805051274

Lambropoulou, E. (2008). About corruption and anti-corruption. In *Essays in honor of Anna Benaki-Psarouda, Penal Sciences-Theory and practice* (pp.1274-1303). Athens-Komotini: A.Sakkoulas Publ. (in Greek).

Léauté, J. (1972). *Criminologie et Science Pénintentiaire*. Paris: PUF.

Magganas, A. & Lazos, Gr. (1997). *Social values of delinquents and non-delinquents*. Athens: Panteion Univiersity of Social and Political Sciences (in Greek).

Magganas, A. (Ed.). (2003). Human rights-Crime-Criminal Policy. In *Essays in Honour of Alice Yotopoulos-Marangopoulos*. Athens-Brussels: Nomiki Vivliothiki-Bruylant.

Magganas, A. (2004). *The criminal phenomenon in the practice*. Athens: Nomiki Viliothiki (in Greek).

Mavris, M. (2008). Probation officers' service- An institution under "probation". In *Essays in honour of Anna Benaki-Psarouda, Penal Sciences-Theory and practice* (pp.1305-1335). Athens-Komotini: A.Sakkoulas Publ. (in Greek).

Panoussis, Y. (1988). *The "requested" in Criminology*. Athens-Komotini: A.Sakkoulas Publ. (in Greek).

Panoussis, Y. (1994). Teaching Criminology in Greece. *Eurocriminology*, *7*, 111–118.

Panoussis, Y. (2008). Central Scientific Council of Prisons. In S. Vidali & P. Zagoura (Eds.). *Consultative and prison*, (pp.121-140). Athens-Komotini: A.Sakkoulas Publ. (in Greek).

Panoussis, Y. (2008). What is criminology? First plan of an answer. *Youths, crime and society, 1*, 13-19, (in Greek).

Panteion University of Social and Political Sciences (2003). *University Guide*. Academic year 2002-2003.

Panteios Higher School of Political Sciences (1957). *Twenty five years seniority-Eikosipentaetiris, 1930-1955*, (in Greek).

Papathanassopoulos, E. (2006). Remarks-Brief presentation of basic points of the presidential decree 195/06 about the organisation and the function of the services of probation officers. [Penal speech]. *Poenikos Logos, 3*, 1069–1084.

Spinellis, C. D. (1995). Center for penal and criminological research, Section of penal sciences, University of Athens. *European Journal on Criminal Policy and Research*, 100–103. doi:10.1007/BF02243137

Spinellis, C. D. (1997). *Crime in Greece in perspective*. Athens-Komotini: A.Sakkoulas Publ.

Spinellis, C. D. (2000). Memories from the teacher K. G. Gardikas or the Criminology, the penology and the Criminalistic from yesterday in our days. In C.D. Spinellis (Ed.). *K. Gardikas the founder of Criminology in Greece* (pp.47-67). Athens-Komotini: A.Sakkoulas Publ. (in Greek).

Spinellis, C. D. (2005). *Criminology, Contemporary and older trends*. Athens-Komotini: A.Sakkoulas Publ., (in Greek). Papathéodorou, Th. & Mary, Ph. (Eds.). (2006). *Mutations des politiques criminelles en Europe*. Athènes: Éditions Papazissis.

Yotopoulos-Marangopoulos, A. (1981). La criminologie en Grèce. In *Actas del XXIX Curso International de Criminologie* (pp.104-127). Spain: Fundacion Bartolomé de Carranza.

Zagoura, P. (2008). Consultative in minor delinquents and inmates. In S. Vidali & P. Zagoura (Eds.), *Consultative and prison*, (pp. 171-117). Athens-Komotini: A.Sakkoulas Publ. (in Greek).

Zarafonitou, Ch. (2002). *The fear of crime. A criminological approach and inquiry based on an empirical study of the phenomenon within the city of Athens*. Athens-Komotini: European Studies in Law, A.Sakkoulas Publisher (in Greek and in English).

Zarafonitou, Ch. (2006). La peur du crime parmi les immigrés et leurs attitudes face aux institutions de la justice pénale. In Th. Papathéodorou & Ph.Mary (Eds.), *Mutations des politiques criminelles en Europe* (pp. 91-138). Athènes: Éditions Papazissis.

Zarafonitou, Ch. (2006a). Criminological approaches of fear of crime and (in)security. [in Greek]. *Poeniki Dikaiosyni, 8-9*, 1031–1039.

Zarafonitou, Ch. (2009). Fear of crime in contemporary Greece. In L. K. Cheliotis & S. Xenakis (Eds.). *Crime and Punishment in Contemporary Greece: International Comparative Perspectives*. Oxford: Peter Lang AG (forthcoming).

Zarafonitou, Ch. & Courakis, N. (2009). *Unsafety, punitivity and criminal policy.*, Athens-Komotini: A.Sakkoulas publisher (in Greek).

## WEBSITES

Aegean University: www.aegean.gr

Aristotle University of Thessaloniki: www.auth.gr/law

Center of Safety Studies: www.kemea.gr

Criminological Journal "The art of crime": www.theartofcrime.gr

Democritus University of Thrace: www.law.duth.gr

Kapodistrian University of Athens: www.uoa.gr

National Center of Social research: www.ekke.gr

National School of Judges: www.esdi.gr

Panteion University: www.panteion.gr

Research Center for Gender Equality (KETHI): www.kethi.gr

TEI of Messolongui: www.teimes.gr

University of Crete: www.uoc.gr

University of Peloponnese: www.uop.gr

## ENDNOTES

1 The purpose of this paper is not to proceed in the exhaustive description of all the existing criminological courses, research or publications but to present the context in which Criminology is evolved in Greece and its main characteristics.

2 According to Professor C. Spinellis (2005, p. 33), more than 12 books and many papers on Penology/Criminology have been published before 1900 (see S. Anagnostakis, 1964, p. 71).

3 About the teaching of Criminology in Greece, see especially Yotopoulos-Marangopoulos, 1981; Panoussis, 1988, 1994; Spinellis, 1997, 2000, 2005; Lambropoulou, 2003, 2005; Alexiadis, 2004, Farsedakis 2008a, 2008b.

4 Panteios School of Political Sciences was founded in 1930 and in 1937 it was renamed Panteios Higher School of Political Sciences. Two years later (1939) the School was once again renamed Panteios Higher School of Political Sciences and Public Administration. By virtue of Law 540/1943 the School reassumed its old name of Panteios Higher School of Political Sciences under which it operated until 1989 when the School acquired its current name, Panteion University of Social and Political Sciences (P.D. 377/1989), see the University Guide, 2003.

5 Along with M. Bakatsoula, associate of Gardikas mainly on issues of Penology (Spinelli, 2005, p. 35).

6 http://www.panteion.gr.

7 National and Kapodistrian University of Athens, founded on 3 May 1837, was the first University not only in the modern Greek State but also in the Balkans and the Eastern Mediterranean in general (www.uoa.gr).

8 The information which is found at this point comes from Courakis, 2000.

9 The significant contribution of the ancient Greeks in the history of Criminology is described analytically in the work of J. Farsedakis, 1990, p. 15s.

10 The seminar "Social control and penal repression: criticism and comparative approaches".

11 http://web.auth.gr/law.

12 http://www.law.duth.gr.

13 The Aegean University is established in 1984 (http://www.aegean.gr).

14 The University of Crete is established in 1977. Courses in Criminology are taught in the School of Philosophy of the University of Crete (http://www.uoc.gr).

15 The University of Peloponnese is founded with the P.D. 13/2000 and started operating in 2002 (http://www.uop.gr).

16 The Research Centre for Gender Equality (KETHI), a Legal Entity under Private Law, was founded in 1994 and functions centrally

in Athens and regionally in Heraklion, Kalamata, Komotini, Patras, Preveza, Thessalonica and Volos. KETHI is supervised and funded by the General Secretariat for Equality of the Ministry of the Interior (http://www.kethi.gr)

[17] About this laboratory see C. D. Spinellis, Center for Penal and Criminological Research, Section of Penal Sciences, University of Athens, in *European Journal on Criminal Policy and Research*, 1995, pp. 100-103.

[18] About its aims and a report of its activities, see N. Courakis, *The Laboratory of Penal and Criminological Research of Athens University*, http://www.law.uoa.gr/crime-research/ergastirio.htm

[19] See also the research studies included in Magganas, 2004.

[20] As for example the collection of social and Educational Policy of the European Group of Research on Penal Justice and of the University of Peloponnese (Papathéodorou, M. (Ed.), 2006).

[21] The last issue of this review was V.11-16/1993-95. It is worth to mentioning also the recent establishment of the *Association of Greek Criminologist of Panteion University.*

[22] See Lambropoulou (2003, p. 838).

[23] Greece participated only in the last European Victimization Crime Survey which was funded and transpired by the European Union (see Zarafonitou, forthcoming 2009).

* The series is published by A. Sakkoulas publications, Athens-Komotini, and edited by Professor N. Kourakis.

Section 2

# Criminology and Victimology:

## Operational Tools for New Social Problems

# Chapter 5

# P. E. N. T. A. C. R. I. M. E.: Project on Electronic 'NTensive Advanced Teaching For Criminological Research & Intelligence in Media Era

**Arije Antinori**
*"Alma Mater Studiorum" University of Bologna, Italy and "Sapienza" University of Rome, Italy*

## EXECUTIVE SUMMARY

*This chapter introduces the birth of the project named P.E.N.T.A.C.R.I.M.E. based on a dynamic teaching approach. The contemporary Criminology has to face today's complexity, then the Criminologist has to apply a multidisciplinary and interdisciplinary way of thinking to deeply understand the brand-new Criminal and Deviant phenomena. During the latest years Communication has gained a main role in human life especially about the group relationships. The author shows the philosophy, methodology and technology profile of this seminar project that can be represent a new and useful way to grasp the meaning of Media processes and Media technology in the so-called new Terrorism, the Global Terrorism. Thanks to the interconnection between technology mediated teaching and learning it is possible to create an open-source Knowledge model to be used as valuable tool both in research and practice field.*

## CRIMINOLOGY: A MULTIDISCIPLINARY APPROACH TO FACE COMPLEXITY

### Background

The project has arisen from the author's experience as sociologist, criminologist, geopolitical analyst, I.T.C. expert and Police officer.

DOI: 10.4018/978-1-60566-872-7.ch005

Since 2004, he teams up with Professor Gemma Marotta, Associate Professor of Criminology at "Sapienza" University of Rome – Faculty of Communication Sciences.

In these years the author has been Criminology Course Tutor, Social-Change Analysis Course Tutor, and he has taught some lessons in: Criminology and Sociology; Terrorism and Counter-terrorism; Media and Crime; Social-Change and Deviance; Geopolitics, Immigration and Law.

Talking to students during these years, he has realized that they asked and needed more dynamic teaching to let them experience the "taste" of their wished tomorrow occupation.

Mainly today, the Italian University system is based on a very traditional way of teaching which doesn't agree with a rational use of technology to increase at the same time the capacity of teaching and learning.

Oppositely, as the author points out, the complexity of today's social, cultural and political context emphasizes the importance of technology use to promote a multidisciplinary and interdisciplinary characterization of contemporary Criminology, which is able to face the challenges given by the soaring phenomena of Deviance and Crime, especially related to the organized crime as one of the main actor of next future.

So, the author believes that is necessary to reach a systemic theoretical and practical approach. In this way the objective of study can be conceptualized by many points of view as the many fields of interest that focus on it.

It has to be considered that, for this reason, every deviance and/or crime phenomenon happens in a strong-tight functional interdependence between man – as "social actor" – and the social structure or sub-structure, in which he has integrated and he can live together with the other men, sharing his and their interests, or in opposition to shared social norms or - in the extreme – against the Law.

To be more precise, it seems necessary to explicate what is the kind of scientific approach that the author promote during his didactic collaboration, at the above mentioned Faculty of Communication Sciences.

In fact, the author wants to underline, that the object of study: criminal as individual, criminal fact or event, criminal phenomenon - from a micro-level to a macro-level of analysis - has to be studied according to a systemic model and referring to the interaction of the main principles and methodologies of the following disciplines:

- Social-Change Analysis – it studies the changes of social structures together with the relational dynamics of men.
- Sociology of Deviance – it studies the causes and origins of deviant behavior, along with its radicalization into the society. It see into the relationship between man and institutions in charge of social control and safety & security.
- Criminology – studies the origins, ways and causes of events that offend and damage personal and public safety and interests.
- Communication Sciences – study the Communication, not only as transfer of encoded information, but in particular as social relation that can be possible thanks to the sharing of particular meanings.

Therefore, it's clear that the technology – in particular information technology - can help the Criminologist to manage all these specific tools given by the above mentioned theoretical approaches.

According to these analytical perspective, the centrality of Communication Sciences is pointed out especially in the main role taken by this dynamic of interaction during the process named "social unit" construction. In fact, "atomized" men join together thanks to the sharing of a language and/or a set of signs recognized by themselves.

It is the result of the affiliation – "normal"/ deviant / criminal - concept as identity self-recognition through the assimilation of behaviors and/or lifestyles, all integrated into a system of rule-set.

The author has experienced that studying, analyzing and countering the terrorist phenomena, it is necessary, both in research and practice; such as the knowledge of communication dynamics through the deviant and/or criminal behavior is set. That is why the Criminologist has to observe:

- Verbal systems of communication - referring to the relationship signs/symbols;

- Non-verbal systems of communication – referring to the relationship signs/signals.

Talking about non-verbal communication dynamics and future trends, it can be affirmed that today's centrality of internet as mass media strategic platform, catches the attention of the terrorist groups. That confirms the efficacy of the symbols in the terrorist context.

In fact, thank to the symbols, the terrorists communicate their being as a particular "social animals" – their sociality is in opposition to the majority of people - who recognized themselves as a rigorous group built round about a rigorous identity. It can be easily referred to the following processes:

- definition of the affiliation – thanks to the symbols, usually in unconflictual contexts individuals recognized themselves as "Us" between the others. That can be stronger experienced if related to the dicotomic vision of life in each true terrorist mind. So, in this case, affiliation can be represented by the conflict representation: "Us" against "Other" who is the Enemy, the Evil – especially for the religious based terrorist group;
- synthesis of the ideology – usually a name, a number, a tag, or a logo synthesize the principles and values – in this case it has to consider these as disvalues – on the base of the criminal choice of group;
- self-legitimation – the terrorist group tries - first an inside-directed to its members, thanks to the sharing culture, then an outside-directed to all people, thanks to mass media - to legitimate their violent acts due to their self-assigned status of "oppressed".
- rituality - it defines the relationship between reality and ritual. The rituals the group performs construct and improve the perceptions of the world by organizing social, religious, and political acts. That is possible because the rituality is related to an exact meaning-code acted through an exact behavior. For the terrorist group is necessary to make itself "immortal" – being never-ending in time and space. Moreover, the rituality appears to be very effective as a kind of self-protection against the outside-world, to ensure the maintenance of secrecy and "invulnerability".

For all that, nowadays, the ability of creating a communicative strategy is an important resource for the terrorist groups acting in the global system. They can use it to control, manipulate and make propaganda with the objective of acting a strategic persuasion which can predetermine the socio-political context both at local and global level.

To understand that, Criminology has to uses a very dynamic approach in particular oriented to Media and Media technology.

For all that the author wants to elaborate a kind of Criminology teaching which – thanks to the essential support of technology - can be strongly connected to crime-investigations and safe & security activities and studies. In this way, he intends to promote a "creative osmosis" between social-sciences and police-activities, useful to deep understand, prevent, and counter the terrorist phenomenon.

As mentioned before, now to clarify the field in which the present project was born, the author proceeds to make some conceptual distinctions. That can help the reader to find-out the most superficial key-elements of each terrorist structure, behavior and modus operandi. In fact, about the study of Terrorism, the author affirms that consider the terrorist events as a unique and "monolithic" phenomenon, causes the lost of numerous important singularities, and that can only be a way to fall through the complexity of information, without any chance to find the way back.

To clarify that, let's look some useful examples: in Europe the '70s - '80s have been characterized by the presence of terrorist structures having reference to an hyper-ideologized interpretation on one hand of the Marxist-Leninist thought, on the other hand of the nazi-fascist thought. In Italy, the so-called "Years of Lead" – referred to the lead of bullets – the "Red Brigades" have completed many terrorist acts in particular against representatives of the institutions and labor unions, to overturn with violence the constitutional order. So, proceeding to analyze the strategic and tactical dimension of this terrorist group, it can be asserted that the "Red Brigades" are characterized by a "columns" structure which ensures a hard compartmentation in few operative micro-groups appointed to violently act.

So, the group affiliation is set by militancy and characterized by a strong ideal. At the organization and communication level, it is possible to find a top-down, plus feedback dynamic.

While in another case, for example analyzing post-colonial terrorism developed especially in the Maghreb and Mashreq, it is possible to see the presence of a paramilitary pyramidal model of organization determined on a strong pan-African and/or pan-Arab ideologization. The groups that can be associated to that are substantially homogeneous and standardized and are characterized by a hard familiarization and territorialization. Their relationship with institutions is characterize by dimorphism, and inside the group there is a macro-sharing dynamic based on a top-down organization and communication model. An example of that is the so-called political-cultural pan-Arabic movement and its history that in this instance, even if militancy has reference to ideology, it is also characterized by a strong ethnicity component and familiarity in anthropological sense.

The application field of this case study, focused on technology for Criminology teaching, is represented by the contemporary International Terrorism, also known as Global Terrorism. The groups that can be referred to this new kind of Terrorism are structured in a pyramidal form, but it is connected to some peripheral satellites that act as "points of contact" as "door to the world" that open on sensible geopolitical areas. These new terrorist groups are characterized also by political-strategic bipolarity which inside can be possible to find the presence, at the same time, of top-down and bottom-up dynamics. In these groups there is a strong ideologization and a total and violent opposition to institutions, that are based on a faitheistic military membership through the confluence of idealistic ethnic and religious component.

The so-called Qaedism, very often mistakenly considered a homogeneous phenomenon, deserves a different dissertation. In fact, Al'Qaeda terrorist structure dynamic evolution has passed through three development steps and likewise three structural models. The first is characterized by low territorialization associated to an operative collective-vertex connected to a basic multicellular structure. Stands out the institutions rejection against the creation of a transnational Umma. The militancy is based on a faitheistic membership added to an ideological and religious component. So, the chain-network model is the most representative of the first Al'Qaeda communication and organization profile. This is why it can be considered relatively vulnerable. In the second step, Al'Qaeda undergoes an evolution in which is recognizable just a temporarily territorialization structure, where the strategic vertex gradually transform itself into a star-network dynamic form, characterized by a fideistic militancy and/or affiliation added to online "virtual-antagonistic" support, too. This kind of terrorism structure is like a big brand franchising.

Finally, the current step of qaedism features a deterritorialized full-matrix-network, in which the head-vertex consists in a ideological-media center inside a wide virtual network. Operatively, there is the presence of worldwide expanded sleeper-cells. So, in this last step, the strategic planning is global and globalized such as characterized by real and virtual - but concrete, sharing pseudo-militancy fideistic form.

In the field of Criminology applied to investigation and related to safety & security, oriented to the analysis and interpretation of this new criminal phenomenon, it highlights today complexities of social, political and cultural context characterized by heterogeneity and dynamism. That is why it is so important to underline the interdisciplinary and multidisciplinary theoretic approach, so far proposed.

In this scenario, it emerges the role of technological progress on a tactical and strategic level, both as a distinctive feature of "neo - terrorist" action, both as essential resource to be operatively used in the above mentioned creative osmosis process which must interconnect scholars to police.

Therefore, today it shows the increasingly importance of information, especially in the management of so-called "open source" and "gray source", in an era characterized by hyper-informatization due to the Information & Communication Technology pervasiveness. There is, in fact, a progressive growth of virtual networks and "new" kinds of relationship set as protagonists in the today's dawn of hyper-networking age.

Besides, are emerging new, free and different platforms of social-networking that, in the next future, will become an extension of human three dimensional life, a new model of social life, so a new model of Deviance and Crime, too.

For all that, the scholars have the necessity to invest in technology which can be possible to reduce the gap between social-change and research in action. To do that the author wants to adopt - at the Faculty of Communication Sciences - a new way of teaching based on a innovative mix of methodology referred to the quality/quantity synergic approach and technology interfaces to apply that. In this way it will be possible to understand Terrorism and support the counter activity.

## MEDIA DIMENSION OF TERRORISM

### Setting the Stage

Then, the following experience is based, as above mentioned, on a new technological methodology to Criminology teaching based on the open source software technology that will allow the student to take totally part to a learning activity that conjugate at the same time practice and research.

For a long time the author had the purpose to organize a workshop that could give to the students simultaneously criminological skills and tools to operate in the safety & security field, but mainly to let them understand that every-day technology, can be a useful tool, although for initial analysis.

A further target was to focus on creativity, synergies and teamwork very strongly.

In the broadest sense, it is necessary to identify terrorist phenomenon environment. But Terrorism is integrated in complex context named Life. So, how to elaborate a useful model which consent to point out all the key-elements? In Life it can be experienced complexity: the "noise". But, why don't try to understand the complexity of Terrorism analyzing its Media dimension?

But the Net is dynamic so we have to keep in mind that the starting situation (time = 0, space = 0) is modified by the Net itself because it is characterized by continuous change.

First of all, to decrease the complexity is necessary to create a model which can be useful to know the underling elements, actors and dynamics of the studied phenomenon. In this light it is important to focus on the communication process, on the language.

In a model, thanks to the use of indicators, it is possible to represent the phenomena through the concepts. This leads to create the indicationing relationship as the act of signification. Now, it emerges the importance of measurement as the complex process of translation from concepts to the indicators. So a valid and useful indicator has to have:

*Figure 1. The metaphor of complexity*

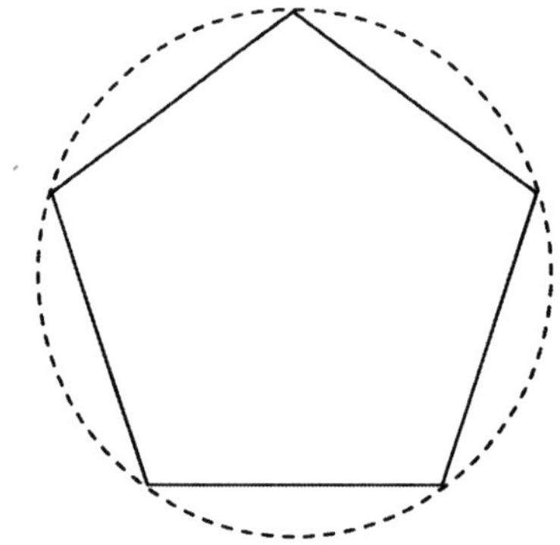

- a sign value;
- a specific relevance, that is why the indicator has not to be flexible;
- a specific contextualization.

Given that, there is the need for choosing one or more rigorous points of view (P.O.V.) from which the observer can operate a constant monitoring through the previously developed indicators. The dynamism of the present model involves the need to let the operator get additional information directly from the practical side of the investigation field related to the analyzed phenomenon. It is necessary to verify, in a "practical" way too – thanks to the operative feedback - the fulfillment of the chosen indicators, as testing their ability to provide a satisfactory representation of the phenomenon. Then the students are led to the use of technology to apply quantitative and qualitative methodology for understanding Terrorism by its Media dimension. As it will possible to read in the next chapter, Pentacrime is a project in which the participant work at last to implement Knowledge, using Internet and open source softwares. Finally, is important to remember that the whole process should ensure a close correlation between data and theories.

## APPLICATION OF PENTAGON PHILOSOPHY: P.E.N.T.A.C.R.I.M.E.

### Case Description

The author regarded that a maximum of 15 - 20 students was the right measure to enable a successful project's fulfillment, both for logistics and also considering the learning purpose that is the essential point for any university project realization.

He was thinking about every day "sea of information" which flows around all of us. Trying to represent metaphorically this situation with a two dimensions draw, the author has chosen for a circle that describes all the existent.

Considering that it was useful to organize three groups of five students, the author immediately thought them as a single flexible and dynamic entity; that is why it has been represented in a regular pentagon form.

The regular polyhedron idea grew up from geometry passion of the author, but above all from the desire to give instantaneous representation of today's context complexity and human determination in ruling 360 ° complexity with technology help. (See Figure 1)

The figure above (Figure 1) represents a inner regular Pentagon circle, in which it is drawn an isosceles triangle.

*Figure 2. The never-ending Pentagon*

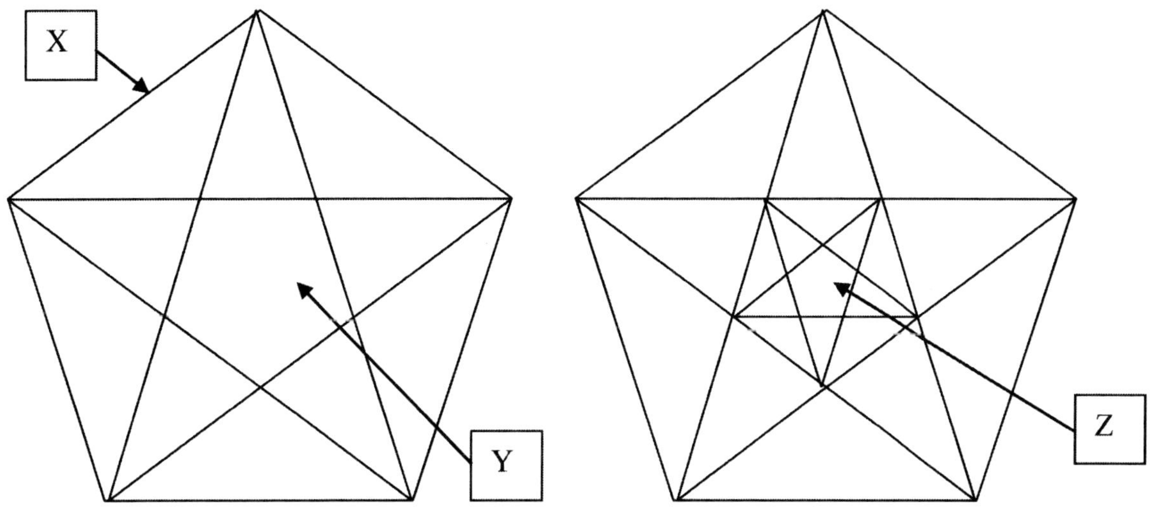


The Pentagon (Figure 2) is special because diagonals lead to a new never-ending Pentagon.

This well represent working group involve to decrease low - level analysis in order to get the core of the study.

Besides, the regular Pentagon can be divided into equal portions (Figure 3) that represent members group equality condition because they interact in a leaderless structure given by the regular pentagon. It can be observed that if the regular pentagon could be open projecting its vertex to the outside it will change in a starfish, as above shown. So, the group operativity can be imagined as a continuous two-step movement: the starfish with his independent and self-generating tentacles is wide open to receive the information coming from outside, then it will close, changing in the polygon during its activity of multilevel analysis. In the personal opinion of the author, dehierarchization makes learning enjoyable and reduce the distances. Team spirit collaboration and cooperation oriented can be useful to the whole

*Figure 3. The leaderless Pentagon and the starfish*

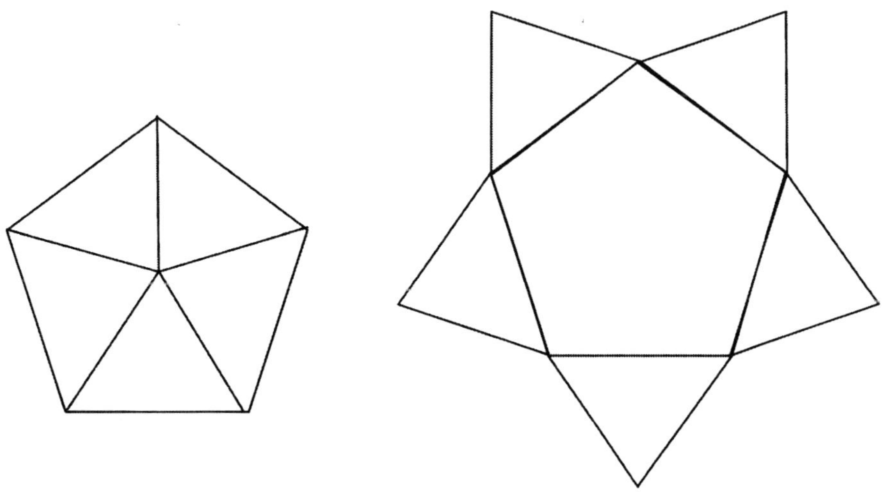

*Figure 4. Pentagon Group*

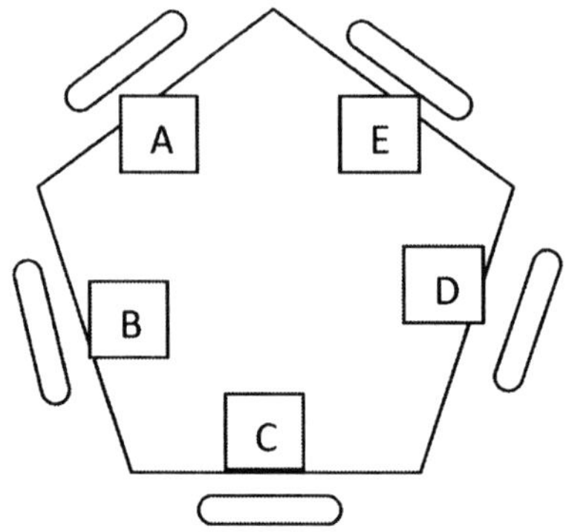


group in which the teacher has to explain the used methodology, has to give appropriate tools, has to explain the working ability and, above all, has to experience a totally technological mediated teaching.

It was chosen to articulate teaching in this way also to bring to light what technology has become. In the course of time, in fact technology changes into a central element of human behave and went beyond the simple human - machine interaction, through networks and interconnections, in other words towards new perception patterns, interaction and socialization that seem to open the doors to the future.

Considering creative thinking and synergy the basis of a dynamic approach to "an operative way" oriented criminology to investigation and safety & security, the author has organized a interactive seminar called P.e.N.T.A.C.R.I.M.E. - Project on e-lectronic Ntensive Advanced Teaching for Criminological Research & Intelligence Era in Media – in which <'ntensive> give the high degree evidence of interactive teaching involvement, made possible through the use of technology.

For logistical reasons the three days full-immersion seminar were hosted by an information technology company, based in Rome, who has kindly offered to provide the necessary technological support.

Fifteen student were asked to take part in a free Criminology training seminar. It has to specify that if a student wanted to participated he before needed to demonstrate of having passed Criminology I (First Level Course) exam and Criminology II (Second Level Course) exam. The students involved, joined with great satisfaction, showing curiosity for the seminar. The students were average 25 year old and they fifteen group consisted by nine women and six men.

They were randomly divided into three pentagonal groups, so each group was formed by five students (Figure 4). It was decided to call them respectively RED Pentagon, GREEN Pentagon and BLU Pentagon, referring to three - colour system (R G B) that determines all the possible colors. The purpose of this seminar was to make the students learn, through the support of a technology widely accessible to them, support, some useful concepts and techniques in crime-investigation activity. The following step was to experience, through information technology mediated interaction, the work of a professional team-up called to support an institution in the understanding of the so-called Terrorism and its related culture. Studying the analysis research process of media contents, looking at contemporary terrorism, to develop a wider point of view to implement the process of knowledge.

Each polygonal team has to be characterized by the ability to collect, select, analyze and systematize some media files.

In particular, each group (RED Pentagon,

*Figure 5. The big Pentagon*

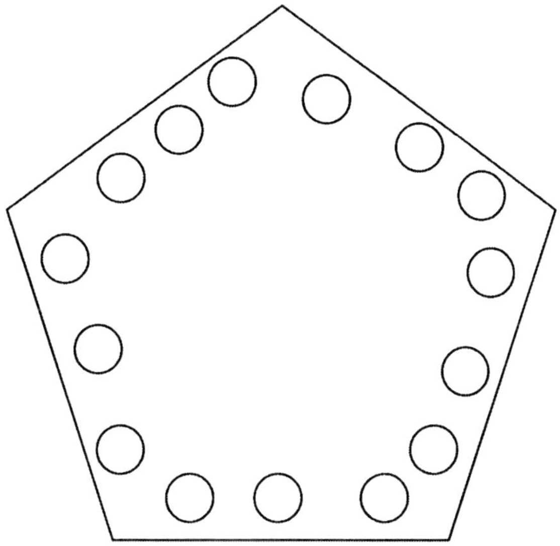

GREEN Pentagon and BLU Pentagon) is thought as a pentagonal leaderless team-up .In fact, to favor that, the author provided to arrange fifteen tables forming three different pentagons, in which were arranged five chairs - one for each component.

Every student is on one of the five polygonal face, inside the polygon (Figure 5). Each of them has a set workstation made up by a hard disk, monitor, mouse, keyboard and microphone headset. Any workstations has a free open-source software installed, easily available on Internet. Therefore, every student has a web browser, a graphic editing software, an audio editing software, a video editing software, a software for writing and a sheet notes. They have an access suchlike workstation profile with user and password, generated in random order. These three groups are interconnected through the author and coordinator who use his laptop as server of a network. So, the author, as designer, organizer and project coordinator of PeNTACRIME uses his laptop to manage all the activities of the group.

It is important to specify that the author is not inside the room where are the Polygons, because he coordinates the seminar from a different room place beside, separated by a big window.

Each group, in respect to the author guidelines, has its own autonomy in decision-making process and functional independence from the other two, instead the simulation management is lead by the author. The three groups network hierarchy, RED Pentagon, GREEN Pentagon and BLUE Pentagon, are connected "in parallel" with each other, creating, with the server, a whole small intranet. Therefore, as it is clearly shown, the communication flow moves on two different ways: one defined internal (intranet) and the other external (internet).

## Day 1

### Step 1

The coordinator has organized a 27 video files directory, taken from his personal database which contains internet videos since 2000. Selected from 2004 until 2008. For this kind of teaching the author has chosen files related to several events that are not exclusively produced by a terror media network. In fact, more of them show just the cultural side of Terrorism. On account of this the author wants to stimulate the reach of a creative thinking. In this way it will be possible to face Terrorism In a more rationale and professional way.

These are the selected files list:

1. 20040411 Atocha Station Madrid Al-Qaeda Bombing Amateur Footage. mpg (time 00: 01': 08" – Audio + Video - color - 11.617.676 bytes – mpg file) – it's an amateur videoclip in Spanish language, about the 2004 terrorist bombing in Madrid;
2. abu ghraib terrorist torture pigs apes cia military snuff human rights behead decapitate decapitation pau (time 00: 02': 50" – Audio + Video + Text - color - 28.770.304 bytes – mpg file) – it's a shocking collection of torture scenes in Arabic language and edited in an English subtitled file;
3. Afganistan - Bombing 2 Vehicles.mpg (time 00: 00': 24" – Video – black & white - 5.361.680 bytes – mpg file) – this nocturnal video shows, from above, a vehicle that has bombed in a rural context;
4. Al Qaeda Trains Children.flv (time 00: 03': 32" – Audio + Video – color - 8.500.363 bytes – flv file) – this video in Arabic language shows some armed black-hooded children during a war training camp. In the videos it can be noted the presence of a black-hooded man who seems to train the above mentioned children.
5. al-Qaeda's New Tactics.flv (time 00: 02': 33" – Video + Text - color - 2.325.818 bytes – flv file) – this video is probably realized by US Force in Iraq and it shows some war scenes that illustrated the difficulties that Americans experienced.
6. Dirty Kuffar - DIGIHAD (ORIGINAL). mpeg (time 00: 04': 28" – Audio + Video + Text – color 46.754.232 bytes – mpeg file) – this video, in Arabic and English language, is a very interesting product because is similar to the music videoclips but the content is a mix of snuff war scenes, documentary scenes and morphing effects that offers a very catchy product in particular for young supporters not yet militants. It's seems to be an interesting way to make propaganda of terrorism using the tools and communication strategies of marketing.
7. Do You Know What You're Watching. flv (time 00: 05': 34" – Audio + Video + Text – color - 12.072.471 bytes – flv file) – this video, in Arabic language and English language dubbed and subtitled, shows a suicide–bomber since the organization of his attack to his death during it.in the second part the video seems to be a documentary about the relation-ship between suicide-bombing and Internet culture.
8. Faces of Death – R P G gunman killed by machinegun fire during street fighting.mpg (time 00: 00': 12"- Audio + Video - color - 2.307.732 bytes – mpg file) – this video, in a Spanish language, shows a man who has been killed during a war scene in Iraq.
9. Faces Of Death - Taliban Execution 3.mpeg (time 00: 01': 10" – Video + Text – color - 7.776.135 bytes – mpeg file) – this video shows a public execution of a Taliban probably in Afghanistan.
10. Farfour martyred by Israelis in final episode. flv (time 00: 04': 42" – Audio + Video + Text – color - 11.205.892 bytes – flv file) – this video is an episode of "The pioneers of Tomorrow" A Children's Show on Hamas TV – Al-Aqsa TV (Hamas / PA) in which "Farfour", a co-host character similar to Walt Disney "Mickey Mouse", promotes hatred of Israel and preach about world Islamic supremacy. It is edited in Arabic language with the add of English subtitles.
11. Hamas Blows Israeli Terrorists in a Tank. wmv (time 00: 08': 57" – Audio + Video – color - 6.723.778 bytes – wmv file) – this video, in Arabic language, shows the organization of an attack against an Israeli tank since its blast.

12. Hamas Mickey Mouse Teaches Terror to Kids.flv (time 00: 03': 27" – Audio + Video – Text – color - 8.334.439 bytes – flv file) – it's another episode of "The pioneers of Tomorrow" A Children's Show on Hamas TV – Al-Aqsa TV (Hamas / PA) with the protagonist "Farfour". This Video is in Arabic language with subtitles in English language.
13. Hamas Mujahideen In Palestine - Jihad Islam.wmv (time 00: 26': 19" – Audio + Video – color - 37.147.822 bytes – wmv file) – this video shows, in Arabic language, the life of a Hamas fighter together with is people and his fighter-friends. At the end some war scenes and martyrs scenes, too can be seen.
14. Hamas propaganda.wmv (time 00: 00': 57" – Audio + Video + Text – color - 2.360.958 bytes – wmv file) – this video in both Arabic and English language describes the training of some Hamas fighters.
15. IRAQ marine corps M1 Abrams tank destroyed by 250kg IED irak road side bomb. mpg (00: 01': 22" – Audio + Video – color - 3.999.748 bytes – mpg file) – this video, in Arabic language, shows the organization of an attack against a USA tank since its blast.
16. Iraq Resistance Video Suecide Bomber Prepare Mission Falluja Banned Usa Face Of Dead Ogrish Behead Kummel (00: 01': 56" – Audio + Video + Text – color - 19.853.316 bytes – mpg file) – this is a spoof video of the suicide-bombing life and acts. It has been banned in many Islamic Countries. Characters talk in Arabic language.
17. London Attack 7-7-2005 Bnp Tv.wmv (time 00: 01': 41" – Audio + Video – color - 13.007.044 bytes – wmv file) – this video is made by some live shots taken during 2005 attack in London. People talk in English language.
18. Marsho - Russian TV Studio Capture By Chechen Mujahedeen (Chechnya, Cecenia, Czeczenia, Ichkeria).wmv (time 00: 09': 34" – Audio + Video – black & white - 16.426.857 bytes – wmv file) – in this interesting video, a group of Chechnya mujahedeen fighters attack the office of a probably russian TV studio. All of them seem to speak Russian language.
19. Ogrish - Suicide Bomber Still Alive.asf (time 00: 00': 30" – Audio + Video – color - 887.497 bytes – asf file) – It is a very raw movie in which it can be seen a suicide-bomber, probably in Colombia, after his explosion who is without some parts of his body but still alive.
20. Ogrish – dot – com - head_of_suicide_bomber.wmv (time 00: 00': 20" – Audio + Video – color - 530.998 bytes – wmv file) – it is a short raw video which shows the head of a suicide-bomber lied on the ground surrounded by some U.S. marines.
21. Suicide Bomber Blowing Up A Us Checkpoint In Iraq (Terror, Attack, Assault, Bomb).wmv (time 00: 04':09" – Audio + Video + Text - color - 3.045.088 bytes – wmv file) – this video narrates the organization, the progress and the finalization of a suicide-bomber attack against a U.S. checkpoint in Iraq.
22. Suicide bombing aftermath 2 – 28 - 2005. wmv (time 00: 01': 53" – Audio + Video – color - 1.906.610 bytes – wmv file) – in this video has shown the chaos created after the explosion generated by the attack of a suicide-bomber. It is used the Arabic language.
23. Taliban sniper training 11.mpeg (time 00: 00': 28" – Audio + Video - color - 6.168.326 bytes – mpeg file) – in this video can be seen a young Taliban during his ballistic training in presence of an occidental guy. Can be listen some phrases in Arabic language and some short phrases in English language.

24. Top 20 al ansar attentati mujahedeen. Wmv (time 00: 07': 17" – Audio + Video + Text – color - 111.264.212 bytes – wmv file) – This is one of the most interesting video, because it has a very good quality and is fully realized using digital tools. So, it is a demonstration of the maker capacity to manage the technology for creating catchy videos. This product has the same structure of a video made by a music or sport broadcasting service. In particular, it is very similar to a music top chart or a chart which shows to you the top 20 goals of the week. This video made by Ansar Al-Sunnah terrorist group, starts with a 3 dimensional golden logo. Watching it the observer can note the progress in the ability of bombing, from the $20^{th}$ position to the $1^{st}$. Another peculiarity is that some seconds before each bombing, a banner written in English language illustrates what is playing on the screen while the observer can listen some Arabic songs playing background.
25. VW Polo Suicide bomber. flv (00: 00': 21" – Audio + Video + Text – color - 904.940 bytes – flv file) – this video is a product of viral marketing. It describes a suicide-bomber who make himself explode inside a famous German car.
26. Women with Down's Syndrome used as Suicide Bombers in Iraq.flv (time 00: 01': 43" – Audio + Video + Text – color - 3.637.122 bytes – flv file) – it is a video fragment captured by CNN. The journalist narrates that a woman affected with Down's Syndrome has completed a suicide-bombing in Baghdad.
27. WQ2RX Sexy War Propaganda Bunny Explains Suicide Terrorism (time 00: 05': 54" – Audio + Video + Text – color – 13.322.000 bytes – flv file) – this video is realized by mixing several media sources: a cartoon, a children tv-show, some 9/11 live streaming, a soft-porn clip and some sequences of a videogame. One of the main protagonist of it is a live-puppet pink Bunny, similar to the famous Warner Bros "Bugs Bunny". In this product has been used both English and Arabic language with some English language banner for the text messages.

In this starting step, the decision to supply the material without the student evolvement research on the web, it is due to put the student in front of the media product avoiding any web setting influence and any comments and / or remark referable to it. That allows the students to watch, make an analysis and experience a more "purified" have an understanding as possible in order to assess the operative capabilities and to highlight the emotional stress.

Each student has on his PC screen. They have just to login (user and password).

Next, the student had access to a Graphical User Interface (GUI) set up by a panel that has a files list numbered since 1 to 27, in alphabetical order.

After checking the box corresponding to the files number, the student starts an open source software player who plays the selected full-screen movie. In this step, the user has no opportunity to move back and forward, neither to stop the video. This would egg on the user to a first straight view. Every time the user ends the view, the open source software restart from the beginning or shows the next videos list. The coordinator manage a control procedure that shows students working state of the watched view.

After few minutes of cooling-off period, the author allows the students to "metabolize" what they have seen, so, the coordinator enable the student workstation on name-files. In this way they can have some short references about the files.

At this point, the coordinator shows simultaneously on each user's video six slides, with the following information: the identification file date, the file source, the file extension and its spread and a short description of geopolitical context.

It was specifically chosen a different teaching system in opposition to the traditional Italian methodology, in which the teacher lead the lesson from a workspace connected to a big screen, it was used this methodology because:

- it allows the users to become more comfortable with their workspace and this will be useful to promote the attention of all participants;
- it simulates the analysis process that usually takes place at professional level;
- it permits the user feel to be a part of a highly structured task group simulating the joint work of five experts;
- it leaves student creativity free to be involved in the process of analysis.

**Step 2**

After this first view, the students are called to a second different view, in fact, now they can use the full player interface, they can slow down, speed up, pause and stop watching.

Viewed all the files, the students are asked to argue about the files posting in a “polygons” discussion forum especially created for this purpose. So they can share their emotional impact and their opinion.

**During Training**

The coordinator, in multi-user sharing, project on the screen of every user the video named “Dirty Kuffar” and, after the view, thanks to a graphic board, shows the break up methodology in different level to get systemic outputs from different methods of analysis, such as visual, symbolic, content and standard communication. The author’s purpose is to explain to the students how-to use, thanks to open source software, the resources given by the Net and the technology they usually use for delight, to apply criminological operative concepts using an appropriate methodology as the one here proposed. The outputs of the on-line multimedia surveys, filled by the students, have been used to select data that will implement a database that constitute the core of the analysis model as mentioned in the previous chapter.

**Step 3**

To each students of the pentagon is assigned a randomized analysis of videos: 4; 6 and 16, in order to verify the level of learning related to what the author has taught before.

**Step Text – Audio - Video (T.A.V.)**

For a correct review feedback of reading (T - text), listening (A - audio) and viewing (V - video), the group starts to breakdown and use separate languages, so the coordinator, in a random way, shall identify each student in the pentagon that will deal only with audio, only with video and eventually with text:

Pentagon RED

Users: Ra and Rb shall listen; Rc and Rd shall view; Re shall read.

Pentagon GREEN

Users: Ga and Gb shall listen; Gc and Gd shall view; Ge shall read.

Pentagon BLUE

Users: Ba and Bb shall listen; Bc and Bd shall view; Be shall read.

In this step, contiguous users work in pairs. Thus, the outputs of each Pentagon are three: Text, Audio and Video, corresponding to the three dimensions form. This procedure is formalized through the filling of a qualitative and quantitative multimedia form. The structure of this form consists in a text-box and check-list in which the user can write notes and comments.

The forms are collected in the system database to enable further elaboration.

## Day 2

**Step 1**

The coordinator, after acquiring the survey results, shows to the students, through a multi - transmission, the outputs report obtained from each pentagon operative session just to highlight the critical identified points.

**Step 2**

In order to encourage students to share and to achieve a common form among the three pentagons, the coordinator fill out the final form sharing the reasons for its choices, and release on the net the final form version that will implement the reference database.

## Day 3

**Step 1**

In the same logistics way, only one big pentagon is set up and it gather 15 students inside, on each side of the pentagon there are two workstations with an amount of 10 workspace.

Aim of this meeting is to:

- increase complexity;
- promote team-up;
- set free working activity from educational practice, to check macro - Pentagon tendency and organization on Internet.

In fact, the coordinator ask to the team to find on the Net 3 video files, giving as reference only some major search keys of them, which are:

- "marines firing" - actually matching the file - "Raw Video: Marines in Gunbattle With Taliban" on Youtube.com.
- "Benazir" actually matching the file – "KARACHI BOMB BLAST VIDEO RALLY BENAZIR BHUTTO 18TH OCT 2007" on http://pakistanpakistan.blogspot.com
- "LTTE woman" actually matching the file - "LTTE woman suiside Bra bomb"- on Youtube.com

The Pentagon students must identify the above mentioned files, search them, and download them into a folder. To increase the complexity of learning and training, they will analyze them in a new way. The students in fact are asked to use open source software, available on their workstations to stimulate creative learning and to test their skill level. They can edit the files using audio and video software, using picture-box, as shown by the coordinator on the network. The picture-box are remarkable useful because allows video - captured screenshots intake, gained by the user for its meaningfulness. Same chance is allowed for audio samples for a 5' maximum.

In this step, the coordinator will stimulate self-functional organization of the working group, avoiding tasks assignment and / or any kind of support.

**Step 2**

Now the users within the Pentagon decide by their selves to create 3 working groups, each one composed by 5 students, to research the files on the Net. The author notice this self-organization and gather than this structure is functional to the goal to be achieved. In this way the students draw on work synergies, and the author observe that this involvement remove either critical situation and any conflict.

At this point, the students begin their research and when someone has found the file immediately share the result.

In the following step, the students organized their selves to proceed in this way:

5 students constitute a sub-group view;

there is a languages TAV (Text, Audio, Video) distribution inside the sub-group;

15 students score the total view of all the video;

the filling output form is collective and they use the new multimedia tools.

**Step 3**

The coordinator analyzes collective output form and discusses it with the whole group on the network.

## CONCLUSION

### Authors Remarks

It is highlighted the substantive improvement of decreasing working time, but especially, on a quality level, the accuracy results that shed light on the individuals ability in information technology interaction. This new kind of interaction in based on individual consciousness in human-computer relationship, characterized by technology interaction and collaborative work.

Finally, in to this project, emerge that the removed role of leadership has promoted groups activities during the work sessions.

### Students Remarks

As reported by the students in the following interviews:

- they felt a strong sense of responsibility and competition;
- this new way learning was very challenging for two reason: the use of every-day technology close to their personal computers habit, the operative approach of the seminar;
- they show wonder at open source software flexibility and at its actual use;
- they highlighted the organizational step in teamwork importance;
- they assign greater relevance to relationship between terrorism and Media.

The author makes the point that currently, further study are in progress for pointing out more development and analysis log-files acquired during the seminar. This is to highlight both aspects of degree participation and interaction, beneath organizational dynamics.

## CURRENT CHALLENGES FACING THE ORGANIZATION

During the developing of a Terrorism knowledge model, are found at least two important operational guidelines related to the social-sciences approach:

1. Exploratory - phenomenical description by identifying the dimensions that composite it.
2. explanatory – an already known analyzed phenomenon can be related or compared to another one. The explication of problem related to the phenomenon consists mainly of three steps:
    - definition of the phenomenon - as mentioned before, it is characterized by an extremely dynamic and complex context;
    - identification of sources - here it emerges the recurring problem to identify the levels of reliability of sources and the problem to share the information they have provided

- creation the universe of indicators - which requires, as already seen, a balanced operation of synthesis.

The first approach of this project has been the creation of a semantic and taxonomic reference set. In this way it has been useful to analyze with students the many Net-found definitions of Terrorism. So, the question "Which interpretation adopted?"

example: "Action and method of political struggle (to defend, or more often, to subvert or destabilize an institution) that, to impose itself uses acts of extreme violence such as bombings and sabotage, hijacking, robberies, kidnappings and murders, urban guerrilla warfare against the police but especially against innocent people in order to arouse panic and emotional reaction of the population." [Treccani - Dictionary of Italian Language]

That shows how difficult it is to find a large share on the concept of Terrorism, which is not closely tied to Law .

- Inspired to the so-called "rule of 5 W" (Who? What? Where? When? Why?) - as a basis of Anglo-Saxon journalism - students were now asked to interpret and represent a summary of a terrorist event. Subsequently, through the use of a open source online surveys software, the author has asked students to fill a survey, with the aim to know the main questions to connote a terrorist act. So, the result of the survey filling points out the main dimensions of a terrorist act:
- what is it for the actor who causes it? – by the side of the offender;
- what is it for the actor who is harmed by or made to suffer from the act? - in relation to the important role of the victim;
- what is it in concrete terms? - in a very objective sense, referred to the role of police and other institutions that have to counter the terrorist group, identify the subject involved and catch them soonest;
- media relation – the act is considered as a significant act of a dynamic interaction – crime act, in this case - between the perpetrator, individual and / or group, the victim, individual and/or collective subject and/or institution;
- media sight - set of possible effects, whether or not predetermined, as the echo effect useful to propagate overtime and multiply the effectiveness of the single act;
- actors field - the frameset of all individuals involved in the act
- why – voluntary or unvoluntary, explicit or unexplicit reason given by the offender.
- statistical significance - the presence in the current act of key-elements that can be found in other past acts. It gives the possibility to create links and statistical inferences;
- trend - the possibility that this act is conformed to some other brand new acts. In this case, it highlights the born of a new sub-phenomenon;
- victim reaction – the active-role of the victim who has taken part in the act;
- goals - subjects or objects against who is planned and /or oriented the act;
- physical damages – organized in primary, secondary and / or collateral damages;
- Strategy - as an opportunity to connect this act to a broader plan useful to spread the terrorist group power;
- implications social / political / economic – emotional effects in the main spheres of human life.

For all that, it's necessary ask the question:

What are the concepts representative of the phenomenon? To answer, it has to operate a procedure of conceptualization consist of five main step:

- Conceptual deconstruction;
- Figurative representation;
- Empirical dimensions specification;
- Semantic concepts - indicators assignment;
- Indicators – variables - indexes choose;

Moreover, considering the terrorist act as a "social fact", then it is possible, first of all, to distinguish analytically two separate profiles - individual and social – then identify several dimensions - cultural, religious, political, economic, family - friends, media, etc. - of analysis. Finally, it also shows, within each dimension, a useful set of operational indicators, related to the so-called "Lazarsfeld paradigm" approach which affirms that a phenomenon can be deconstructed in its main dimensions to elaborate a representative indicator or a set of these for each representative dimension.

So, according to that, a terrorist act can be deconstructed in three main and representative dimensions: a) the aggressive ability; b) the organizational skills; c) the vulnerability of the target, in which can be developed three groups of macro-indicators, as explained:

- aggressive capacity - indicators relating to: A) techniques - murder, kidnapping, suicide-bombing, contamination, hijacking, cyber-attack, etc; B) agents, substances, materials - nuclear, bacteriological, radiological, etc; C) Carriers, vector - aircraft, car, ship, food supply networks, etc; D) Media resources - tv, internet, radio, mobile, telephony, etc;
- organizational skills – indicators relating to: E) mobility in the territory; F) Virtual Mobility; G) war Supply; H) training; I) recruiting; L) Economic availability; M) subsistence food;
- target vulnerability - indicators relating to: N) Target centric profile – sensible targets, structural damage, human presence, collateral damage, symbolic value, systemic features, etc; O) Geostrategic profile - level of managing local and global, countering capacity, emergency management capacity, presence of public events, geographic profile, area stability, etc.

As shown in the past chapter, now, to obtain good outcomes is necessary the perfect joint between the Pentagonal work outputs - given by the students - and the develop of more sophisticated models and indicators - given by the teacher - to realize a deep level of Criminological analysis and at the same time of technology support to teaching Criminology. Finally, the author is working to use open source technology to develop interfaces that make it possible the project of new and more interactive system of technological teaching and learning in Criminology.

## REFERENCES


AA. VV. (1995). *Il dilemma dell'Islam. Politica e movimenti islamisti nel mondo arabo contemporaneo*. Milano, Italy: Franco Angeli.

AA.VV. (1998). La tutela della sicurezza nel settore economico. Il ruolo dell'intelligence. *Per aspera ad veritatem, 12*, 783-796.

AA.VV. (1999). Intelligence e analisi strategica. *Per aspera ad veritatem, 14*, 447-498.

AA.VV. (2000). Intelligence e statistica. *Per aspera ad veritatem, 16*, 21-54.

AA.VV. (2001). La comunicazione istituzionale e la comunicazione dell'intelligence. *Per aspera ad veritatem, 20*, 449-476.

AA. VV. (2002). *Erased in a moment: Suicide bombing attacks against israeli civilians*. New York: Human Rights Watch.

AA. VV. (2002). *Suicide, martyrdrom, terrorist attacks, or homicide – a debate in Arab media.* Germany: Middle East Media Research Institute (MEMRI).

AA.VV. (2003). Fondamento, fondamentalismo: uno sguardo dal profondo. *Rivista di psicologia analitica, 15*(67), 111-167.

AA. VV. (2003). *The profile of the suicide bomber. An ICT Research project*. USA: ICT.

AA.VV. (2004). Progetto Jihad. *Limes*, Gruppo Editoriale L'Espresso, 1/2004.

Acquaviva, S., & Pace, E. (1996). *Sociologia delle religioni. Problemi e prospettive*. Roma, Italy: La Nuova Italiana Scientifica.

Amadori, A. (2002). *Bin Laden. Chi è, cosa vuole, come comunica il profeta del terrore*. Milano, Italy: Libri Scheiwiller.

Andrew, C. (1997). L'intelligence in un mondo multipolare, *Per aspera ad veritatem, 8*, 307-328.

Andrew, C. (2001). L'intelligence nel XXI secolo, *Per aspera ad veritatem, 20*, 437-448.

Antonelli, C. (1984). *Cambiamento tecnologico e impresa multinazionale: il ruolo delle reti telematiche nelle strategie globali*. Milano, Italy: FrancoAngeli.

Aruffo, A. (1995). *Il Mondo islamico. Movimenti Stati e rivoluzioni da Maometto ad* oggi. Roma, Italy: Datanews.

Aruffo, A. (2002). *L'islamismo militante. Dal Maghreb all'Asia Centrale*. Roma, Italy: Datanews.

Atran, S. (2003). Genesis of suicide terrorism. *Science*, *299*, 1534–1539. doi:10.1126/science.1078854

Balloni, A. (1983). *Criminologia in prospettiva*. Bologna, Italy: Clueb.

Balloni, A. (Ed.). (1989). *Vittime, crimine e difesa sociale*. Bologna, Italy: Clueb.

Balloni, A. (Ed.). (1998). *Criminologia e sicurezza*. Milano, Italy: Franco Angeli.

Balloni, A. (2004). *Criminologia e psicopatologia*. Bologna, Italy: Clueb.

Balloni, A., & Bisi, R. (Eds.). (1996). *Dalla criminologia alla security*. Bologna, Italy: Clueb.

Balloni, A., & Bisi, R. (Eds.). (1998). *Criminologia applicata per l'investigazione e la sicurezza*. Milano, Italy: Franco Angeli.

Balloni, A., & Sette, R. (Eds.). (2000). *Didattica in criminologia applicata. Formazione degli operatori della sicurezza e del controllo sociale*, Bologna, Italy: Clueb.

Bauman, Z. (2000). *La solitudine del cittadino globale*. Milano, Italy: Feltrinelli.

Bauman, Z. (2005). *La fiducia e la paura nella città*. Milano, Italy: Mondatori.

Benedetti, A. (2004). *Decisione e persuasione per l'intelligence (e la politica)*. Genova, Italy: Erga.

Benedetti, A. (2004). *L'osservazione per l'intelligence e l'indagine*. Genova, Italy: Erga.

Berardino, F. (1997). Modalità e strumenti dell'attività di informazione e sicurezza tra legittimità ed illegalità. *Per aspera ad veritatem, 9*, 697-706.

Bertaccini, D. (2006). *Modelli e strategie di polizia nelle società di sicurezza*. Roma: Italy: Carocci.

Bettetini, G., & Colombo, F. (1996). *Dall'alfabeto alle reti*. Roma, Italy: SEAM.

Caligiuri, M. (2000). Intelligence: un problema di comunicazione istituzionale?. *Per aspera ad veritatem, 16*, 57-80.

Caligiuri, M. (2003). Università e intelligence. Un punto di vista italiano. *Per aspera ad veritatem, 25*, 85-119.

Canetti, E. (1981). *Massa e potere*. Milano, Italy: Adelphi.

Clarke, R. V. (1992). *Situational crime prevention. Successful case studies*. New York: Harrow.

Clarke, R. V., & Felson, M. (Eds.). (1993). *Routine activity and rational choice*. New York: Transaction Books.

Cooper, A. (1999). *Disagio tecnologico*. Milano, Italy: Apogeo.

Durkheim, E. (1991). *Il suicidio. Studio di sociologia*. Milano, Italy: Rizzoli Libri.

Etienne, B. (2001). *L'islamismo radicale*. Milano, Italy: Rizzoli Libri.

Fallace, P. (2000). *La psicologia di Internet*. Milano, Italy: Raffaello Cortina.

Fiorani Piacentini, V. (2003). *Islam - Logica della fede e logica della conflittualità*. Milano, Italy: FrancoAngeli.

Gannon, J. (2001). Il ruolo dei servizi di intelligence in un mondo globalizzato. *Per aspera ad veritatem, 20*, 493-508.

Garland, D. (2001). *La cultura del controllo*. Milano, Italy: Il Saggiatore.

Gatti, U., & Barbagli, M. (2005). *Prevenire la criminalità*. Bologna, Italy: il Mulino.

Germani, L. S. (Ed.). (2001). *L'Intelligence nel XXI secolo*. Roma, Italy: Quaderni del Centro Studi Gino Germani.

Goffman, E. (1969). *La vita quotidiana come rappresentazione*. Bologna, Italy: il Mulino.

Goffman, E. (1988). *L'interazione strategica*. Bologna, Italy: il Mulino.

Guerrero, L. K., et al. (1999). *The Nonverbal Communication Reader: Classic and Contemporary Readings*. Illinois: Waveland Press.

Guevara, E. (1996). *Opere scelte 1. L'azione armata*. Milano, Italy: Baldini&Castoldi.

Habermas, J. (1974). *Storia e critica dell'opinione pubblica*. Roma-Bari, Italy: Laterza.

Habermas, J. (1980). *Teoria dell'agire comunicativo*. Bologna, Italy: Il Mulino.

Ingrassia, G. (1990). *Comunicazione sociale: crimine e devianza nel post-moderno informatico*. Torino, Italy: Giappichelli Editore.

Jacobelli, J. (Ed.). (1996). *Dall'analogico al digitale*. Bari, Italy: Laterza.

Jean, C. (2001). *Guerra, strategia e sicurezza*. Bari, Italy: Laterza.

Jean, C. (2004). *Geopolitica del ventunesimo secolo*. Bari, Italy: Laterza.

Juergensmeyer, M. (1993). *The new Cold War? Religious nationalism confronts the secular state*. Berkeley, CA: University of California Press.

Juergensmeyer, M. (2003). *Terroristi in nome di Dio*. Bari, Italy: Laterza.

Kahn, D. (1996). *The Codebreakers: The Comprehensive History of Secret Communication from Ancient Times to the Internet*. New York: Scribner.

Knapp, M. L., & Judith, A. H. (1996). *Nonverbal Communication in Human Interaction*. Orlando: Harcourt College Publishers.

Leathers, D. G. (1996). *Successful Nonverbal Communication: Principles and Applications*. Boston: Allyn & Bacon.

Marotta, G. (Ed.). (2004). *Tecnologie dell'informazione e comportamenti devianti*. Milano, Italy: Led.

Marotta, G. (Ed.). (2004). *Temi di criminologia*. Milano, Italy: Led.

Marotta, G. (2004). *Teorie criminologiche. Da Beccaria al postmoderno*. Milano, Italy: Led.

Mazzoli, G. (1998). *Profili sociali della comunicazione e nuove tecnologie*. Milano, Italy: Franco Angeli.

Morris, D. B. (1995). *The Meaning of Human Gestures*. New York: Crown Pub.

Pace, E. (1999). *Sociologia dell'Islam. Fenomeni religiosi e logiche sociali*. Roma, Italy: Carocci Editore.

Rankin, J. A. (1995). *Body Language in Negotiations and Sales*. Springfield: Rankin File.

Rapetto, U., & Di Nunzio, R. (2001). *Le nuove guerre*. Milano, Italy: BUR.

Rapetto, U., & Di Nunzio, R. (2002). *Atlante delle spie*. Milano, Italy: Rizzoli.

Selmini, R., & Braccasi, C. (Eds.). (2005). *Sicurezza urbana e ruolo della polizia locale*. Bologna, Italy: Maggioli.

Wainwright, G. R. (2000). *Teach Yourself Body Language*. Columbus: McGraw-Hill.

Williams, F. P., & McShane, M. D. (2002). *Devianza e criminalità*. Bologna, Italy: il Mulino.

# Chapter 6
# GIS:
# A New Tool for Criminology and Victimology's Studies[1]

**Elena Bianchini**
*"Alma Mater Studiorum", University of Bologna, Italy*

**Sandra Sicurella**
*"Alma Mater Studiorum", University of Bologna, Italy*

## EXECUTIVE SUMMARY

*The advent of the GIS technology has revolutionized the traditional field of information and cartographic production. The GIS, indeed, enables the management of much more numerous and more complex data and it is able to overcome the static and the traditional two-dimensional cartography. The Geographic Information Systems (GIS), that is used in various fields and disciplines, represent, also, in the university research, a valuable tool for investigation. In criminology, in particular, it has facilitated, regarding the city of Bologna, on the one hand, a kind of crime mapping on the nature of the so called "petty crimes" within the jurisdiction of the criminal Justice of the Peace, and the creation of a city's map on which have been identified support centers for victims operating in them. The use of GIS software is the basis in order to realize and put into practice not only operational measures designed to combat and to prevent crime, but it is also of help to social control measures, to public policy and to security. To the end of ensuring public safety, nowadays, it is essential, to have a clear, spatial and graphics representation, of the high concentrations of crime areas and of the degraded ones, in which there is a greater likelihood that some type of crime is committed.*

## ORIGINS

The history of cartography has very ancient origins; the first evidences, even still elementary, in fact, date back to primitive civilizations: their tendency to nomadism seems to have refined the ability to draw maps on stone or wood.

The production of maps was already known among Egyptians and Babylonians (III millennium BC) who built rudimentary maps of property and territorial representations of the known world, with decorative or religious function.

DOI: 10.4018/978-1-60566-872-7.ch006

Between the VII and VIII BC among Persian, Phoenician and Chinese developed the use of trace land and sea routes as a guide for commercial routes.

In classical times were the Greeks to give a scientific basis to the cartography applying mathematical and geometric notions to the geographic representations.

The first map of the known world is to be traced back to the philosopher Anassimandro (VI century BC) and Eratosthenes of Cyrene (III century BC) calculated with great approximation the circumference of the globe and created maps marked by a perpendicular grid of lines to measure distances. In the second century AD Claudius Ptolemy brought changes to the cartographic system introducing a network of meridians and parallels.

The Roman cartography, instead, pursued administrative and military purposes (http://digilander.libero.it/diogenes99/Cartografia/Cartografia01.htm).

These first cartographic representations used methods based on perception and subjective reconstruction and the surveying of the earth could vary depending on the point of observation of the cartographer.

During modern times occurred the problem of representing the spherical Earth's surface on a flat surface that was resolved, initially, using geometric solutions and, subsequently, using analytical performances, which the principles of modern projections maps are based on. To represent a three-dimensional space on a two dimension's map, is necessary to recall the concept of map projection; it refers to a series of geometric, mathematical and empirical transformations of geographical points expressed in geographical and Cartesian coordinates. Through the projections or representations we can approximately represent the spherical surface of the Earth on a plane surface, managing to maintain some geometric properties such as isogony, equivalence and equidistance (http://digilander.libero.it/diogenes99/Cartografia/Cartografia02.htm).

Over the last century the aerial photos, the ortho-photos (Image solution system) and satellite images later, made it possible to achieve real representation of the earth, before unknown.

Today the most widespread cartography is no longer representing only places, spaces and geographical distances, but, it is also representing data and information of all sorts, associated with many different disciplines.

Among the many uses of thematic maps we can include agriculture, services to citizens, environment, statistics, tourism, transport, cultural assets and university research.

## THE USE OF GEOGRAPHICAL MAPPING IN CRIMINOLOGY

Within the criminological research, geographical mapping has ancient origins. Already Quételet and Guerry, after a careful consultation of official data, had prepared a "paper crime" and Guerry in particular, in 1833, created a "social cartography" of relative crime on analyzing the socio-structural data belonging to different French departments (Melossi, 2002). However it is with The Chicago School of Sociology, in the first half of 1900, that are carried out systematic studies on the city, as an organic whole, making use of maps.

One of the recurring themes of this School is that of development and change of human behavior induced by the physical and social environment. According to the thought of Matza, The Chicago School of Sociology thought to individuals as complex creatures, able to adapt very different lifestyles and it considered the community as the main element of influence on the individuals' behavior. The community was to be regarded as the natural human environment and it was the main factor of influence on the behavior of individuals. The natural human environment was to be considered the city, a microcosm of the human universe (Williams & McShane, 2002). The Chicago School of Sociology had to face with a social-historical context characterized by many social phenomena until that time unpublished, such as the development of large cities, rapid industrialization, mass immigration, the effects of the First World War, the prohibition, the great depression.

The theorists of The Chicago School of Sociology developed an attempt of scientific approach to the study of deviant behavior. These scientists, in addition to data obtained from the life stories and the ecological studies, made use of official data on crime, of the results of the census and of data on housing accommodations. This type of information was collected and analyzed for each different areas and districts of the city. They realized in this way a crime mapping that allowed the identification of areas of social disadvantage. The geographical statistic descriptions of social phenomena, repeated several times, showed stability, which revolutionized the explanation of the causes of crime: it underlined that certain areas of the city were prone to crime despite repeated changes of their social and ethnic composition (Williams & McShane, 2002).

These researchers, inspired by the idea of the study of plants and animals in their natural environment, tried to rebuild a human ecology, to study people from how they naturally behave over time and space. It is for this reason that The Chicago School of Sociology is also commonly defined as the Ecological School: because it studies the correlation of organism between them and the environment.

The most important contribution of The Chicago School of Sociology was certainly the organic approach to the life of the community, led by Robert Park who, together with his collaborator E. Burgess, arrived at the conception of the city as a set of separate concentric circles, which radiate from the central business district.

Park and Burgess located three areas: a central businness area (characterized by few residents, but a lot of factories and offices); the second area was called "transitional area" because of the presence of immigrants (it was the cheaper one); and then the "worker area", without urban decay.

The mapping of the city allowed to show how the incidence of social problems and crime was inversely proportional to the distance from the center. The basic idea was that the growth of the city, but also the location of areas and different social problems, do not occur by chance but obey to a specific model; the theory established that there are dominant land uses within each zone. The concept of growth of cities according to a model with concentric zones provided, later, The Chicago School of Sociology, of the groundwork for explaining crime and delinquency (Melossi, 2002).

A few years later C. Shaw and H.D. McKay, on the basis of these premises, put in relation the spatial structure of the city of Chicago and its various types of settlement both with particular demographic characteristics, such as the composition of the immigrant population, and indicators of various social diseases, for example the crime rate and the rate of mental illness considered area by area. The comments of researchers described the city as a place where social life were superficial, the people were anonymous, the relations were transitional, the friendship and parental ties weak. The Chicago School of Sociology read the weakness of social relations as a primary process of social disintegration: if there is a social disruption within a community or a neighborhood, for example a low economic status, a mix of ethnic groups, a high mobility of residents inside and outside the district, disadvantaged or broken families, then it is possible a correlation with the distribution of crime's rates and delinquency (Williams & McShane, 2002).

Shaw and McKay subdivided the city of Chicago in five concentric zones, which radiated from a commercial business center (central), then there are transition areas, the workers' houses area, the residential area and the area of commuters.

They considered the study of an individual only as an approach to the study of crime. The authors, so, developed an analysis of "delinquent areas" as special type of natural area and found that the incidence of crime was significantly higher in certain areas, precisely defined delinquent (Berzano & Prina, 2004).

The method used was to locate the criminal acts marking on a map of Chicago the place of residence of the offender or the place where the crime took place, the resulting paper was subsequently corrected in relation to the population's density of the area.

Thanks to this method, they formulated the "law of the gradient", reaching the same conclusions of Park and Burgess: the delinquency rate is inversely proportional to the distance from the city center, that is more increased the distance from the center more decreased crime rates; furthermore, areas with high crime rate have other symptoms of social disorganization (for example high number of attended, suicides): according to the ecological point of view, the forms of "social pathology" does not arise so much from the individuals proper qualities, but from attributes of the socio-cultural context they live in. So, the inhabitants of the central region of Chicago had higher rates of social pathology since resided in an area where turnover, mobility and anonymity were higher (Balloni, 1983).

A further contribution of Shaw and McKay is the explanation of the process through which the disintegration influence young people and lead them to delinquency. This conceptual elaboration is defined as theory of cultural transmission: deviant behavior is determined by a subsystem of knowledge, beliefs that make possible, permit or require special types of deviant behavior in specific situations. Those knowledges and beliefs must exist first and foremost in the actor's social contest and are taken and incorporated into the personality in the same way as the other elements of local culture Balloni, 1983, p.104).

The two experts put in evidence how the youths who lived in socially disrupted areas were more likely to come into contact with individuals who embraced criminals and delinquents values, and how in these areas developed a delinquent tradition, through which deviant values were transmitted. They focused that most delinquent acts take place in small groups, that the crime and deviance were aspects that in neighborhoods with high crime rates, had become, more or less, a traditional part of the social life. These traditions of delinquency were transmitted through personal or group's contacts. Shaw and McKay provided an important contribution on the process by which the social disintegration influences young people and leads them to delinquency (Williams & McShane, 2002).

The experts researches of The Chicago School of Sociology have, over the years, maintained their influence. Exhaustive it is to say that some police departments take over from the tradition of The Chicago School of Sociology, the use of a geographical map of the city (spot map) over which they put in evidence the criminals streets. The more recent approaches are no longer referring to the spot map, but to the analysis of the so-called hot spots ("hot spots" describe urban areas characterized by criminality and degrade), which are defined, empirically identifying on a map, their geographic centers and then tracing their borders (Williams & McShane, 2002, p.195).

The interpretative and methodological implications of this school have had special influence on the development of that part of the "crime analysis" known as "crime mapping". The crime mapping can be defined as an investigative technique that allows to graphically display on a map a set of data, a technique certainly valid to provide a detailed imagine of the urban areas most affected by crime or degradation .

The use of maps, as known, was experienced for some time (according to the police department of New York it dates back to early 1900), however, over the years, numerous limits have been exceeded, thanks to the development of tools ever more advanced. The first crime maps used in the United States, representing the various jurisdictions, as well as presenting logistic difficulties and resulting hardly manageable due to their extension, they were static, presenting difficulties to store unless they had been photographed, and when containing many data, they were not easy to read. In addition, from the logistical point of view, the old maps occupied much space on the wall, for all these reasons they had a limited duration. In the first maps used by U.S. police departments, the information from various sources regarding the crimes (for example, where was the crime committed, the place of residence of the author and the victim of crime) were placed manually, using the pins in different colors. The technique of maps "on pins" has taken, in recent decades, to computerized mapping: the computers' elaboration was certainly faster and mapping became a common activity in the police districts (Harries, www.ncjrs.gov).

A transformation in qualitative terms revealed itself with the advent of the technological instrument of GIS (Geographic Information System), which allows not only to overcome the typical two-dimensional display of maps and provide a space - temporal dynamic framework, but also allows to enter different data in connection with crimes that occur in a certain place. The American tradition, in fact, shows that the use of GIS by creating maps of reality under study enables to show when and where the crime occurred, what kind of weapon was used, whether there was a victim, if the victim was a man or woman and so on (www.ojp.usdoj.gov/ovc/publications/infores/geoinfosys2003/191877.pdf), so, the union between crime mapping and GIS tools should allow professionals to obtain a number of valuable information that they can use in a preventive viewpoint, providing a clear interpretation of reality and of the problems closely related to it.

## THE GEOGRAPHIC INFORMATION SYSTEM

The Geographic Information Systems (GIS) have led to a revolution in the field of information and cartographic production.

These systems are based on the merging of two programs: computerized design systems (CAD) and relational database (DBMS - Database Management System-), which are also among the first creations of computing. The first system has fostered the computerized geographical entity design, the second to storage data and information related to these entities. The merging of these two systems in GIS has enabled the overcoming of the compromise inherent in any cartography: in fact, every representation of geographical entity is always somewhat symbolic and in scale, or rather it is based on paradigms of representation according to which a particular symbol (for example a small rectangle) in the paper is a real object with certain geometric properties (for example a house). (...) With these new systems, the applications of cartographies are proliferating: each figure can be represented in a map through its geographical position, defined by the coordinate system adopted and together with all the information concerning it, which are stored in a database. In this way the analysis of the geometric properties of the entities represented on a map (for example their exact physical dimensions), could be combined with the general properties of other cartographic entities (for example the reciprocal distance between houses, residences, between schools and hospitals, etc.), and of any chosen entity it will be possible to analyze in detail all the information concerning it (http://www.geotecnologie.unisi.it/Geotecnologie/gis.php).

According to Burrough's definition (1986), GIS is composed of a series of software tools for capturing, storing, extracting, processing and displaying spatial data from the real world (p.194); Mogorovich (Mogorovich & Mussio, 1988) instead defines it as the complex of men, tools and procedures (often informal) allowing the acquisition and distribution of data within the organization and making them available when they are required to those who need to carry out any activities (p.503).

The GIS technology allows the integration of the typical operations of databases, such as data's storage, research and statistical analysis, with the specific advantages of geographic visualization and analysis provided by the cartographic tools. These innovative capabilities make it an indispensable tool for a wide range of public and private users who need to view and analyze information, to plan events, to foresee scenarios, to define strategies. The GIS provides wide opportunity for interaction with the user and a set of tools that facilitate its customization and adaptation to specific issues.

A GIS system, contrary to a purely geometric representation of reality, must be able to handle information concerning the spatial relationships between different elements, while defining the topology.

The characteristic of GIS, as well as geometric and topological dimension, is entering data on its internal, defined as attributes that describe the individual real objects.

Another key aspect of this software is its ability to geo-reference data; or rather to assign to each element its real space's coordinates. This means that the coordinates of an object are stored in their concrete size (not to scale) and following the coordinates of the reference system in which the object is actually located and thus, the information is not recorded in relation to an arbitrary reference system.

In the GIS system, there are three types of information, which are managed in a relational database:

- **geometric:** On the mapping of the objects represented, such as shape (point, line, polygon), the size and location;
- **Topological:** Referring to relations between objects (connection, adjacency, inclusion etc ...);
- **Information:** About the data (numeric, text and so on ...) associated with each object.

GIS is characterized by geometric features: it stores the position of data using a real projection system that defines the actual location of the object.

The real world is represented in a geographic information system through two main types of data: the vector data and the raster data.

The vector data consists of simple elements such as points, lines and polygons, encoded and stored on the basis of their coordinates. To each element is joined a record of information database that contains all the attributes of the represented object. A vector is a system of storing graphic data according to which the objects are stored in conformity with Cartesian coordinates of points and lines used.

The raster consists of a set of identical small areas (pixels), ranked according to lines and columns, such as to constitute a matrix. The values associated to each cell in the matrix can express both graphic information (color, gray tone, etc.) and descriptive ones (temperature, slope, etc.). It therefore allows to represent the real world through an array of cells called pixels, which is a contraction of picture elements and it is the primary component of a raster characterized by an associated value containing the relevant information to what it represents in the territory (http://it.wikipedia.org/wiki/Sistema_informativo_territoriale).

GIS have functionalities that allow us to transform and develop geographical elements of attributes. Some examples might include: topological overlay consisting of a spatial analysis procedure which allows to overlap and intersect the information layers (layer) joining, thus, the associated information with each of them, to the purpose of producing a new layer of synthesis;

the buffering: it is a process of analysis belonging to the topological overlay that allows to create polygons within predefined elements.

## USE OF ArcGIS

ESRI's ArcGIS (Environmental System Research Institute, world's market leader for GIS, of which it is the Italian official distributor) is an integrated collection of software for creating a complete geographic information system (GIS).

The ArcGis, thanks to a comprehensive set of tools, processes geographic data on three different approaches:

1. the Geo-database through a specialized data model allows the management of vector elements (features), raster images, topologies, networks and so on. This approach is represented by the Arc-Catalog, a whole of geographic data-set, synthesized in a number of shape-file (a popular vector format, developed and regulated by ESRI. "Shape-file" usually refers to a set of files with an extension .shp,. dbf, .shx., often, with shape-file is indicated only the ". shp." The shape-files describe spatially points, polygons, usable poly -lines, for example, to represent respectively institutions, buildings and roads. To Each item may be associated additional attributes that describe the items (for example name or address).

In a geo-database there are some fundamental components:

- the geographic representation, which specifies with what kind of geometry the real elements are represented; for example, territorial portions are represented as polygons, lines as roads, trees as points;
- descriptive attributes are included in tables relating to specific geographic objects describing their characteristics;
- the spatial relationships affect the topology and networks. The topology is a set of rules to define clearly the relations, reports of connection and continuity between the spacecraft and to connect those details to the relevant descriptions (attributes). In a topological data model, for example, it is possible to recognize contiguous areas and identify lines that surround each area (borders). A network is generally described by a graph, namely a set of interconnected arches (linear elements in vector format);
- thematic layer: the layer is the whole of homogeneous elements that make up a map, such as roads, rivers, forests, etc..

2. the Geo-visualization, achievable thanks to the assistance of ArcMap, enables to draw up complete and complex maps that show the elements (features) and their spatial relationships on the hearth's surface. Such maps can be stored and reused to support the question, the editing and the analysis of the data. "Geo-visualization" means the ability of a GIS to visualize geographic data in various ways, including: interactive maps, three-dimensional models, charts and tables, representation of temporal events and schematic views of relations within a network.

The maps are the main tools for presenting the geographic information to users and for allowing their interaction. The maps of a GIS system differ from those printed because these are dynamic and at the same time we can interact with them; this allow to exceed the limit of traditional maps which allowed the creation of static maps only.

An interactive map can be so explored, enlarged, cut and the information levels (layer), represented in it, can be "turned on" and "turned off" from the table of contents, according to the specific needs of the user. We can also select (click) any geographical object on the map and get more information about it or make search and spatial analysis. The maps are used to communicate geographic information, and at the same time, to perform several complex tasks, including the compilation of data, mapping, analysis and data collection.

3. Geo-processing, corresponding, from an operational point of view, to ArcToolbox. The Geo-processing is another approach based on a set of operational tools for analyzing and processing data in a dataset.

A GIS software includes a rich set of tools for working and processing geographic information. The merging of features associated with geodatabase and the use of tools, Geo-processing instruments, allows us to create new data from those already stored (http:// www.esriitalia.it/gis/index.htm).

After a purely theoretical complaint of functionality and technical characteristics, we can deepen the operative contribute of the GIS software in the University of Bologna's research.

Among the researches included in the following paragraphs, in fact, one of the tools used is the ArcGis - ArcView 9.x. This tool has facilitated, on the one hand, a kind of crime mapping of the city of Bologna which refers to petty crimes under the responsibility of criminal Justice of the Peace, and the other, creating a reality map of the city of Bologna on which have been identified centers victim support that operate in that context.

The useful data for the creation of the city map, found at municipal offices, relate to different shape-files, such as roads, buildings, hydrography, urban furniture, street numbers, etc ... According to the purposes of the research, the shape-files were selected, framed on the program and moved into the contents, in order to obtain the graphical display on the main screen map.

In this way it was possible to obtain a representation of the city containing: the border, roads and street numbers with their labels, neighborhoods, buildings. Subsequently, have been created by the Arc Catalog, new shape-files matching to the points of interest for each search, i.e. crimes and support centers for victims of crime. New items can be placed spatially (obviously based on their position in the real world) on the map, thanks to the Editor that allows us to modify the map.

The new maps thus obtained, offer a representation of the reality under study: in fact, in the first search, the crimes were located exactly where they had been perpetrated, in the second, instead, the services to assist victims were identified and reported in the corresponding address.

The maps, to be more understandable, need a title, a legend that can interpret the information within, a scale and guidance (for example, a compass or a rose of the winds).

## THE CRIME MAPPING UNDER THE JURISDICTION OF THE CRIMINAL JUSTICE OF THE PEACE IN BOLOGNA

As has been already noted, in many fields where GIS can be applied, crime mapping founds a privileged place, that is the description of the distribution of the facts of crimes that occur in a given reality in an interactive map. For example, we can put in connection the analysis and distribution of certain types of crimes to the presence of specific areas and urban elements, such as closed roads, crumbling buildings, public parks, unattended car parks.

A sort of Bologna's real crime mapping was performed thanks to a research conducted by the University of Bologna, Department of Sociology, on "Criminal Jurisdiction of the Justice of the Peace and author- victim crime interaction in a party law suit; a criminology and socio-victimology analysis".

The study was conducted at the Court of Justice of the Peace of Bologna and it is designed to analyze the data found in the archives of the tribunal related to all measures defined by storage decree or *judicata res* in criminal matters following the entering on force of Legislative Decree No. 274 of 2000 delegating powers precisely at the criminal Court of Peace.

The data found in the Court cover the period from 2002 (the first year it became operational on Legislative Decree No. 274/2000) to 2006. There are party law suit, and reports of crimes by security forces.

It is important to dwell briefly on the news introduced by the new legislation in the Italian legislative scene. From a substantive point of view, it offers a slenderness through the procedural process of redress for lawsuit proceedings crimes, in which is the person offended by the crime, assisted by a defender, to deliver the summons directly to trial before the Justice of the Peace (immediate claim to the Justice of the Peace), being that, a judicial response, quickly given to the person offended by the crime, by two institutions that fall under the so-called alternative definitions to the proceedings (the low degree of seriousness of the event and the crime's release as result of reparatory conducts), it offers also sanctions with a rehabilitation and not merely afflictive function (work of public interest and house arrest), and finally, give a chance of reconciliation between the parties and a renewed importance recognized to the victim.

As a result of the above mentioned decree, the Justice of the Peace is now responsible for a series of crimes that relate to the sphere of criminal law concerning a micro inter-individual conflict which, although it generally produces not particularly serious illegal behaviors, it ends with nourishing situations of significant social disadvantage (Vezzadini, 2006, p. 229). Indeed, in the case of conviction, the court applies the fine (not more than prison sentence) and, in more severe cases, the house arrest or work of public interest.

Moreover, precisely because of the petty crimes, the penalty is imposed only after the failure of the conflict reconstruction: so, a reconciled solution to the dispute becomes the basic principle of the proceedings before the Justice of the Peace (Marzaduri, 2002).

The widespread crimes, those of Justice of the Peace's competence and only in the most mild cases (the responsibility for aggravated hypothesis is included in the functions of the Court), concern the person's sphere (such as blows, bodily harms, failure to rescue), the honor (such as insult and slander), the property (such as damages and squating other people's property), the animals (such as hurting or killing someone else's animals).

From an operational point of view, the procedural files were reviewed taking into account: the lawsuit's date of filing and the date of reporting it, the decision of the Justice of the Peace, the motivation of the incident, the perpetrated crime, the place where the victim reported a complaint, the decision of the court (archiving, conviction or acquittal), some features regarding both the victim and the offender (such as sex, age, nationality, marital status, the municipality of residence, the profession and academic titles) on the basis of which a kind of identikit has been drawn, the exact location and address in which the crime occurred, any relationship and knowledge which exist between the two actors, finally, the presence or absence of witnesses.

The research has a double purpose: on the one hand the task is to investigate the relation between the author and the victim, to examine the different degrees of kinship (for example parents-children, brothers, cousins, father-in-law /daughter-in-law /son-in-law, brother-in-law, grandparents-grandchildren), the acquaintance (for example friendly, co-workers, employee-employer, neighbors, buyer-dealer), affective-sentimental relations (for example spouses, cohabitants, partners, separated, divorced) or situations with no type of relationship between the two actors of a criminal scene. With only a brief mention, it was found that with regard

*Figure 1.Map in 2002*

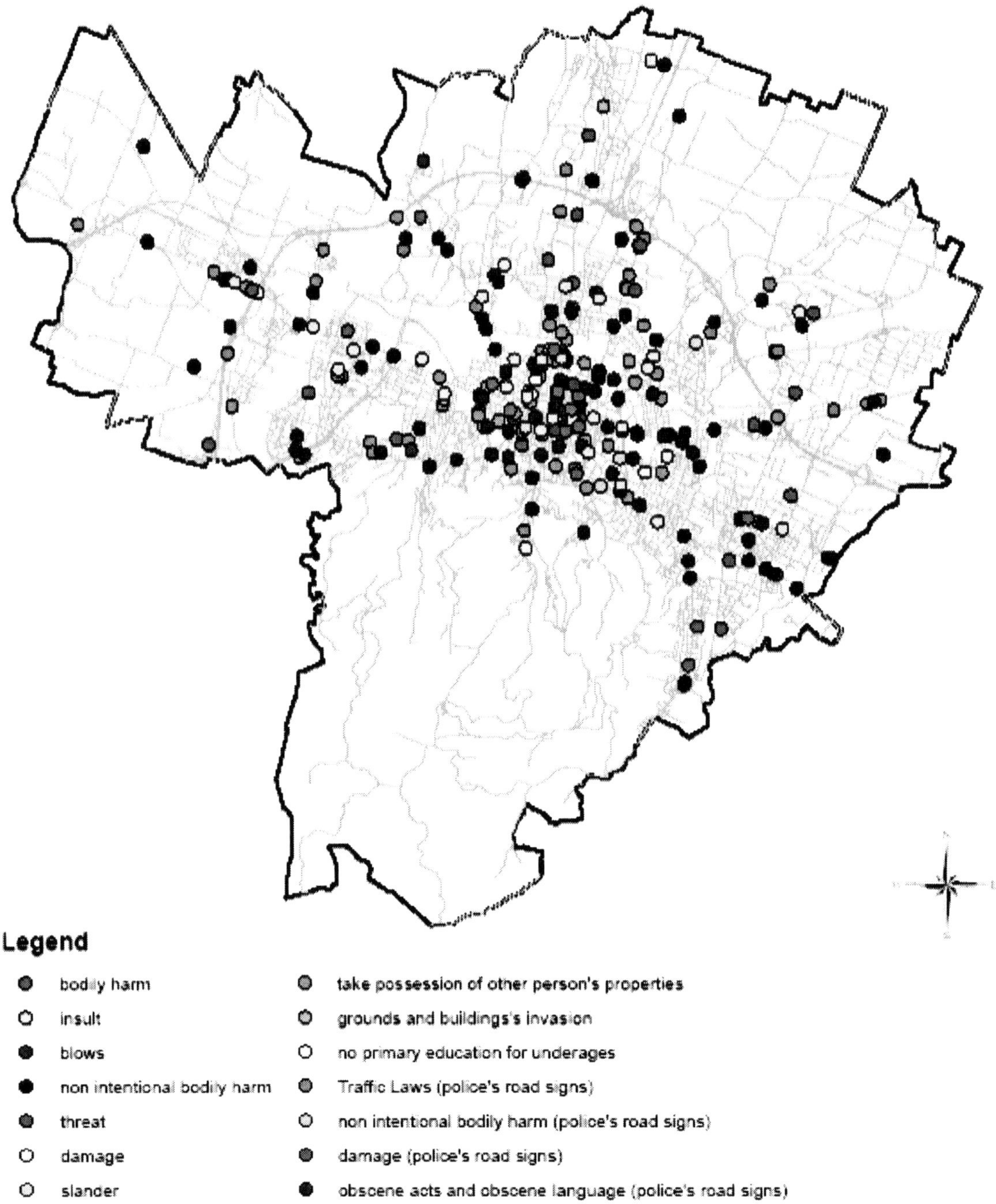


to the relationship, it moves from 3.2% in 2002 to 4.9% in 2003 to 7.6% in 2004 to 9.4% of 2005 up to 7.1% in 2006; besides, there is knowledge between author and victim of the crime of 28.4% in 2002, in 35% of cases in 2003, in 39.7% of cases of 2004,45, 6% of cases in 2005, in 33.3% of cases

*Figure 2.Map in 2003*

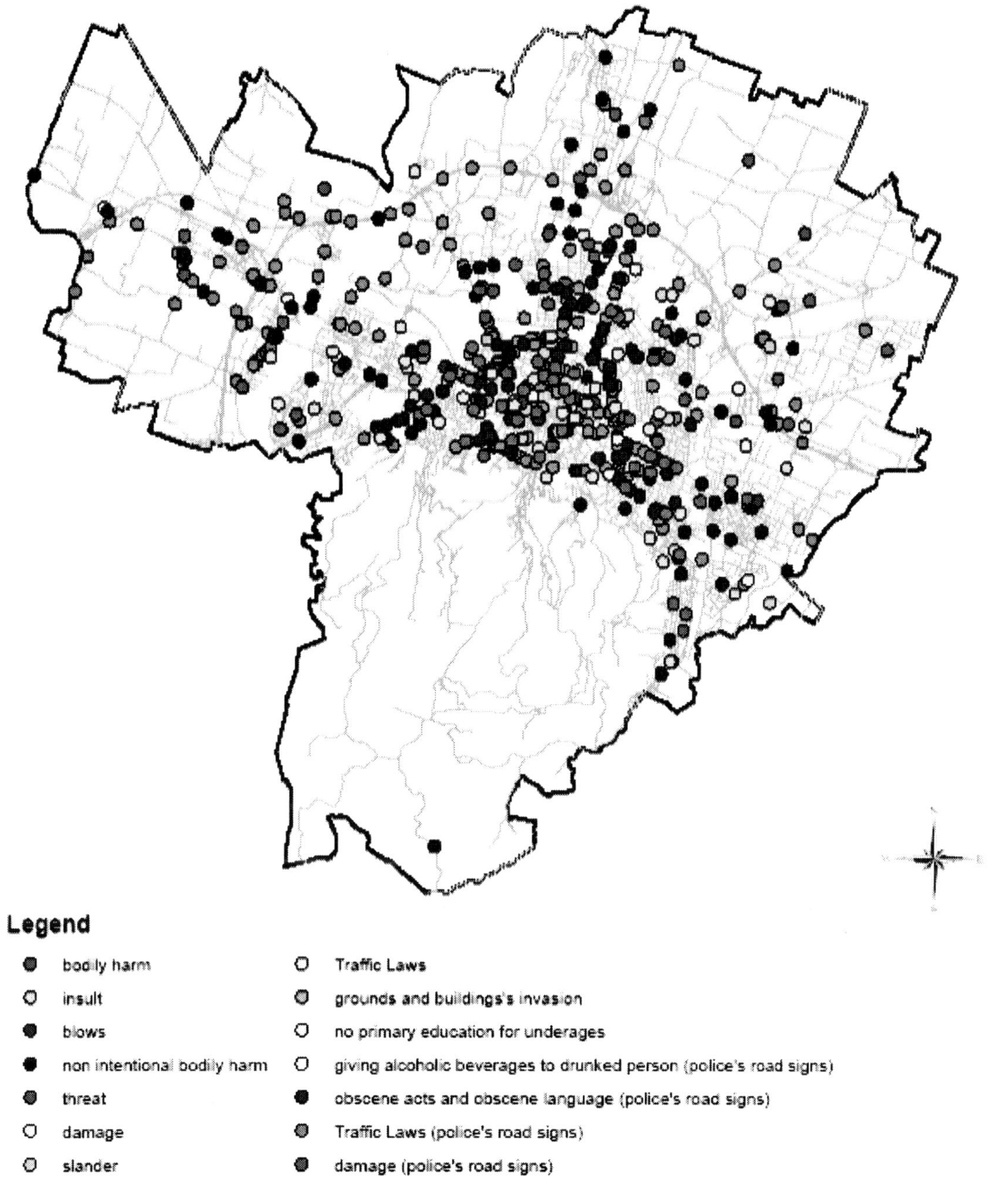


in 2006. So, while just over half of crimes within the jurisdiction of the magistrate was committed by people who did not have any relationship with the victim, on the other hand, almost half of crime is perpetrated by members of the same family or by people linked by a relationship of friendship and more or less close.

The second purpose of research, achieved thanks to the use of GIS software, is to put on an interactive map of the City of Bologna a crime (for

*Figure 3. Map in 2004*

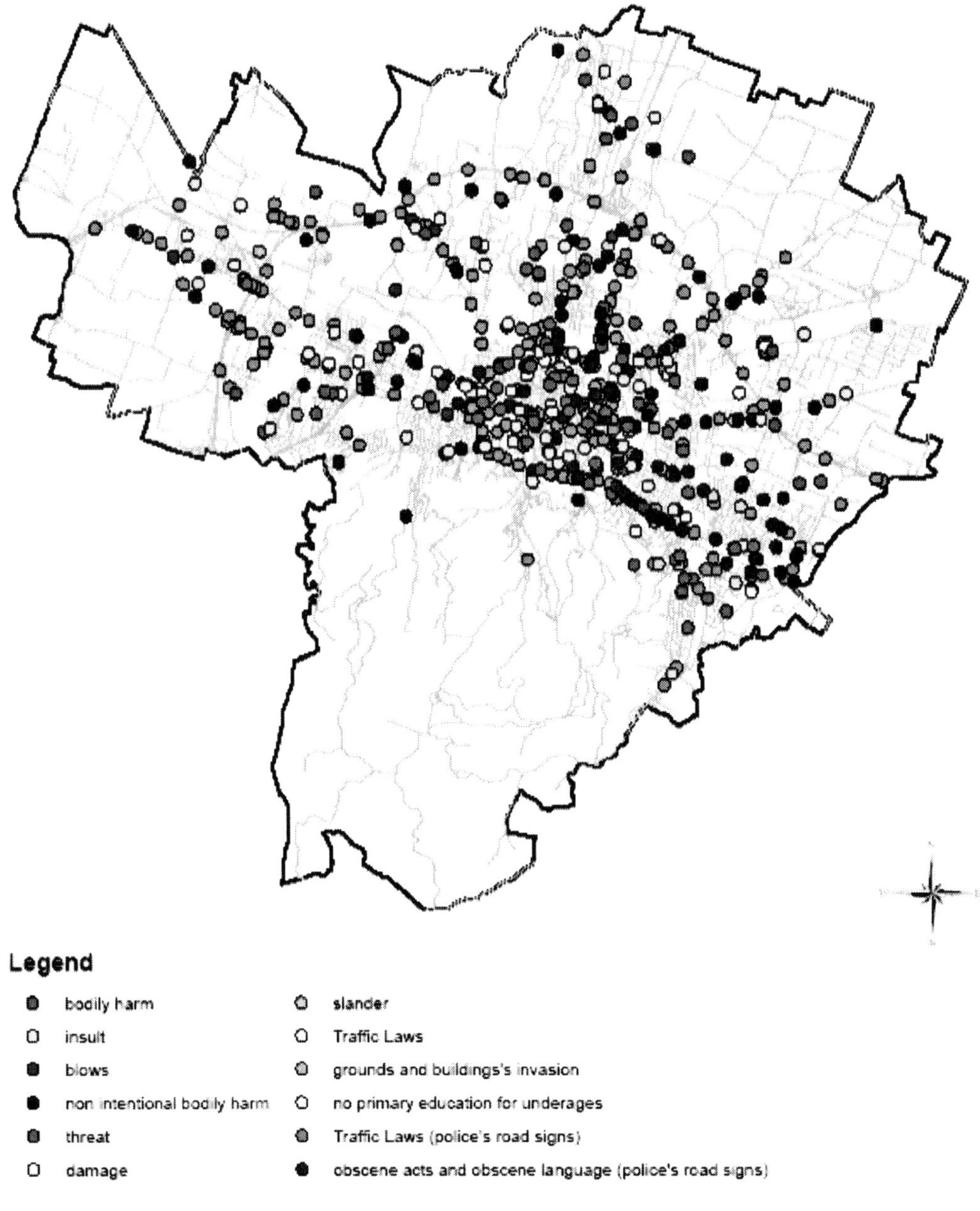


example, non intentional bodily harm, a slander, threats, etc..) exactly in the location (road, building, public park) where it happened.

Indeed, the GIS program allows us to produce, only inputting on it data of the location where the crime occurred, computerized maps which give the chance to see real-world data. In this way have been highlighted the areas, the neighborhoods and the roads most affected by this crime under the responsibility of the Justice of Peace, called "petty crimes", which are certainly less serious than other types of crimes, but significantly and adversely affecting the perception of safety and quality of people's life.

*Figure 4. Map in 2005*

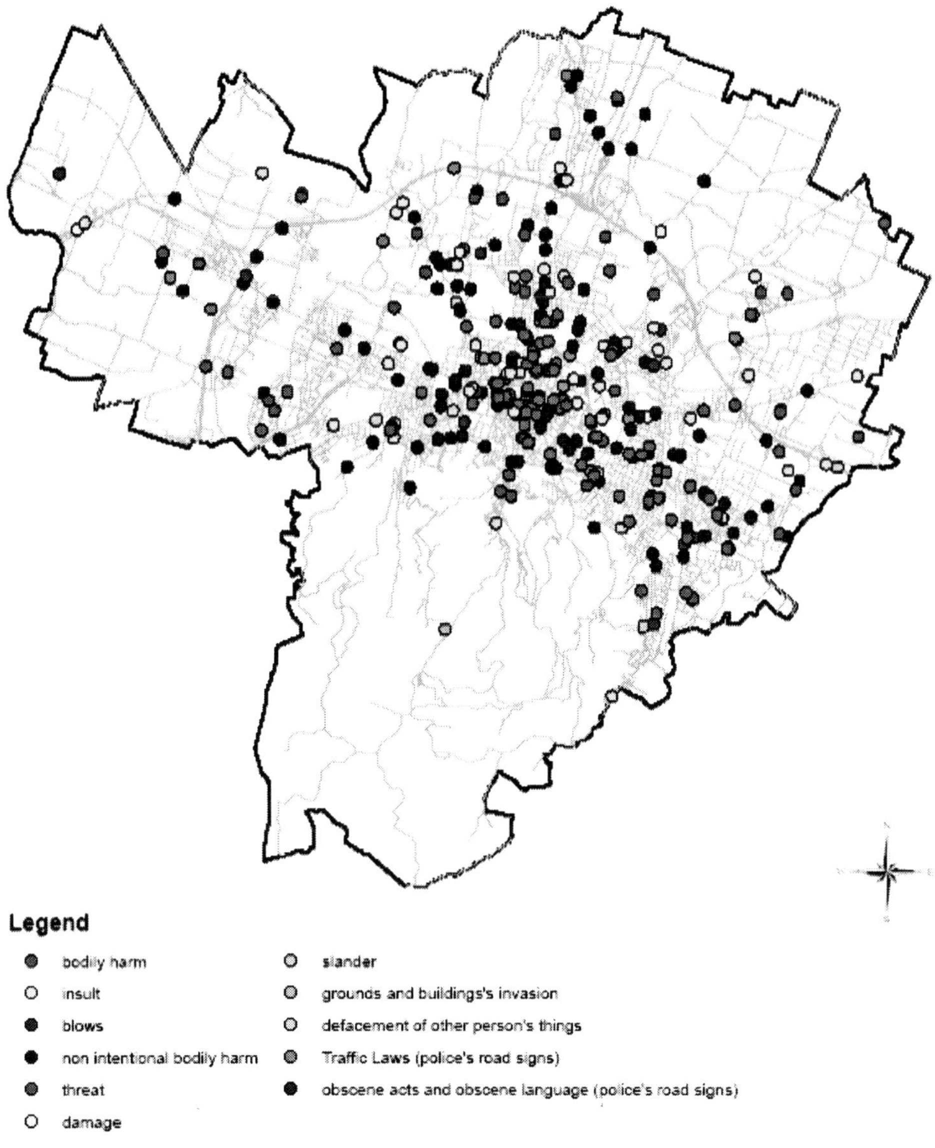


Indeed, the criminal offences included in the so-called "petty crime" category, are the ones that generate fear, influencing the collective imaginary and causing those feelings of concern affecting the quality of life and connecting to the fear of crime (...) Hence the need of a relevant experimentation on an operating model that addresses to the better management of information and to the establishment of a data network to provide security to citizens, and especially to provide cooperation to all agencies of social control (Sette, 2003, p.80).

It was built, in this way, a sort of crime mapping of the city of Bologna's reality, divided in the five years under consideration (2002, 2003, 2004, 2005, 2006 - look at figures 1, 2, 3, 4 and 5), which provides a picture of areas, neighborhoods, and of the roads most affected by the crimes under

*Figure 5. Map in 2006*

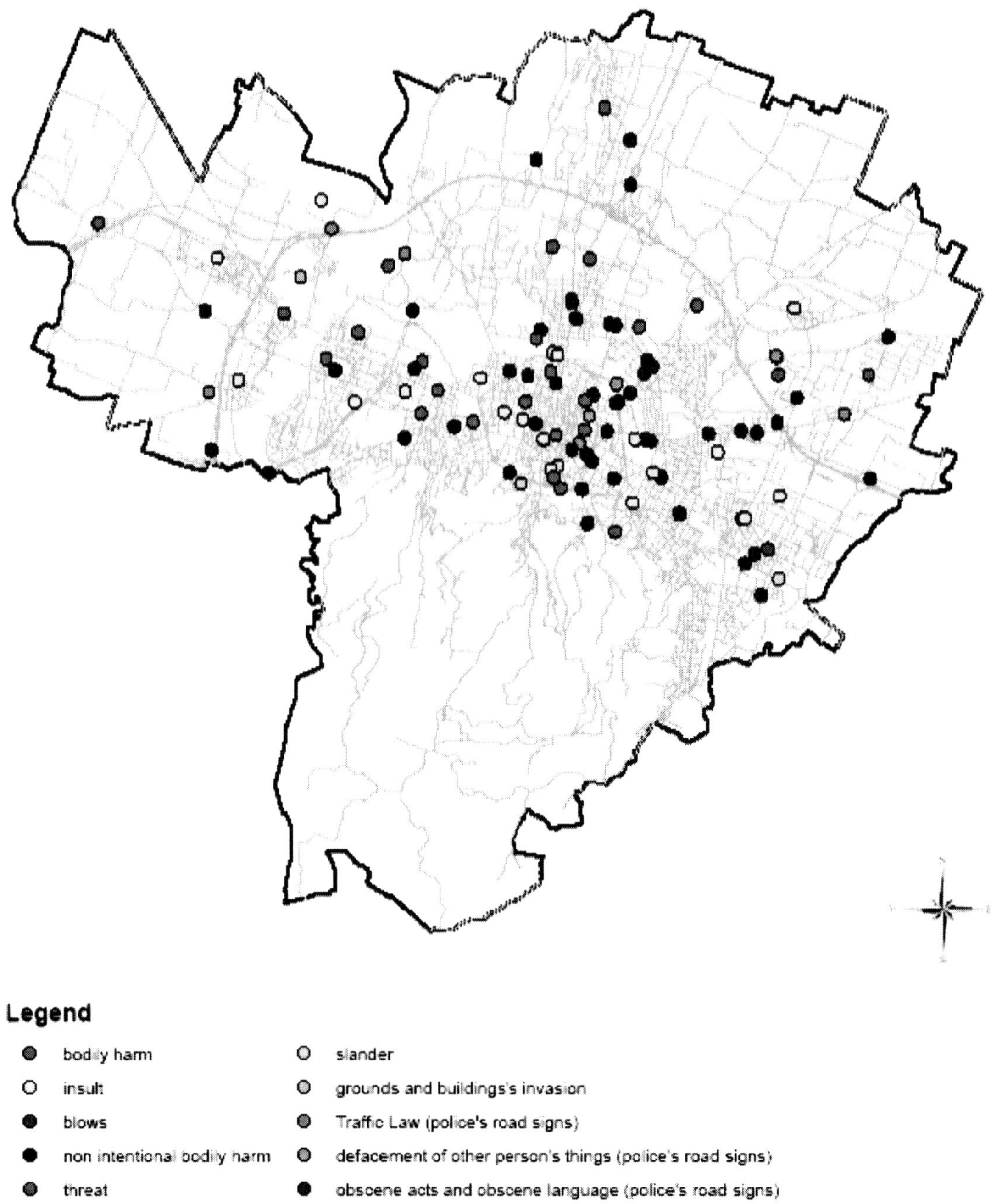


the responsibility of the Justice of Peace.

Thus, only with a widespread and detailed knowledge of the territory, through awareness of offenses known, and with a proper management of the information will be possible to carry out prevention policies. Therefore, the crime is not a phenomenon neither isolated nor random and, due to this reason, it should be studied in relation to certain space-time conditions (Sette, 2003, pp.80-81).

The use of GIS software constitutes the basis to be able to realize and implement operational measures to combat crime; it has precisely the aim to prevent crime. Only through the knowledge of the territory and the areas at most risk, the local administrators can, for example, decide the location of police stations, the development of activities of Public Forces, or the creation of centers for victims' support; besides, it may be highlighted the presence or the absence of public institutions, and agencies responsible for social control.

Precisely for this reason, the identification of hot spots of the city of Bologna, in addition to providing detailed image of urban areas most affected by crime and delinquency, offers a solid basis both for the police to product a social control, and for those who formulate policies for the security in a city like Bologna that, in recent years, has seen an increase in crime and the emergence of troubling feelings of insecurity in the population. Finally, the mapping of areas with a high criminal concentration should allow the elaboration of strategies to minimize the risk of victimization of all citizens and, particularly, of certain categories of individuals most exposed, and should also help the decrease of the victimization impact of crime by encouraging the design of places for supporting the victims and their placement in the most disadvantaged areas (Vezzadini, 2006, pp. 93-94).

The use of crime mapping, and as in the Bologna research, the GIS software, can become a valuable aid for managers and staff working in centers, for local administrators, for criminologists, for psychologists . But above all, it becomes an instrument of high importance for the victims: it is also through the way of new technologies that they can find the right help, the right assistance, the right support.

## THE MAPPING SERVICE IN BOLOGNA

As part of the research on mapping services, have been identified, in Bologna, the institutes involved in supporting the victims. They are, first of all, but not exclusively, victims of crime (such as terrorism, extortion, usury, rape, pedophilia, mobbing); among the centers taken into consideration, in fact, are also included those which look after, for example, the victims of drug or prejudice.

After a necessary selection, given the numerous number, such centers were divided into two categories: institutional centers, referring, therefore, to the municipality, to the Province and to the Region and voluntary associations. Once selected the centers, their representatives were contacted by phone to ascertain their willingness to grant an interview and possibly set a appointment.

Now we go on with a brief excursus to understand what the centers object of our research are dealing with.

1. Public Services:
    - FONDAZIONE EMILIANO-ROMAGNOLA PER LE VITTIME DI REATO (the Emilia Romagna foundation for the victims of crime);
    - IL FARO (The Lighthouse, local center specialized in child abuse);
    - SERVIZI SOCIALI PER MINORI E FAMIGLIE DEL COMUNE (Social Services for minors and local families);
    - UFFICIO SICUREZZA DEL COMUNE (Local security office);
    - UFFICIO VITTIME DELL'USURA E DEL RACKET PRESSO LA PREFETTURA – UFFICIO TERRITORIALE DEL GOVERNO – (The office for victims of organized crime).

*Figure 6. Bologna*

2. Private Services:
    - ASSOCIAZIONE FAMILIARI VITTIME DELLA STRAGE 2 AGOSTO 1980 (The Association for victims of terrorism);
    - ASSOCIAZIONE FAMILIARI VITTIME UNO BIANCA (The Association for the victims of "The White Fiat Uno" – armed attacks in Italy in the 90's where the perpetrators used a white Fiat Uno);
    - ASSOCIAZIONE PRIMA contro il mobbing e lo stress psicosociale (The First Association against physical and psychological harassment at work);
    - CASA DELLE DONNE per non subire violenza (Refuge for women victims of domestic violence);
    - CODICI ONLUS: contro l'usura e il racket (for victims of organized crime);
    - Gruppo giustizia UDI (Refuge

*Figure 7. Private Services*

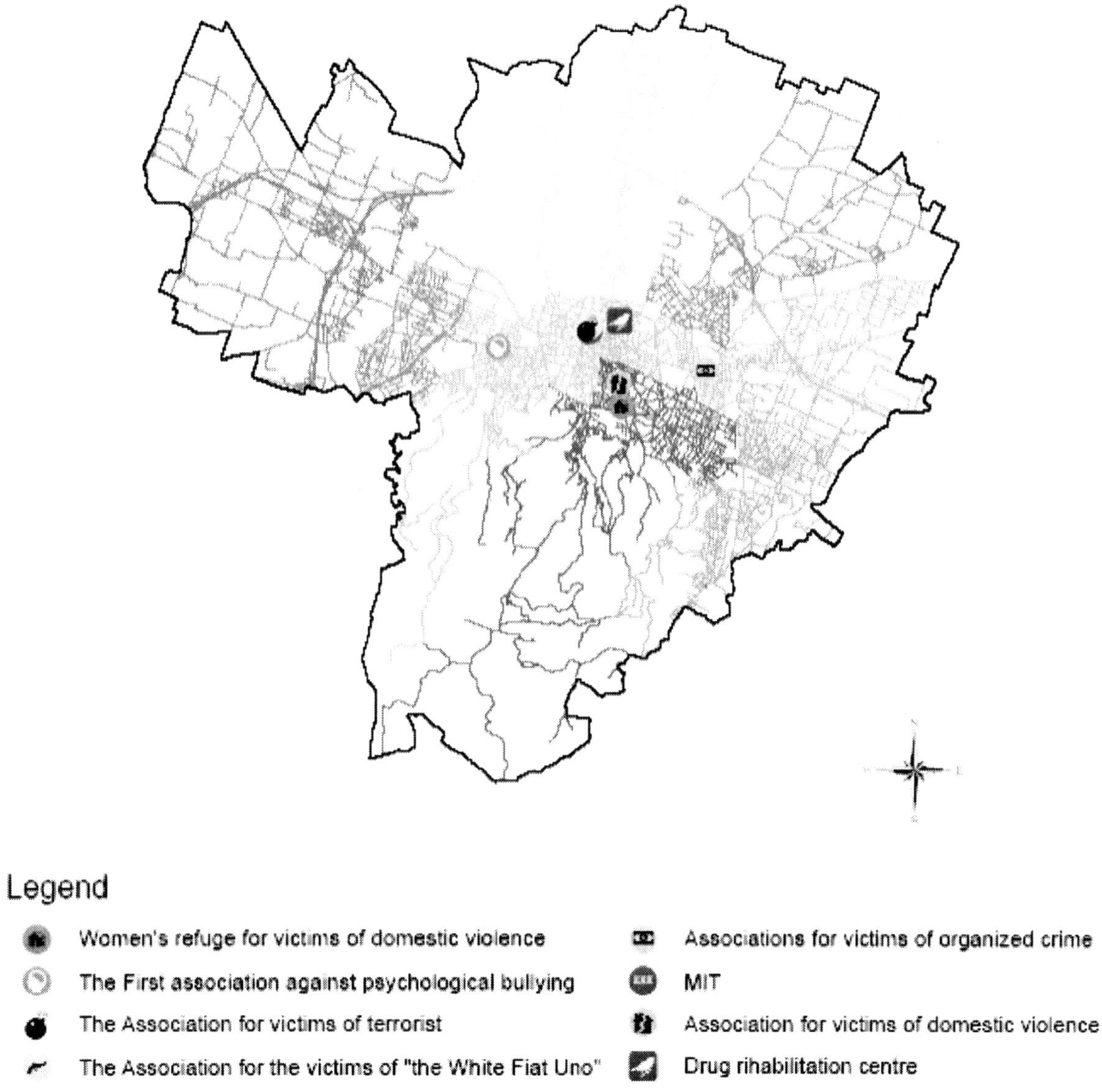


for women victims of domestic violence);

- IL PETTIROSSO: per il recupero della tossicodipendenza (Drug rehabilitation center);
- MIT, movimento italiano transessuali: contro la stigmatizzazione della diversità (Movement for Italian Transexuals: against the stigmatization of marginal groups).

Afterwards, the leaders of each center were submitted to a semi-structured interview focused on issues particularly relevant in terms of victimology, such as the difficulties encountered in setting up and managing the centers, the definition of victim, the types of harms observed, the applications received concerning the satisfaction of needs, the operators' training, the integration between public and private, the prevention of the risk of victimization, the criminal mediation, the contact with the other groups in their areas, etc.

The semi - structured interview, subjected to privileged and selected witnesses, had, in fact, the purpose of investigating and deepening, whenever possible, topics related not only to the life of the association and/or public service, thus, to the history, to the handled issues and to the types of services offered, but also related to the condition of victims in our country considering the European directives issued in this matter.

The interviews were subjected to particularly representative characters, which may be the presidents of voluntary associations and representatives of public institutions, who by choice or professionals, deal with the victims of crime (Sicurella, 2008, p.81).

Starting from the foreign experiences of the victims' supporting centers, and continuing with a careful consultation of the existing literature on the subject, the aim of the research is to analyze the reality of the region Emilia-Romagna, particularly of the city of Bologna and its province, to understand strengths and limitations of the first centers of support for victims on the national territory, and to describe the type of victims more represented in these centers.

But what are the centers of support for victims?

The supporting centers for victims have the purpose to provide material, legal and psychological assistance to who, unfortunately, has been object of a crime, remaining victim of the same.

In Great Britain, Country forerunner in this institution, the support to the victims dates back to 1974 in Bristol, and today it is primarily known as Victim Support.

The "Victim Support" (Sette, 2003) is a national non-profit service. It is an attending center and a place of first aid which works in close collaboration with the Ministry of Interior and Police.

The staff, which has received the necessary training, provides a psychological assistance, information and practical help to all the victims of crime.

The Victim Support of Britain has three main aims:

1. to provide support and assistance to the victims, to their relatives and to their friends;
2. to increase the public awareness about the effects of crime;
3. to promote the victims' rights.

Following the English example, the Italian centers for victims' support, could offer a range of services to the victims of crimes, that include not only the psychological support, but also the answer to other problems of various kinds (such as being followed during the trial, or to have the chance to ask for professionals and craftsmen, who are, following the provision of turnovers, always available, and for example, able to replace a forced lock or a broken glass) that the victims are suddenly forced to confront with, often, without having the right means.

The support to the victims and the possibility of their psychosocial treatments are not only useful to implement attempts which, with success, may have the effect to heal the wounds as a result of the self-pitying experience, but also are to be considered in order to prevent new victimization.

Supports of this kind for the victims of any crime are, undoubtedly, essential if we imagine the severe inequality of treatment between the offender, the guilty, and the one who suffers the criminal act (Sicurella, 2008, p.78).

We must emphasize here that the Italian situation is quite unique compared, for example, to what happen in United States. In our country, in fact, there are no real victims' supports and, anyhow, the initiatives that can be read in these terms are light years distant from the overseas experiences, using the creative realism, centers for the

*Figure 8. Public Services*

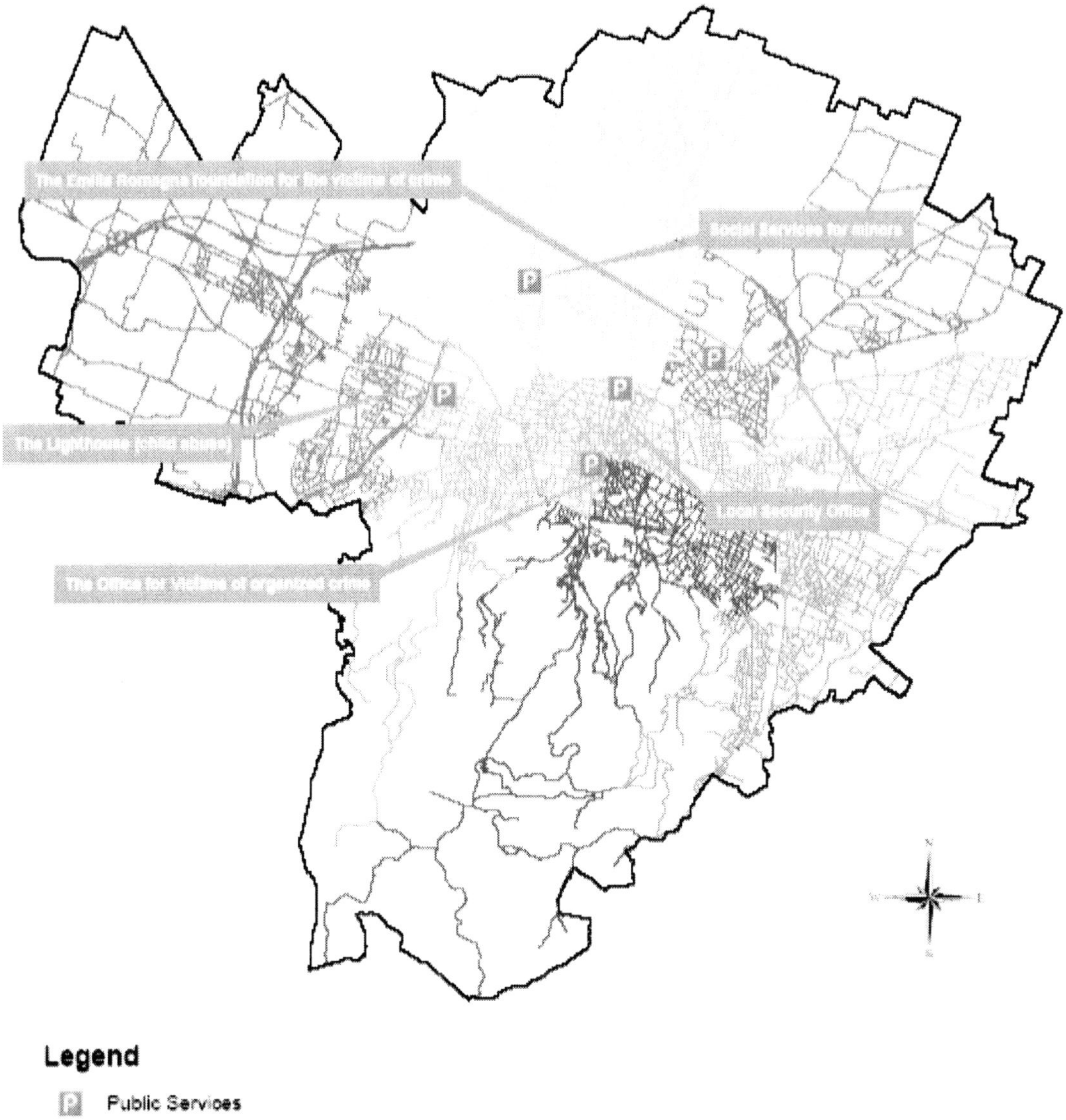


victims' assistance should be set up, along with centers for the youth social deviance and for the adults perpetrators of crime (Sette & Vezzadini, 2008, p.96).

Emilio Viano has recently underlined many changes that, over the time, have focused the scope of supporting and helping the victims. Compared to the '70s, in fact, the United States of America, although there remain serious weaknesses as, for example, the existence of a certain racial and ethnic barriers in providing assistance and services to some part of the population (Sette & Vezzadini, 2008), nowadays, they can boast a qualified professional training, financing more stable and secure, successful integration between the various sectors that operate differently in this field such as police, judges, doctors and psychiatrists; there are also significant changes within the judiciary contest. The police receives a greater awareness in terms of assistance and support to the victims of

*Figure 9. Public and Private Services*

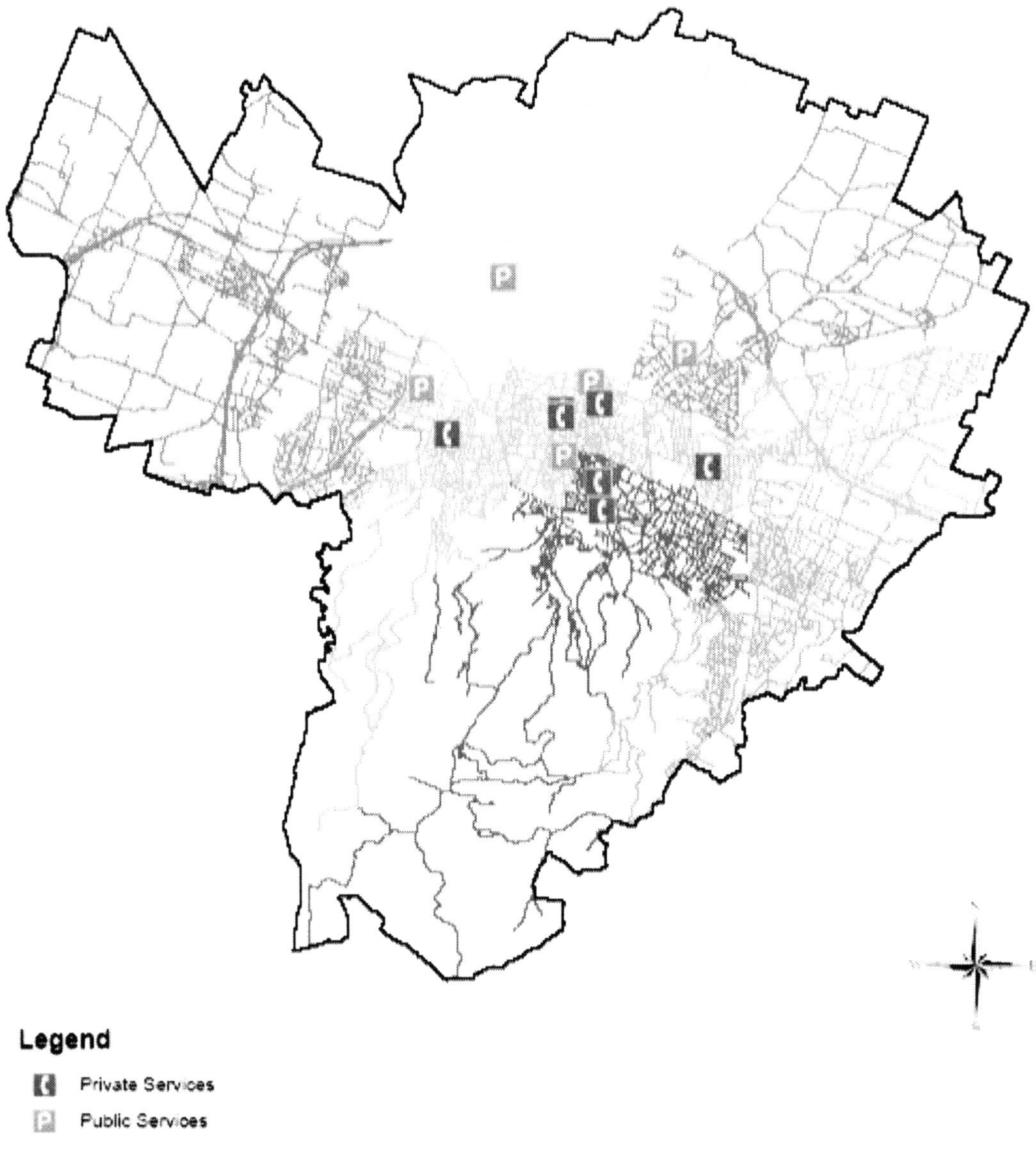


crime, and the logistical arrangements, then, allow greater protection to victims, such as the creation, in the courts, of separate waiting classrooms for defendant and witness, for family members or for the victims themselves. Information concerning the judiciary procedure, the reimbursement costs for the participation to the trial and the assistance to disadvantaged persons (Sette & Vezzadini, 2008) are all a series of conquests that Italy is not yet able to boast.

During the research, the technological instrument, named GIS, has given a spatial location to the structures in the area of Bologna, the leaders of which were interviewed.

In truth, it would be appropriate, to achieve a complete mapping of the present structures, considering each existing, but actually they are too numerous to be surveyed in this work and also, our aim was to have the perception, certainly realistic, of what happen in Bologna and what it was done specifically to help the victims.

The computerized mapping of the territory and areas with high criminal concentration, should allow the development of strategies act to minimize and to reduce the risk of victimization which all citizens suffer from, in particular, some groups of people exposed to more risk, it should help to decrease the self-pitying crime's impact, it should encourage the generation of centers for the victims' support, and their placement in the most disadvantaged areas, thus, trying to fill the gaps and to cover the absence, which are the result, in most cases, of this type of service on our territory.

In order to realize a map of Bologna (look at figure 6) on which to place spatially the support services, have been used, as mentioned above, the ESRI's ArcGIS software which consists of three main modules: ArcCatalog to manage data and display them in preview; ArcMap to create maps, to display geographic data and make some space operations and Arctoolbox to convert data and enable editing functions.

On the map of the city of Bologna were so created (edited) some points corresponding to the physical location of the structures object of our interviews.

Specifically, for example, have been identified centers relating to private services (look at figure 7) or public services (look at figure 8) and each of them has been identified with an icon, which, in some way, could visually bring to the history or to the activities of the association.

The use of GIS technology in this case can be considered experimental because it represents an attempt to graphically illustrate and spatially place on the map of the city of Bologna, the centers of support for victims involved in our interviews. The ultimate aim is, in fact, to obtain a complete, public and private services' mapping, of the territory of Bologna (look at figure 9).

This work, as mentioned above, should be combined with a kind of crime mapping, namely a study on a crime's mapping, with its different types and its hot spots, which might find a useful feedback on social control, public policies and security. In this way, the institutions could intervene, having an accurate and not only mental representation, especially spatial and graphics, supported by appropriate and effective tools, of the areas with high concentrations of crime and of the degraded ones, in which there is a greater probability that a certain crime is committed, not only in a timely, that is, making appropriate interventions in disreputable areas, or increasing surveillance by security forces in some districts. They could, at the same time, prepare, in strategic positions, for example where is more necessary, the creation and placement of support centers for victims, to intervene, if the victim so wishes, after the occurrence of a crime.

## REFERENCES

Aprile, E. (2007). *La competenza penale del Giudice di Pace.* Milano, Italy: Giuffrè.

Baldi, F. *(2000).* Manuale del giudice di pace. Tutti i reati di competenza del giudice di pace, con ricchi richiami di dottrina e giurisprudenza; il nuovo processo ed il nuovo sistema sanzionatorio introdotti dal D.lgs. 28 agosto 2000, n. 274. *Milano, Italy: Giuffrè.*

Balloni, A. (1983). *Criminologia in prospettiva.* Bologna, Italy: Clueb.

Balloni, A. (Ed.). (1989). *Vittime, crimine, difesa sociale*. Bologna, Italy: Clueb.

Balloni, A. (Ed.). (2006). *Cittadinanza responsabile e tutela della vittima.* Bologna, Italy: Clueb.

Balloni, A., & Bisi, R. (2004). The evolution of Victimology: a view over Italy and and Europe throught Research. *International Persepectives in Victimology, 1*(1), Tokiwa International Victimology Institute Journal.

Balloni, A., & Bisi, R. (Eds.). (2008). Processi di vittimizzazione e reti di sostegno alle vittime. *Rivista "Salute e Società", VII*(1). Milano, Italy: Franco Angeli.

Balloni, A., Mosconi, G., & Prina, F. (Eds.). (2004). *Cultura giuridica e attori della giustizia penale*. Milano, Italy: Franco Angeli.

Balloni, A., & Viano, E. (Eds.). (1989). *IV Congresso Mondiale di vittimologia. Atti della giornata bolognese*. Bologna, Italy: Clueb.

Berzano, L., & Prina, F. (2004). *Sociologia della devianza.* Roma, Italy: Carocci.

Bianchini, E. (2008). Processi di vittimizzazione e competenze penali del giudice di pace. In A. Balloni, & R. Bisi (Eds.), *Processi di vittimizzazione e reti di sostegno alle vittime* (pp. 27-29). Milano, Italy: Franco Angeli.

Bisi, R. (1996). Vittime, vittimologia e società. In R. Bisi, & P. Faccioli (Ed), *Con gli occhi della vittima.* Milano, Italy: Franco Angeli.

Bisi, R. (Ed.). (2004). *Vittimologia. Dinamiche relazionali tra vittimizzazione e mediazione*. Milano, Italy: Franco Angeli.

Bisi, R. (Ed.). (2006). *Scena del crimine e profili investigativi. Quale tutela per le vittime?* Milano, Italy: Franco Angeli.

Bisi, R., & Faccioli, P. (Eds.). (1996). *Con gli occhi della vittima: approccio interdisciplinare alla vittimologia.* Milano, Italy: Franco Angeli.

Bisi, R., & Sette, R. (2002). Victimes de tragédies en Italie. Ombres et lumières d'une réalité oubliée. *Revue Francophone du Stress et du Trauma, 2*(1).

Burrogh, P. A. (1986). *Principles of geographical information systems for land resource assessment.* Oxford, U.K: Clarendon Press.

Cernetti, S., & Spriano, M. (2006). *La sentenza penale del giudice di pace.* Torino, Italy: G. Giappichelli.

Chiavario, M., & Marzaduri, E. (Eds.). (2002), *Giudice di pace e processo penale. Commento al D. lgs. 28 agosto 2000 n. 274 e alle successive modifiche.* Torino, Italy: UTET.

Cipolla, C. (Ed.). (2003). *Il ciclo metodologico della ricerca sociale.* Milano, Italy: Franco Angeli.

Corbetta, P. (1999). *Metodologia e tecniche della ricerca sociale*. Bologna, Italy: il Mulino.

Guidicini, P. (Ed.). (1991). *Nuovo manuale della ricerca sociologica.* Milano, Italy: Franco Angeli.

Guidicini, P. (1995). *Questionari, Interviste, Storie di vita: come costruire gli strumenti, raccogliere le informazioni ed elaborare i dati*. Milano, Italy: Franco Angeli.

Gulotta, G. (1976). *La vittima.* Milano, Italy: Giuffré.

International Perspectives in Victimology (2004). *Tokiwa International Victimology Institute Journal, 1*(1).

Lana, M. (2004). *Il testo nel computer*. Torino, Italy: Bollati Boringhieri.

Losito, G. (1993). *L'analisi del contenuto nella ricerca sociale.* Milano, Italy: Franco Angeli.

Marzaduri, E. (2002). L'attribuzione di competenze penali al giudice di pace: un primo passo verso un sistema penale della conciliazione? In M. Chiavario, & E. Marzaduri (Eds.), *Giudice di pace e processo penale. Commento al D. lgs. 28 agosto 2000 n. 274 e alle successive modifiche* (pp. 17-19). Torino, Italy: UTET.

Mattevi, E., Panizzo, F., & Pongiluppi, C. (2007). I reati di competenza del giudice di pace. *Il giudice di pace, Quaderni, 8*. Milano, Italy: Ipsoa.

Mazza, F.A., & Caruso, R, (2006). Giudice penale di pace protagonista fra conciliazione e giurisdizione. *Diritto e giustizia, 1*, 58-76.

Melossi, D. (2002). *Stato, controllo sociale, devianza.* Milano, Italy: Bruno Mondatori.

Migani, M., & Salerno, G. (2008). *Manuale ArcGis*. Palermo, Italy: Dario Flaccovio editore.

Mogorovich, P., & Mussio, P. (1998). *Automazione del Sistema Informativo territoriale. Elaborazione Automatica dei Dati Geografici* (Vol 2). Milano, Italy: Masson.

Nappi, A. (2004). *La procedura penale per il giudice di pace.* Milano, Italy: Giuffrè.

Pavone, M. (2005). *Le nuove competenze del Giudice di Pace.* Matelica, Italy: Halley.

Piccialli, P., & Aghina, E. (Eds.). (2001). *Il procedimento penale davanti al giudice di pace. Manuale teorico-pratico per gli operatori giudiziari.* Napoli, Italy: Edizioni Giuridiche Simone.

Saponaro, A. (2004). *Vittimologia.* Milano, Italy: Giuffrè.

Sette, R. (2003). Sicurezza urbana e centri di victim support. In A. Balloni (Ed.), *Il vigile di quartiere a Milano* (pp. 80-81). Milano, Italy: Franco Angeli.

Sette, R. (2008). *Controllo sociale e prevenzione. Un approccio criminologico*, Bologna, Italy: Clueb.

Sette, R., & Vezzadini, S. (2008), Quale sostegno per quali vittime? tavola rotonda con: Augusto Balloni, Gemma Marotta, Monica Raiteri, Raluca Simion, Emilio Viano. In A. Balloni A., & R. Bisi (Eds.), *Processi di vittimizzazione e reti di sostegno alle vittime* (pp. 89-118). Milano, Italy: Franco Angeli.

Sicurella, S. (2008). Processi di vittimizzazione e centri di ascolto alle vittime. In A. Balloni, & R. Bisi (Eds.), *Processi di vittimizzazione e reti di sostegno alle vittime* (pp.73-87). Milano, Italy: Franco Angeli.

Stella, F. (2003). *Giustizia e modernità. La protezione dell'innocente e la tutela delle vittime.* Milano, Italy: Giuffrè.

Taylor, I., Walton, P., & Young, J. (1975). *Criminologia sotto accusa.* Firenze, Italy: Guaraldi.

Turnaturi, G. (1991). *Associati per amore: l'etica degli affetti e delle relazioni quotidiane.* Milano, Italy: Feltrinelli.

Venafro, E., & Piemontese, C. (2004). *Ruolo e tutela della vittima in diritto penale.* Torino, Italy: Giappichelli Editore.

Vetere, E., & David, P. R. (2005). *Victims of Crime and Abuse of Power (Bangkok, 18-25 April 2005): Festschrift In Honour of Irene Melup.* New York, NY: United Nations.

Vezzadini, S. (2006). Profilo geografico e crime mapping. Il contributo della criminologia ambientale allo studio del delitto. In R. Bisi (Ed.), *Scena del crimine e profili investigativi. Quale tutela per le vittime?* (pp. 83-94). Milano, Italy: Franco Angeli.

Vezzadini, S. (2006). *La vittima di reato tra negazione e riconoscimento.* Bologna, Italy: Clueb.

Viano, E. (1989). *Crime and Its Victims: international research and public policy issues.* New York, NY: Hemisphere Publishing Corporation.

Wertham, F. (1949). *The show of violence.* New York, NY: Doubleday.

Williams, F. P., & McShane, M. D. (2002). *Devianza e criminalità.* Bologna, Italy: Il Mulino.

## WEBSITES

Harries, K. Mapping Crime: principle and practice, from: http://www.ncjrs.gov

Using Geographic Information System to map crime victim services – A guide for State Victims of Crime Act, from: http://www.ojp.usdoj.gov/ovc/publications/infores/geoinfosys2003/191877.pdf

http://digilander.libero.it/diogenes99/Cartografia/Cartografia01.htm

http://digilander.libero.it/diogenes99/Cartografia/Cartografia02.htm

http://www.esriitalia.it/gis/index.htm

http://www.geotecnologie.unisi.it/Geotecnologie/gis.php

www.giustizia.it

www.altalex.it

www.interno.it

## ENDNOTE

1 This paper is a collaboration between the authors. In particular Elena Bianchini redacts the paragraphs "The use of geographical mapping in criminology", "Use of ArcGis" and "The crime mapping under the jurisdiction of the criminal Justice of the Peace in Bologna"; Sandra Sicurella redacts the paragraphs "Origins", "The Geographic Information System" and "The mapping service in Bologna".

# Chapter 7
# How to Train Professionals to Effectively Manage Child Abuse Cases:
## The Case-Example of a University-Based and Multidisciplinary Training Program in Italy

**Ernesto Caffo**
*Telefono Azzurro, Italy*

**Barbara Forresi**
*Telefono Azzurro, Italy*

**Gianluigi Lepri**
*Telefono Azzurro, Italy*

## EXECUTIVE SUMMARY

*Despite the increasing number of child psychological, physical and sexual abuse cases, and the subsequent need for interagency interventions, professional knowledge about the dynamics, nature, strengths and difficulties of the integrated response to child abuse is not universal. In addition to this, training programs for the delivery of a multidisciplinary approach to child abuse cases has always received little attention. The purpose of this chapter is to describe the postgraduate training course "Assessment and treatment approach when handling child abuse cases and paedophilia", developed by the University of Modena and Reggio Emilia (Italy), as an example of a university based and multidisciplinary training to child abuse professionals. This program is aimed at assisting graduated communities' professionals - such as child psychiatrists, psychologists, social workers, educators, law enforcement officers, judges and lawyers - to develop evidence based strategies to respond to child abuse. First the training program will be presented, describing contents and methods used to facilitate critical reflection and analysis of practice/policy: lectures, case studies, work-groups and team-building, web-based and experiential learning. Furthermore, the impact on trainee knowledge, attitudes, and behaviors will be described and discussed on the basis of the existing literature. Barriers to multidisciplinary work such as work style and communication differences among professions, attitudes and behaviors toward children, will be also critically discussed.*

DOI: 10.4018/978-1-60566-872-7.ch007

## CHILD ABUSE AND NEGLECT: THE NATIONAL DATA

Child maltreatment is one of the major public health issue and a worldwide concern. The knowledge about nature of child abuse has changed dramatically since Kempe and Caffey in the 1960s identified child abuse as a medical problem. If in the 1960s the term *child abuse* normally referred to only physical maltreatment, since then its application has expanded to include sexual and psychological abuses as well as neglect and the failure to provide children with proper care.

Today, new areas of victimizations such as sexual tourism (defined as travelling to a foreign country with the intent to engage in sexual activity with children and adolescents), ritual abuses, child pornography and sexual offences via the Internet have been recognized. Internet, in particular, as a potential mean for paedophiles to stalk and seduce children as well as to make child pornography widely available, has raised several new demands.

Although there is growing awareness among the public and professionals about this issue, the prevalence of victimization among youth remains a source of ongoing debate and controversy. What percentage of children and adolescents are exposed to abuse and neglect in Italy? Unfortunately, Italy lacks of a national register and the only available official data concern sexually abused children. According to the Italian Police database, in 2005 approximately 699 reports of sexual abuse cases were made and approximately 605 children were referred for investigation.

More data are made available by Telefono Azzurro, a non-profit Italian organization, dedicated to enhancing children and adolescents' well-being, especially for those living situations of developmental difficulties, abuse and trauma. Telefono Azzurro manages several projects and initiatives, being involved in primary prevention, emergency intervention, treatment, research and training activities. One of the main project is represented by the helpline for children and adolescents. Launched in 1987, this help-line is a confidential service that enables children, adolescents and adults to talk to professional counselors, toll free, 24 hours a day. The service provides assessment, emotional support, information, and whenever necessary referrals to local agencies.

From 2000 to 2007 Telefono Azzurro's helpline received 11,545 phone calls concerning child abuse cases (27.9% of the total number), with more than 1,400 cases per year (Table 1).

## RECENT FINDINGS IN "CHILD ABUSE AND NEGLECT": IMPLICATION FOR TRAINING

Nowadays, the notion that children are widely subject to abuse and exploitation is firmly fixed in the public consciousness and research has contributed much new information about the etiology of child abuse, the mechanisms of risk

*Table 1. Telefono Azzurro's phone calls concerning abused and neglected children (Source: Telefono Azzurro, 2008).*

| **Abuse (2000-2007) N.** | | **%** |
|---|---|---|
| Physical | 4,083 | 35.4 |
| Sexual | 1,733 | 15.0 |
| Psychological | 3,084 | 26.7 |
| Neglect | 2,645 | 22.9 |
| Total | 11,545 | 100.0 |

and protection, and the consequences of maltreatment on children's physical, emotional, and social development (Caffo et al, 2006).

It is now increasingly accepted that abused and neglect children are an "at risk" population for a wide range of mental health disorders and adjustment difficulties. According to some interesting reviews, victims of abuse and neglect shows higher rates of substance abuse, depression, PTSD and anxiety disorders, suicide, conduct disorders, oppositional disorders, ADHD and eating disorders (Paolucci et al., 2001; Kendall-Tackett et al., 1993; Berliner & Elliot, 2002; Cohen et al, 2003; Rogers, 2003; Evans et al, 2005; Levitan et al., 1998; Gisese et al.,1998; Zlotnick et al, 2001; Miller et al 1993; Kaplan et al, 1999). Researchers have also documented a higher incidence of general health problems among adult survivors of victimization: more medical consultations (Felitti, 1991), more surgery (Kendall-Tackett et al, 2000), higher risk of having one or more chronic pain syndromes (Kendall-Tackett, 2000). Apart from physical and mental health consequences, the experience of having been abused or neglected may be significantly associated with a wide range of psychological difficulties, that may persist in adolescence and adulthood.

In the last two decades a growing body of research concerning child testimony has also been published. The reliance of many child sexual and physical abuse cases on the testimony of children about abuse, in fact, has led to continued research into the extent to which children provide reliable and accurate testimony. These studies clearly suggest that although potential inaccuracies and biases can afflict a child's report, under appropriate conditions reports of children are relatively accurate. Therefore the credibility of child testimony depends on the interviewing process that must be careful, supportive and not biased (Ceci & Bruck, 1993).

Finally, the multidetermined nature of child abuse and neglect, has been explicated by decades of research. Risk factors for child maltreatment, as for other forms of violence, occur on multiple levels, ranging from biological and individual-level factors, to family and community levels. Teenagers, girls, and those who live in dangerous communities, for example, appear to be at increased risk for being sexually victimized as children. Similarly children at higher risk of child abuse appear to come from families characterized by multiple sources of difficulties and dysfunction, including marital conflict, parental separation, step-parenthood, parental psychopathology and impaired parent-child relationship (Caffo et al, 2006; Forresi 2003, Fergusson and Mullen 1999). Family and social variables including poverty, unemployment, low education and lack of social support can contribute to increased risk for physical abuse, neglect and emotional abuse (Krug et al, 2002; Zelenko et al, 2001) but seem to have much less impact on CSA (Finkelhor, 1993).

If a problem is multidetermined, in order to optimize the probability of favorable outcomes, intervention should address the complex array of factors that are related to the problem (Henggeler et al. 2002; Cohen and Caffo, 1998). This is the reason why, in many cases, a single mental health professional cannot be expected to effectively address the broad range of challenging problems presented by abused children and families. Managing a case of child abuse is a complex process, demanding collaboration among different and specific agencies (school, social services, court, law enforcement) and different professionals, such as doctors, psychologists, social workers, lawyers, judges, and policemen. This is particularly evident in emergency situations in which the child/adolescent is acutely and imminently in danger or is at high risk for abuse: safe and effective interventions can be best developed working on individual, family, and community factors.

As a result of these considerations, over the past 20 years an increasing emphasis has been put on multi agency cooperation and joint working practices. As highlighted by Horvath and Morrison (2007, p.56), different levels of endeavor can be identified within the complex concept of "collaboration":

1. Communication: individuals from different disciplines talking together.
2. Co-operation: low key joint working on a case-by-case basis.
3. Co-ordination: more formalized joint working, but no sanctions for non-compliance.
4. Coalition: joint structures sacrificing some autonomy.
5. Integration: organizations merge to create new joint identity.

At the simplest level, the focus is on collaboration among individuals, while the highest degree of integration occurs when whole systems collaborate with regard to the planning, commissioning and management of services. The highest objective of a multi agency approach is therefore to bring together all relevant statutory and voluntary sector agencies in order to build joint responses in child protection matters, sharing of policies, procedures, and practices on a wider interagency basis.

Nowadays there is a growing awareness that the ability to collaborate within a network of services, sharing common language, methodologies, and goals represents the real challenge for the successful care of abused and neglected children. According to the literature, coordinate efforts are effective in protecting children from further abuse and trauma, for example reducing the number of times a child must be interviewed (Werner & Werner, 2008). The positive outcomes of collaboration include also faster responses, reduced anxiety for workers (Hetherington, Baistow, et al, 2002), a significant increase in the provision of mental health services to abused children (Jaudes & Martone, 1992), faster access to services (Cottrell et al, 2000), greater continuity of care (Williamson, 2001), and improved cost-effectiveness (Johnson, Wistow, et al, 2003).

However, despite this awareness as well as the increasing number of child abuse and neglect cases, the knowledge about the dynamics, the nature, and the strategies for an integrated response to child abuse is not universal. As stated by Darlington et al (2005, p.1086):

*"There are many forms of interagency relationship, ranging from a low level of joint decision making with limited shared resources (e.g., loose single-issue coalitions) to multifaceted integrated services (Gardiner, 2000; Walter & Petr, 2000). Integration of services, including the 'one-stop-shop,' has been proffered as the ideal for meeting the needs of families with complex problems (UK Department of Health, 1999). However, it is still more common to see less integrated modes of joint working (Johnson, Wistow, et al., 2003), such as consultation (i.e., talking to a worker from another agency about services that may be available, or seeking general information) or collaboration (i.e., in-depth shared work in relation to a client)".*

According both to Goad, and to Horvath & Morrison, the situation is even more critical:

*"Rather than a response that combines the expertise of all involved, there are multiple parallel, but often uncoordinated, efforts. Furthermore, CPS workers, health care providers, police, and others have an understanding (not always an understanding that facilitates an effective process) of his or her role in the response to an abuse/neglect report. This "understanding" is often individually held (eg, different CPS workers from the same agency may have very different views of the role of the CPS worker in a case that involves medical issues). Similarly, role expectations across disciplines vary (eg, different doctors from the same hospital may have very different views of the role of the CPS worker). The result is that no one really knows what to expect from each other. Inevitably, confusion and the belief that others are not doing their job is the result" (Goad, 2008, p.7)*

*"The rationale for collaboration appears obvious in as much as it is aimed at promoting multidisciplinary practice in order to meet the needs of the vulnerable child. However, collaboration, whilst a useful and motivating concept, is in reality far from straightforward and contains complexities and ambiguities" (Horvath & Morrison, 2007, p.55)*

With regards to training courses, there are just few data on the quantity and quality of multi-professionals education in child abuse. According to the most recently published scientific articles, it is evident that current education in the field of "child abuse and neglect", instead of being focused on multidisciplinary and multi agency practices, is mostly focused on identification, and reporting child abuse and maltreatment cases.

Even in this field, the lack of preparation is "immeasurable in terms of missed abuse and subsequent childhood morbidity and mortality" (Botash, 2003, p. 239). We know for example that school personnel fails to report many cases of suspected abuse a year (Reiniger et al, 1995). Similarly, 40% of mental health professionals resulted not being successful in reporting suspected abuse or neglect, at some time in their career (Brosig & Kalichman, 1992). This failure to report is often due to a poor knowledge of both signs and symptoms and the process of reporting (Alvarez et al 2004). Interviewed teachers usually report their training in child abuse to be minimal and consider themselves unprepared to report child abuse (Kenny, 2001). Similar results have been shown by Christian (2008) reporting that physicians feel they are not adequately trained to identify and report child abuse and by Lazenblatt & Freeman (2006) evidencing that professionals fears and lack of knowledge act as barriers to recognizing and reporting abuse in primary healthcare professionals.

Although the lack of a multidisciplinary assessment team is often considered as one of the reason for which some professionals (e.g., primary care physicians, nurse practitioners and paediatricians) find it difficult to decide whether to report child abuse or not - the important role played by consulting other professionals in the decision-making process has been recently highlighted (McCarty, 2008) - only few studies are focused on training programs promoting a multidisciplinary approach to child abuse (Palusci and McHugh; Hibbard et al). It is not surprising, then, that the multidisciplinary model of care has been recently defined as "a relatively new paradigm for physician education and practice"(Christian, 2008, p15).

Although, systematic data concerning training programs are lacking, the current situation in Italy could be described with the same words used by Gallmeier and Bonner in 1992 when describing the USA:

*"Although a great deal of information related to child maltreatment has been compiled over the past three decades, it is generally reported that academic training for professionals such as physicians, psychologists, nurses, attorneys, and social workers has not kept pace with the demands for expertise"(Gallmeier & Bonner, 1992, p. 513).*

Until now, little efforts in Italy have been put into establishing multidisciplinary training programs in child abuse and neglect. In addition to this, differently from USA, nor Italy does have laws mandating multidisciplinary teams, neither federal money are dedicated to the establishment of multidisciplinary teams. Moreover, the majority of training courses on child abuse in Italy are not university-based and tends to be in the form of unstructured in-house training and on the job experience, supplemented by attendance at occasional conferences and workshops.

In the following paragraphs we therefore describe the postgraduate training course "Assessment and treatment approach when handling child abuse cases and paedophilia" - developed by the University of Modena and Reggio Emilia (Italy), together with the Italian NGO Telefono

Azzurro - as an example of a university- based and multidisciplinary training to child abuse professionals. This program is aimed at assisting communities' professionals - such as child psychiatrists, psychologists, social workers, educators, law enforcement officers, judges and lawyers – in adopting evidence based strategies in order to respond to children when an abuse is disclosed as well as to prevent child abuse. To our knowledge, this is the only Italian second level master's degree on child abuse and one of the few Italian university-base training program.

First the training program will be presented, describing contents and methods used to facilitate critical reflection and analysis of practice/policy: lectures, case studies, work-groups and team-building, web-based and experiential learning. Furthermore, the impact on trainee knowledge, attitudes, and behaviors will be described and discussed on the base of the existing literature. Barriers to multidisciplinary work such as work style and communication differences among professions, attitudes and behaviors toward children, and various forms of conflict will be also critically discussed.

## A MULTIDISCIPLINARY TRAINING ON CHILD ABUSE: THE EXPERIENCE OF THE UNIVERSITY OF MODENA

In an effort to fulfil the above mentioned training needs, the University of Modena and Reggio Emilia developed in 1997 the training course "Prevention and intervention in cases of child abuse", which in 2001 turned out to be a post-graduate Master's degree[a]. The training program is based in the Paediatric Departments of Medical University and the academic director is from child and adolescent psychiatry discipline.

The faculty is from the targeted professions: medicine, psychology, social work and related disciplines such as law, public health, child development, and education. Community professionals from law enforcement, child protective services, and the judiciary are also members of the faculty.

Since the beginning the training program was built up in collaboration with Telefono Azzurro, a Italian Ngo working in the field of child abuse. The Scientific Committee of the Master, in fact, was firmly convinced of the necessity of a multidisciplinary and multi agency approach as well as of the need to mix research method and theory with practical experience. If the first two were guaranteed by the University of Modena and Reggio Emilia, the third could have been offered by Telefono Azzurro, a well known association working with abused children and families since 1987 through its helpline.

The experience of Telefono Azzurro goes far beyond the helpline: in fact in 1999 Telefono Azzurro, with the collaboration of the Province of Rome, developed the "Tetto Azzurro", a center for diagnosis, treatment, and residential care of abused and neglected children. Children are referred by the Juvenile Court, social services, and national health system, for a second-level, clinical intervention. Tetto Azzurro also provides a psychosocial help-desk for parents, teachers, or other professionals who deal with abuse or maltreatment cases: evaluate, investigate, treat, and provide care for maltreated children.

The Center Tetto Azzurro also organizes training programs to professionals working in social services, health and mental health services, law enforcement, courts, and schools being located in the Province of Rome. These courses are focused on the management of child abuse as well as on a multi agency and interdisciplinary network approach.

This training experience (only published in Italy, Lepri et al, 2005) developed within the Province of Rome was particularly important and represented a good starting point for the development of a university-based training program. In fact, characteristics, attitudes and practices of community practitioners working with abused children and families informed the training program "Assessment and treatment approach when handling child abuse cases and paedophilia" developed by the University of Modena and Reggio Emilia.

It was developed as a 12 months certificate program for students in medicine, psychology, law, social work, public health, nursing, education, and related disciplines. The training program is designed for graduate and postgraduate students sufficiently trained in their own discipline to benefit from interdisciplinary education in child abuse and neglect. Ten monthly workshops (three days each) are aimed to increase both professional knowledge and skills regarding the handle of child abuse and neglect cases .

The number of students be limited to 15-20 in order to provide intensive faculty involvement in instruction, supervision, and research. To date, bout 150 students from child psychiatry, psychology, law, medicine, education, have completed this interdisciplinary training in child abuse and neglect. Female represented the majority of the total student population. The largest number of students are from psychology, Although medicine was a targeted discipline, it is interesting to note that just a few students from medicine participated in the training: it could be the result of a widespread underestimation of child abuse by medical professions.

The training programs has a length of 12 months and required 250 hours of classroom instruction. Discipline-specific practice requirements is of 450 hours. In the end of the training course, students are asked to complete a special project such as a literature review, or research project.

This program is designed to provide professionals from multiple disciplines (social workers, law enforcement, child psychiatrists and psychologists) with current empirical knowledge, skills, tools, techniques, strategies to enable effective interventions within a multidisciplinary approach. These strategies are based on current research and accepted standards of practice for intervention.

The specific clinical and didactic components of the program's curriculum include: information on child abuse and neglect definition and prevalence; legal issues and mandated reporting law; dynamics and warning signals of child abuse; psychopathological sequelae of child abuse and neglect; medical and forensic aspects of child and physical sexual abuse; techniques for interviewing the alleged victim and evidence gathering; prosecuting and defending child abuse and neglect cases; assessment instruments and evidence based treatments; treatment of child victims and adult survivors of child maltreatment; treatment of perpetrators and non-abusing parents; cultural issues in child abuse and neglect; becoming a professional in the field of child abuse and neglect; roles and responsibilities; interdisciplinary perspectives in child abuse and neglect; preventive intervention, and well being therapy; ethical issues in child abuse and neglect.

Professionals involved in the training program participate in activities that include besides lectures, mock interviews, role plays, videos, discussion groups, and case studies. Practical exercises and simulated practices are very relevant, particularly during the sessions on child interview (Powell et al, 2008).

The approach incorporates a CMI (Computer Managed Instruction) and CML (Computer Managed Learning) techniques to manage and track student progress. Every participants is given a password via email to allow access to the training contents on Internet and is given the chance to:

- send his/her exercises and get the results via email;
- ask the tutor information concerning specific topics and the on site training course;
- take part in forum on line;
- access to university of Modena and Reggio Emilia databases and online journals;
- get references of most relevant articles, constantly updated by the Faculty;

Participants are assigned a tutor who can help them with questions or concerns they may have about the content or the exercises. Participants can also contact their tutor by phone or email.

The most interesting part of the web-site is represented by case studies. As experience is the best teacher, students are introduced to the reality of decision making, including cases characterized by incomplete information and conflicts among agencies. Case studies stimulate students' thinking, challenge their knowledge and competences, and prepare them for future decision making.

The training course web-site makes it easy for professionals to find articles and get information on specific topics, to find recent sentences and laws, to link to international organizations working in the field of child abuse and neglect, but also to learn how to manage a case, to learn how to write good or bad referrals or forensic evaluations. They will also find videos and other relevant materials concerning "on site" training: in fact, course materials including streaming lecture video and slides will are put on the web-site.

Key outcome of this training program is to ensure that professionals:

- are capable of identifying child abuse cases, recognizing behavioral signs and physical indicators.
- are able to address the concern with families,
- take whatever actions are needed to safeguard children,
- report suspicions to the proper authorities,
- assist investigators with interpretation of information,
- manage medical and health consequences of child abuse and neglect,
- work with families affected by child maltreatment,
- advocate for the child.

According to the literature establishment of joint training and good information exchange processes can facilitate multidisciplinary for effective ways to bridge these gaps (see, e.g., Hetherington et al., 2002; Johnson, Zorn, et al., 2003; Pietsch & Short, 1998; Tye & Precey, 1999), a specific part of the training is focused on the barriers to multidisciplinary collaboration such as work style and communication differences among professions, attitudes and behaviors toward "child abuse" and "multidisciplinary work" are always critically discussed.

These barriers may involve either the agency or the professional level (Johnson, Wistow, et al., 2003; Fowler et al, 2000). As far as agency interactions are concerned, barriers may include different philosophies and organizational structures, conditions of service and conflicting priorities, time pressure, inadequate resources and competitive funding arrangements, differences between agencies' confidentiality policies and practices, different training levels, and values of organizations (Darlington et al, 2005; Patterson, 2004; Johnson, Zorn et al, 2003; Hudson, 2002; Hetherington et al, 2002). When considering professional interactions, work-style differences, communication problems, sexism, racism, age differences, differences in authority, in power/status and areas of expertise, mistrust and lack of respect, need for recognition can be included (Reder & Duncan, 2003; Lardner, 1992). Sometimes these barriers are due to lack of information about the other agency (in terms of availability, role, or contact points) that can lead to unrealistic expectations or negative stereotypes (Darlington et al, 2005). One source of conflict comes about because different agencies may have different tasks to accomplish and limited resources. School teachers ore paediatricians, for example, usually express frustration about the fact that social services don't follow up enough on their referrals about abused or neglected children. The fact that it isn't possible for a social worker to follow up every child, as there are too many cases to take care of, could be meant as negligent or uncaring behavior by another agency. These negative

*Table 2. Some attitudes about "child abuse" and "multi agency collaboration".*

| | |
|---|---|
| **Schools** | School teachers and school professionals seem to underestimate risk factors and report to social services and courts just in case of severe abuses. They give three different explanations to this attitude, mostly related to their past experiences with social services and courts: first of all they say they are worried about the possibility for the child to be immediately removed from his/her family as a consequence of their referral; furthermore, they are not willing to become involved in a child abuse trial. Finally, they feel frustrated by the lack of information concerning the child and his/her family after their report. |
| **Mental health services and hospitals** | Health and mental health services rarely collaborate with social services. In case of severe abuses, as a consequence of the mandatory report law, an immediate report to the Court is made. They usually make emergency report as they underestimate the role of social services in preventing severer abuses, therefore not giving much importance to risk factors for child abuse. |
| **Law enforcement** | Law enforcement operators are used to work in emergency contexts, when social and mental health services are not always available. They usually describe themselves as not enough prepared to manage psychological aspects of children and adolescents involved in emergency situations. They feel frustrated by the lack of resources (e.g., foster care centers) that, according to their opinion, prevent them to make the best for the child. They acknowledge that wrong emergency interventions may cause further trauma to children. |
| **Social services** | They usually express a high emotional involvement and commonly refer a feeling of "loneliness": their intervention come last, after those usually made in the immediate aftermath of an abuse by law enforcement and ER. Social workers are often critical toward child interviews made by law enforcement and decisions made by judges, believing that these interventions make the case more complex, sometimes confused and difficult to manage. |
| **Lawyer and Court** | Juvenile court and Family Court are usually not well coordinated. As an example, the same request can be made to social services by different Court professionals or a child can be interviewed many times without any good reason. |

perceptions of one another may lead to distrust and hostility. Therefore, a special attention should be paid either to the different points of view, and to difficulties and pressures every agency has to deal with.

The training experience of Telefono Azzurro with the Province of Rome's agencies similarly evidenced that some factors facilitate, while some others hinder, effective interagency collaboration in the management of child abuse cases. According to this particular experience, practitioners from nine different agencies who have worked with child abuse cases were asked to complete focus group discussions on their attitudes concerning "child abuse" and "multi agency approach". The following table report the most frequently observed attitudes in different agencies (Lepri, Genovese, 2003).

As practitioners' behaviors and attitudes may facilitate or impede the transportability of evidence-based interventions and evidence based treatment (EBT) from research settings to community settings (Goad, 2008; Baumann et al, 2006; Aarons, 2005; The National Advisory Mental Health Council Workgroup on Child and Adolescent Mental Health Intervention Development and Deployment, 2001), these issues should be paid higher attention.

It is evident that these barriers must be considered in the development of a multidisciplinary training program. For this reason the training program developed by the University of Modena and Reggio Emilia addresses specific issues such as improving understanding of roles, communication among different agencies and trust between agency professionals. Professionals are encouraged to explore some of the ways in which different perspectives impact upon the ability to work together effectively and how different practices might develop out of different theoretical understandings of "child", "child abuse", "care", and "protection". By sharing different ideas about how multi agency working might successfully address child abuse problems and professional perspectives, participants are encouraged to reflect on their own experiences of working within and across professional boundaries, building new collaborative relationships.

The aim of the course is to provide participants with the knowledge of the legal framework of a multi agency intervention, as well as on how child abuse assessment is inter-linked. Participants are also provided with the opportunity to explore responsibilities, strengths and tensions of working together, to consider the experience of parents and teachers and the need to work in effective partnership with them. In summary, as to multidisciplinary and multi agency collaboration, this training course is aimed at teaching professionals to:

- Understand legal and organizational frameworks
- Be familiar with local services for supporting families and children
- Communicate and develop working relationships in the interests of children
- Understand the need to share information in order to safeguard children
- Understand contribution made by others to safeguarding children
- Understand the impact of own decisions and actions on others
- Appreciate their own role and that of others
- Co-work on complex tasks or particular areas for example, investigative interviews and complex assessments.
- Establish and maintain relationships based on mutual trust and respect.

The idea of a multi-agency and integrated training model is necessary in order to build a MIN - Multi-agency Intervention Network. In practice we created a training system able to go over the inter-professional equip model. In our experience we have noticed that intervention in child abuse and neglect challenges the equip framework. These sort of cases need assessment and treatment able to involve not just professionals working in the same contest but professionals working in different agencies, with different rules and epistemological point of view. In our research we underlined the necessity of sharing common paths of knowledge and learning in order to provide treatments. The training experience is the framework where to built up the assessment and the treatment model.

The integrated training is complex model, as it means networking, common guidelines, sharing procedures of intervention, sharing expertise in the territories by:

- Reducing the gap between working practice and training experience,
- Sharing methodology and working practices between Social Services, NHS, etc. etc.,
- Building a shared technical and methodological language,
- Case work,
- Process consultation.

## DISCUSSION AND CONCLUSION

The number of studies on children and adolescents exposed to abuse and neglect has increased steadily over the past 25 years, allowing us to gain a greater understanding of the psychological and biological consequences of early exposure to this events/conditions. These studies also let us know that sound assessment and case management are multi-dimensional and multi-professional activities.

However, quoting a recent article by Christian (2008) we could say that research on education in child abuse and neglect has been limited and suggests that improving knowledge is easier than influencing professional practice.

It is generally accepted that no profession alone can effectively deal with the complexity of child abuse and neglect. To date, university education has typically failed to prepare professionals to meet the demands for expertise that these cases present.

The goal of the postgraduate multidisciplinary training program developed by the University of Modena and Reggio Emilia was to train new professionals the field of child abuse and neglect, identify a body of information that is necessary for intervening effectively in this field, and provide training in the mechanics of working in an interdisciplinary and multi agency setting.

Despite the limited available resources this training program in the last years exhibits adaptation to new challenges in the field of child abuse, either adopting new training technological solutions or focusing on new topics such as sexual abuse via the Internet, grooming and ritual abuses.

However, there are still many limits and open questions that should be addressed (and we already working on them) in the near future. First of all, this is a postgraduate training program and under-graduated professionals who work in the field of child abuse (e.g. teachers and other school professionals) cannot take part in. To broaden the spectrum of detection and to reach more abused children and adolescents, who are less likely to be referred to social services, it will be necessary to develop a new university based training program for undergraduate community professionals because many of them frequently have contacts with children and adolescents.

Secondly, although from a qualitative point of view we always observe a high impact of the training course on participants' ability to collaborate, this multidisciplinary program lacks of a quantitative evaluation of training effectiveness.

Up to date there is no consensus about the effectiveness of multidisciplinary training programs. While according to Rodgers (1994) and Pence and Wilson (1994) multidisciplinary training may reduce the barriers to a multi agency approach, by improving understanding of and respect for differences, according to some others (Davey & Hill, 1995) these differences may be resistant to joint training

The real difficulty, of course, is not the transmission of knowledge but the skill training, which needs continuing expert supervision and ongoing education. There are obviously many challenges in assessing the impact of training efforts as practice is influenced by multiple and confounding variables: recent studies, for example, evidence that professional efforts are often hindered by a lack of supportive structures and practices at the organizational level (Darlington et al, 2005). However, there is an evident need to defining a set of outcomes and indicators in order to evaluate the impact of this training program.

Unfortunately, this topic is internationally a source of debate and standardized trainings - either university-based or not - with empirical evidence are lacking. A number of training and educational programs in child abuse have been implemented throughout USA and Europe over the past two decades, but there have been few studies regarding the effectiveness of these programs with little rigorous evaluation of their impact (Carter et al, 2006).

Gallmeier and Bonner (1992) described 10 university-based training programs that were aimed at educating future professionals about child maltreatment (these programs were funded by the National Center on Child Abuse and Neglect in 1987 in an attempt to incorporate child abuse training into graduate programs), but have not been empirically validated. Further, Donohue, Carpin, Alvarez, Ellwood, and Jones (2002) used a controlled multiple baseline design across behaviors to evaluate skills acquisition, but it was only employed with a single subject. Positive results were also obtained by Palusci and McHugh (1995) who evaluated interdisciplinary team-based training program on sexual abuse consisting of didactic lectures, case discussions, videotapes and direct participation in patient evaluation

Two weeks and six months after a multidisciplinary training in child sexual abuse for medical and social work professionals, improved knowledge about child sexual abuse was observed but as the study lacks of a long term follow up we don't know if knowledge were sustained over time (Hibbard et al, 1987).

Botash et al (2003) developed and assessed a study course for physicians by using case studies. Knowledge was evaluated by using multiple-choice pretests and posttests and an essay examination after the completion of the training program. A knowledge improvement emerged for the 64 physicians who completed the course as well as the pretests and posttests, but more than half of them misinterpreted important medical topics, and 39% did not show an appropriate comprehension of legal implications of child sexual abuse.

The only study suggesting a set of outcomes that might measure the training effectiveness is that by Carter et al (2006); among the others, they suggest to use referral rates to child protection and the number of identified abused children seen as indicators.

In addition to the issue of evaluating the impact of training, it is necessary to identify more precisely training needs of every professional category and agency. What need for training for which agency?. What types of training social workers need about physical abuse? What kind of information they need to know? What are the barriers to training, and the gaps between current knowledge and expected level of knowledge? As outlined above, training coursed should be informed on important variables such as characteristics and common intervention practices, professional attitudes, and organizational climate of community agencies.

It is also evident the need for finding the best and cost-effective way to train professionals. The Web is gaining popularity as a teaching tool in academics (Owston, 1997) and until now has shown many strengths and some weaknesses. On the positive side, the Web-based format allows for independent learning, access to the information at almost any time, and may be helpful with students with varying learning styles (Button & Payne, 2008).

On the other side, however, it is not completely clear what kind of content is more adapt to be transmitted via Internet. Up today, the only existing study on a web based training in child abuse demonstrated that Internet can be an effective and convenient method of teaching content related to referrals and mandatory reporting law (Kenny, 2007). On the post-test, in fact, participants' showed a self-reported increase in acquired knowledge as well as significantly improved scores, demonstrating that in a relatively short period of time, teachers and counselors were able to assimilate knowledge related to the detection and reporting of child maltreatment. It is worth noting that the majority of participants referred statistical data, reporting procedures, and legal issues/penalties as the most useful information they learned.

Whether it is possible to learn a multi agency and multidisciplinary model of working via the Internet, is still an open question.

To sum up, it is evident that in the specific area of multidisciplinary training in child maltreatment, a variety of needs in future professional education still exist. More consistent and sustained education of professionals is needed as well as improved clinical research funding for the generation of new knowledge.

## REFERENCES

Aarons, G. (2005). Measuring provider attitudes toward evidence-based practice: consideration of organizational context and individual differences. *Child and Adolescent Psychiatric Clinics of North America, 14*, 255–271. doi:10.1016/j.chc.2004.04.008

Alvarez, K., Kenny, M. C., Donohue, B., & Carpin, K. (2004). Why are professionals failing to initiate mandated reports of child maltreatment, and are there any empirically based programs to assist professionals in the reporting process? *Aggression and Violent Behavior*, *9*, 563–578. doi:10.1016/j.avb.2003.07.001

American Psychological Association Child Abuse and Neglect Working Group. (1996). *A guide for including information on child abuse and neglect in graduate and professional education and training*. Washington, DC: American Psychological Association.

Baumann, B. L., Kolko, D. J., Collins, K., & Herschell, A. D. (2006). Understanding practitioners' characteristics and perspectives prior to the dissemination of an evidence-based intervention. *Child Abuse & Neglect*, *30*, 771–787. doi:10.1016/j.chiabu.2006.01.002

Berliner, L., & Elliott, D. (2002). Sexual abuse of children in the field of child maltreatment. In J. Myers, L. Berliner, J. Myers, et al (Ed.), *The APSAC Handbook on Child Maltreatment* (55-78). London: Sage.

Botash, A. S. (2003). From curriculum to practice: Implementation of the child abuse curriculum. *Child Maltreatment*, *8*(4), 239–241. doi:10.1177/1077559503257960

Brosig, C., & Kalichman, S. (1992). Clinicians' reporting of suspected child abuse: A review of the empirical literature. *Clinical Psychology Review*, *12*, 155–168. doi:10.1016/0272-7358(92)90112-L

Button, D. M., & Payne, B. K. (2008). Training child protective services workers about domestic violence: Needs, strategies, and barriers. *Children and Youth Services Review*. doi:.doi:10.1016/j.childyouth.2008.08.011

Caffo, E. (2003). *Consulenza telefonica e relazione d'aiuto. La qualità dell'ascolto e dell'intervento con i bambini e gli adolescenti*. Milano, Italy: McGraw-Hill.

Caffo, E., & Forresi, B. (2005). L'abuso all'infanzia e all'adolescenza: prospettiva storica e questioni aperte. In M.L. De Natale (Ed.), *Pedagogisti per la giustizia* (795-818). Milano, Italy: Vita e Pensiero.

Caffo, E., Ghiringhelli, B., & Forresi, B. (2007). Minori stranieri vittime di abuso: quale ruolo per il pediatra? In G. R. Burgio, S. Bertelloni (Eds.), *Una pediatria per la società che cambia* (pp. 279-288). Milano, Italy: Edizioni Tecniche Nuove.

Caffo, E., Strik Lievers, L., & Forresi, B. (2006). Child abuse and neglect, a mental health perspective. In M.E, Garralda, M. Flamant (Eds.), *Working with children and adolescents: an evidence based approach to risk and resilience* (pp. 95-128). Oxford, UK: Aronson, an imprint of Rowmans and Littlefield publishers.

Carter, Y. H., Bannon, M. J., Limbert, C., Docherty, A., & Barlow, J. (2006). Improving child protection: a systematic review of training and procedural interventions. *Archives of Disease in Childhood*, *91*(9), 740–743. doi:10.1136/adc.2005.092007

Ceci, S. J., & Bruck, M. (1993). The suggestibility of the child witness: A hystorical review and synthesis. *Psychological Bulletin*, *113*, 403–440. doi:10.1037/0033-2909.113.3.403

Champion, K., Shipman, K., Bonner, B. L., Hensley, L., & Howe, A. C. (2003). Child maltreatment training doctoral programs in clinical, counseling, and school psychology: Where do we go from here? *Child Maltreatment*, *8*(3), 211–217. doi:10.1177/1077559503254139

Christian, C. W. (2008). Professional education in child abuse and neglect. *Pediatrics*, *112*(1), 13–17. doi:10.1542/peds.2008-0715f

Cohen, D. J., & Caffo, E. (1998). Developmental Psychopathology: a framework for planning child mental health. *Epidemiologia e Psichiatria Sociale*, *7*, 156–160.

Cohen, J. A., Berliner, L., & Mannarino, A. P. (2003). Psychosocial and pharmacological intervention for child crime victims. *Journal of Traumatic Stress*, *16*(2), 175–186. doi:10.1023/A:1022851324044

Cottrell, D., Lucey, D., Porter, I., & Walker, D. (2000). Joint working between child and adolescent mental health services and the department of social services: The Leeds model. *Clinical Child Psychology and Psychiatry*, *5*(4), 481–489. doi:10.1177/1359104500005004003

Darlington, Y., Feeney, J. A., & Rixon, K. (2005). Interagency collaboration between child protection and mental health services: practice, attitude and barriers. *Child Abuse & Neglect*, *29*(10), 1085–1098. doi:10.1016/j.chiabu.2005.04.005

Davey, R. I., & Hill, J. (1995). A study of the variability of training and beliefs among professionals who interview children to investigate suspected sexual abuse. *Child Abuse & Neglect*, *19*(8), 933–942. doi:10.1016/0145-2134(95)00055-D

Department of UK Health. (1999). *The NHS plan*. London, UK: The Stationery Office.

Donohue, B., Carpin, K. M., Alvarez, K. M., Ellwood, A., & Jones, R. W. (2002). A standardized method of diplomatically and effectively reporting child abuse to state authorities: A controlled evaluation. *Behavior Modification*, *26*(5), 686–701. doi:10.1177/014544502236657

Evans, E., Hawton, K., & Rodham, K. (2005). Suicidal phenomena and abuse in adolescents: a review of epidemiological studies. *Child Abuse & Neglect*, *29*, 45–58. doi:10.1016/j.chiabu.2004.06.014

Felitti, V. J. (1991). Long-term medical consequences of incest, rape, and molestation. *Southern Medical Journal*, *84*, 328–331.

Fergusson, D. M., & Mullen, P. E. (1999). *Childhood sexual abuse: An evidence based perspective*. Thousand Oaks, CA: Sage Publications.

Finkelhor, D. (1993). Epidemiological factors in the clinical identification of child sexual abuse. *Child Abuse & Neglect*, *17*, 67–70. doi:10.1016/0145-2134(93)90009-T

Forresi, B. (2003). Un nuovo approccio alla relazione d'aiuto: la psicopatologia dello sviluppo. In E. Caffo (Ed.), *Consulenza telefonica relazione d'aiuto. La qualità dell'ascolto e dell'intervento con i bambini e gli adolescenti* (pp. 53-70). Milano, Italy: McGraw-Hill.

Fowler, P., Hannigan, B., & Northway, R. (2000). Community nurses and social workers learning together: A report of an interprofessional education initiative in South Wales. *Health & Social Care in the Community*, *8*(3), 186–191. doi:10.1046/j.1365-2524.2000.00241.x

Gallmeier, T., & Bonner, B. (1992). University-based interdisciplinary training in child abuse and neglect. *Child Abuse & Neglect*, *16*, 513–521. doi:10.1016/0145-2134(92)90067-2

Gardiner, J. (2000). *Literature review on models of coordination and integration of service delivery*. Perth, Australia: Women's Policy Office, Domestic Violence Prevention Unit.

Gisese, A., Thomas, M., Dubovsky, S., & Hilty, S. (1998). The impact of a history of childhood abuse on hospital outcome of affective episodes. *Psychiatric Services (Washington, D.C.)*, *49*, 77–81.

Goad, J. (2008). Understanding roles and improving reporting and response relationships across professional boundaries. *Pediatrics*, *122*(1), 6–9. doi:10.1542/peds.2008-0715d

Henggeler, S. W., Schoenwald, S. K., Rowland, M. D., & Cunningham, P. B. (2002). Serious emotional disturbance in children and adolescents. *Multisystemic Therapy*. London, UK: Guilford Press.

Hetherington, R., Baistow, K., Katz, I., Mesie, J., & Trowell, J. (2002). *The welfare of children with mentally ill parents: Learning from inter-country comparisons*. Chichester, UK: John Wiley & Sons.

Hibbard, R. A., Serwint, J., & Connolly, M. (1987). Educational program on evaluation of alleged sexual abuse victims. *Child Abuse & Neglect*, *11*(4), 513–519. doi:10.1016/0145-2134(87)90077-9

Horwath, J., & Morrison, T. (2007). Collaboration, integration and change in children's services: Critical issues and key ingredients. *Child Abuse & Neglect*, *31*, 55–69. doi:10.1016/j.chiabu.2006.01.007

Hudson, B. (2002). Interprofessionality in health and social care: The Achilles' heel of partnership? *Journal of Interprofessional Care*, *16*(1), 7–17. doi:10.1080/13561820220104122

Jaudes, P. K., & Martone, M.(1002). The importance of interdisciplinary evaluations of alleged sexual abuse cases. *Pediatrics*, *89*, 1164–1168.

Johnson, L. J., Zorn, D., Kai Yung Tam, B., LaMontagne, M., & Johnson, S. A. (2003). Stakeholders' views of factors that impact successful interagency collaboration. *Exceptional Children*, *69*(2), 195–209.

Johnson, P., Wistow, G., Schulz, R., & Hardy, B. (2003). Interagency and interprofessional collaboration in community care: The interdependence of structures and values. *Journal of Interprofessional Care*, *17*(1), 69–83. doi:10.1080/1356182021000044166

Kaplan, S. J., Pelcovitz, D., & Labruna, V. (1999). Child and Adolescent Abuse and Neglect Research: A Review of the Past 10 Years. Part I: Physical and Emotional Abuse and Neglect. *Journal of the American Academy of Child and Adolescent Psychiatry*, *8*(10), 1214–1222.

Kendall-Tackett, K. A. (2000). Physiological correlates of childhood abuse: chronic hyperarousal in PTSD, depression and irritable bowel syndrome. *Child Abuse & Neglect*, *24*, 799–810. doi:10.1016/S0145-2134(00)00136-8

Kendall-Tackett, K. A., Marshall, R., & Ness, K. E. (2000). Victimization, healthcare use, and health maintenance. *Family Violence & Sexual Assault Bulletin*, *16*, 18–21.

Kendall-Tackett, K. A., Williams, L. M., & Finkelhor, D. (1993). Impact of sexual abuse on children: a review and synthesis of recent empirical studies. *Psychological Bulletin*, *113*, 164–180. doi:10.1037/0033-2909.113.1.164

Kenny, M. C. (2001). Child abuse reporting: Teachers' perceived deterrents. *Child Abuse & Neglect*, *25*, 81–92. doi:10.1016/S0145-2134(00)00218-0

Kenny, M. C. (2007). Web-based training in child maltreatment for future mandated reporters. *Child Abuse & Neglect*, *31*, 671–678. doi:10.1016/j.chiabu.2006.12.008

Krug, E. G. (Ed.). (2002). *World Report on Violence and Health: Summary*. Geneva, Switzerland: World Health Organization.

Lardner, R. (1992). Factors affecting police/social work inter-agency co-operation in a child protection unit. *The Police Journal*, *65*, 213–228.

Lazenblattt, A., & Freeman, R. (2006). Recognising and reporting child physical abuse: a survey of primary health care professionals. *Journal of Advanced Nursing*, *56*(3), 227–236. doi:10.1111/j.1365-2648.2006.04030.x

Lepri, G. L., & Genovese, M. R. (2003). La formazione nel corso della pratica professionale: costruzione e sviluppo di gruppi operativi integrati. In P. Patrizi, M.S. Di Tullio D'Elisiis, B. Del Vecchio (Ed.), *Strategie della formazione,* (pp. 145-163). Roma, Italy: Carocci.

Levitan, R., Parikh, S., Lesage, A., Hegadoren, K. M., Adams, M., Kennedy, S. H., & Goering, P. N. (1998). Major depression in individuals with a history of childhood physical or sexual abuse: relationship to neurovegetative. *The American Journal of Psychiatry, 155*, 1746–1752.

McCarty, C. (2008). Doing the right thing: a primary care paediatrician's perspective on child abuse reporting. *Pediatrics, 122*(1), 21–24. doi:10.1542/peds.2008-0715h

Miller, D. A., McClusky-Fawcett, K., & Irving, L. M. (1993). The relationship between childhood sexual abuse and subsequent onset of bulimia nervosa. *Child Abuse & Neglect, 17*, 305–314. doi:10.1016/0145-2134(93)90050-F

Owston, R. O. (1997). The World Wide Web: A technology to enhance teaching and learning. *Educational Researcher, 26*(2), 27–33.

Palusci, V. J., & McHugh, T. M. (1995). Interdisciplinary training in the evaluation of child sexual abuse. *Child Abuse & Neglect, 19*(9), 1031–1038. doi:10.1016/0145-2134(95)00065-G

Paolucci, E., Genuis, M., & Violato, C. (2001). A meta-analysis of the published research on the effects of child sexual abuse. *The Journal of Psychology, 135*, 17–36.

Patterson, G. T. (2004). Evaluating the effects of child abuse training on the attitudes, knowledge, and skills of police recruits. *Research on Social Work Practice, 14*(4), 273–280. doi:10.1177/1049731503262390

Pence, D., & Wilson, C. (1994). *Team Investigation of Child Sexual Abuse: The Uneasy Alliance*. London, UK: Sage.

Pietsch, J., & Short, L. (1998). *Working together in families in which a parent has a mental illness: Developing 'best practice' for service provision and interagency collaboration*. Melbourne, Australia: Mental Health Research Institute.

Powell, M. B., Fisher, R. P., & Hughes Scholes, C. H. (2008). The effect of using trained versus untrained adult respondents in simulated practice interviews about child abuse. *Child Abuse & Neglect, 32*(11), 1007–1016. doi:10.1016/j.chiabu.2008.05.005

Reder, P., & Duncan, S. (2003). Understanding communication in child protection networks. *Child Abuse Review, 12*, 82–100. doi:10.1002/car.787

Reiniger, A., Robinson, E., & McHugh, M. (1995). Mandated training of professionals: A means for improving reporting of child abuse. *Child Abuse & Neglect, 19*, 63–69. doi:10.1016/0145-2134(94)00105-4

Rodgers, J. (1994). Collaboration among health professionals. *Nursing Standard, 9*(6), 25–26.

Rogers, J. R. (2003). Sexual abuse and suicide: Why we may not know what we think we know. *Archives of Suicide Research, 7*, 83–91. doi:10.1080/13811110301564

Scott, D. (1997). Inter-agency conflict: An ethnographic study. *Child & Family Social Work, 2*, 73–80. doi:10.1046/j.1365-2206.1997.00048.x

The National Advisory Mental Health Council Workgroup on Child and Adolescent Mental Health Intervention Development and Deployment. (2001). *Blueprint for change: research on child and adolescent mental health*. Washington, DC: The National Advisory Mental Health Council Workgroup on Child and Adolescent Mental Health Intervention Development and Deployment.

Tye, C., & Precey, G. (1999). Building bridges: The interface between adult mental health and child protection. *Child Abuse Review*, *8*, 164–171. doi:10.1002/(SICI)1099-0852(199905/06)8:3<164::AID-CAR556>3.0.CO;2-G

Volpe, R. (1981). The development and evaluation of a training program for school-based profession- als dealing with child abuse. *Child Abuse & Neglect*, *5*, 103–110. doi:10.1016/0145-2134(81)90027-2

Walter, U. M., & Petr, C. (2000). A template for family-centered interagency collaboration. Families in society. *Families in Society*, *8*(5), 494–503.

Werner, J., & Werner, M. C. (2008). Child sexual abuse in clinical and forensic psychiatry: a review of recent literature. *Current Opinion in Psychiatry*, *21*(5), 499–504. doi:10.1097/YCO.0b013e328305e4b0

Williamson, V. (2001). The potential of project status to support partnerships. In S. Balloch & M. Taylor (Ed.), *Partnership working: Policy and practice* (pp. 117–141). Bristol, UK: Polity Press.

Zelenko, M. A., Huffman, L., Lock, J., Kennedy, O., & Steiner, H. (2001). Poor adolescent expectant mothers: can we assess their potential for child abuse? *Adolesc Health*, *29*, 271–278. doi:10.1016/S1054-139X(01)00272-5

Zlotnick, C., Mattia, J., & Zimmerman, M. (2001). Clinical features of survivors of sexual abuse with major depression. *Child Abuse & Neglect*, *25*(3), 357–367. doi:10.1016/S0145-2134(00)00251-9

# Chapter 8
# Technologies for the Safety of Adolescent: The "Between School and Family Project" Case Study

**Daniela Passaro**
*Suor Orsola Benincasa University of Naples, Italy*

## EXECUTIVE SUMMARY

*The focus of this paper is to describe a case concerning the key role of security technologies to observe, describe and some way record teenagers' behaviors and social action at school, at home and in the daily life as a whole. A kind of security "public eye" to protect/control them is pivotal especially according to some High School Policies in Italy aimed to cancel each "blind spot" or "black hole" from the youngsters' daily life to facilitate cross double checking among parents, relatives, social networks and teachers. In Italy the deviance of youth is increasing and the crime cases involving very young boys, like baby gangs and teenagers working for organized crime are growing rapidly. Among robberies, theft, and dang pushing the juvenile criminality in the Campania Region (an Italian Southern Region) continues to represent a critical point in this society and is unfortunately increasing. The family plays a key role and inside it often baby gangsters, whose parents are completely unaware of what is happening in their children's lives. "Between school and family" is a project that aspires at tracing a connection between the school and the family thanks to the influence of new technologies and the way in which they influence the interpersonal relationships. What will be, for example, if every school place a fingerprint reader?*

## SCENARIO

In the recent years, the phenomenon of child deviance increased and assumed rather severe proportions and characteristics such as the growing involvement of juveniles in criminal organizations. The concept of deviance changes according to the changing realities in which it is contextualized.

The Italian traditional juvenile deviance has gradually experienced a "qualitative leap" with forms of exploitation and organic integration of children into criminal organizations, including those similar to the Mafia. The link that connects the attraction of criminal models of young people

DOI: 10.4018/978-1-60566-872-7.ch008

with the socio-economic deterioration and/or the lack of future perspectives has also been noted, which pushes many children to act more and more criminally in the hope of leaving the condition of marginalization and lack of identity in which they live (Boffi, 1981, p. 24).

If, as Becker says, "*the deviant is the one on which the operation of labeling was successful*" (see: Ciappi & Becucci, p. 73), then the deviance takes the substance of the attributes of a negative or marginal status.

Goffman states that the term stigma is generally associated with a purely derogatory attribute, or better, "*the attribute is a stigma when it produces profound discredit*" (Goffman, 1963, p. 3).

Crimes carried out by minors in Italy are continually rising: robberies, rocks from overpasses, rapes, beatings. In short, a real war bulletin. Most become part of gangs, when they should be in the classroom, and society does not know how to deal with this real emergency.

Particularly in Campania (an Italian Southern Region), juvenile crime continues to be a critical point of today's society and is unfortunately growing strongly.

One might consider that behind this violence, for some young men, reigns the fear of not equaling his peers, of not being "cool." Teens today live in groups and their appearance within these groups is essential. Money, success, the latest cell phone or PC, make them feel like they're winners.

This is because for a teenager who is part of a gang, the sense of inferiority is unbearable. This, then, could inspire in the young man the idea of being accepted by the others at any price. In addition to the school and the family, society should give its support to make new rules and propose positive models for children.

The fact that nowadays we lost important values, such as family, respect of authority, respect for others, does not help, especially if there is also a change in the way of life: a model of individualistic life gains ground more and more, which pursues success, money, and power. It is no longer important to be strong, but merely appear to be strong. Today's adolescents are growing up in a society where everything is 'owed' to them. Perhaps they grow up too fast and are too spoiled and pampered, living under a bell of glass which keeps them far away from the outside world. Believing everything is acceptable certainly does not help young men.

Even the statistics suggest a sharp increase – in recent years – of the propensity towards violence among young people.

According to police criminal statistics between 1999 and 2006 (from http://www.bj.admin.ch/bj/it/home/themen/kriminalitaet/jugendgewalt.html) the number of minor suspects for crimes of violence has increased continuously and significantly (personal injury: an increase from 760 to 1525; threat: increased from 405 to 869). Also, the number of rulings (from http://www.bj.admin.ch/bj/it/home/dokumentation/medieninformationen/2007/ref_2007-06-29.html) handed down increased significantly in the same period for young people who committed violent crimes (from 1241 to 2268) (simple injuries: increased from 288 to 638; threat: increased from 148 to 317). The field experts are unanimous in believing that the number of serious acts committed by young people has increased. The problem should not be minimized: youth violence has reached a level that worries most of the population.

The causes of youth violence are many. Many factors increase the risk: a lack of supervision by parents, an incoherent educational style, school difficulties, belonging to a group of young people prone to violence, a social disadvantage, the cultural walk of life or lack of integration of young foreigners. The influence of violent images, pornography, and violent behavior by young people has not yet been clarified conclusively. To try to curb this rampant phenomenon, we must focus on prevention starting from schools and families. It is from there that the fight against juvenile delinquency must begin. Schools and families should create a dialogue to educate and help provide new educational and social models. But, above all, they should supervise the lives of children through the use of new technologies that may affect interpersonal relationships and facilitate control for the safety of teenagers.

## DESCRIPTION OF THE PROJECT "BETWEEN SCHOOL AND FAMILY"

### Its Strategic Value

"Between school and family" is a project that hopes to draw a continuum between the institutions of school and family, thanks to the influence of new technologies and their potential to affect interpersonal relationships.

The goal is to find a technology (in the "Foucaltian" sense) so that, in synergy, the family and the school can monitor and supervise the daily life of teenagers by stimulating communication between the parent and the child and the teacher and the student. This would allow us to understand how so many young adults, who have deserted school due to the influence of groups offering alternatives to school, spend their time, or how and when these teens come in contact with youth gangs in the service of organized crime.

But, is there really a way for the man-machine interface, and the use of new technologies, to facilitate the monitoring of adolescents?

Think about today most popular facility among boys: the Internet. In particular, online diaries of adolescents tell (proceeding by hypothesis) the adventures of X, a boy/girl like many people who, every day, is placed in the position to make choices, create solutions, choose between good and evil, and tell about his/her experiences, fears, and the difficulties that often are not even shown in the family. It is the way of experience, the knowledge of the self and of the world. It is the hard road for building its own identity. It is the difficulty of growing in a world that often bewilders, confuses, and sets traps.

X is the typical young man in Italian schools, the student in desperate search for meaning, who must find within himself the answers to life's adventures. Special seminars held at the school against wastage in cities of Campania might allow, with the help of teachers of schools in the network, an effective job of designing training courses on the issues of legality.

The education of the legality as a guideline to live in social forms and the promotion of a culture of compliance with the rules of social coexistence is not intended to be added as a "discipline" to those already existing, but as a transversal approach to the teaching / learning action.

Connecting to the Web site of the school, every student could have his/her own login and password to access the online personal diary, visible only to the teachers involved in monitoring, mediation, and tracking of the information gathered.

Parents, in turn, would be kept constantly updated by teachers who have the duty to disclose the psychological and emotional state of the student to the families, especially noting the presence of situations where more control needs to be exercised.

The second phase of the project involves the installation of a fingerprint reader at the entrance of school buildings. Within five minutes from the bell announcing the start of classes, if the unit does not record the entry of the student, text messages could be sent from the operating systems of the school secretariat to both parents' mobile phones alerting them to their child's absence.

The dialogue between student-teacher, teacher-parent and parent-child might represent the most strategic way to control the lives of children without having them suffering the pressure.

## THE LIFE CYCLE OF THE "BETWEEN SCHOOL AND FAMILY" PROJECT

The life cycle of the "Between School and Family" project defines the phases that connect the beginning and end of the project (from http://www.tenstep.it/TenStep-PB/2.1ProjectLifeCycle.htm). For example, if the project identifies an opportunity that deserves interest, it will usually authorize a feasibility study to decide whether or not to undertake the project. Defining the life cycle of the project could help the leaders clarify whether it is appropriate to consider the feasibility study as the first phase of the project or a separate and autonomous one.

When the outcome of this preliminary effort is not clearly identifiable, the effort should be considered as a separate project. The transition from one phase to another within the lifetime of the project generally involves a form of technical transfer or transit of deliveries, which usually defines it. The *deliverables* obtained from a phase are usually analyzed in order to verify their completeness and accuracy. Then they have to be approved by the School Executive before proceeding with the next phase of work. However, it is not entirely unusual that a phase, when some possible risks are considered acceptable, can be started before the *deliverable* of the preceding phase.

This practice of overlapping phases, usually carried out in sequence, is an example of the application of the technique of compression of scheduling, otherwise known as *"fast tracking."*

Some organizational structures have adopted rules that allow to standardize all projects through a single life cycle, while other facilities prefer to entrust the group of *Project Management* with the best choice-of-life for the project assigned to the group.

Moreover, the practices commonly adopted in the specific area usually lead to a life cycle of preference for this sector.

The life cycle of the "Between School and Family" project defines:

1. What technical work must be done in each phase (e.g., At what stage the work of communicator must be made);
2. When the deliverables must be produced at each stage and how each *deliverable* must be reviewed, verified, and validated;
3. Who is involved in each phase (e.g., the simultaneous design requires the involvement of leaders of the implementation in the definition of requirements and in design);
4. How to check and approve each phase;
5. The descriptions of the life cycle of the project can be either very general or very detailed. More detailed descriptions of life cycles may include models, charts, and checklists in order to give a structured form and ensure the control.

The "Between School and Family" project will attempt to follow the following characteristics:

- The phases are usually sequential and are commonly defined by a form of transfer of technical information or a transfer of technical components;
- The costs and levels of personnel involved will be initially low, reaching a peak during the intermediate stages and could fall quickly when the project goes to its conclusion;
- The level of uncertainty, and thus the risk of failing to achieve the goals, are more at the beginning of the project. The certainty of reaching the completion should increase gradually with the extension of the timetable of educational offerings.

## GOALS OF THE "BETWEEN SCHOOL AND FAMILY" PROJECT

The "Between school and family" project intends to implement a unified and centralized management of the control and mediation services in support of the many young people involved, unbeknown to their families, in organized crime.

Everything including the design of specific training developing the human, to financial, technical and technological resources.

In addition, the project aims to create an educational network that is present as a strategic way to allow the continued relationship between the parties (school and family) through innovative activities in support of the new technologies.

**Strategic goal:** Establish through technological tools such as an online diary and the fingerprint reader, a continuous network of contacts to facilitate not only the dialogue for students and the consideration of teachers, but also the immediate control by the school in the event of early school departures, and, the following intervention of families.

**Operational goals of communication:** Having outlined the main goals that form the backdrop for the whole project, you will have specific goals for the area of institutional communication, for the scope of internal communication and the communication-marketing.

1. **Target Image (the communication-marketing):** A first goal is, inevitably, to give visibility to the project which, in its nascent stage, requires a strategy that will work to make it recognizable to the market.

It has to promote "Between school and family" as the promulgator of a new constructive way of using the new technologies and has to spread its benefits to the adopters.

2. **The aim of policy (area of institutional communication):** A second goal is to communicate the importance of the project in the dynamics of local politics. "Between school and family", by involving institutions, schools, families, local authorities, contributes to the real improvement of the territory, in terms of reduction in juvenile crime during school hours: communication becomes a key lever for achieving that goal.

Providing greater availability of data relating to crimes committed by young gangs will promote greater awareness of policy makers, but especially more control on the part of schools that, thanks to the involvement of all those involved in the recovery of young people who desert school, could enjoy a real growth of investment in terms of using new technologies for the safety of teenagers.

## IMPLEMENTATION OF THE "BETWEEN SCHOOL AND FAMILY" PROJECT

### Field of Investigation

Analysis of network institutions and organization of a database for the inclusion of documentation on the activities of control, monitoring, and evaluation: boards, indicators, projects, information, services, information retrieval, and so on.

### Type of School

Schools at all levels.

### Type of Project

Create a technology information system for the safety of teenagers.

## Promoter of the Project

The Technical Committee of the schools involved includes:

- The head teachers;
- The people in charge of the project areas;
- The administrative director of schools;
- The co-ordinator of network activities.

## Recipients of the Project

- Teachers;
- Students;
- Families.

## Operating Procedures

- Implementation of training on the use of new technologies aimed at teachers responsible for monitoring activities and control;
- Establish a database of all students' contacts;
- Establish a database of all parents' contacts;
- Acquiring skills for classification, cataloging, standardization and retrieval of information;
- Make use of easy consultation and secure transparency all the data regarding the emotional state of students and frequency of any school dissertations;
- Comparison of methods and resources employed and results achieved;
- Implement a process of recovery for students who take deviant behavior.

## Workers Involved

Operators involved in the project are listed below:

- Teachers internal at schools;
- External operators;
- Co-ordinator of the activities.

## Methodology and Articulation of the Project

The project has four distinct phases of development:

- **First phase:** Convening the families at the school in order to explain the goals of the project and its purpose;
- **Second phase:** Training teachers and tutors who will acquire the skills needed for the design, development and realization of the activities. Design, implementation, installation of the information system;
- **Third phase:** Assigning students their own login and password to access the diary online. Explanation on the use of the technology system and its purposes;
- **Fourth phase:** Illustration for students and families of the new school control procedures: the fingerprint reader at the school's entry;
- **Fifth phase:** systematic collection of data concerning the most important stages of the project for a study of its self evaluation. Publication of results.

Obviously a necessary condition is the technology and computer training of all the school staff. The introduction of Information Technology and Communication in educational process is producing substantial changes in the teaching and control process.

The effectiveness of these technologies requires that the teacher is motivated, qualified and interested, and that is positive towards the technology.

In addition to teaching, we must consider other variables that affect this process, such as school equipment, although the teachers training has a key role in the strategic use of new technologies as a tool for young control.

As regards computer and technological training of teaching staff, closely linked to the development of technological infrastructure and its use, there are various training courses divided into different levels of skills, whose aim is not a simple technique acquisition, but a systematic relationship between technology and teaching, between technology and control processes.

Respect to this process is necessary to provide different training:

- basic general training;
- training in the use of technology resources and multimedia in teaching process;
- training for leaders of technological infrastructure in schools.

## HYPOTHESIS OF IMPACT OF THE "BETWEEN SCHOOL AND FAMILY" PROJECT

In order to analyze the hypothetical impact of the "Between school and family" project, let's depart from the model of Rogers (Rogers, 2003*)*, focusing on the laws by which innovation spreads (or doesn't spread) between people. The Rogers' model allows us to highlight the different types of approach to innovation that characterizes the people who move within the scenario of reference.

The results that emerge from analysis will assist us in choosing the most appropriate strategy to involve colleagues. An effective practice to extend a new way to communicate within an organization is, in fact, the gradual involvement of a progressively wider public.

This requires, first, the identification of the **Innovators** (from http://www.12manage.com/methods_rogers_innovation_adoption_curve_it.html) from which the project originated, those who push the change: we of the "Between School and Family" project. Then the so-called **Early Adopter**, closer for status to innovators and porters of innovation, those who show more enthusiasm and are open to new ideas and can contribute effectively to the process of internal legitimacy of our proposal: the school, the Region, The Ministry of Education, Consortia and all those organizations that for the first time come into contact with the "Between School and Family" project. We can distinguish three different types:

- **Connectors**, i.e., the faculty body. Subjects internal or external to the organizational structure, with no special expertise, but with a broad network of relationships, allowing for easy access to different types of tools and resources needed.
- **Experts**, i.e., the people in charge of the technical-operational aspect of the project. Subjects with high technical skills so as to make their involvement particularly strategic and effective for an internal legitimacy of the proposal.
- **Sellers**, i.e., teachers and tutors that interface with both students and families. Subjects who, by nature, are characterized by a persuasive and seductive approach.

With the help of Early Adopters, we will try to gradually involve the entire organization, affecting increasing levels of public interest:

- **First majority**, teachers and administrative staff responsible.
- **Second majority**, all students (including their families) of year 2008/2009, possibly separable in *sub-targets* for lifestyles; *sub-targets* that would become the possible third, fourth, fifth and so on majorities, to lead to the last majority.
- **Last majority**, i.e., the workforce, both of public and private sectors.

This will come, finally, to the scope of public criticism, excluded from the process of innovation, the so-called **marginal**, including schools and families absolutely not interested in the process of innovation.

Even among the **marginals** it is possible to distinguish different types:

- Those who **want** and **can** take part in the innovation, but due to some mistakes, have been left out: a lack of communication in promoting the "Between School and Family" project;
- Those who **wish** to take part to the innovation, but **can not**: schools that while believing in innovation of the project do not have the money to support it;
- Those who **do not want** to take part in the innovation, even though they **could**: schools that have adequate facilities to support the use of new technologies, but who appear skeptical before the proposal. Or even the families who do not believe in the strategic methodology of the "Between School and Family" project;
- Those who **do not want** to take part in innovation and **can not do** it: schools that not only are not interested in the project but otherwise, would be hampered in being or for economic reasons or because the school executive, for example, absolutely have no intention to support the project.

In the interests of efficiency, you should not involve the latter two types of subjects: the costs of the conviction would be so high that it could not be justified by any results.

## REFERENCES

Boffi, M. (1981). *Immagini di devianza: i giovani tra tolleranza e sanzione*. Milano, Italy: Feltrinelli.

Ciappi, S., & Becucci, S. (2000). *Sociologia e criminalità: prospettive teoriche e strumenti di ricerca in criminologia*. Milano, Italy: FrancoAngeli.

Goffman, E. (1963). *Stigma: l'identità negata*. Bari, Italy: Laterza.

Rogers, E. M. (2003). *Diffusion of Innovation*. New York: Free Press.

## WEBSITES

http://www.bj.admin.ch/bj/it/home/themen/kriminalitaet/jugendgewalt.html

http://www.bj.admin.ch/bj/it/home/dokumentation/medieninformationen/2007/ref_2007-06-29.html

http://www.iard.it

http://www.informagiovani-italia.com/bullismo.htm

http://www.informagiovani-italia.com/cosa-puo-fare-la-scuola-contro-bullismo.htm

http://www.informagiovani-italia.com/aiutare-figli-vittime-bullismo.htm

http://www.istruzione.it

http://www.minori.it

http://www.stopalbullismo.it/

http://www.tenstep.it/TenStep-PB/2.1ProjectLifeCycle.htm

http://www.vedogiovane.it

http://www.12manage.com/methods_rogers_innovation_adoption_curve_it.html

http://www.12manage.com/methods_rogers_innovation_adoption_curve_it.html

## ADDITIONAL READING

Becker, H. S. (1963). *Outsiders: Studies in the Sociology of Deviance*. New York: Free Press.

Braithwaite, J. (1989). *Crime, Shame and Reintegration.* New York: Cambridge University Press.

Cesareo, V. (1979). *Socializzazione e controllo sociale.* Milano, Italy: FrancoAngeli.

Cohen, A. K. (1955). *Delinquent Boys. The Culture of the Gang.* New York: Free Press.

Cohen, L. E., & Felson, M. (1979). Social Change and Crime Rate Trends: A Routine Activities Approach. *American Sociological Review, 44*, 588–607. doi:10.2307/2094589

Cohen, S., & Scull, A. T. (1983). *Social Control and State: Historical and Comparate Essays*, Oxford: Robertson.

Dubin, R. (1959). Deviant Behavior and Social Structure: Continuities in Social Theory. *American Sociological Review, 24*, 147–164. doi:10.2307/2089426

Durkheim, E. (1963). *Le regole del metodo sociologico.* Milano, Italy: Edizioni di Comunità.

Engels, F. (1972). *La situazione della classe operaia in Inghilterra.* Roma, Italy: Editori Riuniti.

Foucault, M. (1974). *Surveiller et punir. Naissance de la prison.* Paris: Gallimard.

Gennaro, G. (1993). *Manuale di sociologia della devianza.* Milano: FrancoAngeli.

Goffman, E. (1956). *The Presentation of Self in Everyday Life.* New York: Anchor Books. Gofffredson, M.R., & Hirschi, T. (1990). *A General Theory of Crime.* Stanford, CA: Stanford University Press.

Hagan, J. (1989). *Structural Criminology.* New York: Rutgers University Press.

Hirschi, T. (1969). *Causes of Delinquency.* Berkeley, CA: University of California Press.

Hyman, H. H. (1969). *Political Socialization. A Study in the Psychology of Political Behavior.* New York: Free Press.

Katz, J. (1988). *Seduction of Crime: Moral and Sensual Attractions in Doing Evil.* New York: Basic Books.

Lemert, E. M. (1967). *Human Deviance, Social Problems and Social Control.* Englewood Cliffs, NJ: Prentice-Hall.

MacIver, R. M., & Page, C. H. (1957). *Society: An Introductory Analisysis.* London: MacMillan. Mantovani, G. (1995). *Comunicazione e identità. Dalle situazioni quotidiane agli ambienti virtuali.* Bologna, Italy: il Mulino.

Mantovani, G. (1995). *L'interazione uomo computer.* Bologna, Italy: il Mulino.

Matza, D. (1964). *Delinquency and Drift.* New York: John Wiley.

Merton, R. K. (1938). Social Structure and Anomia. *American Sociological Review, III*(5), 672–682. doi:10.2307/2084686

Norman, D. (1990). *La caffettiera del masochista: psicopatologia degli oggetti quotidiani.* Firenze, Italy: Giunti.

Norman, D. (1998). *The invisibile computer.* Cambridge, MA: MIT Press.

Park, R. E., Burgess, E. W., & McKenzie, R. D. (Eds.). (1925). *The City.* Chicago: University of Chicago Press.

Parsons, T. (1965). *Il sistema sociale.* Milano, Italy: Edizioni di Comunità.

Platt, T. (1982). Crime and Punishment in the United States: Immediate and Long-term Reforms from a Marxist Perspective. *Crime and Social Justice, 18*, 38–45.

Rasmussen, J. (1981). *Skill, Rules, Knowledge; Signals signs and symbols.* New York: Plenum Press.

Schwendinger, H., & Schwendinger, J. (1985). *Adolescent Subcultures and Delinquency.* New York: Praeger.

Shaw, C. R., & McKay, H. D. (1942). *Juvenile Delinquency in Urban Areas.* Chiacago: University of Chicago Press.

Sutherland, E. H. (1949). *White Collar Crime.* New York: Holt.

Sykes, G. M., & Matza, D. (1957). Techniques of Neutralization: A Theory of Delinquency. *American Sociological Review*, *22*, 664–670. doi:10.2307/2089195

Taylor, I., Walton, P., & Young, J. (1973). *The New Criminology: For a Social Theory of Deviance.* London: Routledge & Kegan.

Thomas, W. (1966). *On Social Organization and Social Personality.* Chicago: University of Chicago Press.

Turk, A. T. (1966). Conflict and Criminality. *American Sociological Review*, 338–352. doi:10.2307/2090822

Turk, A. T. (1969). *Criminality and Legal Order.* Chicago: Rand McNally.

Wilkins, L. T. (1965). *Social Deviance: Social Policy, Action and Research.* Englewood Cliffs, NJ: Prentice-Hall.

# Chapter 9
# Victims of Trafficking and Sexual Exploitation:
## A Video Documentary to Analyze Measures of Prevention and Institutional Interventions

**Silvia Ricci Lucchi**
*University of Bologna, Italy*

## EXECUTIVE SUMMARY

*This chapter shows the production of a video documentary, realized to deepen the knowledge about actual interventions to assist the victims of a particular crime of international interest, namely the trafficking of women for purposes of sexual exploitation. The video documentary has been made in Italy and especially through a restricted area in the North of the Country, Emilia-Romagna region, where particularly widespread are the phenomenon and the heterogeneity of interventions brought against. The dynamics of trafficking and exploitation are described as well as the legislation on them and the interventions brought about in order to give the victims the chance to redeem from the condition of sexual exploitation. This part is accompanied with the step-by-step explanation of how the video documentary has been made. The relevant objective is to define the modalities used to set up the video, in order to examine part of the actual interventions aimed to defend the victims, and to underline how it represents a useful effective document for teaching the dynamics associated with this particular kind of crime.*

## INTRODUCTION

The practices of trafficking in human beings are still existing in the world, even though they evoke distant ages, and they involve different cultures in several parts of the world.

DOI: 10.4018/978-1-60566-872-7.ch009

Actually at present, the discussion on women trade for sexual exploitation purpose is inevitably linked to other three subjects: migrations, prostitution, victims. The three themes are strictly associated with each other, suffice it to say that most part of the prostitutes in Italy are foreigners. On the other hand more difficult is to decide how many of them are really victims of human trafficking. If we speak about trafficking in human beings (for sexual exploitation purposes or others) we of course speak about a crime and, as anticipated, about victims.

Essential is to concentrate our attention on the victim experiencing a series of impositions and abuses; in the specific case, the trafficking of women for purposes of sexual exploitation leads women to be victims both physically and psychologically. In fact the woman becomes the victim of sexual violence, sometimes kidnapping and, not less important, victim of threats and impositions to force her to sell her body.

Moreover we have to consider that, in the phenomenon of trafficking, pimps take advantage from the victim's social cultural condition, depending on its country of origin, in the most deceitful way; in most cases the intermediaries in the trade, or even the promoters, are people belonging to the same ethnic group as the victim.

Women almost never succeed in throwing by themselves off their pimps, being strictly watched, with minimum chances of escape which often they cannot take since they live under constant threat.

How is a woman victim of sexual trafficking and exploitation helped and assisted? What are the answers to meet her needs?

This is the starting point of the present work.

## HISTORICAL NOTES

First of all it is necessary to introduce the subject by some historic examples, in order to stress the persistence and recurring of the problem, changing in shape according to different periods.

Since ancient times women (and not only) have been sold for purposes of sexual exploitation.

In the Middle Ages, in certain areas of France, the rampant poverty produced a multiplication of women "on sale" on the street, as it happens also today in less developed countries or encountering greater economic difficulties. Then existed houses built and governed by public authorities where girls could prostitute themselves paying a rent to the abbess.

In the medieval period prostitution started towards the 17$^{th}$ year of age, even if in some cases before the 15$^{th}$. The sexual exploitation of the woman was often preceded by rape; a victim of such a violence had many problems in reintegrating in society and in her family because if married, at times she was abandoned by her husband, if unmarried then her possibilities to get married were very much little. At this point the situation of the woman was exploited by some individuals (as brothel-keepers) who gave her housing persuading her to sell her body to pay debts.

This pattern was used also with foreign girls, coming from poor lands or regions devastated by wars.

At the early 16th century, the level of immigrants increased so much that it saturated urban areas; farmers moved towards the towns, unsatisfied with the inequality between their income and the local one.

The Authorities tried to obstruct the arrival of new citizens by granting benefits to those who had been living in the urban area for long time, in order to spread a common sense of mistrust towards foreigners.

The number of women on the street and without a home increased; The Refuge of Penitent Girls (Refuge des Pénitentes de Paris) was then founded in Paris. The access to such a structured place was bound to give evidence of an 'immoral' past, and thus a lot of poor girls approached prostitution to be allowed to enter the shelter and several poor families forced their daughters to prostitute themselves.

Another example is represented by the Sing Song Girls, whose traffic probably started towards the middle of 19th century. Very young Chinese women who were 'recruited' in their countries, kidnapped from the street, or even sold by their parents who ignored the real destiny waiting for them. The girls were then brought to United States by ship, trained by the aged ones to attract and gratify clients, and finally sold in a sort of auction. These girls were sold in China by their masters and replaced in America for an amount about ten times higher than the first price.

They were then obliged to sign a contract which bound them to the 'buyer' for a certain period of time, but without having the actual possibility to regain freedom.

In America this phenomenon took root mainly in California, when arrived men from every part in the world looking for fortune, invited by the discovery of precious deposits; this situation led to an increase in the sexual offer, to a proliferation of prostitution, therefore to the traffic of these young Chinese women.

The trade of white women is maybe one of the most famous examples even for modern ages; it raised in Europe between 19th and 20th centuries; European girls were abducted or deceived to be then brought to the colonies and introduced into brothels and clubhouses.

## DYNAMICS OF TRAFFICKING

Before dealing with the interventions, to be actuated after the woman has set herself free from her condition of victim, it is important to analyze her story of life: who are the girls coming to Italy? What countries are they from? How does the trade occur?

To answer these questions we have referred to the existing literature and to some ad hoc interviews, to the sector operators, we will observe subsequently in details.

The modalities of trafficking and exploitation of the prostitution vary according to the origin of the woman and of the pimps. Therefore we can advance different methods of recruitment of the young women; such typologies are changing constantly because of the economic, social, cultural transformations of the countries involved in this traffic, as well as for the eventual national and international rules and agreements restricting or modifying accesses and movements from a Country to another one.

The trade, as well as the exploitation, is managed by highly organized criminal groups.

Firstly the woman brought to Italy for being then sexually used did not know the kind of activity she would be expected to do once arrived there; with time passing by, mostly in the East European countries has become generally known the fact that women are brought to Italy to be sold, even more than once, to be passed from hand to hand and finally coerced to prostitute themselves.

Up to some years ago frequent was the kidnapping of women, who were literally raped and forced with violence, while at present exist other methods which seem to be more used, as deception.

An example of that is the technique of falling in love, used mostly in the East European countries; the pimp seduces the girl and cajoles her to follow him to Italy or to other countries, where she will be sold. It seems that this method is applied in the most deceitful way in Albany: generally the man pretends to be interested in the young woman and officially ask her family to marry her, then, once seduced, he convinces her to move to Italy; it is important to underline that in some areas of Albany still exists a sort of unwritten law, a code of behavior, the remains of a complex of principles dating back to ancient times, the so called *Kanun*.

Among the rules of Kanun, there is one according whom the young girl is 'handed' by her father to the man he judges worthy, she is thus compelled to be submitted to all kind of impositions; in these cases the woman is considered as a property which passes from father to future husband and find herself in a situation of constant submission and servitude. Kanun dates back to $15^{th}$ century and even if it is fallen into disuse towards 1930, still nowadays its influence affects certain areas of Albany; therefore it often risks to be used by traffickers and pimps to their advantage, constituting a point of weakness for the woman who is bound to her own cultural roots.

Usually the Albanian woman is accompanied to Italy by this man pretending to be her fiancé and often she does not realize what she is heading for until the situation becomes evident.

In this way the woman is obliged to prostitute herself, she is often forced by threats, and sometimes hit or sexually raped. The woman coming to Italy as a fiancée or as a wife can have the possibility to act as a controller of the young girls just arrived, and she instructs them on the kind of attitude they have to keep on the street and arranges to collect the money they have earned.

Different is the case of some girls, above all from the East of Europe, who are persuaded by a self-styled girlfriend or acquaintance, assuring them a good work in Italy as maid or dancer, for example.

As far as African girls are concerned, especially those coming from Nigeria, Ghana and Cameroon, their binds with cultural origins risks to favor their involvement in trafficking and exploitation.

The exploitation of young African girls is mainly run by Nigerian women coming from a life dedicated to prostitution who have the knowledge, having personally lived this condition, to manage other less practised girls. The women who manage the exploitation in Italy, usually have four or five girls in charge. The soliciting of these girls is not complex because in different African areas Europe represents a coveted destination both for women and for their families who often live in poor conditions and are very numerous; the illusion of sending a daughter to Italy for working leads the family itself to convince her to migrate. The real destiny of the unfortunate girl is often masked by lies and promises which make her imagine a rich future, depending on a honest well-remunerated job.

In some other cases, the family seems to be conscious that the departure will bring the daughter inevitably to prostitution, but the profits obtained from the girl's earnings are, in spite of everything, very tempting.

Since childhood African women are used to do what is imposed to them, normally they are not asked their opinion, but are simply informed, not existing the custom for women to make questions or ask for explanations; the habit is rather to rely on other people; so often it will be a component of the family to take them into the world of prostitution, or anyway a known person, a friend.

## LEGISLATIVE ASPECTS

It is necessary, at this point, to study the situation in depth at the legislative level, consequently to identify international agreements and conventions, national and possibly regional laws.

The need of creating international agreements for the repression of trafficking and exploitation offences was felt since the beginning of 1900, firstly to face the phenomenon of white-slave trade:

*"The Convention for the Suppression of the Traffic in Persons and of the Exploitation of the Prostitution of Others" (1949) is the first United Nation Treaty against Trafficking;[1] these included International Agreements and Conventions:*

- International Agreement for the Suppression of the White Slave Traffic (1904)
- International Convention for the Suppression of the Traffic in Women and Children (1921)
- The Slavery Convention (1926).

International laws and agreements are, still at present, among the most important means to oppose trade and exploitation of prostitution.

In 1926 the International Convention for abolishing slavery provides for some definitions as far as the same slavery and the slave trade; the situation in the first Twenties was surely different, it was necessary to eliminate a contingent, widespread, visible problem. Also today the phenomenon is contingent and spread up but often it exists in an obscure form, it is a world hidden for most of its part, often difficult to be detected.

However is felt the necessity of fighting the phenomenon which has for its nature an international range.

Extremely important is the 'Protocol to Prevent, Suppress and Punish Trafficking in Persons, Especially Women and Children, supplementing the United Nations Convention against Transnational Organized Crime' (subscribed during the conference in Palermo – 12-15th of December 2000); the title itself shows the importance given to women and children. It is fundamental at this point to report some articles of such protocol in order to underline its objectives and characteristics.

Art. 2 Statement of purpose:

The purposes of this Protocol are:

a. To prevent and combat trafficking in persons, paying particular attention to woman and children;
b. To protect and assist the victims of such trafficking, with full respect for their human rights;
c. To promote cooperation among States Parties in order to meet those objectives.

In the Article 3 some definitions are introduced, essential to identify and fight the crime, and to protect its victims as well:

Art. 3 Use of terms:

For the purposes of this Protocol:

a. "trafficking in persons" shall mean the recruitment, transportation, transfer, harbouring or receipt of persons, by means of the threat of use of force or other forms of coercion, of abduction, of fraud, of deception, of the abuse of power or of a position of vulnerability or of the giving or receiving payments or benefits to achieve the consent of a person having control over another person, for the purpose of exploitation. Exploitation shall include at a minimum, the exploitation of the prostitution of others or other forms of sexual exploitation, forced labour or services, slavery or practices similar to slavery, servitude or the removal of organs;
b. The consent of a victim of trafficking in persons to the intended exploitation set forth in subparagraph (a) of this article shall be irrelevant where any of the means set forth in subparagraph (a) have been used;
c. "The recruitment, transportation, transfer harbouring or receipt of a child for the purpose of exploitation shall be considered "trafficking in persons" even if this does not involve any of the means set forth in subparagraph (a) of this article;
d. Child shall mean any person under eighteen years of age.

The second part of the Protocol is titled *Protection of victims of trafficking in persons,* it provides references and information to Countries. The first article of this second part is n. 6 *(Assistance to and protection of victims of trafficking in persons)* reported hereunder:

1. In appropriate cases and to the extent possible under its domestic law, each State Party shall protect the privacy and identity of victims of trafficking in persons, including, inter alia, by making legal proceedings relating to such trafficking confidential.
2. Each State Party shall ensure that its domestic legal or administrative system contains measures that provide to victims of trafficking in persons, in appropriate cases;
   (a) Information on relevant court and administrative proceedings;
   (b) Assistance to enable their views and concerns to be presented and considered at appropriate stages of criminal proceedings against offenders, in a

manner not prejudicial to the rights of the defence.

3. Each State Party shall consider implementing measures to provide for the physical, psychological and social recovery of victims of trafficking in persons, including, in appropriate cases, in cooperation with non-governmental organizations, other relevant organizations and other elements of civil society, and, in particular, the provision of:
   (a) Appropriate housing;
   (b) Counselling and information, in particular as regards their legal rights, in a language that the victims of trafficking in persons can understand;
   (c) Medical, psychological and material assistance; and
   (d) Employment, educational and training opportunities.
4. Each State Party shall take into account, in applying the provisions of this article, the age, gender and special needs of victims of trafficking in persons, in particular the special needs of children, including appropriate housing, education and care.
5. Each State Party shall endeavour to provide for the physical safety of victims of trafficking in persons while they are within its territory.
6. Each State Party shall ensure that its domestic legal system contains measures that offer victims of trafficking in persons the possibility of obtaining compensation for damage suffered. [2]

Moreover the article 7 provides for every State Party to start adopting legislative measures, taking into account human and personal factors, allowing victims of human trafficking to stay in the territory of the State in appropriate cases, temporarily or permanently.

In Italy there is not a specific exclusive legislation on human trafficking for sexual exploitation purposes, however exist several legislative interventions we can refer and have recourse to, in order to fight such an offence (recognized and punished as a crime in the criminal code) and to protect victims living on the territory.

In this regard, Italy disposes of the *Consolidation Act on dispositions concerning the discipline of immigration and regulations on the condition of foreigners* of 1998; the article 18 in particular is an important instrument for the purpose of assistance and protection to the victims of trafficking and sexual exploitation. Actually it provides for the issue of a special residence permit allowing foreigners to escape the violence and the conditionings of criminal organizations and to take part into an assistance and protection program in Italy.

In that specific instance, a foreign woman victim of sexual exploitation can have recourse to that possibility if cases of violence or serious exploitation towards her are verified, and if arise real concrete dangers for her safety.

The issue of the residence permit for social protection purposes can occur after a denunciation to the Authorities, reported by the victim who helps, in this way, to contrast the criminal organization; anyway the woman can obtain the residence permit and benefit from an assistance program even if effective cooperation with law enforcement does not exist, but the actual presence of danger for the subject's safety is in any case necessary.

The Italian laws provide also, to defend the victims of this crime, for the institution of a special assistance program to grant, provisionally, appropriate housing, board and health care. Assistance programs should be realized by Regions, local authorities and private subjects, should provide for accommodations in buildings at confidential addresses for the safety of the victim, available social-health services and possibilities of actuating programs of assisted voluntary repatriation to the country of origin.

Assistance programs are mostly financed by grant-in-aids.

Much importance is given to the cooperation which should be created among the different government and non-government bodies, in order to form real networks inside the State and through the regions themselves.

## INTERVENTIONS IN FAVOR OF THE VICTIMS

At this point emerges the strong fundamental role of Regions in the administration and organization of the different subjects and institutions attending to the victims of trafficking and exploitation.

Inside Italian territory we have considered Emilia-Romagna region. For a better comprehension, we will explain clearly which is the Italian geographical political set-up. The fundamental law of Italian Republic is the Constitution describing the Republic itself as *one and indivisible*, nevertheless the division of the Country in twenty geographic areas called Regions is recognized and promoted. This organization is not only physical and geographic, but also political and administrative.

Each of the above mentioned Regions is endowed with government administrative powers on the relevant area. The inhabitants of the Region vote for the President of the Region this implying inevitably a political plurality inside the Country, so that regional government bodies are often characterized by a different political stance compared to national government bodies. Each Region is endowed with a statute which determines its fundamental principles of functioning, organization and the form of government.

According to the principles established by the Constitution, Regions have in fact proper functions and powers. Regions enjoy a wide degree of autonomy on the relevant territory, they have legislative powers, valid locally, which must be harmonized with and not contrary to government laws.

Regional legislative competence deals with matters which are not expressly handled by government laws; generally, Region's competences concern territory's government, public life, education, tourism, transports, health protection, civil defense, enhancement of cultural and natural heritage, social services.

For further decentralization, Regions include further self-government bodies (Provinces and Councils) which have not legislative but executive and regulation functions.

The geographical position, the culture, the law and the regulations are aspects which can strongly condition and influence the different subject's way of acting; the choice of analyzing the work of sector operators in the same territory (exactly Emilia-Romagna Region), thus sharing the above listed aspects, has enabled us to render the observation more objective and homogeneous.

Given the above mentioned choice, the first step has been of collecting information by the head office of Emilia-Romagna Region, in order to understand and verify what are the possibilities to reintegrate socially and in work for a foreign woman coming from a situation of trafficking and sexual exploitation. There is not much available literature on the specific subject, we have therefore used some texts published and proposed by the Region itself.

In order to deepen the matter and catch the most practical and meaningful aspects of reintegration programs we have made some interviews to sector operators in the Region. Every interview, we will deal more precisely with, case by case, have been taken by a video camera and edited to produce a video documentary.

From the first interview taken in the Region, we have obtained general information above the organization of the cooperation network present locally. In this contest the Region has mostly the function of co-ordinating the different bodies which, present in territories, operate in favor of the victims, offering support and housing to those who prostitute themselves (voluntarily or coercively) with the purpose of improving their conditions of life and help them to escape from possible exploitation cases.

The existing network acts on three big intervention categories: the reduction of damage, the 'green number', protection and social inclusion programs.

## The Reduction of Damage

The reduction of damage consists in offering the women who prostitute themselves an appropriate support mainly aimed at keeping them in decorous physical and healthy conditions.

The premise is acknowledging that a number of women prostitute voluntarily or do not intend anyway to abandon the world of prostitution; in any case no kind of moral judgement has to intervene on the subject's choice.

The reduction of damage is actuated through the drop-in centers where one can find a direct contact with the operators, and through the Street Units (groups of educators, operators and cultural mediators) who has the function of distributing information material for health protection, accompanying the women who like to the social health services in the territory, and taking contact with the girls who prostitute on the street. This last aspect has a fundamental importance, above all when we deal with exploitation, because it helps also in creating relationships and contacts with women who would like to start a reintegration and protection program.

The world of prostitution has changed in the last years; girls are younger and younger, generally their exploiters keep moving them to other parts of town, to prevent detection and avoid the establishment of too extended contacts in the territory.

This situation hampers enormously the Street Units operators who usually, if they consider it as necessary and if the woman has not asked for it yet, propose a protection program only after a number of meetings, after having gained the woman's confidence.

Another element which makes the Street Unit's work complicated is the indoor prostitution, which generally takes place in rooms and apartments, is not visible on the street, therefore it is not quantifiable and hardly identifiable. The indoor prostitution seems to be increasing and contributes to keep the 'dark number' which characterizes the sexual exploitation offence very elevated.

## The Green Number

It consists in a service, available on the whole Italian territory, financed by the Department of Equal Opportunities of the Presidency of the Council of Ministries; since 2000 Emilia-Romagna Region provides a National Anti-Trafficking Toll Free Number local service (800.290.290)

The phone call is free, and can be addressed by women who are victims of trafficking for sexual exploitation purposes, for getting help and information, as well as by any other person, like friends, relatives, clients of the girls.

The main purpose of this phone line is to help the victim in escaping from a condition of exploitation and forced prostitution, and to facilitate and render the access to prevention services and structures more simple.

Each local service has the task of talking with women who call and educating them about their rights, about the opportunities they would have in case they decided to leave the commercial sex world. Moreover the phone line operators have to explain the possibilities of obtaining regular residence permission in Italy and the operation of social protection programs.

In Rome there is a central service which handles the calls to the service units present in the different Regions.

At a local level, the operators who answer to phone calls are social and cultural mediators speaking the foreign languages related to the Countries most frequently involved in the world of commercial sexual exploitation (English, Russian, Polish, Albanian, Spanish, and Rumanian).

During the first telephone approach, it is necessary to avoid creating any reaction of suspicion or fear towards the service, without posing too intrusive questions. The aim of this first phase is to provide clear and useful information to the subjects who require them, and thanks to a reassuring approach, to push them to call again or to open to talk.

Successively the operator must be able to understand the real need of the subject and to lead the conversation to that direction but without inappropriately forcing it; by respecting the subject's times they have to understand when concrete action must be taken. In this last phase the operator makes the strongest action, he shall solve the problem or act as a psychological support. If the woman demands for an active intervention to get access to the housing projects, the green number service shall have a mediation function with the different services and structures, and proceed to organize a real escape from the exploiters and the place where she is trapped.

This service, obviously very useful and functional, has been unfortunately not much advertised, therefore it is little exploited and used.

## Housing and Social Rehabilitation Programs

First of all it is important to signal the presence of entities or associations operating in this sector without adhering to institutional networks; furthermore, this evidences the actual deployment of forces to oppose the problem of trafficking and sexual exploitation.

The structures involved into reintegration programs, adhering to the same regional network, follow common guidelines, however their operating method is not always strictly univocal, for this reason, as far as the interview subjects are concerned, we have oriented our choice on two Centers in particular, in order to have a wider and more diversified view of the situation and, contemporarily, to assemble the common characters recurring in the different cases.

The involved entities are the Center for Woman Justice in Ferrara and the Association Pope Giovanni XXIII whose head office is in Rimini, both provincial capital cities of Emilia-Romagna region. We have addressed The North Star Project too, active on Trieste territory (capital city in Friuli-Venezia Giulia Region), representing one of the first actions taken in Italy.

Above mentioned centers cooperates with Emilia-Romagna Region for the actual network project, but they exist independently; they have their own life and attend to other activities as well, only part of their work interacts with the Region.

Now we analyze how does the activation of reintegration programs work and which is the role of above mentioned entities, considering their common operating methods; successively we will go into details by observing the differences among action modalities.

The information subsequently discussed make reference to the interviews I carried out, in 2006, in Emilia-Romagna Region.

Cases requiring a drastic intervention, due to the exploiter's violence, have decreased; this because of the continuous changes in trafficking and in exploitation techniques, which seem softer from outside; this does not mean that things have improved, exploitation and trafficking do exist, as well as women who choose to prostitute but succeed in preserving their autonomy.

It is important never to forget that do exist women who choose prostitution, who do not need any help and do not ask to be saved because in fact they are not exploited and do not want to change their life.

On the other hand, when a woman escapes from a situation of exploitation, the danger is real and contingent, there are hence all the preconditions for granting her a temporary residence permit for social protection reasons; often she is helped to escape by Street Units, by the clients, by indications provided by the Green Number; anyway the escape assumes always a number of elements:

- The firm belief of the girl to abandon the world of exploitation, also leaving behind any possible sentimental relationship with the exploiter
- The trust in those who propose her an alternative and in the private or public institutions which will offer her some help
- The woman's courage, because she could risk to be caught by the exploiter during the escape.

If the woman, before deciding to go away, has taken contact with the Green Number, the escape is arranged together with phone operators so that they can grant a support as soon as the action takes place. Then the regional network activates and, if necessary, makes use of its contacts on national level too.

If a real danger exists, generally pondered by law enforcement, the woman is immediately moved to another territory in defense of her safety, protected also by the fact that all the housing structures of this kind have secret addresses; in this way much trust is set in the hands of the woman, who will sign a series of rules providing for the interdiction to tell the address of the house and to house anyone in. For about three weeks will be carried out interviews aimed at reconstructing the migrant background of the woman and the situation of exploitation she comes from.

Meanwhile her health conditions are checked by screenings and tests for sexually transmissible diseases after which she will start any eventual therapy.

In the same context are given lessons of Italian language and practice manual skill exercises according to the attitudes shown by the woman.

The accommodation is safe but temporary, therefore the operators of the center attend to look for lodgings as much appropriate as possible.

It is important to understand if there is any intention to cooperate with the Police by reporting them their exploiters identity; we remind that, on the contrary, the woman gets protection anyway if she is in a real situation of danger.

The report to the law enforcement is important also because it allows to accelerate the legalization of the girl through documents and residence permit. In the meantime it is necessary to respect the times, first of all by offering quietness and security.

Great importance is given to the interview, to the listening of the story, which can provide useful indications to the operator as well in order to start creating an appropriate reintegration program. Who conduct the interview should make the victim feel they are close to them but keeping the right distance to respect the times, the spaces and the freedom of the woman; the interview represents a new contact with the outside world, which is fruitful for the first time and should be reassuring for the victim; the contact with the interlocutor will be the first step to regain their confidence in other people.

At times for girls it is also hard to recover self-confidence because they have often experienced a failure and sometimes the feeling of depression is superior.

The housing centers avail of subjects of different kinds, of psychologists and lawyers for possible advises, but also of cultural mediators, able to face the relationship based on the diversity of the involved cultures. The relationships created with the operators and between the girls are meant to give them back a sense of belonging, to stress the value of affections and of close persons, and to accept other people.

The social reintegration planning is created according to the woman's different needs and agreed with her; it is necessary to consider the different cultures, the different life and exploitation backgrounds, the social relationship established in Italy and the emotional condition.

The programs are aimed to achieve social reintegration (rarely and only on demand of the woman to repatriation) therefore it is necessary to introduce her in the working life, in order to complete her program of emancipation and psychological and material independence. The working rehabilitation is carried out with an orientation period which ends with a stage of a number of hours; if the woman is not employed by the company, she will have to find another job and postpone her independence plans.

On average the social working reintegration program lasts about a year.

The following step is seeking for a flat to rent, but due to high costs, they often share flats with other girls in the same situation.

All the actions taken have the final purpose of giving the woman back her migration plan and independence, providing her the tools to face the new life and leaving prostitution and exploitation back.

Now we see the differences between the various reintegration plans, through a rapid analysis of the two above mentioned interviewed subjects.

1) The Woman Justice Center.

It is situated in Ferrara and is an example of voluntary organization, initially born to provide legal or psychological advice mostly required by Italian women, during the years the situation is considerably changed and at present many foreign women address the association.

Programs and housing centers have been activated both for women coming from abuse and violence situations and for women who want to escape from the experience of prostitution and exploitation; this second case in particular takes part in the regional plan.

Most part of the girls entering this housing center is of Nigerian origin, probably the center has become specialized for this kind of culture, the working methods reconcile with the girls habits and eventually they create a real 'pass the world' between them.

Due to the situation, the attempt has been to keep the prevalence of Africans higher than possible, also to avoid conflicts and divergences among too different and far habits and cultures, in a such fragile moment of the victim's life.

To this program take part about twenty girls every year, a big number of which inside the housing center; sometimes the girl has already a contact and stay living by a friend or by the boyfriend for example; in these cases the accomplishment of the plan will be more complex.

During their program girls attend Italian courses, receive working orientation and have unpaid work experiences in companies with the purpose of being employed. The girls shall know the real existing possibilities of employment and prove their skills with the stage.

On average the program lasts one year, depending on the variables involved, as the possibility of not being employed by the company offering the stage or the difficulty in finding their residence.

2) The Association Pope Giovanni XXIII.

It is an International Association of Papal Law, approved by Vatican and Italian States; now it has reached other 25 countries in the world. At present Italy provides for approximately 230 accommodation centers of different type and for 600 structures and plans in other parts of the world.

During the years have been implemented the accommodation centers for special cases, as for those who decide to leave the commercial sex world.

The Association employs more or less 1700 people, in Italy and abroad, who are members of communities, choosing to share their lives with other accommodated people. Every person will build her or his own life project in order to reintegrate in society or to stay by the Association because she or he has not anymore contacts with the outside world.

The Association begins to work on the phenomenon of prostitution in the Nineties, when Rimini streets are 'invaded' by women selling their bodies, some of them victims of exploitation. At present the phenomenon of commercial sex on the street is particularly decreased on Rimini's province, on the other hand more alarming is the phenomenon of prostitution in flats or night clubs already extended on the national territory.

Currently the contact between the women and the Association occurs through the Police, or thanks to the Street Units. The victim is contacted in order to offer her to evade from the commercial sex world she is part of, by offering her housing and protection.

The Association provides for its own accommodation center, where it hosts women for the first days, waiting for a lodging; when the victims is addressed to a center she starts the real program, meaning the observance of some rules finalized to the security of the woman and of the hosting center.

In this case too, emerges the great importance attributed to the contact with the outside world and the complexity of recreating the confidence in other people and in themselves.

Besides operators, the Association makes also use of volunteers for recreational activities or others; the program lasts from six months to one year and during this period the subject can follow different courses, for example literacy lessons, for working orientation, in order to achieve the economic autonomy while trusting the support of the center. The following step is to live independently. This program is rather long and on average the complete autonomy is reached towards the eighteenth months of hosting.

The Association has implemented also some programs aiming at repatriate victims in their countries of origin, that is why have been established contacts with official entities too, like the Border Police.

The Association cooperates with the regional project as far as part of its activities is concerned in the themes of prostitution, trafficking and exploitation.

3) The Trieste case.

We have considered helpful to make a brief reference to another type of program, actuated in Italy, since it is different from the above illustrated ones, because of the different geographical position. We refer in particular to a program called Stella Polare (North Star) whose center is in Trieste (Friuli Venezia Giulia Region), a city on the border with Slovenia.

The 'North Star' project is proposed by the 'Committee for the Civil Rights of Prostitutes' and is active in social protection planning to encourage self-determination processes and support people who want to come out of serious situations of commercial sex trade.

The projects avails of some local entities cooperation and of the network established with the other services in the North-east of Italy and with the National Green Number.

The project proposes:

- To accommodate victims of trafficking who want to take part in a program for coming out of the commercial sex world,
- To offer support to those who do not want to leave prostitution, encouraging their self-determination, thus their independence and the rupture with the eventual exploiters.
- To reduce the damage, by preventing the diffusion of sexually transmissible diseases and avoiding abortions, by promoting the use of contraceptives.

Even this project uses a mobile unit to create contacts with women on the street and to actuate the reduction of damage, furthermore women are invited to have a complete check up of their health conditions and they are informed about the possibilities of having access to protection plans.

On demand of the woman is foreseen the assisted repatriation to the country of origin, with the cooperation of the associations present in the territory.

The accommodation of the woman is based on the rules dictated by national laws, as in the previously analyzed cases. The planning, agreed with the woman, ends with the complete emancipation of the subject.

Trieste, as anticipated, is situated on the borderline, is therefore particularly multiethnic, Trieste citizens are used to it; it is a city characterized by big trades and population flows, and thanks to its location, is the access way for illegal immigration from Eastern countries. The flow of illegal immigrants succeed in having access to Italy from Trieste, crossing the border by means of a courier, by train or by foot, evading border detections.

There is a train connecting Trieste to Budapest, therefore it occurs that girls victims of exploitation take it with the idea of escaping, but when they arrive at the Slovenian frontier, are sent back since they lack documents. Usually at this point the Border Police or law enforcement address the Project, leading girls to it; then starts the reconstruction of their story, and they are convinced (or they already have the intention) to denounce traffickers.

Often the protection program is activated and it is very similar to those actuated in Emilia-Romagna.

From a brief analysis of the above exposed cases it appears clear that intervention methods can vary between each other but, at the same time, can be effective as well.

Often the interviewed subjects' opinions were in contrast; they have actually revealed that laic centers aim to reach a higher level of emancipation, self-determination, total independence of the victim, above all when the condition of prostitution is chosen by the woman, by avoiding any moral judgement; in particular, Trieste project aims very strongly at the self-determination of the woman who chooses prostitution. This laic projects' trend is demonstrated by the actuation of the reduction of damage (lower the risk of contracting diseases for the woman who prostitutes) through the distribution of information material and also by distributing preservatives, activities which assume the acceptance of the free choice of prostituting.

On the other hand, we have the sensation that the Giovanni XXIII Catholic Association is mostly oriented to reintegrate the woman in a familiar context. If we consider the reduction of damage policy, it is not agreed by the Catholic Association which judges it as limited to assistance, non resolutive, thus not sufficient. It is necessary to remind that the starting assumptions are different since in this case prostitution is seen under another perspective, is not accepted as a free choice, the 'selling' of one's body is not tolerable. Evident is the existence of methods with common and divergent characteristics which nevertheless cooperate and activate to improve such a dramatic and hard to solve situation.

To fight a crime like trafficking, both private and public institutions activate; we consider it as a clear sign of the importance and gravity of this problem. As previously mentioned, in this scenario intervenes also Italian legislation by providing for laws in favor of the victims.

## DIFFICULTIES IN THE STUDY OF HUMAN TRAFFICKING AND EXPLOITATION

The trafficking and sexual exploitation are complex subjects to study and to face.

First of all is very difficult to identify and quantify the phenomenon which is characterized by a high number of hidden cases, which remain unknown by law enforcement, absent from official figures; the dark number is in fact one of the biggest obstacle to a complete study of this reality.

Why do the dark number of this phenomenon is so elevated?

We can try to answer this question by help of different existing factors; firstly we have to understand how prostitution has changed in recent years, starting from 'indoor' prostitution (in flats or night clubs); as previously anticipated it is a spreading phenomenon which makes prostitution invisible to the eyes of people. This situation certainly advantages the sexual commercial crime, which will be hard to be identified and will not be in any way quantified. Therefore it is not possible to carry out effective reliable estimates or statistics to comprehend and study this kind of offence.

Moreover, institutional interventions to fight the crime and to activate in favor of victims have appeared to be very complex.

Another element which increases the dark number related to trafficking and exploitation offences is the lack of reports to the Authorities by the victims. The reasons for such a reserve can be identified starting from the observation of the relationship victim-criminal; we consider that, in different cases, the relationship between the two subjects has changed in recent years, generally the victim is not violated anymore, while she was until some years ago, at present it is more frequent to find women who accept to prostitute themselves, surely coerced by threats or by the fact that they feel 'with no alternative' (due to the lack of documents and to their status of clandestine persons). It appears that these criminal organizations have realized that by avoiding violence and respecting agreements (for example by leaving part of the earnings to the girls) is more difficult to be denounced.

It is important to remember that, also when methods are softer and there is no violence, the woman is anyway kept in a condition of servitude to the exploiters, therefore this situation leads back to the sexual exploitation offence.

In other cases the reality is very different. We take for example African women; to coerce them to prostitute often traffickers play on their cultural roots. Some of them believe in voodoo rituals, then used by criminals to menace them; in this way women are convinced that, refusing to accept prostitution or denouncing traffickers, will cause them very unfortunate events.

Furthermore, it happens that criminal groups, who have contacts in the woman's country of origin, menace her of retaliating against her family.

The mentioned factors provide a clear example of the reason why the woman is reluctant in reporting the offence suffered, keeping to obey to the rules of traffickers. This makes the intervention of the institutions difficult and complicates the study to understand the dynamics and the extent of the phenomenon.

## THE VIDEO SHOT AND THE VIDEO DOCUMENTARY

The video object of analysis has been produced mainly for teaching purposes because, through the audio visual medium, direct evidence of the subjects interviewed can be listened to during courses, without any intermediate.

One objection could be that the interviews, before being screened, are edited to realize the video, therefore potentially manipulated, so that the product is 'polluted' by the hands of filmmakers. However we think that mistrust should be left apart to leave room to curiosity and interest, placing a big dose of trust in the subject who has edited the video.

In the specific case of this video documentary the best solution was to follow personally every phase, of the bibliographical research and documentation, of the interviews and the editing, and also of the final product's presentation.

This can grant a wider and deeper knowledge of the discussed themes. The advantage of following personally the different phases is evident during interviews; in fact it will be easier to carry on an interview, moving freely among many subjects, pressed also by the interviewee, having clearly in mind what are the background and the present situation of the subject in exam. This knowledge derives obviously from the direct acquisition of information and documentation previously occurred.

Essential has been, before starting the shots, to collect a complete documentation and to fix a geographical area of reference. Furthermore, the knowledge of the themes has been useful, in preliminary phases too, for the choice and selection of the subjects to interview.

In this specific instance, therefore, documentation has been found in existing publications; starting from this point clear has been the impossibility of providing a generalized vision which represents the reality related to this phenomenon and the initiatives taken. It has been thus necessary to actuate a geographic delimitation. We chose to take into consideration Emilia-Romagna Region which presently provides for strong services aiming at social reintegration and at preventing women from trafficking and sexual exploitation.

Actually in the Region are available, as previously mentioned, several structures, of different kind, with different operating methods and different philosophies and action policies; nevertheless, they cooperate to the same objective and follow common guidelines, for example the provisions of the law and the actual regulations.

Another factor which contributed in choosing this geographic area is our residence in the zone concerned. Living in the reality analyzed in the survey represents a wider degree of knowledge and orientation necessary to develop the study, but also more simple and deeper and potentially more frequent contacts, when they appear to be necessary.

After having decided to examine Emilia-Romagna Region we went to the relevant head office with the only purpose of collecting information on the modalities of action of actual programs and on the dynamics of the relationships characterizing them. In this way has come to surface the existence of a real working network which links the various structures and subjects operating in the sector, organized and managed by the Region itself. The involved subjects exist and work apart from the Region, but they cooperate with the same to grant the best possible interventions to victims in question.

What has appeared from the presentation of the different projects is the existence of an evident divergence in action strategies between catholic and laic subjects. The different operating method is due to the different policy and philosophy constituting the roots of the various projects.

We have decided then to base on this divergence for the choice of the subjects to interview, in order to describe obviously different typologies which are contemporarily univocal and co-operating with each other; interviews have been addressed to a laic center's persons in charge (The Woman Justice Center) and to a catholic center's (Association Pope Giovanni XXIII). To deepen further the situation we have considered necessary to analyze other realities; basing on the initial documentation, we have oriented our choice to a project, known all over Italy by the sector operators, whose center is in Trieste. It can be counted between the pilot programs in Italy as far as interventions against trafficking victims are concerned, another interesting aspect of this project being the particular geographic position of Trieste, as previously mentioned. It is immediately evident that interviewed subjects are only operators and not girls who benefited or are benefiting from services or actual initiatives.

Surely with their evidence the video would have reported more 'captivating' issues, but for reasons of safety (a number of them lives at secret addresses and take part in protection plans), of respect, and also of sensibility and delicacy towards them, we considered as more appropriate to avoid involving them in this work; moreover we remind that our purpose has been to describe in the best possible way the actuated interventions, that is the work of public institutions and private subjects.

To carry out interviews we have taken phone contacts with the examined associations, explaining our intention of producing a video documentary; then the different dates with the relevant operating units have been fixed.

We have made use of a video camera, a tripod and a microphone installed on the camera. Once arrived by each association center, after having met the person to be interviewed, I have invited the subject to choose the recording location. Interviews have been carried out in the form of conversation, only the interviewee and I were present; I have put the video camera on the tripod, shot the subject and started the recording; I have tried to manipulate the camera as few as possible during the interview, only for changing the tapes and, rarely, to adjust the shot.

To limit the movements around the camera, pretending not to be in its presence, probably helps the interviewed subject to feel more at ease, without constantly reminding him or her we are recording his or her image and voice, and achieving a sufficient level of naturalness.

During the interview I have not used a pre-filled questionnaire but I had clear in mind the information I were seeking; in this way the interview takes a more colloquial and less rigid aspect.

On the other hand there is the possibility to find subjects who hardly express their opinions and commit themselves during the conversation, who give short answers and restrain their personal ideas and considerations. In these cases it is useful to make sufficiently open questions which are supposed to entail more conversational answers (ex. How was your association born? How does it operates in the territory? What is the planning for a girl who needs social rehabilitation? What are the difficulties to face in your work?) otherwise it is possible to ask the subject to tell about past episodes.

The direct exchange with the other person during the interview helps to clarify any eventual doubt and, even more, stimulates the dialogue and the production of new issues the interviewer had not foreseen, enriching the recorded conversations.

Each interview has been filmed in full, by an audio visual medium, offering the possibility of catching the different aspects of the subject showed during the interview, as facial expressions, signs of embarrassment or anxiety, of satisfaction or gratification.

Once the interviews have been collected, we had at our disposal several hours of audio visual material for the editing.

First of all I have thought about a logical thread for the work I intended to realize, by making an exhausting summary of the themes I would like to study: the definitions of 'trafficking' and 'sexual exploitation', the actual laws, the trafficking practices in some European countries, the issues connected to the identification and detection of the crime, the differences between the actuated interventions, the points of discussion and divergence.

As far as the first parts are concerned (definitions, legislation, problems) I have considered necessary to prepare some written schemes summarizing these arguments to be shown on slides during classes, to be integrated with an oral comment.

As regards the more practical and operational aspects, related to the subject's contributions, I have edited the interviews with the purpose of giving them voice on the discussed themes and to have evidence of their direct experience, expressing their different points of view which, through the difference itself, enrich the final product.

Most part of the work is dedicated to the detailed description of the phases which constitute protection and reintegration programs and projects, told by the direct voice of operators who actuate them every day.

Finally I have focused the attention on a number of central points of the argument, discussion points, open questions and controversies, in order to emphasize, directly by the voices of the interviewed subjects, which are the main divergences between the different intervention policies.

The final product will be available to be submitted to students by the mediation of the teacher, who will introduce the different themes to let then the interviewed subjects speaking, through the video documentary. The positive aspects in suggesting an audio visual product to a group of students are manifold.

On the assumption of a careful and appropriate editing, the direct vision of the video, can grant that the interviewee's words are faithfully reproduced, without the risk of misinterpretations.

Furthermore, students have the possibility to watch directly the cases of the subjects in question which, if read on a text, would not have the same impact and would probably arouse less curiosity and interest.

The telling of an experience, by watching and listening to, even through a screen, the person who is living it directly, allow to catch visually emotions and feelings expressed through small movements of the body (impossible to do with an audio recording, by reading a book, or with a lecture given by one teacher); we have therefore the unique possibility of having in class, during the same course, several speakers who could hardly be present at the same time. It could be objected that these speakers (appearing only on the video) cannot give any answer to the possible doubts and clarifications asked by students; it is then necessary to carry out interviews which deal with the possible higher number of themes without ignoring the curiosity they could excite in the future audience, moreover is essential the mediating role of the teacher during the class.

Normally watching the video leads the student interested in the subject to a higher participation and awareness, by reducing, at least apparently, the possibilities of distraction.

The proposal, in the final part of the video, of using more open and controversial questions can enrich the course by suggesting to the teacher and the students the possibility of creating a small discussion or exchange of opinions and considerations during the class.

All this by keeping the same characteristics of a frontal lesson.

In my opinion the use of the audio visual medium to supply with documentary evidence a phenomenon of this kind for educational purposes can be very fruitful.

The medium used (video) does not affect excessively the documentary's production time, but in the editing phase, the more complicated step, because it is necessary to create a thread running through the different opinions and experiences of the interviewed subjects.

## REFERENCES


Angelini, F., & Centonze, S. (2002). *Numero Verde contro la tratta. L'esperienza dell'Emilia Romagna.* Ravenna, Italy: Regione Emilia-Romagna & Cooperativa Sociale il Mappamondo.

Corso, C., & Trifirò, A. (2003). ... *E siamo partite! Migrazione, tratta e prostituzione straniera in Italia.* Firenze: Giunti Gruppo Editoriale.

Donadel, C., & Martini, E. R. (2005). *La prostituzione invisibile.* Ravenna, Italy: Regione Emilia-Romagna, Grafiche Morandi.

Monzini, P. (2002). *Prostituzione, tratta e sfruttamento.* Roma: Donzelli Editore.

Rossiaud, J. (1995). *La prostituzione nel Medioevo.* Roma: Laterza Editore.


## WEBSITES


DESA United Nations, New York. The United Nation Response to Trafficking in Women and Girls. Retrieved from www.un.org/womenwatch/daw/egm/trafficking2002/reports

United Nations (2000). Protocol to Prevent, Suppress and Punish Trafficking in Persons, especially Women and Children, Supplementing the United Nation Convention against Transnational Organized Crime. Retrieved from www.untreaty.un.org/English/notpubl/18-12-a.E.doc

## ENDNOTES

1 DESA United Nations, New York. The United Nation Response to Trafficking in Women and Girls. www.un.org/womenwatch/daw/egm/trafficking2002/reports

2 United Nations (2000). Protocol to Prevent, Suppress and Punish Trafficking in Persons, especially Women and Children, Supplementing the United Nation Convention against Transnational Organized Crime. www.untreaty.un.org/English/notpubl/18-12-a.E.doc

# Chapter 10
# Anthropo-Sociological Approach of the Criminology and Applied Victimology:
## Social Unrest, Insecurity, Fear

**Rosaria Romano**
*Suor Orsola Benincasa University of Naples, Italy*

## EXECUTIVE SUMMARY

*Criminology attempts to explain the causes of crime using two different approaches: the anthropological and the sociological. The anthropological approach focuses on man as the author of crime, and seeks to determine the physical, psychological, motivational, and psychosocial factors, that may have led to the criminal conduct. The sociological approach, on the other hand looks at the macro social factors influencing the insurgence of crime. The problem of social control, namely the way in which a society is able to integrate individuals around a single coherent system of customs, traditions and norms, and thus guarantee community security is connected to the concept of social disorder. The concept of social disorder is also linked to that of marginality, characteristic of the immigrant condition: the loss of cultural roots and the lack of integration in the new cultural context places immigrants in the margins of society. Instances of social problems resulting were reported news broadcasts of events occurring towards the end of 2008 in Italy which suddenly brought to light a series of similar events, evidencing ever more frequent occurrences of racism and xenophobia. These episodes spoke for themselves. Evident as the light of day, it was no longer easy to conceal their true matrix. From the homicide of a Milan boy (from http://www.rainews24.rai.it/notizia.asp?newsid=85897) who had allegedly stolen a packet of biscuits, to the homicides of Castel Volturno immigrants (Castel Volturno is a Southern Italian little city)*

DOI: 10.4018/978-1-60566-872-7.ch010

*(from http://www.corriere.it/cronache/08_settembre_19/rivolta_castelvolturno_immigrati_de6698dc-8635-11dd-bef9-00144f02aabc.shtml), the violent Parma bashings, the injuries sustained by a young man from Ghana, and to those in Rome against a Chinese citizen. But this is not the end of the story. This study will analyze the Abba's homicide. Abba was a young man, an Italian citizen, and the son of Burkina Faso immigrants with Italian citizenship; he was born and grown up in Milan. The theoretical premises on which this case is based are those reported in victimology literature, it has been chosen for it's similarity to other cases of xenophobia and because it brings new insights to present notions existing within criminology and applied victimology, (such as concepts of social disorder and social fear), and as such constitutes a significant contribution to this field of study.*

## BACKGROUND

Today most of the leading scholars in crime research find a correlation between urban decay and the weakening of social relations leading, in turn, to an enfeebling of collective security. In fact, a substantial number of studies in current social science literature have highlighted this nexus, having revealed a significant correlation between individuals' fear of crime and levels of fragility and insecurity, indicating a decline in social integrity.

Terror posed by the prospect of crime and the likelihood of becoming its victim form part of a phenomenon that is becoming more and more a defining feature of contemporary society, having resounding social and psychological repercussions. Further, value judgments proffered by local and government authorities, tending to influence relations amongst various social groups and overall social order, also impact on insecurity levels, making their appraisal difficult (Bandini, 2003).

Results of recent research studies on victimization, regarding illicit behavior which, in common language is referred to as "petty crime", but whose magnitude is often anything but minimal, provide indisputable evidence of the presence of insecurity generated by crime within the Italian population, to the extent that it has become a significant social phenomenon that can no longer be ignored.

Whereas the theme of a social sense of insecurity had been largely undervalued in Italy until a few years ago, in other countries, particularly in the USA and in Great Britain, it has been, over the last 30 years, the subject of copious studies and research. International analyses have found that a mounting sense of personal insecurity, even though concurring with a corresponding increase in petty crimes, seems to be becoming more and more widespread and frequent throughout society, regardless of the circumstances, to the extent of constituting, both from a social and a scientific point of view, a distinct entity.

Researchers have nominated two variables as fundamental indicators of sense of uncertainty: *fear of crime*, i.e. fear of crime on an individual basis, and *concern about crime* or social anxiety about crime or public order (Roché, 1998).

The first is a physiological and emotional response to an intimidation that may be either real or probable, so that a sense of danger based on intuition is able to indicate both the likelihood that a feared event could actually occur and the improbability of such an event happening.

On the other hand, social fear regarding crime is anxiety over the possibility that it could spread to one's own neighborhood.

It is interesting to note that crime does not strike homogenously throughout the population in a uniform manner, but varies according to the genre, age, and type of municipality or geographical area in which subjects live.

Research studies have shown that the most significant variable is genre, given that fear is much more widespread amongst the female population than the male. On the other hand, we find a concave age/personal fear curve, i.e. older people display the most fear, followed by youth in the early teens, leaving the middle aged sector as the most secure. Other interesting considerations can be drawn from the research on groups at risk, or those groups of individuals which by their very nature are most likely to be subjects of crime.

This research approach is entirely different; it concentrates to a greater extent on the offence, on the situational typology in which the offence is perpetrated, an moreover highlights the possible circumstances which could facilitate such and act, together with the structure of opportunities connected with the criminal action (Balloni, 1983).

These types of studies are becoming very important, as their application often dismantles stereotypes such as those built up by media reports regarding the compositional variables of groups at risk of victimization. An example is provided by age and sex variables; according to the stereotype, women and the elderly are more likely to be victims of bag snatchers and muggers. In reality empirical research shows that the risk is spread unevenly amongst the various strata of the population; women are more at risk of being subject to bag snatching or pick pockets, whilst men are more likely to become victims of armed robbery or assaults (Barbagli & Gatti, 2005).

The risk of victimization also varies with age, but this variation changes with the type of offence. Robberies and assaults on the person tend to decline in the upper age groups, and the risk of becoming a victim of any form of predatory crime decreases with increasing age. Another very important variable is urban location, data have shown varying percentages of victimization in different metropolitan zones (Barbagli & Sabbadini, 1999).

Research studies of the last 50 years have consistently shown a close correlation between crime rate and urbanization. International research results show that fear of crime is much more widespread than actual victimization (real crime) and that the demographic slices of the population with greater senses of insecurity are, in fact, the least victimized.

However, even this assertion is worthy of further analysis in the light of changes that have occurred in Italian cities over the last thirty years, and which render obsolete those interpretative models which are being used even up to the present day (up until recently the rate of urbanization in a municipality had been calculated in relation to the number of its inhabitants. However in recent years, due to the rise in, firstly, the number of commuters, and secondly in the number of consumers, [(*city users*) who come periodically to the city not to work, but to consume services], researchers have preferred to make a distinction between daytime and night time population. All of this necessitates a review of the relationship between urbanization and predatory crime; in short, it is no longer enough to refer to the number of inhabitants of municipalities or to crime rates, but it has now become essential to distinguish between where victims actually live and the locations in which the offences against them are perpetrated).

It is important to analyze the relationship between experiences of victimization and personal fear. Numerous research studies carried out in this field in the US, in Great Britain and in other Western countries have drawn conflicting conclusions. Many authors, having found no significant correlation between the two variables, hypothesized that personal experience of victimization can play only a limited role in determining the prevalence of fear of crime, or that after experiencing victimization, subjects become more cautious, resulting in less exposure to dangerous situations and hence to a reduction in their fear (Balloni & Bisi,1996).

It may be stated, thus, that the particular break-up of data adopted in this case, and the striking discrepancies between researchers' predictions and actual results, explain why much of the research endeavor in the area of risk of victimization has been oriented towards ascertaining its determining factors, experimenting both the selection of variables to be examined and alternate ways of partitioning data (Clarke & Felson, 1993).

Results have shown that the more a particular life style (i.e. the set of activities connected with work, school, home or leisure) puts the individual into contact with potential perpetrators of crime, the greater the risk of victimization (Bruno, 1999).

Therefore, when and how often subjects leave their abode, where they go to, the routes they take and the means of transport they use, all contribute to determining the extent of risk the subject is exposed to.

Environmental factors associated with the criminal dynamic are considered in the *routine activity* approach, which asserts that a criminal act may occur only where three essential conditions are concomitant: a subject willing and able to perpetrate a crime, a goal (object or person) that can be easily reached and attacked, and the lack of adequate means to impede criminal actions. This theory analyses subjects' routine dynamics and is able to illustrate the modification of risk not only in space, but also in time. Considering that the absence of even a single one of the three conditions is sufficient to prevent any crime being committed, the routine activities of subjects most at risk of victimization have been closely looked into, underlining: - those habits which most place them in the eye of likely offenders (*closeness);* their place in society - their job, income or place of residence making them advantaged targets *(profitability)* and poorly protected *(accessibility).*

These features relate, in turn, to specific socio-demographic features such as age, sex, and social class (Milanesi & Naldi,2001).

Many authors have found fear of crime to be irrational, in two senses; firstly, fear is disproportionate to the real risk of being subjected to a criminal act (*irrationality with respect to causes*) and secondly, when faced with a real danger, a subject may be 'freeze' or react inadequately (*incoherence with respect to outcomes*).

As regards irrationality with respect to causes, a large number of studies carried out in Great Britain and the United States during the 1980's have shown the absurdity of fear, evidencing how groups in which fear levels were highest, (women and the elderly), proved to be those least at risk; the rate of victimization of these groups was actually lower. Researchers concluded that this result, apparently paradoxical, was due to the amplification of fear through misinformation ensuing from the mass media and regarding the risk of becoming the victim of a criminal offence (Pavarini,1994).

Various studies effected in some Western countries have highlighted how fear of crime may be ignited, may flare up and extend as a reaction to a series of events and facts recurring in the place where one lives, even if these events appear, at first sight, to be of minor importance, and even though they may, in some cases, not quite qualify as criminal offences. Such actions, termed insolent gestures, are perceived, by citizens, as a totality, lying along a continuum of anti social behaviors, and interpreted as signs of a collapsing moral order.

In 1978 Albert Hunter stated that "the fear in an urban setting is above all a fear of social disorder, which can be considered to constitute a threat to the individual"; he emphasized the fact that the origins of social disorder could be traced back as much to minor infringements (incivilities) as to the more serious offences (crimes), and stated that the more the former proves to be a common occurrence, the higher the incidence of the latter.

It was noted, however, that citizens' sense of insecurity originated more from insolent gestures than from actual offences, and that this was to due to the fact that they were much more frequent. (Other authors have stressed the fact that too often too little importance is accorded to "the fear of being harassed by people who violate social order" (Shaw, 1979, p. 9) (disorderly people).

These individuals are not necessarily criminals, or violent, but they live without rules or appear to be unpredictable, 'shifty' characters - addicts, prostitutes, drunks etc.- and as such are disconcerting and may prove frightening to 'respectable' citizens, invoking feelings of indignation and a strong sense of injustice and powerlessness.)

These studies, then, document the dependence of significant manifestations of insecurity on what many scholars term "disorder", i.e. a multiplicity of signs of incivility, present in an individual's neighborhood, which may be social or physical. The former are connected to facts or certain dynamics such as the attitudes of different types of individuals: e.g. drug dealers and their customers, prostitutes, beggars, etc. (Yin, 1985).

The latter, on the contrary refers to persistent elements in the composition of the urban landscape: abandoned or neglected buildings, graffiti, damaged telephone cabins, broken street lights, dirty streets etc. Incivilities may be active or deliberate - vandalism, graffiti etc.-or passive and involuntary, such as neglected buildings or rubbish left uncollected. These diverse situations and behaviors have an element in common: they all constitute a violation of rules and norms common to members of the population regarding the management and use of public spaces. Some researchers have pointed out that these signs of physical and social incivility act to demonstrate how much more easily the police, and other agencies of formal control within the community, display tolerance to antisocial behaviors, leading to a magnification in residents' concern for their personal safety, an increase in levels of fear and senses of isolation, and to a waning faith in the ability of informal and institutional structures to prevent crime. The strong correlation between antisocial behavior and sense of insecurity has been evidenced – not only by research – but also by social experiments. The most notable is the *Foot Patrol Experiment* conducted at Newark (New Jersey) in the mid-70s. In this experiment, police squads went on patrol on foot rather than by car.

They were successful in increasing citizens' general sense of security, and this was mainly because squads were able to deal with problems of social disorder in a different and more effective manner. In fact, the police, immersed in the life and problems of ordinary people in the various neighborhoods, came to be better known and esteemed by the people, and, through a concrete initiative of social conciliation were able to negotiate agreements with residents on the rules of conduct concerning the use of public spaces, setting thresholds for disorder and limiting the number of uncivil actions (Zani, 2003).

According to some researchers, social disorder tends to become diffuse, and, as it spreads out, leads, over time, to an increase in crime, and, in particular, in the number of thefts and robberies. This may be explained by the fact that the sense of insecurity resulting from series of uncivil actions can, over time reduce interaction and cooperation amongst residents, de-motivating them from taking any action to defend themselves and their community.

To give greater credibility to the existing scientific framework and body of literature concerning criminology and applied victimology, it has been deemed necessary to include international research studies, giving priority to exhaustive Italian studies which approach the question of social disorder and social fear from both sociological and anthropological perspectives. In Italy a rising interest in urban security began to emerge in the 90's, later than in other European and non European countries, such as for example France, Great Britain and the United States. The delay may be attributed to various factors. For many years the main focus of public opinion in Italy had been on macro criminality: the two major players being Mafia organized crime and political terrorism, in consequence micro criminality (of the predatory type) presented a minor concern.

General feelings of insecurity amongst the community and a rising demand for institutions to prime up the fight against crime began to arise in the 90's, when an increase in the crime rate (particularly street crime), an increasingly corrupt political system, and public indignation over the *Tangentopoli* (Clean Hands) affairs, shifted community attention towards the necessity of addressing the deficiencies in interior security. In those years sociologists also began to show interest in what came to be known as the "criminality issue".

These years also marked the introduction of the first statistical studies regarding perceptions of public safety and an increase in those concerning crime rates. The data revealed public opinion to be increasingly concerned with micro criminality and, at the same time, served as indicators of illegal immigration phenomena which were features of the late 80's and continue to occur to the present day; the continuous flow of illegal immigrants: Africans embankments on the Sicilian island of Lampedusa, and entry of non European community nationals over the Slovenian border, not to mention the Asian influx.

The tendency of vast sectors of the community, cutting across almost all social strata, is then to perceive these immigrants as vectors of social deviance and disorder.

The consequence is always a greater sense of insecurity within the community, which then makes ever pressing demands on institutions to deal with the problem. But the state finds itself in difficulty: the problem is new and they find they have not yet been able to adequately equip themselves to deal with it. The more established, traditional agencies, constructed around the laws of the penal code, prove to be unable to cope with the new emergency. The penal code crisis thus makes it imperative to find an alternative course of action to contend with criminality. And so a 'new prevention' is conceived, born of the penal system crisis, *which has as a consequence the complete transformation of criminality monitoring strategies and mechanisms* (Selmini, 2004).

The objectives of the 'new prevention' are, firstly, to reduce criminal phenomena, and, secondly, as a consequence, to increase social reassurance. Prevention means the implementation of strategies which limit criminal actions, by intervening before they even have a chance to eventuate. Thus penal code law, which comes into play after the fact must, by definition, be automatically excluded from the new preventative strategies, and alternative, better equipped agencies must step in to tackle the threat of deviance. Such agencies include: - local government bodies, social services, private businesses, voluntary bodies and common citizens. This change in perspective regarding local government bodies, has been termed the "new local government" the necessity of "doing something" has driven an innovation in decentralized administrative structures, leading to the assigning of new tasks and responsibilities to positions in areas in which they previously had no jurisdiction. For example, the mayor, and consequently the local council, today have responsibilities regarding public security which before were exclusively central state government tasks.

Prevention also means a change in the target groups of these new strategies: it now it is not exclusively the perpetrators of crime who become the subjects of study, but also their real and potential victims, and the community, in its widest sense.

Community prevention is one of the forms of new prevention. It means making citizens aware of the problems of criminality, affirming the necessity of forming a society which is able to defend itself through the use of new associative models and new forms of solidarity. One of these models is the pressure group. This phenomenon first makes its appearance in Italian society around the '90's, responding to new concerns regarding immigration, the increase in micro-criminality, the crisis of the First Republic and the ensuing mistrust of community members towards the political classes following the *Tangentopoli* affairs.

*"Pressure groups are organized, but weakly structured groups, formed of citizens that meet within their local areas and, mainly through forms of protest, oppose interventions that they consider would damage the living conditions in their local area, and demand improvement."(Della Porta, 2004).*

But the facts would indicate an expansion of Della Porta's definition, as they reveal a close connection between the emergence of pressure groups, especially in cities such as Turin and Modena, and migration phenomena, the latter being seen as one of the main causes of social unease, itself tied to rising criminality and a sense of community insecurity, and which in some cases, such as that of the Crocetta and Modena neighborhood (Chiodi, 1999), has created tensions which explode in violence and intolerance. This specific case may be seen as an instance of the Neo Chicagoan's labeling theory: the immigrant, as "different" is easily discernable; criminal acts committed by non European community members are given much greater attention than those committed by Italians; with the risk of drawing the conclusion that the terms: - Non European Economic Community member /Drug Dealer / Delinquent are equivalent.

Also in the Turin case, violent protests sparked off by senses of insecurity were at high risk of degenerating into a total urban crisis (Allasino, Bobbio, Neri, 2000). It is no coincidence that improving the social and physical environment can help to motivate citizens to participate in prevention. Also it was no coincidence in the Modena Crocetta neighborhood experience, a clear example of how residents, solely by improving the living conditions within their residential zone, were also able to improve their neighborhood's reputation. Urban decay is seen, therefore to be a further source of insecurity, fertile ground for deviant behaviors. The "theory of the broken windows" (Broken windows) of J. Wilson and G.L. Kelling could be a good example: dysfunctional uncivil behaviors increase in those zones in which formal and informal monitoring systems are lacking. In the end, decay generates further decay. Difficulties encountered by residents and authorities in taking action to improve the living standards in those areas in which there is a strong presence of groups with very distinct identities (residents, students, migrant communities, etc….) may be analyzed in the light of research studies carried out by the American Robert Sampson, in his studies on deviant behaviors as causing urban and social decay, expressed in terms of *collective efficacy*. According to Sampson, the theory of *Broken Windows* of Wilson and G.L. Kelling, is based on a mistaken premise: urban decay, in certain zones, does not increase because formal and informal controls are lacking, but rather because the community in those areas is neither deep-rooted nor homogeneous and above all is composed of individuals who do not know each other, and who do not feel any sense of belonging to those areas. According to Sampson's theory, therefore, one could state that the difficulty of managing those urban zones defined as "free areas" arises because of the varied nature of its "clientele". The composition of these areas being ever more heterogeneous, both in lifestyle and in interests, renders the task of creating any form of dialogue, or of reaching a common point of encounter complex, even when there are attempts to instill constructive interaction between the various categories of users of these city spaces (Thompson, 1998).

It has been noted that the increase in the sense of public insecurity and the corresponding decrease in sense of solidarity and cohesion between citizens tends to result in a reduction of social informal controls, in a spiraling process resulting in a reversal of the traditional relationship in which which more criminality → more insecurity so that on the contrary, more insecurity → more criminality.

Other experiments have confirmed *Broken Windows'* premises.

In fact, its thesis is substantiated by facts regarding the event of Italian citizen Abdul William Guibre's murder, an event which cannot be considered separately from its context of social tensions, built up, deliberately and painstakingly, in the months leading up to the event, by a spate of rumor mongering and bias constructs, which, fanning the flaring up of aggressive instincts, fostered xenophobic and racist actions (Taylor, 2001).

Broadcasts by press agencies fostering this social climate, reported the motive for the crime to be the theft of a packet of biscuits. This fact, even if were true cannot detract either from the seriousness of the crime, nor from its racist undertones. Media coverage of the 18 months previous to the event was full of 'isolated episodes' like this one. That no-one had lost their life up to that moment can only be considered fortuitous. It must be said that the deliberate and irresponsible exploitation of the problem of security (and its perception, presumably generally held throughout the community), is reinforcing racism and supporting the civil use of violence, mainly against nationals of foreign origin. Today the idea and the practice of 'do it yourself justice', for the most part against the innocent and the helpless, seem to form, regrettably, a noxious nexus with the cultural, political and regulatory legitimization of racism, and this is a cause for great concern (Valcarenghi, 2005).

Abdul was a young man, bearing, as many of his peers, the legacy of his parents' migratory travail, a story both of tragedy and prosperity, beginning the moment they decided to leave their native country, and continuing through years of struggle and sacrifice, of being prepared to put up with anything in order to fulfill their dream of a better life.

And Abdul also bore the resentment of one who, though an Italian citizen brought up in Italy, finds that his immigrant status persists; the terminology speaks for itself: "an immigrant of the second generation".

This event is an evident indicator of social unease, the tragic point of the iceberg. It may be seen as a symptom of a deep seated infection: a syndrome of fear; fear of the other, pumped up beyond its actual proportions by political interests through the false ideology of security. Projecting one's fear, one's anxieties and uncertainties on the other, makes it easier to identify the enemy as the cause of all ills. In substance, much of that which occurs in the name of social control and public order becomes reduced into a type of 'different' hunt, sustained by an ideological framework of xenophobia and racism. And this is occurring all over Italy, from North to South, from Milan to Castel Volturno and is no more than the result of an ideology of security which is based on structural insecurity, hopefully to be exorcised in the future, but with no guarantee that this will happen. Scapegoating of all those who are different becomes the order of the day, and manifests in both semantic and physical outbreaks of violence such as reported against Abba, a black Italian citizen of Milan.

Migration has always been a part of human history. In this era of the 'global village', distances have 'shrunk' and travel is effected with much greater ease than in the past.

In addition, a widening of economic and social disparities, throughout the world, has marked this historical period, further encouraging migratory phenomena. This issue cannot be avoided by pretending that it does not exist, or worse, by raising the barriers still higher, closing us up in a fortress until some desperate marginal manages to get in all the same.

So countries hosting immigrants must make a commitment to achieving complete integration, not only for ethical considerations or for promoting solidarity, but also as a prudent investment in the new citizens who will co-operate and make a real contribution to the growth of society.

This last example of Abdul substantiates the theory of the self propagation and transmissibility of aggressive violent and uncivil acts.

The phenomenon of fear of crime is thus integrated in a social sphere that contributes, through its specific dynamics, either to the extension or the contraction of insecurity throughout the society. The approach in this case evaluates fear of crime in relation to both indices of actual crime committed (in turn resulting from an increase in social confusion and linked to the overall sense of insecurity) and to the concept of personal fragility, so that the sense of insecurity and fear are considered as aspects arising from the individuals' sense of concrete " indices of incivility" and are measured strictly on an individual basis (Park,1999).

In short it must be stressed, that from social disorder, and a series of incivilities in general, ensue significant social consequences; above all provoking indignation of residents, who appear unfairly penalized by the social costs of that situation of urban decay. The fear of crime then increases, because even if only *soft crimes* are committed, the recurrence of a series of anti social actions leaves, on residents, the impression that no one in the neighborhood is able to enforce or instill compliance with the principal norms of coexistence, so that anything could happen.

Abdul Salam Guibre, a black Italian citizen, 19 years of age, died from repeated blows to the head, in Milan.

The reality speaks for itself: A dead boy, a father with his son in jail, local citizen groups (*Amministrazione Meneghina*) who propose excluding children of illegal immigrants from public crèches, or blocking access of clandestine immigrants to casualty departments in hospitals.

The city's governing institutions found difficulty in giving an adequate reaction to this event that, long past being an alarm bell, was the sign of an existing miserable social condition, a benchmark against which the efficacy of political decisions may be gauged.

(It certainly is not, as in the recent proposal to oblige doctors to report all illegal immigrants staying in hospital, thus denying the right to health, that one can resolve problems of legality and security) Ever greater levels of urban insecurity generating tensions which result in homicide are certainly not an excellent result for those who expected, through the use of iron fist tactics, to increase levels of security.

At this point, it is important to bring in the concepts of territoriality, defined as a geographical area which is in some way *personalized* or defined by physical and social border signs (markers). Many authors link the concept of "regulation of privacy," to territorial protection, making a distinction between primary and public or secondary space.

The former is delimited by physical markers which are non verbal signs of ownership, monitoring and protection, making a clear division between this area and that in others' dominion (plants, gardens, signs, hedges etc). This concept is of great interest in the study of the fear of crime, as it underlines the strong relationship between possession of territory and its social control, so that it appears obvious that places which are less "territorialized" are subject to less control and may encourage the expansion of social deviance and insecurity. This theory pictures a kind of conceptual map with one's own residence in the centre, as the most important place. The further one moves out from the centre of this map, the more the sense of ownership of areas decreases, and the more the significance of events, occurring in those areas, lessens.

A consequence of this is the creation of interstitial areas which appear dangerous both in reality (evidencing higher rates of victimization) and in social perception (more insecurity). Therefore a well developed "territoriality" means increased social interaction and a higher sense of community with a consequent decrease in fear of crime and less property violations. The concept of "behavioral *setting*" defines, on the other hand a specific place/situation whose physical or social characteristics engender particular patterns of behavior (Selmini, 2004).

Hence the study of these settings and their characteristics may prove more useful for predicting the behaviors of individuals than for discerning their personal characteristics, in as much as roads and housing areas constitute defined spaces that can be seen as places that generate particular behaviors and consistent patterns of social relationships.

Not only does belonging to a social group determine certain prejudices and views, it also influences an individual's choices and shapes his most hidden fears. The acceptance of a risk, such as the risk of becoming a victim, is not, as in Abba's case, a question of personal choice.

It is well known that any person who makes an important choice, without consulting anyone, or heeding advice given by close friends and relatives, will be severely reprimanded and certainly will not enjoy their support in the event of a worst case scenario. Factors forming the perception of risk levels, therefore, are always social; very rarely is it the case that the risk assessment is made by a sole, reasonable individual with no social relations (Douglas,1991).

The appraisal of the magnitude of danger, as an instance of rational individual behavior, constitutes a minimal contribution to the genesis of fear. Rather, it has been found that issues tied to commonly held notions of justice, equity, and the social distribution of obligations and advantages, are implicated in shaping the perception of danger, and thus the insurgence of fear, as in Abba's assailants. It does not result only from the actual circumstances of real danger, but from the conception of being scarcely protected, hence at the mercy of events, abandoned in a world of dangers. The impression of social disorder in some urban areas and the failure of public authorities to deal with it are clearly manifested in the fear of criminality.

It is, then appropriate to speak of "*Social vulnerability*" a concept which describes and analyses the multiple social variables which determine the quality of life (Santinello, Gonzi, & Scacchi,1998).

The expression of fear of crime is, in the end, an indication of one who feels particularly attackable, due to the insecurity of their social position, an example of which is provided by Mr. Cristoferi and his son (the cafe owners), who, without hesitation, chased after and assaulted Abba and his friends for no more than a suspected theft.

In conclusion, levels of social integration and trust amongst community members constitute the "social capital" of a community, and the analysis of these factors serves to illuminate the origin of the fear of crime (Cavalletti, 2005).

Where trust is lacking, fear reigns unchecked. Thus urban insecurity is about the redistribution of social risks; whilst fear of crime is about the social grapevine's amplification of facts and circumstances which original reference was relatively bland.

The complexity of the issue is evidenced when the attempt is made to define fear as a function of rising crime rates. Present studies refer, also to the political influences on fear of crime. Public accusation of insecurity is a sign of rising social unease on the rise, but it is above all means to vehicle the attention of public institutions and authorities to the issue.

The relation between the "*concern for public security*" and "*apprehension lived privately*", that is, in sociological terms, between the actual context lived in and the determination of levels of sanctions regulating inter and intra individual relations, is defined, not by the objective evaluation of fear, but by the 'virtues' that lead to a politicization of that fear.

## SETTING THE STAGE

This work is divided into two sections, one examines the theoretical bases of Applied Criminology and Victimology, using traditional teaching methods (the written text); whilst the other is based on the same theoretical premises as the first but will adopt the FAD (e-learning) methodology, of a course to be delivered online. There are four main phases within the process of creating online content for training purposes:

1. Project Planning
2. Content development
3. Design
4. Overall Review, function testing and usability testing

The Anthropo-Sociological approach of Applied Criminology and Victimology: social unrest, insecurity, fear project-plan includes a preliminary analysis of training needs, such as the development of critical thinking, presenting, in response to this need theories and case studies for reflection by the user. The *project planning* is divided into nine key stages, each of which is to be considered fundamental to the creation of a course on criminology and applied victimology.

- A statement of both the objectives and structuring of the course and the didactic materials to be delivered
- Selection of resources to be utilized has been: quizzes and/or detailed studies, tool bars;
- Definition of characteristics of eventual users of the online course: the *target audience*;
- Establishment of educational objectives to be achieved, both overall, and, as in this case, those of a single unit.
- A detailed description, presented in Power point of the online course content, specifying the types of information to be used, such as information slides, study slides, quizzes (included in this summary, but, for the purposes of complying with APA recommendations, does not appear in the format of a power point presentation, but as a word document.)
- The evaluation strategy, which constitutes, at the same time, a final course assessment and a test of the efficacy of the application; it takes the form of tests and a conceptual map;

## CASE DESCRIPTION

The Education Unit will be divided into the following sections:

- Introduction
- The broad scope of Criminology
- Crime, Social Disorder and Urban Insecurity
- Theory of Cultural Conflicts
- Unit Summary
- References

The use of B. S. Bloom's taxonomy of cognitive objectives when structuring each section is to be recommended, to ensure clarity when expounding

*Table 1. B. S. Bloom's taxonomy*

| | |
|---|---|
| 1. Knowledge: ability to recall memorized material | Easy to teach and to measure |
| Understanding: capacity to understand the meaning of a piece of information and being able to transform it | |
| 2. Application: capacity to use known materials to solve new problems | |
| 3. Analysis: capacity to separate the elements highlighting their relationships to each other | |
| 4. Synthesis: ability to join up elements in order to form a new organized and coherent structure | |
| 5. Evaluation: ability to independently make critical judgments of value and method | Hard to teach and to measure |

arguments, using criteria such as those listed in the following table.

The use of this Education Unit will achieve the following objectives:

- The definition of criminology as an attempt to explain the causes of crime using two approaches anthropological and sociological.
- Definition of the sociological approach, crime and social disorder from the point of view of individual vulnerability using reliable statistical methods to examine mass phenomena. Mass statistics tends to analyze the various macro social factors generating crime; the sociological approach to criminology is a wide-ranging study based on society and on the historical context in general..
- Definition of the anthropological approach, which focuses on studying the individual, and on theories of cultural conflicts that lead to the development of criminal events. Sellin was on of the most important theorists in the field. His cultural conflict view is that man is now suffering from a form of social fear, and one of the major causes is the dilemma generated by the impact between a host culture and that of its new immigrants.

## Introduction

- The subject matters of Criminology are: criminal offences, the perpetrators and the various forms of social reaction to crime, the personality of the victim.
- Criminology is an attempt to explain the causes of crime using two approaches: anthropological and sociological.
- The Anthropological Approach addresses man as the perpetrator of crime, and searches for organic, psychological, motivational, and psychosocial factors that may have led to the illegitimate conduct.
- The Sociological Approach, on the other hand is interested in the macro factors influencing the insurgence of crime.

## The Broad Scope of Criminology

The original development of criminology was along two different schools of thought: sociological and anthropological. Today, this divergence has become attenuated, the two lines of thought are now seen as complementary, and have been incorporated because the insights from research into criminal conduct, have demonstrated influences of social phenomena, such as families, but also the value of the individual approach, which involves monitoring of how environmental influences are reflected on the individual, and clarifies the different individual vulnerability thresholds.

Conditions of extreme poverty, war, over population in cities and outskirts, mass emigration, unemployment, render individuals vulnerable, both physically and psychologically, and such vulnerability tends to be passed on to future generations. Those who have the capacity to emigrate tend, for the most part, to be young, healthy, enterprising

*Figure 1. Synthesis of the text*

| |
|---|
| Today the criminal is studied from the point of view of his vulnerability to socio environmental factors that lead to the formation of a criminal attitude |

*Figure 2. Synthesis of the text*

| |
|---|
| A variety of factors determine individual fragility or vulnerability: unemployment, poverty, mass emigration, factors which prove to be deleterious, both physically and mentally |

and with sufficient personal conviction to be able to make the difficult adjustments to the different social and legal administrations of their country of destination, and this often provides a type of guarantee of survival, and hope for the future.

Thus the influence of both the macro and the micro factors must be determined. Even though originally, the criminological approach, was based solely on discerning a criminal's individual motivations, it was later realized that in order to determine the etiology of crime it was also necessary to incorporate social factors, including the social means of control, prevention and the various profiles of crime.

## Mass Statistics

Mass statistics is the study of events expressed in numerical values; but whereas they are successful in discerning the influence of macro social elements, they are not as efficacious in revealing the influence of micro social factors, or critical personal conditions. Also responsibility for criminal conduct is as much of the society as of the individual: neither can be exempted from liability. For this reason, it is essential to adopt an integrated approach, that takes into account both social factors and the diverse individual reactions to those negative environmental conditions.

This method proves to be indispensable in the understanding of the phenomenon of the dissemination of criminality and to define its features in a general sense, for example: its frequency and the quantitative and qualitative variations in the prevalence and type of crime committed.

Mass statistics usually limits itself to a phenomenological explanation of criminal behavior. It works with data provided by law enforcement bodies, and assesses them in relation to a large number of variables: sex, age, type of crime, employment, marital status, race, religion, etc.

## Study of Individual Factors

Individual based methods within criminological research involve the study of either individuals or small groups, supported by psychological and medical research, in order to reach a better understanding of the phenomenon through a more intense and multidisciplinary analysis, in effect,

*Figure 3. Synthesis of the text*

| |
|---|
| In criminology mass statistics is used to reveal macro social causative factors, thus giving an overall picture of the causes of criminal conduct, but this method of analysis can never manage to determine those factors which lead an individual to choose to perpetrate a crime |

*Figure 4. Synthesis of the text*

| |
|---|
| The individual approach within criminology, unlike the mass or macro perspective, focuses on the individual criminal in order to determine those factors which motivated him to commit a crime |

leading to an holistic approach.

## Crime, Social Disorder and Urban Insecurity

In the mid 1900's, Criminal Sociology in the U.S.A. benefited from significant insights provided by Shaw (founder of the Chicago School) in his studies of *Criminal Areas*, defined as zones in the city in which the majority of criminal activity is perpetrated. These areas are inhabited by people in need of social welfare services (the poorest sector of the population), they are to be found in every major metropolis and feature: overcrowding, poor hygiene, inadequate public utilities.

However Shaw's work is flawed by the inherent contradictions. They are found across the gamma of works, emanating, firstly from the Chicago School, and secondly from the Neo-Chicagoans and in this respect we may also include the work of the labeling theorists. The work of Talcott Parsons is an exception, rather than making deductions from preexisting criminal theory, he took an inductive approach: making objective factual observations of deviant behavior and social control to arrive at theory.

The Chicago school considered criminality as a social disease without adequately taking into account the significance of historical and cultural factors in determining the complex social problem of social disorganization. Notwithstanding this limitation, the Chicago School approach is laudable, as a value neutral and rigorously scientific approach. The ecologists were those who conducted the first systematic studies on youth gangs, the homeless and the various forms of organized crime.

- Areas of greatest criminal activity are those in which the highest rates of suicide, of mental illness, and prostitution *etc.* are to be found and is at the same time an area characterized by a constant turnover within the population, and a predominance of marginals and moral breakdown. To the Chicago school must also be accorded the

*Figure 5. Synthesis of the text*

| |
|---|
| A case to which the individual approach is applicable is that of the two Milan cafe owners who, after seeing three black young men fleeing from their cafe, believed that they had committed a robbery, then they attacked these young men dealing a lethal blow to one of them, Abba |

*Figure 6. Synthesis of the text*

| |
|---|
| A limitation of the Chicago School is that it considers social disorganization without analyzing the influence of historical and political factors. But paradoxically, this is also al merit because it excludes any possible moralistic bias, whilst adopting a rigorous scientific methodology |

merit of having established a value neutral account of the heterogeneous world of deviance. Its extraordinary efficacy is due to its original analysis techniques, in defining not only the environment in which deviance can appear, but also the modus operandi and 'career' of the deviant character.

- Dwellers of overcrowded and marginal zones tend to remain in these areas, being neither capable nor interested in moving due to low levels of personal motivation, and tend to resign themselves to their miserable condition. These neighborhoods become attractive to those seeking a more permissive environment, appropriate to their status as habitual offenders.

Studies have found that, despite continual turnover of residents, the crime rate remains consistently high: demonstrating that criminal events depend on the characteristics of the social environment. So, *the social environment is the single most important factor in determining the genesis of crime*.

But the theory of "criminal areas" has medium-range coverage, i.e. it does not cover all aspects of criminality or more generalized phenomena such as the spread of crime in other types of environments, but is limited to that of petty crime and delinquency.

- Connected to the concept of social disorder is the problem of social control, namely the way in which a society is able to induce its individuals to conform to a single coherent system of customs, traditions, and norms.
- The concept of social disorder is linked to that of marginality, the condition of those who live in areas of urban decay. The immigrant is particularly disadvantaged, the loss of cultural roots and difficulty of integrating in the new cultural context tends to marginalize almost all of them.

To repeat: social disorder occurs when agents of social control lose their effectiveness, in particular the group and the family. And members of lower socio economic status, for example new immigrants who are, more than the more settled immigrants, at the mercy of different sets of social conditions, tend to be most at risk of developing criminal characters.

- Fear of crime and the fear of being its victim are part of a phenomenon that is becoming ever more a characteristic of contemporary society, and leads to serious social and psychological consequences. Many researchers' stress that insecurity could become a critical factor in the processes leading to anxiety and stress, becoming a limiting factor on people's behavior and movements and fundamentally altering the individual's social interactions. Each society experiences different levels of crime and "fear". The relationship between real experiences

*Figure 7. Synthesis of the text*

| |
|---|
| Guibre Abdoul Salam, 19 years old, an Italian citizen, who died in Zuretti street, in Milan from lethal blows to the head. A tragic event which moved vast sector of the Milan's public and of the young people to form a movement of solidarity with Abba and those in a similar condition, calling for a response from law enforcement agencies to protect persons such as Abba who, being colored or marginal, tend to be unjustly accused of criminal actions or behaviors. Hopefully, the solidarity of the young man is a sign that perhaps is in a future society, any policy maker will consider the needs of a multicultural society |

and the phenomena of "anxiety" is rather complex. For instance, in the United States crime rates are much lower today than they were twenty years ago, yet the fear has not diminished. No correlation has been found between fear of crime and direct experience of the phenomenon: fear of crime results from the particular cultural environment in which experience is amplified by socially transmitted constructions and by common sense. One could say that fear of crime has been "institutionalized" having become an integral part of the urban landscape. There is also a huge industry of "security", whose existence depends on the dissemination of fear. Fear of crime does not come out of nothing: it is certainly based on real experience, but blown up by interests that could profit from its magnification.

It will look at the types of crime which affect young people the most and what can be done to reduce the impact of crime and fear of crime.

- In 1978 Albert Hunter stated that "the fear in an urban setting is above all a fear of social disorder, which can be considered to constitute a threat to the individual"; he emphasized the fact that the origins of social disorder could be traced back as much to minor infringements (incivilities) as to the more serious offences (crimes), and stated that the more the former proves to be a common occurrence, the higher the incidence of the latter.

These studies, then, document the dependence of significant manifestations of insecurity on what many scholars term "disorder", i.e. a multiplicity of signs of incivility, present in an individual's neighborhood, which may be social or physical. The former are connected to facts or certain dynamics such as the attitudes of different types of individuals: e.g. drug dealers and their customers, prostitutes, beggars, etc.

The latter, on the contrary refers to persistent elements in the composition of the urban landscape: abandoned or neglected buildings, graffiti, damaged telephone cabins, broken street lights, dirty streets etc.

It has been noted that the increase in the sense of public insecurity and the corresponding decrease in sense of solidarity and cohesion between citizens tends to result in a reduction of social informal controls, in a spiraling process resulting in a reversal of the traditional relationship in which more criminality → more insecurity so that on the contrary, more insecurity → more criminality.

The phenomenon of fear of crime is thus integrated in a social sphere that contributes, through

*Figure 8. Synthesis of the text*

In summary we can say that there are three hypotheses which have been tested in several research studies: according to the first, fear of crime depends on the number of predatory crimes; for the second, it is due also to physical or social disorder in the community and for the third one social disorder creates fear either directly or indirectly, and leads to an increase in the predatory crime rate

its specific dynamics, either to the extension or to the contraction of insecurity throughout the society. The approach in this case evaluates fear of crime in relation to both indices of actual crime committed (in turn resulting from an increase in social confusion and linked to the overall sense of insecurity) and to the concept of personal fragility, so that the sense of insecurity and fear are considered as aspects arising from the individuals' sense of concrete " indices of incivility" and are measured strictly on an individual basis.

In short it must be stressed, that from social disorder, and a series of incivilities in general, ensue significant social consequences; above all provoking indignation of residents, who appear unfairly penalized by the social costs of that situation of urban decay. The fear of crime then increases, because even if only *soft crimes* are committed, the recurrence of a series of anti social actions leaves, on residents, the impression that no one in the neighborhood is able to enforce or instill compliance with the principal norms of coexistence, so that anything could happen.

Fear of crime was created in a social context that is unable to guarantee security because the individual in the face of social disorder is tormented by insecurity.

It is interesting to mention the concepts of territoriality, defined as a geographical area which is in some way *personalized* or defined by physical and social border signs (markers). Many authors link the concept of "regulation of privacy," to territorial protection, making a distinction between primary and public or secondary space.

The individual, living in an unstable and rapidly changing society, finds himself no longer able to regulate his behavior according to the old criteria, and becomes himself disorganized in conduct. This approach has a wider coverage than the ecological theory, as it includes those classes which, even if not afflicted by economic hardships, nevertheless suffer the influence of disorganization.

## Theory of Cultural Conflicts

The Theory of Sellin (1938) nominates two types of cultural conflicts:

*Figure 9. Synthesis of the text*

Fear of crime is generated in a social context that is unable to guarantee security, in fact the individual, finding himself in a context of social disorder, is plagued by insecurity

*Table 2. The theory of Sellin: two types of cultural conflicts*

| |
|---|
| Primary cultural conflicts: direct friction between two cultural systems, occurring when the differences between the two cultures are too vast |
| Secondary cultural conflicts: discrimination and rejection by a host society, who see immigrants as foreign and too different from its own members |

1. Primary cultural conflicts or frictions between two cultural systems which differ widely from each other.
2. Secondary Cultural Conflicts.

Regards those who move into a new cultural system, and find a host society with different rules, customs, and values which are sometimes in conflict with their own. The hosting society, regarding the new individuals as outsiders and different, may discriminate against and reject them.

But this theory does not address the correlation between delinquency and immigration, a complex relationship which involves many variables, even if it is undeniable that cultural conflicts tend to promote the insurgence of delinquency and deviance.

Immigrants are most at risk because they must integrate into a society with a different culture, with different mores and norms.

In order for there to be integrated behavior, there must be harmony between the *normative values of the group to which one belongs and values expressed by the law*. So, in order to avoid criminal behavior, rules prohibiting certain behaviors, other than being interiorized by the individual must be supported by the group he belongs to. Cultural conflicts occur when some traditional values are no longer accepted in the transition from one cultural set of values to another. According to Thorsten Sellin, the American sociologist who, in the late 30s, proposed the theory of cultural conflict, in every society there is a system of values and standards of conduct, transmitted from generation to generation, which identify the actions to be taken towards individuals in certain situations and that are.

The beginning of Sellin's goes back to the U.S. school of the 30's. The term *structural-functionalism* indicates that the *structure*, namely the set of all relations between individuals in that society, must be instrumental to the maintenance and stability of the social system. In other words, that the structure pursues the fundamental aim of the social system, namely the integration of its individual social members to ensure the maintenance of the system itself.

Representatives of structural functionalism were: Parsons, Merton, Johnson.

Social members regulate their behavior through a set of rules which they come to internalize as their own, compliance or otherwise of these standards leads to *conformity* or *deviance*.

- *Conformity* is the lifestyle, consistent with all the rules, that is, a behavior which is

*Figure 10. - Synthesis of the text*

| |
|---|
| The term structural-functionalism suggests that in order to maintain stability, a society must have a very strong structure so as to ensure that all its individuals can be integrated |

permitted and generally accepted, and constitutes a psychological choice. Then there is a clear awareness that makes the subject constantly informed of the conformity or otherwise of his conduct.

The attitude of conformant behavior is formed by:

- Acquisition of standards, by processes of socialization;
- Maintenance and reinforcement learning, using agents of social control, the threat of sanctions, appeals to ideology and interests.
    - There is deviance only if the violation is the result of a clear choice, and only if the violation breaks a rule which has not lost significance. So deviance is defined as the taking of an oppositional stance against a standard.

Therefore, the deviant attitude implies an attitude of *ambivalence* towards the norm: as the deviant is fully aware of the norm, and of its application, he has interiorized it; however he does not accept its authority. Moreover, to be defined as deviant, it is necessary that the non conformant behavior relates to fundamental norms: only the non-compliance with those rules which still retain credibility and are considered highly important, generate deviance.

*Figure 11. Map summary*

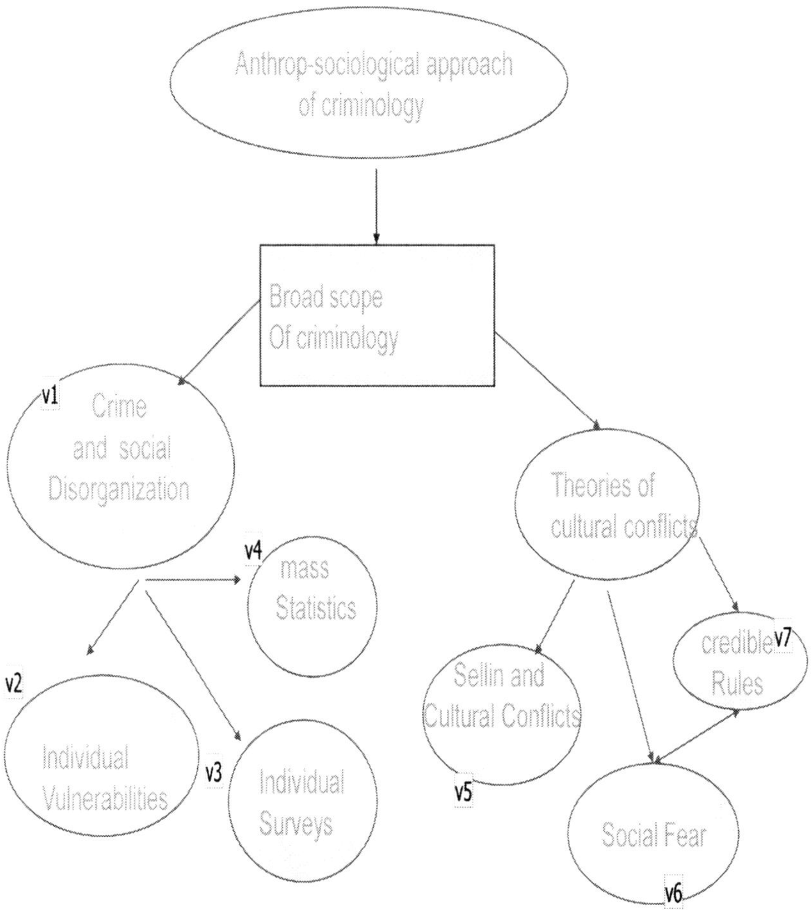

## CONCLUSION

Criminology is divided into two strands: the anthropological and sociological. The first studies the personality of the delinquent subject through the analysis of organic and environmental factors. The other approach looks at crime as a social phenomenon by analyzing the criminal incident in relation to the dynamics of the society in which the criminal finds himself committing a crime.

This is an empirical science and it is thus the observation of actuality which provides the material for analysis: the methodologies are statistical and sociological (mass statistics, individual studies, field surveys, study of sample groups, ...).

1 A tried and tested law of criminology is that the more stable and orderly the social environment is, the less deviant behavior occurs. Criminology finds a correlation between deviance and social disorganization that is, the deviant may be a normal person, who lives in a society, in a community, but when he finds his social environment becoming disrupted, his conduct also tends to be disorganized.

2 Criminal conduct today is studied by analyzing the individual vulnerability, or how the individual, affected by both individual and environmental factors, comes to commit a crime.

3 The individual approach within criminology, unlike the mass or macro perspective, focuses on the individual criminal in order to determine those factors which motivated him to commit a crime.

4 In criminology mass statistics is used to reveal macro social causative factors, thus giving an overall picture of the causes of criminal conduct, but this method of analysis can never manage to determine those factors which lead an individual to choose to perpetrate a crime.

5 Deviance and social disorder arise only if rules are ambiguous and lack credibility.

6 We have primary cultural conflicts where two cultures clash, because the differences between them are too great. The secondary cultural conflicts are cases where a society hosting immigrants sees them as outsiders and too different.

7- Fear of crime is generated in a social context that is unable to guarantee security because the individual, in the face of social disorder, is plagued by insecurity.

## REFERENCES

Balloni, A. (1983). *Criminologia in prospettiva.* Bologna, Italy: Clueb.

Balloni, A., & Bisi, R. (Eds.). (1996). *Criminologia applicata per l'investigazione e la sicurezza.* Milano, Italy: FrancoAngeli.

Bandini, T. (2003). *Criminologia, il contributo della ricerca alla conoscenza del crimine e della reazione sociale.* Milano, Italy: Giuffrè.

Barbagli, M., & Gatti, U. (2005). *Prevenire la criminalità*, Bologna, Italy: il Mulino.

Barbagli, M., & Sabbadini, L. (1999). *La sicurezza dei cittadini.* Bologna, Italy: il Mulino.

Cavalletti, A. (2005). *La città biopolitica – Mitologie della sicurezza.* Milano, Italy: Mondadori.

Clarke, R. V., & Felson, M. (Eds.). (1993). *Routine activities and crime prevention.* New Brunswick, NJ: Transaction.

Milanesi, E., & Naldi, A. (2001). *Cantando sotto la pioggia. Insicurezza e sicurezza urbana*, Milano, Italy: FrancoAngeli.

Park, R. E., Burgess, E. W., & McKenzie, R. D. (1999). *La città*. Torino, Italy: Edizioni di Comunità.

Roché, S. (1998). *Sociologie politique de l'insécurité,* Paris: Puf.

Santinello, M., Gonzi, P., & Scacchi, L. (1998). *Le paure della criminalità: aspetti psicosociali di comunità*. Milano, Italy: Giuffrè.

Selmini, R. (Ed.). (2004). *La sicurezza urbana*. Bologna, Italy: il Mulino.

Shaw, E.(1979). Agenda Setting and Mass Communication Theory. *Gazette International Journal for Mass Communication Studies, XXV*(2).

Taylor, R. B. (2001). *Breaking away from broken windows*. Boulder, CO: Westview Press.

Thompson, K. (1998). *Moral panics.* London: Routledge.

Yin, P. P. (1985). *Victimization and the aged.* Springfield, IL: Chas C. Thomas.

Zani, B. (Ed.). (2003). *Sentirsi in/sicuri in città.* Bologna, Italy: il Mulino.

## WEBSITES

http://milano.blogosfere.it/2008/09/milano-sotto-shock-per-lomicidio-di-abba-in-via-zuretti-fiori-e-biglietti-i-nostri-video-e-foto.html

http://www.repubblica.it/2008/04/sezioni/cronaca/milano-razzismo/corteo-disordini/corteo-disordini.html

http://www.crimeblog.it/post/1259/omicidio-abdul-guibre-convalidato-il-fermo-dei-due-aggressori

## ADDITIONAL READING

Amendola, C. (Ed.). (2003). *Il governo della città sicura.* Napoli, Italy: Liguori.

Amerio, P. (Ed.). (1999). *Il senso della sicurezza.* Milano, Italy: Unicopli.

Bauman, Z. (2000). *La solitudine del cittadino globale.* Milano, Italy: Feltrinelli.

Bauman, Z. (2005). *Fiducia e paura nelle città.* Milano, Italy: Mondadori.

Baumer, T. L. (1985). Testing a general model of fear of crime: data from a national Sample. *Journal of Research in Crime and Delinquency*, 22.

Luhmann, N. (1996). *Sociologia del rischio.* Milano, Italy: Mondadori.

Manunta, G. (1996). Teoria e metodologie di sicurezza. In A. Balloni & Bisi R. (Eds.), *Criminologia applicata per l'investigazione e la sicurezza,* (pp. 88-181). Milano, Italy: FrancoAngeli.

# Chapter 11
# Teaching Criminology and Police Science for Postgraduate Students at the Ruhr-University Bochum, Germany

**Diana Ziegleder**
*Ruhr-University Bochum, Germany*

**Felix Feldmann-Hahn**
*Ruhr-University Bochum, Germany*

## EXECUTIVE SUMMARY

*This case study looks at the postgraduate program in Criminology and Police Science at the Ruhr-University Bochum, Germany. This practice oriented course of study is designed as a distance learning course (blended learning) and therefore focuses on techniques of e-learning. The case study describes the history of origins and examines the educational situation before this master's program was established and how an idea became reality. It is one of the very few possibilities in Germany to receive a deeper insight into criminology and police science. Despite the fact, that the students are all professionals and thus working mostly full time, the technical premises make a discourse possible as in on-campus programs. These innovative forms of learning are the focal point of the following case study. It is our aim to provide insight into how a master's program could be set up and to promote new concepts of e-learning in the field of criminology.*

## BACKGROUND

To date there are two other courses of study dealing with criminology in Germany besides the master's program in Criminology and Police Science at the Ruhr-University Bochum. In addition to two master's programs in the Social Science department of the University of Hamburg (M.A. in International Criminology - consecutive since 2005/as research studies from 1984-2005 & a non-consecutive Master since 2007), a Master of Laws (LL.M.) in Criminology and Criminal Justice is taught at Greifswald since 2006.

DOI: 10.4018/978-1-60566-872-7.ch011

It was a long road to the emancipation of these programs however. The idea of a full and independent course of study in criminology is relatively new in Germany. Whereas in other countries – especially the United States of America (Bufkin, 2004), but also many European countries[1] – teaching criminology (and/or criminal justice) has a long tradition and has therefore brought up almost uncountable programs, a full course of study in Germany was for a long time not in sight. The education of criminological aspects was mostly restricted to basics and, for various reasons, was insufficient or had little practical relevance (Feltes, 2005a, p. 1).

For a long period of time, teaching criminology at most universities was attached to the law schools. Predominantly in the first semester, law students received (and still receive) the possibility to learn about the scientific study of crime and criminal behavior. However, at most universities there only existed one course dealing with criminology – mainly giving the students a brief introduction and supporting the lectures in criminal law. Most other students, although confronted with deviant behavior in their jobs, e.g. of psychology or prospective teachers, did not and still do not get a mandatory criminological introduction during their studies.

Looking at the praxis showed that the situation within institutions such as the police was also not satisfying. There were numerous skill enhancements, which were however mostly orientated on current problems and events. Most students considered the criminological component to be difficult to understand or irritating (Feltes, 2005a, p. 1).

Seldom was there a systematic, theoretical preparation of problems and experiences – especially not with the focus on criminology. For a long time, there was no profound, interdisciplinary reflection of the causes of deviant behavior. The need (as well as the calls [see Löschper, 1986]) for a postgraduate, full course of study grew, after the aspect of interdisciplinarity had developed within the academic discussion (so called "Kommunale Kriminalprävention") and had started to be implemented into every day police work in the mid 90´s. Nonetheless a course of study which was orientated like that in the first place was still missing. These needs also could not be met by police intern study programs (like the German Police University), since they are only open to police officers. Prospects from other occupational backgrounds did not have the chance to attend those programs. Therefore there was a gap in the educational system in both teaching criminology as well as interdisciplinary focused study courses in Germany.

Although having realized that within the respective undergraduate studies the courses in criminology did not present much more than a glimpse (and therefore needing extension) and according to the change in the way of dealing with crime in an interdisciplinary way, it took until the turn of the millennium to change. Since the beginning of the new century these changes are becoming apparent in Germany, too. Slowly, the idea established that knowledge of deviant behavior is important not only to police officers, but also to a variety of other occupations, such as social work, teaching, psychology and that, a postgraduate program was necessary.

In Bochum, this change is irrevocably linked with the name Professor Dr. Thomas Feltes M.A. Feltes holds the chair for criminology, criminal policy, and police science at the law faculty at the Ruhr-University Bochum since 2002. With degrees in law as well as educational science and being headmaster of a police academy for many years, he combines experiences within academia and practice.

The Ruhr-University seemed to be the right place for developing ideas about a master´s program in criminology, because of its history and its geographical position. The city with a population of almost 400.000, is situated in the west of Germany right in the heart of the so called Ruhr Area. The coal and steel industry boomed in the

*Figure 1. Ruhr-University Bochum, Germany*

mid-nineteenth century and made the Ruhr Area Germany's most important industrial region. The industry provided hundreds of thousands of jobs for people coming from all over Europe – mainly the eastern countries – making Bochum and the Ruhr Area a melting pot.

The demand for coal decreased after 1958, and the Ruhr Area found itself in a deep structural and financial crisis. The opening of the Ruhr-University in 1965 was therefore a great hope in the midst of that crisis. It was supposed to push ahead the structural change in the region. Among other things (car industry, etc.) it helped the region to stay the most populated area in Germany and the third largest in Europe[2].

Located in the centre of this cosmopolitan metropolitan region of over five million people, the Ruhr-University Bochum (RUB) recruits students from home and abroad. It combines people from different nationalities as well as backgrounds and does not only assure a good infrastructure (libraries, etc.), but continual improvement of the quality of research and teaching. The university, known as the first new university in post-war Germany, represents innovation and is among the top research universities in Germany. It exceeds excellence in research and diversity in its international contacts. Since it is advanced like no other university in Germany by implementing the Bologna Process (19th June 1999), it seemed like an ideal place for putting the idea of a master´s program in criminology into action. (See Figure 1)

## SETTING THE STAGE

### Planning, Application and Accreditation

The planning and structuring began mid 2003 with the development of a draft for a master´s course in criminology and police science. At this early stage it was important to think of the constituting elements of a new course of study. Besides the curriculum, participants had to be thought of and contacted as well as possible cooperations. The curriculum took an especially long time to be developed. This early stage is probably the hardest one, since it is the basis on which the next steps can be successfully taken.

Besides the principle topic of *criminology*, the developers decided to put emphasis on *police science* and on an interdisciplinary concept. The need for a postgraduate program dealing with criminology results from the current belief that effective measures towards crime prevention and reduction can only be developed in a network between research, police, justice, politics and social work (Feltes, 2008, p. 8). This calls for an integrated concept of learning for professionals coming from these different areas in order to develop their points of view and their knowledge upon the other. Only by understanding the way of working and the way of thinking of other professions, can a problem-free and goal-orientated communication be established. The need of communication between the disciplines (extending beyond the practical everyday contact) is also apparent (cp. Feltes, 2005, 2008). Therefore the idea behind the master's program was to enhance the knowledge and understanding of each other's profession in order to improve everyday's work, but also in order to rethink the daily routine, working conditions, methods of problem solution as well as theories. The combination between criminology and police science meets this demand and assists in supplementing, new approaches and a better understanding into the very often hierarchical institutions such as the police force (cp. Feltes, 2008).

The idea of teaching police science was especially new in Germany, although being a topic of research for several decades in many states of the U.S. The idea to research the connections within and attitudes of the police towards social groups, the coverage of the police on the news, the reputation of the police among the population and particularly the efficiency and way of acting of the police only evolved a couple of years ago in Germany (Schwind, 2007, p. 13). By deciding to include police science into the master's program, this branch of science receives further attention and demonstrates the innovative focus of the program.

After designing, reflecting on and initiating the first steps towards a program on a rather internal level, the next steps for the master's program required the acceptance of the faculty as well as the university. Since the Chair of Criminology had been annexed to the Law School of the Ruhr-University Bochum, the latter was the next to be involved in the process. In July 2004, the Law School Conference decided to apply the master's program as a postgraduate course. Only two months later the committee of teaching of the university discussed the application and finally approved it in November 2004. Another committee (for planning, structure and finance) accepted the request on 6th December 2004.

The procedure then got more detailed. In January 2005 the study conditions had to be worked out, but there was still one bigger step to be taken if the program was to start operating.

The Standing Conference of the Ministers of Education and Cultural Affairs of the Länder in the Federal Republic (KMK) framed, that according the Bologna process new courses of study need to run through a process of accreditation (KMK, 2003/2008). This required the permission of the rectorship for establishing and accrediting the master's program. This was given still in January 2005. The accreditation procedure was opened on 4th April 2005 and covered the full application for accreditation. Based upon this written presentation of the planned program, scientific external experts visited the Ruhr-University on 24th June 2005. After talking to the rectorship and stakeholders included in the design and programming of the master's program, the external experts agreed to recommend the master's program to the accreditation company AQAS. The incoming costs were covered by the university, the faculty and the chair.

*Figure 2. From idea to reality: steps towards the master's program in Criminology and Police Science at the Ruhr-University Bochum (extended overview/original by Feltes 2005b).*

| Time | Measure |
|---|---|
| Mid 2003 - beginning 2004 | Development of a concept for the master's program. Clarification of co-operations; Draft of a curriculum; Preliminary talks with participants |
| July 2004 | Conference at the Law School of the Ruhr-University adopts the application of the master's program as a postgraduate course of study |
| September 2004 | University-commission for teaching (UKL) deliberates on the Law School's application and agrees with the provison of submission of a sustainable financial plan |
| November 2004 | Financial plan is submitted to the UKL |
| 6th December 2004 | University-commission for planning, structure and finances (UKP) enacts the submission |
| January 2005 | Formulation of the study and fee regulations |
| January 2005 | Rectorship of the Ruhr-University finishes the application (for the accreditation) |
| April 2005 | Disclosure of the process of accreditation by AQAS on 4th April 2005; Attendance (perpetration) of the consultants 24th June 2005; dialogues with the principal, the dean of the Law School and the lecturers. Result: the scientific experts will recommend the master's program to AQAS for accreditation (further suggestions for the concrete organization were given) |
| June/July 2005 | The application procedure begins (closing date: 25th July 2005) Selection of the applicants by the examination board |
| 22nd June 2005 | The faculty board enacts the study conditions (preliminary) |
| July 2005 | The examination board chooses 25 students for the semester in Winter 2005/2006. The approval notifications are sent out on 28th July 2005 |
| 10th October 2005 | Conference of the AQAS-commission; official accreditation on 11th October 2005 (date of the certificate) |
| October 2005 | Start of the first course (on campus studies, one year). Start of the lectures on 17th October 2005 |
| July 2006 | Application procedure for the academic year 2006/2007 (deadline 15th July 2006) |
| October 2006 | Start of the second year with two courses: the second on campus year and the first one designed as distance-learning (two years with two phases of attendance per year) |
| February 2007/ February and December 2008 | Graduation of the first (2005/2006 – on campus), the second (2006/2007 – on campus) and the third course (2006/2007 – distance learning) |
| January 2008 | Start of the newly designed "blended-learning" course – basically distance-learning, but with more phases of attendance (four per year and an additional one week at the beginning of the first and the end of the third semester – duration: two years) |
| January 2009 | Start of the second "blended-learning" course |

The main criteria for the accreditation were profile and aims of the program, the quality of the curriculum, the personal resources, the occupational orientation and the quality assurance.

The disadvantage of this procedure lies in the high expenditure of time and money. Nonetheless these disadvantages can also be seen as advantages. Applying for an accreditation requires a detailed and coherent concept. By integrating the "three instances", (law school/ faculty, university, accreditation company) this concept was evaluated by several stakeholders, which in this case led to considerable improvement in quality (Feltes, 2005a, p. 9).

For example, the law faculty discussed whether students without a general university degree but a degree of a university of applied sciences (a second type of post-school university, the graduation mostly obtained by possible students like police officers and social workers) should be able to attend the new program. After a controversial discussion the conference agreed upon a 50/50 regulation, enabling a more diverse structure of students.

The application quality was not only influenced at a primary level (conferences within the faculty), but especially at second (university) and third level (accreditation company). At the third level intense discussions arose and provided the program with a lot of excellent suggestions – e.g. introduction of a module "methods and key skills" and a better balance of social and police items.

After more than two years of planning, the master's program "Criminology and Police Science" finally received accreditation from October 2005 until 2010 as an advanced course of studies for postgraduate students.

## Application Process and the Beginning of the Lectures

Since the program was scheduled to start in October 2005, the application procedure already started in July 2005. Each applicant had to meet the admission requirements – a university or college (university of applied sciences) degree and a minimum one year of working experience. Professionals who were mainly interested to study the MA were police officers, lawyers, teachers, social scientists and social workers. Already the amount and content of the applications in the first year (and the future ones as well) reflected the need for such a program and a variety of personal and occupational motivation.

The analysis of these applications (Feltes, 2005a, p. 8) shows that lawyers for example aspire an additional qualification for their job as an attorney (especially criminal lawyers) or as a criminal judge/public prosecutor. Others regard the program as an appropriate opportunity before starting a career or in between two jobs. Applications however, are not only handed in by people just having passed the legal clerkship and the (second) state examination (bar exam), but also professionally experienced lawyers seeking further education partly to assist in receiving a Ph.D. or during stays abroad. People with a socio-scientific background (psychology, social work, education etc.) mostly apply in order to enhance career options by a specialization. Whereas these groups had different possibilities of getting further qualifications (although not in criminology) before, the occupational group probably benefiting most from the new program are the police officers. The master's program is, from their point of view, the only way to get additional qualification and a possibility to improve their opportunities of advancement as police internal programs are restricted to very few officers

Besides the specific motivations all occupational groups are united by their personal interest in this topic and the desire to improve their daily work. The applications (letters of intent) furthermore mirror the hope for impulses for their work, new perceptions and new solutions or ideas in order to reduce and prevent crime (Feltes, 2008).

The age spectrum varies from mid 20's to late 50's and therefore is as balanced as the professions.

The selection considers according to the guidelines of the accreditation, the overall result of the first degree and the professional experience, the present or the intended profession and the motivation as shown in the application (Feltes, 2008, p. 11).

In the first year, the program was designed as an on-campus program with a duration of one year. Most of the 25 students lived in the Ruhr Area and therefore had the possibility to take part in the program without the need to drive a long way to Bochum. Here again the geographical position of Bochum proved to be helpful. This first group of students graduated in February 2007 with a ceremony. At the graduation they received an internationally accepted master's degree: Master of Criminology and Police Science.

During that first year it became apparent, that the master's program had closed a gap in the Ger-

*Figure 3. Second graduation ceremony in Bochum, Germany (2008)*

man educational system. Since the experiences were good and the feedback of the participants was positive, the master's administration decided to extend the program to a distance-learning course. Therefore in 2006/2007, two groups started: one on campus and the second one distance learning (see below), opening up the program to a larger group of students.

## Current Situation

Since January 2008, the master's program exists in the form of a blended learning course. Therein the MA is completed in four semesters whereas the fourth semester is intended for writing the master's thesis.

These changes, first the extension to a distance learning course and then to the design as a blended learning course of study, were logical consequences from the experiences of the first years. The number of applicants has increased rapidly. With the design of an on campus course of study, the capacity was relatively low and a lot of very motivated and qualified applicants had to be denied. Moreover, the second year (on campus) demonstrated that this design brought the participants (most of them working full-time and having a family) to the edge of their capacities. On the other hand it soon became clear that only two phases of attendance in the distance learning course had a negative effect on the group's coherence and the learning effect.

By combining the idea of on campus and strict distance learning course of study, the new blended learning course – starting at the beginning of January – unites the potencies of the former designs. Today there are maximum 60 students per year. In addition to a complete week at the beginning (and a second one after the third semester), there are four additional phases of attendance per year designed to uphold the contact among the students as well as between the students and the lecturers.

These changes caused an extension of the study time from one year (respectively strictly distance learning 1 ½) to two years. However, this change makes the newly designed program more flexible with time. This flexibility is provided moreover by a reinforced use of e-learning (see below).

The students now have the possibility to work out their own time frame for learning. They are no longer dependent on the times when lectures are being held, but can structure their work according to their personal, familial and occupational needs as well as their reading and working habits.

With all this in mind, the students nevertheless have to complete a full MA Program and the performance of learning has to be organized very well and has to stay on a high level. Statistically it is planned that students need about 15 hours a week (Workload) with seven working days a week. During this time the students acquire not only criminological understanding, research experience and writing skills, they also learn techniques of time management and computer skills. Compared to many other programs the cost is relatively low and varied only slightly during the first years. Currently (February 2009) the overall fee is 3700 Euros. This amount is broken down into 1100 Euro for the first three semesters, whereas the fourth, reserved for writing the master's thesis, only costs 400 Euros.

### Lecturers/Academics and Mentoring/Supervision

The fees are considerably low when looking at the high quality of academics working in the master's program. Coming from many different occupational backgrounds and therefore representing the interdisciplinary orientations of the program, all of them possess a broad range of experience both within theory and practice. Lecturers with an outstanding scientific background as well as experience in practice make the master's program an enrichment for the educational system.

The administrative matters of students and lecturers are organized by two research assistants, also coming from an interdisciplinary background (sociology and law). They take care of the organizational matters concerning the program varying from the planning of the phases of attendance to working on new ideas for further improvement of the master's program. An additional student assistant cares for the technical support and all matters concerning the status of the students. This team is the first contact in case of arising questions, problems or needs of students and lecturers.

## CASE DESCRIPTION

The master's program includes nine modules and the master's thesis, for which the students acquire a total of 60 credit points (CP's) (Workload: 1.500 hours, 1 CP = 25 hours).

The focal point of the applied studies is to build up the following skills and competences:

- Specific expertise in connection with theoretical knowledge, which enables the adoption of scientific insights within the occupational practice
- Methodological and analytical skills of a context specific application of methods and knowledge
- Specific occupational key qualifications, especially the ability to cooperate with stakeholders from other fields and the debate with external, non-scientific, demands.

The content of the studies serve the goal to identify problematic constellations (being relevant for practitioners or/and academia) and to solve them – next to a substantiated knowledge and the acknowledgement of different scientific schools.

This goal is reached through:

- Relevant practical/occupational setting of priorities within the training of basic and subject-specific knowledge.
- Case studies and project work as examples for the solution of problems
- Practical oriented master's thesis, especially in cooperation with external professionals/experts.

According to the goals of studies the lecturers do not only have scientific qualifications but also have the experience to use them in their practical work.

The master's program contains the following basics:

- Modules in form of courses
- Master's thesis and oral examination.

The courses consist of the following didactic elements:

- **Lectures** (video lectures, connect files)
- **Projects**
- **Lecture seminars** - guided reading; basic readings (classic and modern works) in order to deepen the understanding of the theoretical background and at the same time to facilitate the transfer towards current practical questions.
- **Compendium letters** and **exercises.**

Efficiency controls are made with oral and written exams in between and at the end of each module.

The program combines elements of distance learning as well as on-campus learning. This allows the students to continue working. Most lectures are available for the students on the internet since the courses are implemented with the help of modern e-learning techniques. The use of modern e-learning methods enables students to study this field exceeding their regular lectures. Lectures and readings as well as exercises and small research projects are discussed via the specialized e-learning platform "Blackboard". Furthermore, most courses are broadcasted on the internet via the Multimedia-Web-communication-system „Acrobat Connect". Additional seminars at the Bochum University take place where personal contacts are deepened, special courses are taught in person (e.g. scientific work, training of soft skills) and exams are written.

## Content

There are nine mandatory modules on topics surrounding criminology, police science, research methods, social science (including sociology, psychology, educational studies) and legal studies (including constitutional law, criminal law and police law).

*Module 1 "Introduction to Criminology"*: The students learn about conditions, correlations and interactions between offence, offender, victim, social environment and societal control of deviant behavior. They discuss basics and theories of criminology as an independent scientific field as well as the measurement and review of criminality. The students become acquainted with the institutions of social control and prosecution. Further topics are criminal geography, crime and age, gender and nationality as well as repression and prevention. The courses impart scientific and additional practical knowledge in the fields of criminology, deviant behavior, criminal policy and police science. Additional to theories and new insights from research, the students are trained in methodology and soft skills for the critical grading of scientific findings and for the practical implementation in a criminological oriented profession.

*Module 2 "Criminolgy, Criminalistics and Prevention – single offences"*: Based upon the selected single offences or groups of offences aspects of criminology as well as criminalistics are discussed and deepened. Additionally the students are acquainted with current developments in criminalistics. A special emphasis is put on the

*Figure 4. Modules within the two years program*

| 01/09 | 02/09 | 03/09 | 04/09 | 05/09 | 06/09 | 07/09 | 08/09 | 09/09 | 10/09 | 11/09 | 12/09 |
|---|---|---|---|---|---|---|---|---|---|---|---|
| Module 1: Criminology I | | | | | | | Holidays | Module 2: Criminology/Criminalistics | | | |
| Module 9/1: Key Qualifications<br>Module 9/2a Academic Writing and Working (I) | | | Module 3: Juvenile Law, Applied Criminal Policy and Prognosis | | | | | Module 8: Police Law/Sociology | | | |
| | Module 4: Reading course criminology and Police Science | | | | | | | | | | |
| 01/10 | 02/10 | 03/10 | 04/10 | 05/10 | 06/10 | 07/10 | 08/10 | 09/10 | 10/10 | 11/10 | 12/10 |
| Module 5: Applied International Police Science | | | Module 6: Current Problems in Criminology | | | Masterthesis<br>Editing time 3 Months, flexible start | | | | | |
| Module 7: Applied Methods in Social Science | | | | | | Module 9/2b: Academic Writing and Working (II) | | | | | |
| Februar to April 2011: oral exams, graduation ceremony | | | | | | | | | | | |

rework of current relevant cases within the latter, criminology or criminal policy. Further aspects are concepts, tasks and methods of criminalistics, starting from offence to intelligence (e.g. involved actors, measures, investigative approaches). Police measures (e.g. observation, questioning) are discussed from a criminological and a criminalistics point of view. The students additionally learn to compare criminalistics perceptions and work versus criminological-sociological and legal methods of perception.

*Module 3 "Juvenile Law, Applied Criminal Policy and Prognosis"*: The students ascertain the importance of the basic rights and their impact upon other legal areas. Juvenile law (JGG) comprises aspects of youth welfare as well as youth penal law. The students are taught the premises of the use of single measures according to the JGG and learn to connect juvenile penal law with youth welfare and the institutions or stakeholders of youth criminal justice. They reflect critical decisions in the areas of juvenile criminal justice and develop strategies for the improvement of the procedures. The module additionally comprises the complete area of single offence criminology. This includes scientific basics for the criminological survey of individual offenders in their social relations. It takes up case history, analysis, diagnosis, prognosis, police work and special preventive intervention as well as the implementation of this knowledge in expertise, opinions or special preventive decisions (including legal background). The students are trained in criminological methods like exploration techniques or document analysis, as a foundation for diagnosis and prognosis (including forensic psychiatry and psychology).

*Module 4 "Classic and Modern Criminology and Police Science"*: The students discuss basic problems, theoretical approaches and developments in criminology and police science and turn their obtained knowledge into practice. Therefore the students work in-depth through classical and modern readings, which have a special meaning for the development of the scientific disciplines or/and for practice.

*Module 5 "Applied International Police Science"*: Together with the students, elements and aspects of an independent police science are debated and developed. Therein the students gain knowledge of different national and international approaches towards police science and they learn to assess their relevance towards practice. The students are taught the central definitions, history, legal background, organizational and working means, and strategies of policing, as well as problems with police science in a national and international context. A focal point is made on transformation of knowledge into practice and on international comparative police sciences. Furthermore the module includes several lectures on "Policing (all over) the World", which is an e-learning project initiated by the Chair of Criminology at the University Bochum as well as the Centre of Criminology at Cape Town University, South Africa. The students watch an interdisciplinary series of video lectures from police research and police science. The contributions are composed by experienced police scientists and experts in the English language, which originate not only from criminology and police science but also from such fields as law, social science, philosophy or psychology. Learning contents deal with police procedures and the understanding of police work in different cultures and societies. Other learning points comprise work procedures, structure and forms of training and education of state and private security agencies as well as the comparison of juridical systems and philosophies regarding police work.

*Module 6 "Current Problems in Criminology"*: The students learn to understand the current criminal proceeding of crime according to international law within a historical perspective and to describe essential tendencies within the development of crime. They debate basic problems of criminal proceedings on the basis of the work and jurisprudence of established ad hoc tribunals and courts as well as the International Criminal Court (ICC). They critically discuss the relevance of criminological-sociological contents and methods. Additionally the students get to know the work of NGOs in the areas of policing and penal system. They deal with national and international mechanisms of violating human rights and discuss current cases of violations of human rights. Based upon concrete projects the students deal with the development and the methodological implementation, and assess the results of projects. Along with selected material, they gain knowledge of the historical influence/reception within the field of politics "home security and police". Next to this the students develop frameworks of the stakeholders and actions of this policy field, in order to get to know and realize chances and barriers of action. Finally, methods in consulting police and politics are presented and discussed (including controlling and project management).

*Module 7 "Applied Methods in Social Science"*: This module integrates three parts. First, the students engage in a content- and methodological-specific discussion on criminological regional analysis/research on dark figures as preparation for the independent design and implementation of an empirical study project (7c). Second, the students learn basic theoretical and methodological implications for research in social sciences. They develop an understanding for methods, their usefulness and their function. The students gain knowledge of objectives, history and streams of interpretative sociology, approaches, definitions, concepts and ideas, quantitative and qualitative methods of research, including data analysis. They develop scientific question wordings and design a research plan in order to generate knowledge. Third, the students train their learned knowledge of methods and apply it with the help of an individually designed and implemented research project.

*Module 8 "Police Law and Sociology"*: In police law the students address danger defense by the police and other factors of policing. They learn the basic definitions of danger defense as well as public security. They study the different forms of the concept "danger" and the assignment of dangers towards responsible persons. References towards the law of criminal proceedings as well as international, especially European police work are made. Additionally, the law of intelligence services is presented in overview. In sociology the students get to know a variety of basic sociological perspectives, theories and findings. The students read basic texts of sociology and learn sociological ways of thinking. Basic questions are "What is Sociology?", "What does Sociology deal with?". Along current questions and discourses within criminal sociology students acquire knowledge and train the application of theories.

*Module 9 "Key Qualifications and Academic Writing and Working"*: The students get a tool box for effective communication and negotiation. They learn the basics as well as different styles of negotiation. The students are trained in strategies, tactics and mechanisms of success for leading a negotiation. The reflection of their own style of communication leads towards an optimization of future reactions in different settings of communication. The students learn the basics of conflict resolving, the analysis of conflicts and methods of problem solving and they find out about the classical setting of "mediation". The promotion and development of competences in this field enables the students to integrate the learned mechanisms of conflict solving within their professional life. Next to social key qualifications the students train the basics of academic writing and working – techniques fundamentally for writing the master's thesis. The students acquaint themselves with and train themselves in techniques for scientific reading, writing, literature research and training in composition and formulation of important sorts of texts (e.g. excerpts, exposé).

## SPECIALITIES

### E-Learning with Blackboard

Although designed first as an on campus course of study, the master's program "Criminology and Police Science" is now a full distance learning program (blended learning). Whereas former distance learning courses were based on printed material sent by mail, the multimedia revolution of the past years has made postal exchange almost unnecessary.

Recognizing that almost 70% of the German population use the internet nowadays (DESTATIS, 2007), almost the whole course now runs online. The fact is due to the innovative adjustment of the Ruhr-University. Especially since the turn of the millennium the university has steadily expanded its multimedia equipment.

The most important accomplishment was the introduction of the program *Blackboard*. This e-learning platform makes the internet a virtual lecture room and therefore constitutes the basis of the master's program. First tested during the introduction of criminology for law students in 2002/2003, Blackboard has now become irreplaceable for the on-campus, as well as the distance learning courses of the university and consequently for the master's program in Criminology and Police Science.

Blackboard (a system by Blackboard Inc., US) however, offers much more possibilities than just putting learning material online in a compressed and well-arranged form, therefore making it accessible for the students from any place at any time. The lecturers can create their own courses and therefore have influence on the structure as well as the material put online and the time when the material should be unlocked (and therefore be visible to the students).

Besides information about themselves (vita etc.) they can write announcements or contact the students via a discussion board. On the other hand the students can chat among themselves so that the discussion boards, up to a certain stage, replace the discussions within the lecture halls. Furthermore, there is the possibility to arrange working groups with only few students which allows the lecturer to output several assignments which are dealt with by certain students at one time.

Even tests can be arranged with Blackboard, covering a lot of essential functions (such as a time limit). Because these tests cannot fully replace a real testing situation (because of the control needed) the important tests in the pictured master are normally carried out during the phases of attendance. However, running these online tests for minor tests will be a further notion in the future.

*Figure 5. Screenshot Blackboard*

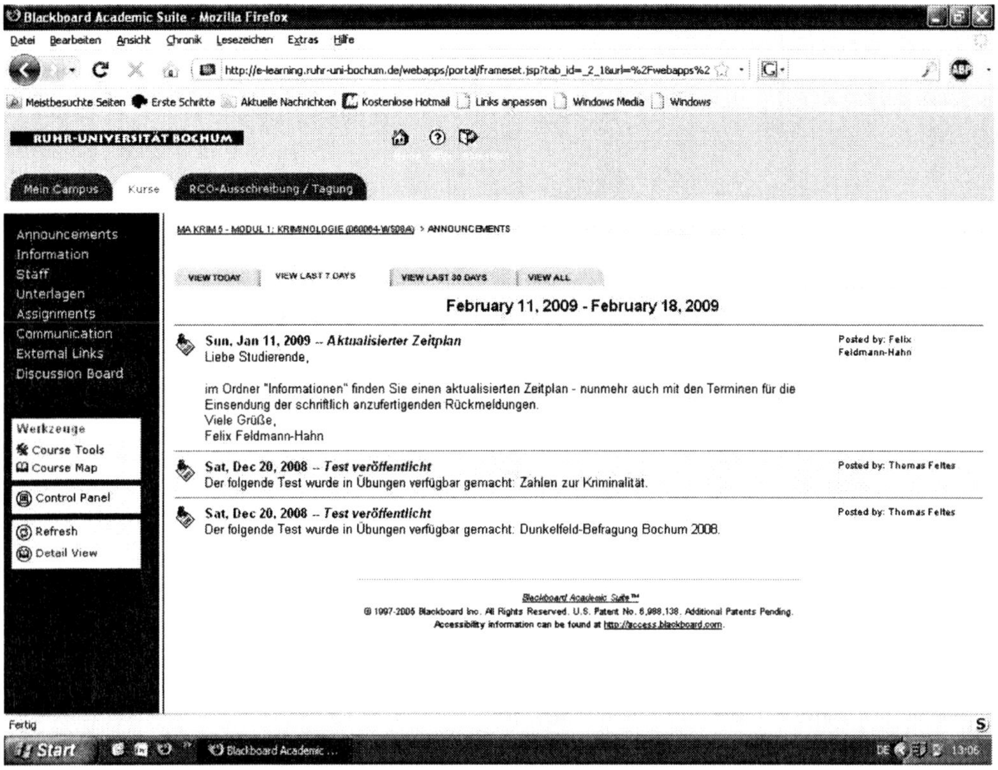


## Acceptance of Blackboard

Today the students have the possibility of getting used to Blackboard even before the master's program starts. The students chosen by the administration committee get an e-mail including a PowerPoint presentation with an explanation of how to create an account and to login to the system.

Because of its constituting character, the students get a further introduction during the first week of attendance at the beginning of the program. At this point, they can ask questions which arose during their own experiences at home.

Because of these previous introductions, the experience with Blackboard is, both from administration's and the student's view, very pleasing.

## Usage of Blackboard

This positive acceptance of Blackboard is reflected within the statistics of its usage.

Looking only at the accesses to Module 1 (Introduction to Criminology), more than 100.000 hits within four months mirror the interests, the motivation and the curiosity towards Blackboard as well as the master's program in general. With 75 users in total (including lecturers) this means there are more than 1000 accesses per person within that period.

Because of the program's design as a blended learning course of study it is interesting to take a closer look at the exact time when the students access Blackboard. The fact that most students are working full time is reflected in the time-frame in which the students accessed the system. Whereas during the day (10 am – 5 p.m.) the activity was high (around 3000), it even increased between 6 and 8 p.m. During this time 3500-4200 accesses were recorded by the program – some 30 per cent of all daily accesses (Feltes & Feldmann-Hahn, 2008). Not till after 10 p.m. did the accesses decrease – even the most assiduous student needs to sleep or at least have some time off.

Surprisingly the weekends do not show a higher access rate than weekdays. Still high with 6100 accesses they are nonetheless used more seldom for studying than the working days. It seems, as if some students prefer studying after work during the week to studying at the weekend. This assumption was proven true when evaluating the habits of studying of the students. Most of them quoted that they need the weekends (at least Sunday) for the family or other private matters.

The obviously higher rates on Thursdays probably have their cause in the fact that the working material was unlocked weekly on this day. Therefore it can be assumed that most students have directly downloaded the material on Thursdays.

## Adobe Connect

In addition to Blackboard, the master's program uses the software "Adobe Connect", also financed by the Ruhr-University.

This software enables to put recorded lectures online so that the students can watch them literally from their own living room. The lectures are recorded in advance, edited later by staff at the chair and then put online. The finesse is that the recording comes along with the PowerPoint presentation used in the lecture. A typical lecture is presented to the students in the form of a three part "Split screen" (see Figure 7). There is the PowerPoint presentation, a "talking-head-video" of the presenter and moreover the structure. With this the students get the possibility to navigate within the lecture, to repeat or respectively skip certain sections, or to stop the presentation and continue at a later point of time.

Although the videos cannot be downloaded, they are available with an adequate internet access from anywhere in the world since they are saved on the university's server.

As well as with Blackboard, the acceptance of Adobe Connect is overwhelming. Students appreciate that the disadvantages of actually being inside the lecture hall (such as chatting of the person sitting next to you, not having the possibility to repeat a certain passage) are not transferred to the presentation. Therefore recently one of the students announced Connect is "simply genius" (Feltes, 2008, p. 14).

*Figure 6. Usage of Blackboard (Feltes/Feldmann-Hahn, 2008)*

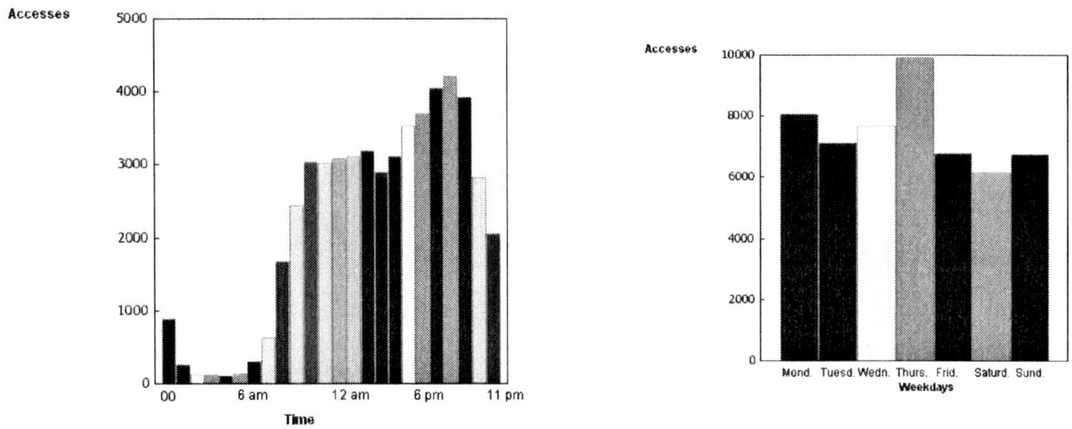

*Figure 7. Screenshot Adobe Connect*

The combination of Blackboard and Connect constitutes a complete new era of distance learning courses. Whereas in former times distance learning students only received material printed per mail (which took time), nowadays they have this material online with the possibility to access anytime (Blackboard), and anywhere.

## Police Science

An additional focus on Police Science (additional to criminology) takes into account the changed view on the role of private and state actors of social control. Therein the program recognizes the importance of interdisciplinary studies as well as the understanding between the different professions dealing with crime. Lecturers from research and practice guarantee an interdisciplinary access to criminology and police-science with focus on theory and methodology as well as practice-orientation.

## EVALUATION

All courses are evaluated in order to ensure the quality of the courses and lecturers as well as to survey the current demand of the students. Therefore the students fill out a questionnaire via the online platform "unipark" (a change to a questionnaire within Blackboard is planned). The questions lead from more widely spread questions on the use of the online-tools towards more specific questions on each module. Therein the students evaluate the concept of the module, the lecturer and the use of media. They review their own conduct of study for this module, their learning outcome and finally the major course assessment. This evaluation is an important tool for the improvement of the quality of the master's program.

## CURRENT CHALLENGES

In the framework of the re-accreditation of the master's program, many data and documents around our program are being collected. The number of applicants, the high number of alumni and the results of the evaluations allow us to conclude that "it works". So far, acquiring students has not been difficult, but with the changes in BA/MA in Germany (Bologna Process) we have to prepare for new paths towards new programs in order to integrate BA graduates. Further considerations are related to more cooperation with other institutions as well as an internationalization of the program. As everybody who has established a new program knows, changes always need to be made, starting from the first project idea in mind until the implementation the actual program. These changes (e.g. more meetings, more e-learning etc.) have to be documented and justified. The thoughtful comments of our students have helped us to improve our program. Being still a program with a small institutionalized administration, we stay flexible to react with improvements. Our greatest challenge is to uphold the good quality of lecturers and students and we try our best to fulfill this. We see ourselves as a learning institution, whereas we constantly adjust to new scientific contents and methods as well as to the requirements of the students (cp. Feltes, 2008, p. 11).

## REFERENCES

Bufkin, J. (2004). Criminology/criminal justice master's programs in the United States: Searching for commonalities. *Journal of Criminal Justice Education*, *15*(2), 239–262. doi:10.1080/10511250400085971

*DESTATIS* (Statistisches Bundesamt Deutschland) (2007). Fast 70% der Bevölkerung ab 10 Jahren nutzen das Internet. *Pressemitteilung Nr. 486*. URL: http://www.destatis.de/jetspeed/portal/cms/Sites/destatis/Internet/DE/Presse/pm/2007/11/PD07__486__63931,templateId=renderPrint.psml (27.02.2009).

Feltes, T. (2005a). Kriminologie als interdisziplinäre Wissenschaftspraxis – wie der Masterstudiengang „Kriminologie und Polizeiwissenschaft" an der juristischen Fakultät der Ruhr-Universität Bochum eine Brücke zwischen Theorie und Praxis schaffen will. *Bewährungshilfe, 52* (4), 359-369. URL: http://www.thomasfeltes.de/pdf/veroeffentlichungen/Bewaehrungshilfe_MA_Studiengang.pdf, p. 1-14 (27.02.2009)

Feltes, T. (2005b). *Stand eines Masterstudienganges „Kriminologie und Polizeiwissenschaft" an der Ruhr Universität*. URL: http://www.kriminologie.com/neues.htm (27.02.2009).

Feltes, T. (2005c). *Studiengänge im deutschsprachigen und nichtdeutsprachigen Bereich*. URL: http://www.kriminologie.com/studiengaenge.html (27.02.2009).

Feltes, T. (2008). Kriminologie und Polizeiwissenschaft im Verbund: Erste Erfahrungen mit dem Masterstudiengang „Kriminologie und Polizeiwissenschaft". In H.-G. Jaschke (Ed.), *Polizeiwissenschaft an der Polizei-Führungsakademie und der Deutschen Hochschule der Polizei – Eine Zwischenbilanz,* 142-163. URL:http://www.thomasfeltes.de/pdf/veroeffentlichungen/2007_Feltes_Beitrag_fuer_Jaschke_Endversion_1.pdf, p.1-14 (27.02.2009).

Feltes, T., & Feldmann-Hahn, F. (2008). Kriminologie aus der Ferne - Der weiterbildende Masterstudiengang setzt auf Blended-Learning. *Rubens*, *15*(127), 5.

*KMK* (Kultusministerkonferenz) (200372008). Ländergemeinsame Strukturvorgaben gemäß § 9 Abs. 2 HRG für die Akkreditierung von Bachelor- und Masterstudiengängen (Beschluss der Kultusministerkonferenz vom 10.10.2003 i.d.F. vom 18.09.2008). URL: http://www.akkreditierung-srat.de/fileadmin/Seiteninhalte/Dokumente/kmk/KMK_LaendergemeinsameStrukturvorgaben.pdf (27.02.2009)

Löschper, G. (1986). Kriminologie als selbständiges, interdisziplinäres Hochschulstudium: Internationales Symposium vom 8. - 10. Mai 1986. Pfaffenweiler, Centaurus-Verlagsgesellschaft.

Schwind, H. D. (2007). *Kriminologie. Eine praxisorientierte Einführung mit Beispielen*. 17. Edition, Heidelberg, Kriminalistik Verlag.

## WEBSITES

Website of the Master´s program "Criminology and Police Science" at the Ruhr-University Bochum. URL: http://www.makrim.de (27.02.2008).

## KEY TERMS AND DEFINITIONS

**Blended Learning:** Blended Learning unites on campus and distance learning courses of study with the help of new and innovative forms of e-learning.

## ENDNOTES

1 Overview in German language on URL: http://www.kriminologie.com/studiengaenge.html - e.g. Leuven/Belgium

2 Cp. Official Web site of the Ruhr-University Bochum, RUL: http://www.ruhr-uni-bochum.de/profil/portrait/regionale_verantwortung_en.htm

Section 3

# Criminology and Victimology:

## Disciplines that Look at the Professionals (of Teaching)

# Chapter 12
# The Present Cybercrime: Operational and Instructive Experiences

**Antonio Apruzzese**
*Italian National Police, Italy*

## EXECUTIVE SUMMARY

*The preponderant role played by the computer means, which is the more and more direct aim of the criminal action through sophisticated computer technologies, incites to reconsider the classical criminological and victimological patterns. In fact, new kinds of criminality linked to the use of sophisticated computer technologies, which are taking up the state agencies in the activities of prevention and repression, have recently assumed aspects of great and worrying importance. So, the need to formulate suitable training course of the personnel of those police branch (Postal and Communication Police of the Italian National Police), specialized in countering the high tech crime, is becoming more and more compulsory.*

## BACKGROUND

The Italian National Police, since few years, has prepared and activated in the Police Communication Brach an agile and specific agency to counter those new threats of cyber criminality. To the creation of high specialized investigative units, which are widespread distributed on the whole Italian territory, this structure combines the activation of international links with analogous agencies that are operating in almost every country in the world. A constant monitoring of the computer networks aims to the surveying and the prevention of any new kind of danger. The constitution, within the central service of the Postal and Communication Police, of the C.N.A.I.P.I.C. – National Anti-cybercrime Center for the protection of the critical infrastructure-, is particularly significant. The center is directed to the carrying out of efficacious forms to counter terrorist criminal computer attacks toward the so called critical infrastructures like, for instance, those of the energetic area, of the transport, of the communication and that of the e-government.

DOI: 10.4018/978-1-60566-872-7.ch012

## INTRODUCTION

New kinds of criminality connected with the use of the high-tech information technology have recently assumed very important aspects.

The well known phenomenon of the "phishing", the more and more frequent improper use of credit cards and other electronic means of payment have almost reached spreading and pervasiveness levels able to cause well-grounded worries in the whole economic and financial area, even because of the widespread fear of the rise of uncontrollable sensations of insecurity in the large number of the users.

The new criminal emergencies are seriously taking up the public agencies, which develop countermeasures and repression activities aiming, first of all, to the most complete global comprehension of the phenomenon, so to the definition of the most profitable investigative protocols.

In this context, the need to formulate suitable training courses of the human resources attached to the production departments becomes more important.

The topic is evidently stimulating the criminological scientific community too, very interested in new reformulations of the traditional concepts of offender typology, victimological profiles, the diversified aspects of the offender-victim of the crime relationship and the innovative kinds of criminal associative patterns which are now emerging.

The professional experience that we want to bear witness in the research came out, on the one hand, from a long term work in the police field (The Police Communication Branch of the Italian National Police) specialized in the fight against the high-tech crime, and, on the other hand from the training activities both of the personnel that is already employed in the operational units and the young people that are attending the Police Academies.

## THE NEW CRIMINAL BUSINESS

The need to outline a general profile of the new kinds of cyber crimes issued from the concrete operational activity, which has been carried out in the field, cannot be postponed no longer.

Once it was the sole prerogative of subjects (for instance the well known hackers, crackers and others) with excellent computer and technical abilities who operated alone and autonomously and, very frequently, without any direct profit purpose. Nowadays, more and more frequently, those criminal events are closely linked with heterogeneous organizations that, having recourse to the most uncommon forms of recruitment of the essential technical experts, conduct the ranks of "corporations" that assure huge financial revenues pointing out new structural models in areas that are undoubtedly transnational.

## NEW CYBERCRIMES

The new crimes, especially based on the digital identity theft, are mainly oriented to the sector of the online banking services, the monetics (automated monetary system composed by credit cards and electronic money in general) and the e-commerce.

The common and substantial characterizing element is the embezzlement of the confidential data, which permit the access and the availability of online bank accounts and the use of credit cards and other electronic means of payment.

In the e-commerce the digital identity theft is often used even to commit frauds in behalf of unaware third parties.

We clearly believe that transnational organized criminal groups are conducting the ranks of those innovative criminal activities insuring the highest profit and the lowest risk concerning the whole occidental world.

Among the most familiar online banking system attacks there is the so called "phishing".

Thousands of victims every year are robbed of the confidential cyber credentials to access to bank and post accounts.

It follows considerable illicit withdrawals of total amounts equal to millions of Euros.

The recycling systems of the considerable stolen amounts are particularly original and sophisticated, based on real online recruitment of hundreds of followers interested in the complex stages of money disposal without leaving any trace.

The opening of convenient online bank accounts is required to the hundreds of recruited "tin soldiers" in order to flow the amounts that have been stolen from the victims.

Afterwards the same "tin soldiers" are charged, once a considerable commission has been appropriated, to send generally the received amounts toward remittees who are in the ex soviet system countries through ordinary international transfer services (Western Union – Money Gram).

From the carried out inquiries came out that in those countries another specular network of receiver followers who, once the amounts received, send them to the bosses of the organizations.

Other innovative forms of recycling usually conducted by gangs that, like the Rumanian ones, can rely on widespread presence on the national territory, provide the "disposal" of the amounts obtained illicitly through systematic "top-up" of particular bank or post electronic debit cards (poste-pay and the like).

In some more sophisticated forms the recycling is carried out by the top-up of prepaid phone cards that are successively employed to call exclusively the so called special rating numbers or added value number that are intentionally activated.

The issue will be to perceive as recycling earnings the net rates of the telephone traffic activated upon those special telephone subscriptions.

## DEVELOPMENT OF THE PHENOMENON

In order to outline properly the evolution of the phenomenon we will point out three typical cases: the phishing, the monetics and the botnet.

- **The phishing:** If during its first stage the phishing was implemented only through the e-mail fraud scam sending whose aim was to cheat the receivers in order to swindle their confidential access data to online accounts, recently it is carried out through complex techniques on a large scale of cyber infection of thousands of computers. The machines are cheated by now, new victims of fearful "virus" deliberately widespread with the largest diffusion, which by producing computer malfunctions, leak out the confidential account access data leaving the users totally ignorant. We have well-grounded suspicions to believe that the essential computer experts to implement the sophisticated technical procedure needed be recruited by internet as well, by very important international criminal gangs by now. It is well known, on the other hand, the existence of a real black market of computer virus.
- **The monetics:** Even the monetics sector is pointing out radical evolutions. Besides the more and more widespread and serious cloning events of credit card and other electronic means of payment, the theft of millions of confidential credit card codes are now implemented through computer attacks to the more and more widespread (and more and more rich!) databanks that process and conduct the huge e-commerce flow. The current inquiries have pointed out, which have been confirmed, that heterogeneous criminal gangs conduct by now real worldwide markets of confidential online bank account codes and also credit cards.

- **The botnet:** The botnet (acronym of the English terms robot and network) are above all very fearful, they are real new entries in the panorama of the cyber crime. The cyber-criminal gangs show off and estimate their power from the point of view of the extent and the size of the computer (robot) networks (net) violated, of which they acquire their availability. Those herds of hundreds and sometimes thousands of compromised machines, skillfully conducted at a distance by able operators, are now employed to carry out the boldest computer attacks by concealing totally the source. Completely useful, for instance, to the activity of the phishing and to the virus spreading, the computer violated are apparently and materially at the holders' disposal who are unaware about the fact that others are using without their knowing the computer for the most wicked actions. The American police experience already reports events of real extortions carried out by zombie computer networks that are used to attack and damage corporate systems in order to demand afterward a kind of cyber protection money.

## THE PHENOMENON PROPORTION

The real proportions of the phenomenon are now hardly quantifiable because of the obvious resistances of the interested financial sectors to provide precise survey data at national and international level.

The only concrete confirmation is provided by the proportion of the worldwide black market concerning the confidential data of bank accounts or credit cards objectively found by internet too.

On the basis of the analysis of one among the most renowned and reliable cyber security company in the world (Symantec) the volume of data potentially offered on the black market would be equal to more than 270 million dollar only for the period July 2007 - June 2008.

In general, as far as monetics is concerned, the most meaningful witness of the virulence and the high organizational level of the criminal attacks, which is the object in the international field, is provided by the latest news that refer to cyber attacks against companies' data bank that conduct e-commerce flows, with theft, in a sole episode, of millions of credit card codes (we refer to the recent case in the U.S.A. of the Heartland Payment System).

Anyway the data are increasing noticeably and steadily at the same rate with the more and more wide basic computerization of the country, the continuous growth of the e-commerce, the more and more stimulated spreading of the online banking services and the general employment of electronic means of payment that are inspired by the widespread "war cash".

The global outline that is sketched out allows us to delineate the edges of new criminal companies that conduct in a quite innovative way the cyber criminal business.

Refined minds head them skillfully by exploiting completely their huge economic capacities. The same Internet "network of the network" and its multiform relational potentials (consider the chat-rooms, the forums and the more and more frequented social networks) are the most practical ways to select and recruit the best computer experts, in order to place the most refined virus at their disposal.

In addition the network makes very easy the individualization and the engagement of experts, and it is also useful, as mentioned above, to support the engagement of the specialists in the recycling activities like the phishing.

The old hackers or crackers seem no longer as the main and autonomous perpetrators of cyber crimes but as merely laborers sometimes permanently included in the new criminal companies, and sometimes engaged, like the virus creators, when necessary.

The clear knowledge and the more effective fight against the rising criminal companies need by this time an absolutely necessary holistic approach that borrow excellent inquiry experiences in a classic way, of refined computer and technical abilities, not least of consolidated abilities of orientation through the complex paths that are the head of the Internet handling of the financial flows, of the monetics and the e-commerce.

## FROM THE COMPUTER CRIME TO THE COMPUTER-RELATED CRIME – THE APPARENT AND THE REAL INNOVATION OF THE PRESENT CYBER CRIMINALITY

A thorough analysis of the computer crime (now computer-related crime) drives only to the discovery of its apparent innovation.

Seemingly the computer crime, in its present proportions, seems as the exclusive field of super experts who act in absolute autonomy following the most recent computer technology innovations.

The computer-related crime, as above analyzed in details, is by now come back tightly "in the hands" of the usual criminals.

Like able puppeteers, they move as best they can their ranks of puppets (computer experts, recyclers and different followers) according to the criminal project directed to the exclusive, and well known by then, illegal enrichment.

Even though those new deviances are led in the classical criminological canal of activities aiming to the mere profit, they outline new particular connotations however. Firstly the singular relationship established among boss and followers. In fact, very frequently, as above outlined, the latter can never meet the first.

Very innovative is also the relationship offender-victim that such criminality tends to shape. Typical examples are the new generation phishing that cheats the machine without the knowledge of the holders, the global black market of credit card codes swindled from huge data banks, finally the attempt at fraud on a large scale carried out by the massive mailing of millions of e-mail fraud scam.

The direct contact between the aggressive criminal and the victim of the cheat seems to move away profiling, as far the organizational managers are concerned, the clear outlines of white collar criminals of new generation.

## NEW OPERATIONAL AND TRAINING NEEDS

Summarizing everything has been above minutely outlined, the new computer criminality appears with peculiar business characteristics where the boss, with marked managerial abilities, recruit and engage in many ways, by rotating them as necessary, on the one hand technical experts specialized in the preparation of clone sites, in the use of botnet, in the creation and diffusion of malware and fearful virus, on the other hand many ranks of followers with merely executive tasks charged with the monetization activities of the huge incomes coming from the cyber theft and then with their dealing and recycling.

A clear role division into compartments marks the structure, so that very frequently the followers do not know even who their bosses are.

The new criminal corporations, on the other hand, do not know limits or territorial barriers any more, pointing out on the contrary marked transnational aspects.

Any suitable operational answer must consider those specific features.

The present inquiry realities seem to suggest more and more resolutely the implementation of fight teams with a balanced cooperation jointly with policemen trained under traditional patterns and others with marked computer and technical knowledge.

The first would be able to organize as well as

possible the criminal contexts where operate. The latter would be able, with attentive police eye, to go over a strictly technique interpretation of the malevolent computer strategies employed by the criminal gangs.

Expert detectives with marked managerial inclination will coordinate and combine the activities of the groups.

The same teams must be able to operate in strict synergy with the corresponding foreign investigative structures and the police as well.

Once the operational and organizational outlines of the fighting units, which are currently being formed, have been defined, we must mention the relevant need of new training models to apply to the employed human resources.

By the reversal of trend that has characterized the first stages of the institutional answer to the cyber crime on the basis of training patterns directed prevalently to the hyper technical specialization, now training and updating multidisciplinary models must be favored.

The first stage of the training will aim to a wide and common awakening of the members of the team in relation to the global complexity of the organizations to counter.

The second and differentiated training stage will aim to the updating of the elements in a classic and more traditional way concerning the new technical strategies employed by the criminal organizations and to awaken the operators with marked technical knowledge concerning the new global criminal aspects of the new gangs.

From the first stage the training will have constant references to aspects clearly transnational of the new criminal phenomenon. From the very first moment, during the preparation, the cyber-policemen will have the knowledge of the operational realities where colleagues inserted in homologue departments of other countries are operating.

Besides the suggestion and the orientation of more incisive counter answers, this enlargement of the "cognitive horizon" will constitute the first and the strongest basis of any following concrete cooperation in the operational activity that young agents will carry out.

## REFERENCES

Apruzzese, A. (2007). Dal computer crime al computer-related crime (Electronic version). *Rivista di Criminologia, Vittimologia e Sicurezza, I*(1), January-April, 55-60. Retrieved from http://www.vittimologia.it/rivista.

Cimini, B. R. (2006). Il contrasto della criminalità informatica. In AA.VV., *Diritto penale europeo e ordinamento italiano*. Milano, Italy: Giuffrè.

Flor, R. (2008). Art. 615 ter c.p.: natura e funzioni delle misure di sicurezza, consumazione del reato e bene giuridico protetto. *Rivista italiana di diritto e procedura penale,* 106.

Luparia, L., & Ziccardi, G. (2007). *Investigazione penale e tecnologia informatica.* Milano, Italy: Giuffrè.

Perri, P. (2008). Profili informatico-giuridici della diffusione, mediante strumenti telematici, di materiale pedopornografico. *Cassazione penale*, 3466.

Picotti, L. (2004). Sistematica dei reati informatici, tecniche di formulazione legislativa e beni giuridici tutelati. In L. Picotti (Ed.). *Il diritto penale dell'informatica nell'epoca di Internet.* Padova, Italy: Cedam.

Picotti, L. (2008). Ratifica della Convenzione Cybercrime e nuovi strumenti di contrasto contro la criminalità informatica e non solo. *Diritto dell'internet*, 437.

Scopinaro, L. (2007). Furto di dati e frode informatica. *Rivista italiana di diritto e procedura penale*, 363.

Vaciago, G., & Giordano, M. T. (2007). La qualificazione giuridica del phishing in una delle sue prime applicazioni giurisprudenziali. *Diritto dell'Internet*, 62.

Vulpiani, D. (2007). La nuova criminalità informatica. Evoluzione del fenomeno e strategie di contrasto (Electronic version). *Rivista di Criminologia, Vittimologia e Sicurezza, I*(1), January-April, 46-54. Retrieved from http://www.vittimologia.it/rivista.

# Chapter 13
# The Professional Training of the Italian Surveillance Magistracy:
## The Useful Knowledge of Criminology and Victimology for a Working Italian Prison System

**Giovanna Fanci**
*University of Macerata, Italy*

## EXECUTIVE SUMMARY

*The Italian prison system is characterized by a sort of schizophrenia (Ferrajoli, 2000) due to two opposite principles of legal framework: the certainty of sentence and the re-educative purpose of imprisonment. The action of the Surveillance Judge (Magistrato di sorveglianza) – a relevant authority for the enforcement of a criminal judgment – takes its place in the heart of such tension. In fact, he must ensure a right implementation of the sentence and, at the same time, he has to attend that the sentence serving is realized in accordance with penal rules and, particularly, with the re-educative aim. Therefore this study will highlight the importance of professional training for serving sentences judges whose educational programming would provide for inputs of criminology and victimology studies. They supply the Surveillance Magistracy (Magistratura di sorveglianza) with cognitive tools to identify the right treatment program for the convicted personality and to promote a mediation process between offenders and victims.*

## THE ITALIAN PRISON SYSTEM AND THE SURVEILLANCE JUDGE

The Italian prison system has the peculiarity of having the help of the Surveillance Magistracy (*Magistratura di sorveglianza*). Its institution dates back to 1930, in the fascist regime, when the law maker introduced new criminal code and that of the penal procedure which brought up the detention orders – laying on the so-called «double binary » («*doppio binario*») – and assigned a task of surveillance and of a working administration within the phase of penal serving sentence (Ferraro, De Stefanis, 1995:7). This authority constitutes originality not only for the Italian legal system, but also for the foreign ones: in fact, it has been introduced in France and in Spain. Such introduction could be understood keeping in mind various

DOI: 10.4018/978-1-60566-872-7.ch013

features, some of them having legal roots, others socio-political ones.

As to the first, we have to consider that the Italian legal system can be traced back to an institutional model commonly called «civil law»; therefore, also judicial authorities are founded on a legal structure distinguished first by a clear powers separation and, then, by the provision for relevant procedures of selection and training. For these reasons it isn't casual that an authority quite similar to our Surveillance Magistracy has been introduced in the French legal framework, as well as a «civil law» system (Vichnieswky, 1980; Mestitz, 1990). Actually, courts having jurisdiction on serving sentence are not instituted in those legal systems which could be traced back to an institutional model commonly called «common law». On the contrary, in these last contexts competence on penitentiary matter it is attributed to independent agencies that are not judges. So they aren't screened by competition procedures and don't return verdicts. Very often penitentiary experts are appointed by government organisms.

As regards the socio-political roots, it's right to hint at the historical context in which the Surveillance Judge has been drawn up and instituted.

This framework can be analyzed during a long period of time. In the first years of the 19th century the prisons looked as places of despair and totally neglected, though the authorities decided to intervene ordering the construction of new prisons and many researchers led a large campaign to raise public and political class awareness of the appalling conditions of the jails[1]. Over the years, we have been watch the revival of the punitive stance according to which punishment could have a reward aim to the community in proportion to the harm; and it has been partnered the abolition process of capital punishment. All this has produced a rigorous idea of the prison which is conceived as an institution distinct and autonomous from judicial guarantees of the legal system; the prison control were firstly assigned to military and police forces; then it has been recognized to administrative authorities. By the strengthening of this feeling of «social defense» the prisoner was thought of as a man excluded by society and by all rights and guarantees that lawmaker was recognizing to free people.

After the enactment of the Italian Constitution a change process got off, that, although long and difficult, produced a modernization of the penitentiary system: it firstly means that an innovation has established itself as a result of new methods, equipment and ideas which involved the actions of judges, prison workers and police men. This process, made easier by the consolidation of the constitutional principle of re-educative purpose of imprisonment[2] - which Italian prison system must primarily obey – was formalized in 1975 through the drafting of the Prison System Act *(Ordinamento penitenziario)*[*ord. penit.*] (26 July 1975/354 Act) and it is fully working. If we think over the interconnection pointed out in this brief retrospective, it appears readily understandable the clear change materialized by the 1975 reform which held in store a role of undoubted prominence for Surveillance Magistracy (Della Casa, 1998:2). It is possible to single out some weighty corollaries of this change: the punishment meted out can be modified qualitatively and quantitatively during serving; as prisoners separateness has produced self-defeating outcomes, the use of adequate instruments is spreading to develop contacts with the territorial institutions; finally, the prisoner is regarded as owner of legal statement towards to penitentiary service in full obedience of re-educative aim of punishment.

As a consequence in the field of trial, the judge has to enforce penitentiary laws (code of criminal procedure, Prison System Act and prison regulations), but his task is not so easy as it could seem. In fact, over the last thirty years after the Prison System Act[3], several reforms of judicial system have changed the role of Surveillance Judge[4]: the phase of serving sentence has been transformed into a fourth judicial step characterized by the power to produce substantial effects on the freedom of the sentenced (Zaniboni, 2004:31). This wider discretional authority has gone along with a further change: the Surveillance Magistracy – instituted as relevant authority for being involved in *intra moenia* questions – is in charge of free people too which are convicted to spend a short period of time in prison (three or four years according to circumstances). Discretion is the heart of the matter of this study, to which we will go back below.

Transversely this change, a gradual and firm process of «jurisdictionalisation» has got off thanks to judgments of the Italian Constitutional Court which have heightened the primary role of the re-educative principle as a «Pole Star» of prisons system, and thanks to political goodwill to restructure the criminal serving proceedings as a true effective trial. Equalizing serving trial to court has implied that lawmaker has assured that decision making process could get out according to rules of judicial procedure, that is those principles which lay down the participation in the decisional process of Prosecutor, lawyer, offender, if this one applies for it, and two experts in penitentiary subject who are appointed by the Ministry of Justice. The above involves that the decisional making process represents a very important feature of the prison system recognizing room to discussion and ending with an ordinance which could be appealed to the Supreme Court.

Now, we think it advisable to investigate firstly what matter falls under jurisdiction of the Surveillance Magistracy; and then, to illustrate how decision making process takes place. It is possible to divide its subject jurisdiction into two big groups referable to the constitution of judicial authority. So we have distinguished between monocratic judge jurisdiction and the court one.

Before dealing with jurisdiction questions, it is appropriate to outline data which are essentially procedural. We can note down the coexistence of the monocratic judge (Surveillance Judge) with collegial one (Surveillance Court). The Former has essentially a role of watchdog of law as regards work of penitentiary service[5]. The Latter has got jurisdiction over the new alternative measures introduced by the 1975 Prison Act (release on probation, early release and part-time detention). The latter has a «"protected" position in comparison with prisons dynamics» (Della Casa, 1998:4) working in conformity with precise procedural rules. Fundamentally, the subjects which fall under the jurisdiction of the Surveillance Judge concern the *intra moenia* treatment, alternative measures if they are urgent and preliminarily to subsequent judgment of the Court, and, finally, detention orders. Going into details, it is possible draw up a list:

- Involvement with guarantee function as regards actions of prison workers for implementing constitutional principles. This area includes the control of prisoners' mail[6]; release on temporary license for good behavior or particular circumstances[7]; taking or not a period of release into account as serving time in prison[8]; admission to mental criminal hospital[9]; transfer of prisoner to nursing home, also without escort[10]. Next to this, there is another area of jurisdiction identified on the basis of advisability reasons: remission of debt for proceedings and support costs[11]; license of entry into prison for the community[12]; license of using telephone service[13]; control of prisoner's money management from governor[14]; giving order for exclusion from penitentiary representatives of jailed because of mental disorders[15].
- Monitoring moves of prison workers through ruling on prisoners complaints[16] about work and disciplinary matter; but, just to set the record straight, Surveillance Judge has no authority over the governor; in the case of a law breaking, he can only set out the fact to the top of penitentiary Service, unless his duty is to go

to court if governor action takes criminal significance[17].

- Checking treatment program and granting to prisoner to work outside on initiative of prison governor[18]. As regards the former jurisdiction[19], the authority of the Surveillance Judge is less wide than it seems to be (Della Casa, cit., 62) because of vagueness of rules regulating treatment plans content[20].
- Preliminary decisions in matter of alternative and suspended measures: the subject in hand regards reconsideration of treatment conditions[21] of release on probation[22], home detention[23] and part-time detention not only for the worse, but also for the better. The spirit of the law wants to assure a judge participation and certainly the Surveillance Judge is the authority nearer to prisoners' needs.
- Judgment in matter of detention orders for which the Surveillance Judge must anyway check the social dangerousness of the person although it should have already been checked by the judge of first instance yet [24].

Now, we are going to present jurisdiction area of the Surveillance Court. Also in this case, it seems useful to classify the judge actions in two groups: the case in which the Court rules «in the first instance» and the case in which it decides on the basis of a previous order of the Prison service or the Surveillance Judge.

As regards the former class, rehabilitating measures take the lion's share. They are: Release on Probation, Ordinary[25] and Therapeutic[26], Part-time Detention[27], House Detention[28] and Rehabilitation Order[29]. Good behaviors in prison and job opportunity for prisoners outside are necessary requirements for the granting of the Ordinary Release on Probation and of the Part-time Detention. The concentration at the head of the same body gets legitimacy in the interconnection amid various alternative measures: for example, in a case of lacking conditions for granting an Ordinary Release on Probation (wider measure as to prisoner's freedom), the Surveillance Court could apply a Part-time Detention. As well, propaedeutical relation between a Part-time Detention and a Conditional Release is not to be denied in view of a reintegration perspective. Finally, the Court has the power to block the serving sentence if the convicted is a drug addict and the treatment program is already set up[30], and in case of petition of pardon[31].

The second class of rulings regards judgments given on appeal. This is made up of:

- Claim about a Special Surveillance[32] provided by the Ministry of Justice for the penitentiary dangerousness of prisoner.
- Claim about reject of a Temporary License for good behavior or particular circumstances[33] and refuse taking period of release into account as serving time in prison[34].
- Appeal against a refusal for detention orders or a grant for a different measure from the one requested [35].

As regards the decision making process, it sounds interesting to describe how a collegiate body works, because, as we will see below, it represents a weighty environment to allow the usefulness of a good professional training of judiciary to come to surface. Primarily, it detects the presence of two experts who collaborate with judges in decision making process. So the court is made up of the President of Surveillance Court, a Surveillance Judge[36], the Chief Appeal Court Prosecutor and two experts. It is defined "expert" a person that is very knowledgeable and particularly skilled in a specific subject (Caso, Josi, 2006:340). Studies about expert competences concentrate on professional practices and identify an important indicator of expertise in the «expert thinking» (Scribner, 1985), that is competency to outline the "area of the problem" by means of implementing cognitive strategies having a high degree of flexibility. This allow expert to adjust to context applying solving problem procedures and considering all variables involved, what Yrio Engeström (1987) calls a «polycontextual» feature. It is obvious that the presence of so-called not stipendiary members could give an interdisciplinary nature to decision making process, particularly suitable for the complexity of the various occurring problems which Surveillance Judges are appointed to solve, that is why they come from particular professions marked by articles n° 70(3) and n° 80(4) *ord. pen.*, among which they point out the following categories: professors in criminology, experts psychology, social sciences, education, psychiatry and clinical criminology. The involvement of this expertise is relevant to analyze the prisoner's personality.

Experts are assigned by the Superior Council of Magistracy (*Consiglio Superiore della Magistratura*) [*C.S.M.*][37] (an Italian self-governing agency of the Bench) on indication of the court President. Criteria to nominate are extraneous to magistracy and rather developed expertise than to hold a degree[38].

Decision making process covers three steps.

During the first step the Judge rapporteur reads the file on a particular case and an expert constructs the "area of the problem" on the basis of the various data emerging by the judge report: first of all, the terms of admissibility or no admissibility and requirements of legitimacy to be admitted to alternative measure claimed by the prisoner; then, information regarding good conduct of interested on the strength of police force and prison workers reports. In this case the statements of the jailed could be very important: he can ask for being present at the trial. His presence could provide the court with information.

In the second step Chief Appeal Court Prosecutor pronounces application of rejection or granting, and then the lawyer tells the court the statement of reasons being at the root of the claim. During the first and the second steps the expert carefully writes down all the pieces of information which could be relevant for decision making.

Chambers go off in the third phase. This is a very relevant moment in the serving sentence proceedings, not only because it pronounces a collective judgment according to specific rules of procedure, but also because in its course the necessity of a multidisciplinary and integrated approach comes out for solving the complexity of case in hearing. Actually, experts may take an active part at chambers in decision making process bringing their own expertise in a dialectical relation. "From setting out a case it arrives at an interdisciplinary decision in which every member's knowledge converges on a common judgment" (Caso & Josi, 2006:364). Furthermore, trial in camera is a very important step because it gives panel of judges the opportunity to debate the case through determining legal obligations and questions, and evaluating different decisions to encourage a right carrying out of prisoner treatment program, designed on his personality.

## THE NECESSITY OF A JUDICIARY PROFESSIONAL TRAINING: THE USEFULNESS OF VICTIMOLOGY AND CRIMINOLOGY

The framework outlined is the starting point for our research on professional training for Surveillance Magistracy. As we presented above, the Judge and the Surveillance Court are called to judge about serving sentence with inevitable consequences for prisoners' freedom. The judgment, actually, produces different outcomes: on the one hand it causes results in punishment serving about both imprisonment duration and way of serving it; on the other hand, granting rehabilitative measures (as Release on Temporary License for good behavior, Release on probation, Part-time Detention or Rehabilitation Order) implies delicate personality analysis: in short, these are the reasons for which jurisdiction over these measures has been appointed to a "skilled" (Della Casa, cit., 74) judge. The prisoner resettlement requires expertise and dedication. The Surveillance Judge – for its role of watchdog of law as regards work of penitentiary service – above all runs every day into difficulty of prison system encouraging inmate's reintegration into the community. Moreover, regarding in detail the Rehabilitation Order, the judge has to evaluate the real reformation of prisoners and their relationships with victims, that is if it is at their satisfaction or not. It is not an easy task, mostly for the complex personality of prisoners and for structural and institutional shortage. The cultural roots and a structural-economic background can be the base of this institutional inefficiency.

It is difficult to define the terms of the problem because different factors intervene in the working of the penitentiary system. Firstly, it is necessary to highlight the concurrence of two constitutional principles: on the one hand the value of punishment certainty (under that final judgment must be served in the ways fixed by judge); on the other hand the assumption of the rehabilitative aim of punishment which involves an inevitable reassessment of the treatment program (Margara, 1995). The discretional power of the Surveillance Magistracy goes just in this direction: it is trying to implement penitentiary policies respecting the two constitutional principles.

In this connection, Stephen Schafer wrote: "If it were realized that a kind of spiritual satisfaction is implicit in any system of punishment, a new concept of the purpose of punishment might arise, strengthening the restitutive character of punishment on the one hand and, on the other, infusing compensation with a punitive quality" (Schafer, 1975:45). To require of the offender to pay money as a punishment is not something new. The origin of the present-day fine is the restitution. The only difference between compensation and fine is that the former (originally called "composition") reimburses the victim while the latter serves as a source of income of the state. Compensation presents good aspects, significant for rehabilitative purpose of punishment: "Few systems of reforming the criminal do not include among their aims the arousal of this understanding and expiation of guilt. While this sort of psychological process can be initiated and assisted by others, it cannot be performed *for* him [the offender]; it must be carried out by the criminal himself. The proposed restitution in the form of compensation is something *he* does, not something done by others *for* him or *to* him, and, since it requires him to make an effort, it may be especially useful in strengthening his feelings of responsibility" (Schafer, cit.:46). Something of the sort is provided for by the Italian penitentiary system: the convicted Rehabilitation Order for whose granting it is required getting in touch with the crime's victim and asking him what could be an adequate compensation, either by money or by doing voluntary work. Personality evaluation of prisoner and punitive progression in connection with outcomes of their treatment program assure implementation of re-educative principle from enforcement to serving sentence (Patrizi, 1996:151). Just on this point there is a serious risk of introducing an «indefinite punishment» in the Italian legal system.

The exercise of the decisional authority is much criticized. We can quote some of the more authoritative Italian opinions. Luigi Ferrajoli, for example, points out that our prison system works under «schizophrenia» conditions as the result of an institutional hypocrisy for which, behind the reassessment aim of punishment, there is an institutional need of managing penitentiary population. In this way, the system works on synallagmatic relation between institution (prison operators, police force and Surveillance Magistracy) and inmates: if the behavior of these last ones is good, the duration and the way of serving sentence will be changed. This synallagma entails the notion of a prison as a control instrument and an unrestrained power assigned to judicial authority (2000: 406-7).

Another critical analysis has been made by Massimo Pavarini, who, looking into penitentiary system, spoke about a strict Prince on the surface, a lenient Judge in facts and a people "inattentive" to political actions. As a consequence, the prison environment is based on discrepancy between judiciary ruling and law making actions: the primary criminalization process produces a severe criminal policy clashing with the secondary criminalization one which outcomes look benevolent and, sometimes, even indulgent (1980:45).

Next to these technical and legal problems, the frantic social change is as well concerning the penitentiary framework and the Italian Bench itself asks for gearing its education to new social complexity: professional training places itself over a mere refresher need, but it is a real cultural activity, close to social changes and expectations (XXIX Congress of National Judges Association - *Associazione Nazionale Magistrati*, [*A.N.M.*] 2008:11). Judges claim the responsibility of *C.S.M.* putting up a steady updating system because they are called to do a job more and more skilled (*A.N.M.*, 2003).

Certainly an essential factor of social change is traceable in a new process called by David Garland «return of the victim»: the victim is at the core of attention of the criminal policies. Up to some years ago, the victim's interests were included among those of the community and they certainly were not conflicting with those of criminal. Everything is changed now. Victims feelings are always invoked supporting punitive reclusion[39]. According to Garland, the prison's system running has become a zero – sum game: when a criminal wins, the victim necessarily is a loser; and intervening in victim's favor means being automatically inflexible to the perpetrator of a crime. In Garland's opinion a new idea of victim is now spreading together with a new definition of relation amid real victim, symbolic one and institutions appointed to criminal control and dispensation of justice (Garland, 2004: 70-72).

This reasoning concerns victimization and the collective value given to the idea of what a victim is; these sort of social processes are mostly widespread in the United States and the Great Britain, and in common law's countries in general. Such phenomena are not accidental, but they are the immediate consequence of their legal framework in which the public support for politics has clear, important and often significant impact on the effectiveness of police operations. When speaking about this subject, the research of Darlene Walker about public support to policies looks interesting. The expert, starting from other important studies, even though infrequent, which have suggested that system outputs might be major variables in explaining the system inputs of support (Ostrom and Whitaker, 1973), reverses the normal independent-dependent variable relationship between public opinion and policy and she investigates the proposition that the level of public support for political institutions is related to policy outputs and outcomes: "Public support for jails and prisons may determine how innovative prison policy will be and may have an impact on determining whether the philosophy of corrections will be essentially rehabilitative or punitive. Beyond these obvious influences, public perception may be an intrinsic part of the quality of justice itself" (Walker, 1977: 4).

What we have said until now is witnessed by Emilio Viano's study, which confirms that "one of the group that has emerged in recent years seeking recognition and respect has been the *victim's rights "movement"*. (…) The success of these groups concerned with particular crimes and crime victims has served to highlight the general importance of "victims" as an effective political symbol and as a rallying point for a variety of grievances, dissatisfactions, and political agendas" (Viano, 1987: 440)[40]. In the United States and in the Great Britain numerous researches have been carried out into victimization[41] because it is a true real problem. But, even though victims support services are institutionalized by now, several issues have been raised about the last ones, or, in general about the action of the criminal system workers. As long ago, that is in 1979, Herman Goldstein denounced, on this point, that the police have been particularly susceptible to the "means over ends" syndrome, placing more emphasis on their improvement efforts on organization and operating methods than on the substantive outcome of their work. "What is troubling is that administrators of those agencies that have succeeded in developing a high level of operating efficiency have not gone on concerning themselves with the end results of their efforts" (Goldstein, 1979:239). Focusing on problems is attractive – he argued –both to citizens and the police, because it is a practical and concrete approach. In the following years we find several studies on how victims support agencies work and on their satisfaction or dissatisfaction. The International Crime Victimization Survey (ICVS) proceeds in this direction; it is the most far reaching program of fully standardized sample surveys looking at householders' experience of crime in different countries[42]. Its conclusion on servicing victims is that there has been an undoubted growth in specialized services to victims since the early 1980s, and "previous sweeps of the ICVS have indicated an increasing proportion of victims receiving help" (Van Kesteren, Mayhew and Nieuwbeerta, 2000:101).

Paying attention to victim begins to crop up in Italy too, even though still at an embryonic stage. This phenomenon is pointed out by one of Claudio Sarzotti's studies. He examines inaugural reports pronounced by chief appeal court prosecutors on the occasion of the opening of judicial years. When we analyze these documents several references to victims come out. According to Sarzotti the above-stated logic of contradiction between criminal and victim is combined in legal terms with the Italian discussion about the so-called reform of «fair trial», which is turned into changing article 111 of our Constitution. But, some prosecutors advocate that such reform has forgotten victims' rights leaving out any constitutional reference to them and largely upsetting the balance of penal system in criminal's favor (Sarzotti, 2006:116). Not affecting perpetrator enough has another harmful effect: it leads a victim to not reporting the crime suffered (*ibidem*:117).

If it is true that studies on the relation among the victimization, the victims' support agencies and the professional training are numerous in countries of common law, it is also true that their findings cannot be extended to the legal systems of civil law, where serving victims fall within judicial authority. This aspect is not a minor issue; you only have to keep in mind the different selection procedures and the different roles within the legal system: the position of the Surveillance Magistracy is totally different from the serving victim agencies one. But we know that also judges need professional training; when considering the great help from an interdisciplinary problem oriented approach; at this propose, a major contribution could come from victimology and criminology researches in view of a decision making process and the rehabilitating purpose of punishment. The Judge and the Surveillance Court have to get to a judgment which considers outcomes of treatment program in light of inmate's personality and which evaluates the real reformation of the prisoner also by means of victim's money compensation or through some sort of voluntary activity. Speaking of the victim's compensation, we have to remember that it is a required condition for granting Rehabilitation Order under the Italian legal system.

The positivist theories, spread at the beginning of the 20th century, gave a considerable boost to the development of criminology which have transformed prison population into a «laboratory» (Pavarini, 1995). Criminology has got a clinical approach which supports the exam of the single case for diagnostic and prognostic purposes and for the formulation of the resocialization treatment: it is a pragmatic and concise science that makes use of a multidisciplinary knowledge to understand the individual reasons of crime in order to prevent recidivism (Ponti, 1987). Instead, victimology is a scientific study of the reasons, the nature and the outcomes of the victimization caused by a behavior or a criminal action, included the interactions between the victim and the deviant, the victim and the judiciary system and the victim and the social reaction in terms of support and aid to them (Saponaro, 2004). We need to specify that a deviant action is not only the behavior formally forbidden by the state law, but also all the deviant actions defined by the international institutions[43]. Victimology borrows multidisciplinary and interdisciplinary scientific method from criminology. In fact, the victimology approach is multidisciplinary because it tries to solve crime victims' problems through sociology, psychology, psychiatry, medicine and law; and it is interdisciplinary because it wants to integrate the issues deriving from these several scientific points of view into one only explanatory model (Saponaro, 2004:66).

## EDUCATIONAL EXPERIENCES AND METHODOLOGIES DEVELOPED

Owing to cultural and socio-political features of the common law legal systems, we find a great attention to the professionalization of penal operators (policemen, prisons social workers, judges, lawyers, etc.). This is not the right place for investigating adequately the concept of «professionalization» or of «professional socialization», both of them examined in detail by eminent scholars of the organizations sociology. We can just mention some of major researches. The word «socialization» means a social process by which a cultural heritage is handed on to the members of a social group. Two conditions are required to make this process work well: the existence of institutions and practices that hand on a cultural heritage to the members of a community, and a high degree of flexibility of such institutions. A «cultural heritage» is the melted result of all sorts of art, buildings, traditions and beliefs that a society considers important for its history and culture. «Professional socialization» means a social process by which the professional skill and the vocational training are passed on. We have to be careful to distinguish vocational training from professionalization. The former refers just to a constituent part of the socialization, namely the acquisition of skills, know-how and techniques useful in the practise of a professional role. The latter includes the phase of the «selection». This last is the rating of members' qualities and skills before their entry into an organization or a profession (Mestitz, 1990:12). Herbert Simon and other scholars underline that selections and training processes are tools by which an organization control its members. Training, in fact, represents a social process intended for the improvement or the growth of the personal skills and powers, and for the development of members' beliefs and values. Effectively, a professional training fosters the internalization of the organizational influence (Simon, H. A., Smithburg, D. W. and Thompson, V. A., 1961:367). When we speak about the internalization of values, we invade a true treacherous arena: one of the arguments in favor of the kind of legislation or common law-making process – that the Right calls "social engineering" – on the one hand, or "activist" on the other, is that, like any other powerful disciplinary and institutional discourse, law has the power to change the terms of the conversation that produces our everyday life if it itself changes. The professionalization could start up "mechanisms by which hegemony is inscribed, reproduced, and accorded value by a range of practices having to do with disciplinary texts and their production within US legal institutions" (Pether, 2005:5). The risk feared is that cultural studies work towards wondering about subject-formation and critically positioning and problematizing the scholarly subject and the various institutions, discourses and practices. This reasoning is extensible to any kind of job and any sort of professional training. "Defining competent practice is an exercise in 'squaring the circle'. Extrapolating the criteria of 'component practice'44 in relation to any occupation may run the risk of placing the social scientist in the role of prescriptive evaluation" (Fielding, N., 1984:568). Studies using naturalistic research methodologies have shown that the strength of an occupational culture is explicable as a response to the everyday working situation. Penelope Pether writes something more: "The structural subordination of "others" in US law schools produces, just as it is produced by, judges who are blind to the ways in which they have come not to see or hear how their culture of writing and publishing the texts of the common law compounds the discrimination that desegregation was supposed to do away with, albeit with the plangent irony that has come in retrospect to characterize the phrase 'with all deliberate speed' (Brown v. Board of Education, 1954:301)[45]" (Pether, 2005:7).

Since the early 20th century most of educational and training courses have undoubtedly been addressed to police force both for cultural reasons and for institutional ones: we have constantly to remember that the serving sentence has been beyond police's authority, partly because it is not provided for a jurisdiction of a court; consequently, the policemen have a leading position in the prison system.

At the Third Annual Meeting of the Society for the Advancement of Criminology held in Berkeley, on December 29, 1948, a resolution was adopted authorizing a survey of the curricula of American Universities and colleges to determine what institutions had pre-professional training programs in the field of criminal justice administration. Frank M. Boolsen was appointed by the President of the Society as Chairman of a Committee to conduct the survey[46]. He and his Committee have released one of the most exhaustive reports of its kind, where we can find an inventory of the organized programs of instruction and research in twenty universities and colleges which offer degrees or their equivalent in this area. August Vollmer, a noted social scientist and a police authority (see below), states: "(…) Professor Boolsen (…) has made careful inquiries throughout the nation with the end in view of discovering how active the institutions have been in the promotion of knowledge concerning the cause and the prevention of crime and the management and the development of law enforcement and correctional agencies. It is hoped that this directory will serve not only as a supplement of what already has been done, but will contribute to the further advancement of criminology in this country" (Leonard, 1950:202). In fact, the general purpose of such survey is being an indispensable guide for future research on these problems: standardization of criminology curricula; standardization of course content; evaluation of existing training programs; transference of students and credit from one institution to another[47]; and coordination of pre-employment and in-service training programs.

Taking a step backward, in 1908 Vollmer established the Berkeley Police School, marking one of the first instances in which formal training was made available to police officers (Carte & Carte, 1975). Vollmer's efforts greatly contributed to the establishment of formal police training protocols and he is given credit for helping found the School of Criminology at the University of California at Berkeley. The establishment of this program launched an animated debate that has last with varying intensity during the intervening years. This debate centers on the proper content and role of criminal justice education and its relationship with formal training for entry-level police personnel.

In the meantime, in 1950 the Police Training Institute of the University of Louisville offered three twelve week terms a year in the fundamentals of police science to police officers of the southern part of the United States financed by grants from the General Education Board of the Rockefeller Foundation and the Carnegie Corporation of New York48. The course of instruction included not only such subjects as investigation, identification, patrol, communications, records, etc, but also administration, law, crime prevention, human relations, and police problems of the South (Leonard, 1950:201).

There is a relevant agreement on the structure and the value of formal vocational police training in a real police classroom. Less concurrence, however, is observed as regards the intent and content of academic preparation for prospective police officers. Such curricular disagreements with the link between academic and professional education are common across academic disciplines (Johnstone, 1990; Ward & Webb, 1984). "In the absence of broader consensus about goals and content of Criminal Justice Education (CJE)[49], it is the faculty of individual institutions who play a major role in shaping individual degree programs and their institutions. Groups such as the Academy of Criminal Justice Sciences (ACJS)[50] have promulgated 'academic standards' intended to bring greater consistency to the teaching of Criminal Justice; there is also a movement within ACJS to develop a certification process for programs which award degrees. At the same time, Criminal Justice remains a discipline that lacks clear consensus on what and how its graduates should have learned" (Schafer & Castellano, 2005:302).

We can quote other researches on professionalization of police force done in various countries. Paula Poncioni underlines that in Brazil an examination of the public security question reveals that, at least since the 1970s, there has been a continuous growth of criminality and violence and that the judiciary system and, in particular, the police have been ineffectual at facing this problem: "In this scenery, one of the topics frequently pointed out by public security specialists, by public policy makers, by government authorities and even by the policemen/women is the necessity to professionalize the Brazilian police as a resource to qualify the force in a more efficient, responsible and effective way to maintain order and public security" (Poncioni, 2005:585). This exigency is connected to global social changes and to complex needs of prison population: inevitably the transformation of the society reflects upon the multidisciplinary training of control and security actors because the «cohabitation of different approaches» can support their updating and the constant evaluation of the effectiveness of their actions (Bisi R. and Sette R., 2006:554). Another weighty matter, as suggested by Roberta Bisi and Raffaella Sette, concerns the motivational side of the day-to-day activity meant to have some chance of success: a performance is the result of the conjunction of the individual effort to reach the institutional objective and the level of skill that the operators of control have (information, grounding and training) (Bisi R. and Sette R., 2006:554).

Similar questions are pointed out by Peter Jen Der Pan, Shi-Hua Chang and Chi-Wei Lin, whose study explores, in Taiwan, 23 correctional officers' perceptions of the training program in the point of view of the Grounded theory: "This training program results in positive feelings about the significant learning experience, greater theoretical knowledge, and a greater understanding of the counseling work" (Der Pan, Chang & Lin, 2004:523).

If this institutional attention to police force professionalization contributes on the one hand to develop teaching methodologies and good practices for professional educational courses, on the other hand it faces the risk of not considering the need of training programs for the other workers of the penitentiary system. Such worry is a true problem for the fundamental action of the judiciary.

When we speak about the training courses for judges, the research done by Christina Murray can be regarded as an interesting idea for our analysis; she focuses on the relation existing among the racism, the sexism, the legal system and the professional training of Courts in South Africa. She describes the work of the Law, Race and Gender Research Unit in Cape Town, which was established in order to examine race and gender bias in the administration of justice, and to explore the possibility of a judicial training. The Author firstly analyzes the racist discourse in the magistrates' courts and gender bias in divorce cases, and more recently, she undertakes an empirical study on gendered allocation of housing and family violence's, and finally the authoress concludes: "(…) Judicial education has not been appropriate in South Africa for political reasons" (Murray, 1995:36): she also suggests that something is changing and that the unit can be involved in training programs.

If we pay attention to what happens in the European Community, the institutional effort is still inadequate for planning a chain of educational and training programs for prison workers, with particular reference to the Italian Surveillance Magistracy. Continental universities mainly set up post degree courses for those who wish to enter into the judiciary career. We can quote the following educational experiences: the Certificat de Criminologie et de Sciences Pénales of Université des Sciences Sociales (France) organized by the Institute of Criminology and of Penal Science; the Licence en Droit of Université Pau et des Pays de l'Adour, Centre de Sciences Criminelles (France) with a course on criminal science which facilitates the enrolment for the vocational training schools for the judiciary career and for the specialization course in criminal science organized by the Centre de Science Criminelles of the Law Faculty and of the Economics one of the Pau University; Certificat de Sciences Criminelles at the Bourdeaux I University (France); and, the Attestation de Sciences Criminelles of the Poitiers University (France) (Sette, 1999:15,16).

Concerning Italy, we have to underline that criminology teaching has been run and is being run in different degree courses: "(...) For instance, within the Faculty of Medicine, in the past, criminology teaching appeared as Criminal Anthropology. Now it appears as Legal Medicine. Criminology also appears in the Political Science degree course (Department of Social Politics), in the faculties of Law, Psychology, Sociology and Educational Sciences" (Bisi, 1999:107). When we concentrate on the professionalization of the Italian Bench, the framework that we can draw up is poor and inadequate to the judicial need of professionalization. The object of our research is the C.S.M. reports[51] on recruiting and vocational training because it is in charge of providing for the teaching of judges. It emerges at a first analysis that young judges, newly appointed, choose to be assigned to the Surveillance Magistracy. This event makes us think over it, especially if we keep in mind that the judiciary of serving sentence has got little social regard from the legal culture's point of view: it is thought as a «second rate» institution within judicial environment. The reason of this choice is linked to a personal motivation: it is very likely that the young judge will work in a place in his residence town, or near it. Such consideration masks obviously a lack of motivation to this profession and, as we said above (and suggested by Roberta Bisi and Raffaella Sette) it is a major matter. If, in addition to these reasons, we also weigh substantial inadequacy of professional training course for the Surveillance Judges the picture is quite discouraging.

If we concentrate on C.S.M. documents, we have to underline that it claims the necessity of an educational plan for 1981 when a special issue of its official review was dedicated to the recruitment and the professionalization of our Bench. Starting from the analysis of the institution of a training period for the judge newly appointed, Enrico Ferri affirms the will of the C.S.M. to look for a building where locate a durable academy open to all the Italian judges and scholars (Ferri, 1981:29). In the following special issue explicitly dedicated to the Surveillance Magistracy, the C.S.M. again pronounces a statement of intentions through various essays of leading scholars and experts without reaching any positive result. The paper of Maria Rosaria Marino – Surveillance Judge in Santa Maria Capua Vetere (Italy) – is the only voice which could stimulate the discussion on the necessity of a training planning for the Surveillance Judges. In fact, she stresses the importance of this educational intervention reporting the difficulties into which judges run every day (Marino, 1995). In particular, she concentrates on conflicting interventions of legislative reforms which have passed from a high openness to change to acceptance new ideas and methods, the so called period of the "prison of the hope" (Marino, 1995:457), to a restrictiveness of the granting conditions and judicial practices to fight organized crime and the increasing narcotraffic. The entry of this new sort of criminal people into the prison has caused a lot of trouble to manage them. The problem of dealing with people whose behaviours are difficult represents the main concern for our Bench. The necessity to update the professionalization on developments of the social change and of the valiant effort to realize a pluralist society inside the penal institution is the leitmotif of all C.S.M. reports. The trouble is that for many years the C.S.M. has never seriously faced the educational problem. The first official document that testifies a new institutional position on this matter is the 1996's one where it is reasserted the necessity to update the professional training both by the point of view of methodology and by the subject's one which are easily identified by means of "detecting the real needs" (Quaderni del Consiglio Superiore della Magistratura, 1996: 24). We also read that there are several points to develop:

- it is necessary to plan the continuous education on the basis of international experiences, especially that developed by the French École Nationale de la Magistrature[52] (ibidem: 25).
- The planning has to consider the level of education and experience (ibidem: 29).
- A scientific attention must be paid to the methodology of the educational course: it is necessary to program a differential training course as regards the seniority, the office and the education. All these elements must be correlated with the development of criminal law, informatics and the European Community law and the comparative one (ibidem: 35-36).
- It is essential that new teaching methodologies are picked out though with flexible teaching schemes (ibidem: 37). The educational pattern used is modulated in different ways: on a report with a discussion amid people attending the meeting; on short reports with debate on separate questions highlighted by the teacher; on study groups and, hardly ever, on round-table conference (ibidem: 38).

All that we have said till now concerns the educational planning generally addressed to the whole of Italian judges. But, we can read an opening signal towards a change in the 1996 report where special training programs are provided for the Appeal judge (penal field) and for the Juvenile court (ibidem: 102, 103). This new development allows us to hope for a specialized educational programming for the Surveillance Judges. Contrary to our expectation, nothing has been provided for this case till now. In fact, if we read the reports for 200553, 2006 and 2008, we do not find any mention of a specialized course, even though something new can be foreseen as to educational subjects, criteria of their selection and teaching methodologies.

Speaking about educational subjects, we underline a course entitled "The victim in the judicial system ". It was organized by the French Ecole Nationale de la Magistrature and was held in April 2006 in Paris. Its purpose was to examine major measures taken in victims favour within the back-up policy and to suggest development prospects (Quaderni del Consiglio Superiore della Magistratura, 2006). To conclude our survey we have to mention a noteworthy course about "The penal treatment between the Surveillance Magistracy and the Cognizance Judge" within the educational plan for 2008.

As for criteria of subjects' selection, we like emphasize the start of a participatory decision making process that can be traced back to the so called «bottom up» mould. In fact, subjects of the training course are pointed out by judges themselves. So, the C.S.M. states that we are in front of a vocational training circuit. Judges skill has to be pursued by a "autocreated" training (Quaderni del Consiglio Superiore della Magistratura, 2005: 16). Only this circular process can exploit best practices developed within local Courts. The prospect is a "dialogic creation of the knowledge" (ibidem, 16). The methodologies and the criteria by which the C.S.M. choice the teacher go in the same direction: training organs at local level are composed by judges who know educational needs and are in close contact with users. In connection with that there is a system for surveying teachers vocations by means of a periodic questioning at local level. The C.S.M. and its Ninth Committee – body of the Head Office dealing with training guidelines – have contacted others authorities and non-profit organizations to carry out shareable educational activities since 2007 (Quaderni del Consiglio Superiore della Magistratura, 2008)54.

When we are interested in new teaching methodologies, we can testify a changeover to the new technology. The training program provides seven courses e-learning, among which a "Laboratory of Practices" about penal matters (Quaderni del Consiglio Superiore della Magistratura, 2008). The Ninth Committee's objective is to reduce face-to-face lectures and to promote discussions between the discussant and judges about a singular case or a specific topic, laboratories and work groups. For these reasons, the teacher or the coordinator will take care to arrange the teaching equipment before the course start; so that the people attending will be able to participate and intervene (Quaderni del Consiglio Superiore della Magistratura, 2008).

## DEVELOPMENTS AND CHALLENGES: THE ITALIAN SCHOOL OF MAGISTRACY AND THE EUROPEAN JUDICIAL TRAINING NETWORK

In spite of an almost total absence of inputs of criminology and victimology essays we can draw the attention on the creation of new canals for the development of professional training.

The institution of the Italian School of Magistracy (*Scuola Superiore della Magistratura* [*SSM*]) certainly represents a milestone in the judiciary professionalization considering that its institutional role bases itself on arranging a professional training program for Italian judges according to their needs.

The first attempt at its establishment dates back to 1993. Actually, the educational activity of C.S.M. started since 1973 and it went on till the early 1990s in an occasional and disconnected way and without an educational plan. The institutions involved in this rudimental professionalization were the C.S.M. and the special reporting parliamentary Judicial Reform and Justice Administration Commission (*Commissione per la Riforma Giudiziaria e l'Amministrazione della Giustizia* [CRGAG]). The Commission pinpointed the prominent subject under discussion and proposed organizing a study meeting to deal with these new important matters. In the early 1990s the CRGAG and the C.S.M. formulated, for the first time, an organic educational policy broaching thorny questions about the organization, the structure and the content of training courses. On the plenary session on 19th November 1992 the CRGAG suggested that the C.S.M. should approve a structured training plan for the following years and should get in touch with the competent bodies of the Ministry of Justice [MJ] to institute a "School" for the Italian Bench. The C.S.M. accepted the proposal and established relations with ministerial bodies. So the MJ and the C.S.M. signed a convention for an experimental establishment of a School for judges on 23rd September 1993. This School – which was an articulation of the C.S.M. – was solemnly opened on 11th April 1994 in the presence of the President of the Republic. But it was short-lived because the State Auditors' Department, particularly the Control Division, refused the check and the registration of the Convention. However, this document represents a point of no return for the judiciary professionalization: it concludes a collective reflection about the value and the institutional meaning of the skill and of the necessity of an educational planning to reach it (*Quaderni del Consiglio Superiore della Magistratura*, 2005: 20).

The C.S.M., been in office from 1994 to 1998, was working at the educational plan; so, it established the Ninth Committee (about which we said above) with the task of organizing and coordinating professional training courses[55].

At last, the SSM has been instituted by the 30th January 2006/26 legislative decree. The School has the exclusive competence on teaching planning and professional training for Italian judges, included promoting international learning exchanges and evaluating the attending judges for their career promotion. The SSM is a self-governing educational center with a legal public status, a civil capacity and an organizational, managerial, contractual and accounting autonomy. The members of the SSM are judges, lawyers and professors. Its establishment was not carried out painlessly. The C.S.M. has pointed up several questions about the constitutional legitimacy of these rules, before their passage: in detail, the C.S.M. has underlined doubts about the composition of the board of governors, the procedure of their appointment, the regulation of the evaluation role of the attending judges to their career promotion, the financial banking of this institution, the absence of clear criteria for the selection of teachers and tutors (Resolution, 10th November 2005)[56]. In spite of this, the C.S.M. reaffirms the necessity of a serious and specialised professionalization confirming its pledge in this direction. The SSM will most probably work throughout 2009 and the question concerning the relation between the SSM and other institutions seems unsolved, above all as for the hardly acceptable involvement of the Ministry of Justice in the appointment of the Executive Committee and in the definition of educational guidelines (*Magistratura Democratica*, 2008)[57].

Another way, by which allow us to start a new development of judiciary professionalization, is the agreement of our Bench with the European Judicial Training Network [EJTN][58]. The EJTN was founded on 13th October 2000; it is a non profit making international organisation with its headquarters in Brussels and comprises the institutions specifically responsible for the training of the professional judiciary within the European Union [EU]. Today, it has 31 members from 26 of 27 member countries of the EU and 7 observers among whom the institutions of the EU and the Council of Europe[59]. The adoption of a Strategic Plan (2007 – 2013) on 21st September 2006, allowed for the specification of objectives and priorities of the EJNT, permits to develop an efficient strategy and thereby to give more visibility to initiatives and activities implemented by the Network. For the period 2007 – 2013, three main directions have been defined:

1. to guarantee the quality of judicial training in Europe;
2. to contribute to the realization of three objectives defined at the European level for judicial training (to improve the knowledge of European judicial systems, European law and cooperation tools, as well as the languages);
3. to reinforce the EJNT in order to make its structure and its networking more efficient.

These aims involve analyzing and identifying training needs, designing programmes and methods for collaborative training, developing exchanges and disseminating experiences in the field of judicial training, coordinating programs and providing training expertise and know-how.

If we focus our attention on the exchange program, we find that its main objective is "to develop a mutual trust between judicial authorities in order to promote the mutual recognition of judicial decisions by getting to know each other better and working together" (EJNT, 2008:8)[60]. In order to achieve the ambitious objectives of the Program, the EJNT has drafted administrative and financial procedures in close cooperation with its network of contact points appointed by each partner of the Program. It also recruits the necessary staff, working under direction of the EJNT Secretary General, Gilles Charbonnier, and ensures the design, implementation, coordination and evaluation of the Program. The EJNT is planning to organize 550 exchanges. Once again, the Program will allow European judges and prosecutors – from the youngest to the most experienced – and judicial trainers at national and decentralized levels to share the work of their colleagues in another European country, to become acquainted with a judicial system that is different from their own, to understand how it works and thus to assess their own professional practices, deontology, as well as the way they deal with the main societal issues[61].

The C.S.M. joins, at least seemingly, the Network enthusiastically (Programma dei corsi di formazione e aggiornamento professionale a carattere internazionale per I magistrati, anno 2006).

The establishment of the *SSM* and the foundation of the EJNT are two weighty opportunities for judges to develop an earnest professionalization. Always keeping in mind that the professional training is a process which moves uninterruptedly from an opening learning to a progressive training leading to a continuous professional growing according to social needs, "it is clear that the new necessities for safety and the necessity to oppose crime globalization impose the creation of specialized disciplines that, (…), train in techniques that may be of service to the community and both public and private sectors for the prevention and repression of any form of crime and offence" (Bisi R., 1999:109).

As regards Italian Surveillance Magistracy, we hope for a professional training planning which considers the usefulness of criminology and victimology in front of new sorts of crimes and the increasing victimization. We wish also to remind that, according to the latest studies on institutional environments, the growing complexity of the justice system has shifted the attention from a technical specialization to an acquisition of integrated relational skills. This integration of various abilities will allow our Surveillance Magistracy to manage convicts and other problematic expressions of crime through a suitable reconstruction of them and to promote the reconciliation between victims and their perpetrators for the restoration of social order.

## ACKNOWLEDGMENT

A special thank-you to my aunt Elisa Fanci, a teacher very keen on English, whose help has been useful to write this chapter.

## REFERENCES

Academic Credit for police training. *Journal of Criminal Justice Education, 16*(2), 300-317.

Associazione Nazionale Magistrati [ANM] (2003, March 23). *Magistrati e la sfida della professionalità*, from http://www.associazionenazionalemagistrati.it/public/File/Convegni/proposta.doc.

Bisi, R. (1999). Teaching and professional training in criminology. *European Journal of Crime Criminal Law and Criminal Justice*, *7*(2), 103–129. doi:10.1163/15718179920518763

Bisi, R., & Sette, R. (2006). Trasformazioni sociali e nuove esigenze di formazione professionale. In A. Febbrajo, A. La Spina, & M. Raiteri, (Ed.), *Cultura giuridica e politiche pubbliche in Italia*, (pp. 553-568). Milano, Italy: Giuffrè.

*Brown v. Board of Education*. 1954.349 U.S. 294 from http://www.nationalcenter.org/brown.html

Carte, G. E., & Carte, E. H. (1975). *Police Reform in the United States: The Era of August Vollmer, 1905-1932*. Berkeley, CA: University of California Press.

Caso, L., & Josi, E. (2006). Lo psicologo criminologo come giudice esperto: riflessioni sul tribunale di sorveglianza. In G. De Leo, & P. Patrizi, (Ed.), *Lo psicologo criminologo* (pp. 339-368). Milano, Itlay: Giuffrè. Consiglio Superiore della Magistratura [CSM] (n.d.). Retrieved from http://www.csm.it/circolari/ & http://www.csm.it/documenti/.

De Leo, G., & Patrizi, P. (Eds.). (2006). *Lo psicologo criminologo.* Milano, Italy: Giuffrè.

Della Casa, F. (1998). *La magistratura di sorveglianza. Organizzazione, competenze, procedure*. Torino, Itlay: Giappichelli.

Der Pan, P. J., Chang, S., & Lin, C. (2007). Correctional officers' perceptions of the competency-based counseling training program in Taiwan. *International Journal of Offender Therapy and Comparative Criminology*, *51*(5), 523–540. doi:10.1177/0306624X06294134

Engeström, Y. (1987). *Learning by Expanding. An Activity Theoretical Approach to Development Research*. Helsinki, Finland: Orienta-Konsultint.

Ferrajoli, L. (2000). *Diritto e ragione. Teorie del garantismo penale*. Roma-Bari, Italy: Laterza.

Ferrario, B., & De Stefanis, C. (1995). *Procedimenti e provvedimenti della magistratura di sorveglianza.* Padova, Italy: CEDAM.

Ferri, E. (1981). Il tirocinio degli uditori giudiziari nella realtà normativa della Repubblica Italiana. Consiglio Superiore Magistratura [Special Issue]. *Il magistrato. Dal reclutamento alla formazione professionale. Esperienze in Italia e nel mondo* (pp. 15-30).

Ferrua, P. (2005). *Il 'giusto processo'*. Bologna, Italy: Zanichelli.

Fielding, N. (1984). Police socialization and police competence. *The British Journal of Sociology*, *XXXV*(4), 568–590. doi:10.2307/590435

Garland, D. (2004). *La cultura del controllo. Crimine e ordine sociale nel mondo contemporaneo*. Milano, Italy: Il Saggiatore (original title: *The Culture of Control*. Oxford, UK: Oxford University Press, 2001).

Goldstein, H. (1979). Improving policy: a problem oriented approach. *Crime and Delinquency*, *25*(2), 236–258. doi:10.1177/001112877902500207

Idem, XXIX Congresso. (2008). *Un impegno per un'Europa dei diritti.* Retrieved from http://www.movimentoperlagiustizia.org/filedload/opuscolocongresso1.pdf.

Johnstone, D. B. (1990). Looking at New Links: New Models of Transfer and Articulation between Two-Year and Four-Year Campuses. *Journal of Criminal Justice Education*, *1*, 51–57. doi:10.1080/10511259000082051

Leonard, V. A. (1950). Current notes. *Journal of Criminal Law and Criminology*, Jul/Aug(41), 201-2.

Lurigio, A. J. (Ed.). (1987). Criminal Victimization and Crime [Special issue]. *Crime and Delinquency*, *33*(4).

Margara, A. (1995). L'evoluzione della normativa e la situazione penitenziaria dopo la riforma del 1986. In Quaderni del Consiglio Superiore della Magistratura [Special Issue]. *La magistratura di sorveglianza* (pp. 94-117).

Marino, M. R. (1995). La magistratura di sorveglianza e l'esecuzione della pena. Le rispettive funzioni, le conseguenti problematiche. In Quaderni del Consiglio Superiore della Magistratura [Special Issue]. *La magistratura di sorveglianza* (pp. 449-460).

Mestitz, A. (1990). *Selezione e formazione professionale dei magistrate e degli avvocati in Francia*. Padova, Italy: CEDAM.

Murray, C. (1995). Interrogating justice: Research on race and gender bias in the South African Court system. *International Journal of Discrimination and the Law*, *1*(1), 29–38.

Ostrom, E., & Whitaker, G. (1973). Does Local and Community Control Make a Difference? *American Journal of Political Science*, *17*, 48–76. doi:10.2307/2110474

Patrizi, P. (1996). *Psicologia giuridico penale*. Milano, Italy: Giuffrè.

Pavarini, M. (1995). L'articolazione del sistema punitive: novità e prospettive. In Quaderni del Consiglio Superiore della Magistratura [Special Issue]. *La magistratura di sorveglianza* (pp. 43-65).

Pether, P. (2005). Negotiating the structure of violence; or, on not inventing "The Sullivans". *Social Semiotics*, *15*(1), 5–28. doi:10.1080/10350330500059080

Poncioni, P. (2005). The professional police model and the professional formation of the future polireme in the Police Academies of Rio de Janeiro State. *Sociedade e Estado*, *20*(3), 585–610. doi:10.1590/S0102-69922005000300005

*Riflessioni, proposte ed approfondimenti* (XXIX Congress of *Associazione Nazionale Magistrati*, 2008, June 6-8), from http://www.movimentoperlagiustizia.org/filedload/opuscolocongresso1.pdf

Saponaro, A. (2004). *Vittimologia. Origini, concetti, tematiche*. Milano, Italy: Giuffrè.

Sarzotti, C. (2006). *Cultura giuridica e culture della pena. I discorsi inaugurali dell'anno giudiziario dei procuratori Generali*. Torino, Italy: L'Harmattan Italia.

Schafer, J. A., & Castellano, T. C. (2005). Academie versus academy: Faculty views on awarding academic credits for police training. *Journal of Criminal Justice Education*, *16*(2), 300–317. doi:10.1080/10511250500082229

Schafer, S. (1975). The proper role of a victim-compensation system. *Crime and Delinquency*, *21*(1), 45–49. doi:10.1177/001112877502100106

Scribner, S. (1985). Knowledge at work. *Anthropology & Education Quarterly*, *16*(3), 199–231. doi:10.1525/aeq.1985.16.3.05x1486d

Sette, R. (1999). *L'insegnamento della criminologia nelle Università e in altre istituzioni*. Bologna, Italy: CLUEB.

Simon, H. A., Smithburg, D. W., & Thompson, V. A. (1961). *Public Administration*. New York: Knopf.

Van Kesteren, J., Mayhew, P., & Nieuwbeerta, P. (2000). *Criminal Victimization in Seventeen industrialized Countries*. The Hague, the Netherlands: Wetenschappelijk Onderzoek – en Documentatiecentrum.

Viano, E. (1987). Victim's rights and the Constitution: reflections on a bicentennial. *Crime and Delinquency*, *33*(4), 438–451. doi:10.1177/0011128787033004002

Vichnieswky, L. (1995). Le misure alternative nei paesi CEE con particolare riferimento alla legislazione francese. In Quaderni del Consiglio Superiore della Magistratura [Special Issue]. *La magistratura di sorveglianza* (pp. 527-585).

Walzer, D. (1977). Citizen contact and legal support system. *Social Science Quarterly*, 3–14.

Ward, R. H., & Webb, V. J. (1984). *Quest for quality*. New York: University Publications.

Zaniboni, A. (2004). *Magistratura di sorveglianza o tribunale della pena?* from http://www.sestaopera.it/home/CORSO_VOLONTARI/4_art.Zaniboni_Dignitas2004_MagistrSorv.pdf.

## ENDNOTES

1 See Di Gennaro & Vetere, (1933), I diritti dei detenuti e la loro tutela, Rassegna di storia penitenziaria, p. 5; Petitti Di Roreto, C.I. (1840). Della condizione attuale delle carceri e dei mezzi di migliorarla, Torino; Scalia, M. (1967). Sul governo e sulla riforma delle carceri in Italia, Saggio storico e teorico, Torino.

2 It is ruled in the Italian Constitution, article n° 27, which provides that imprisonment and fine must not lie down on inhuman treatments, but we have to tend to the reeducation of sentenced.

3 From now on ord. penit. when it's quoted an article of Italian Prison Act.

4 The most important are the 24 November 1981 no. 689 Act, which introduced substitute sanctions, and, primarily, the 10 October 1986 no. 663 Act, commonly called Gozzini's Law: it increased power of the Surveillance Magistracy and established new alternative measures to promote the reintegration of ex-convicts into society.

5 Article n° 69 ord. penit.

6 Article n° 18(7, 8) ord. penit.

7 Articles n° 30 and n° 30-ter, and n° 52 and n° 53 ord. penit.

8 Article n° 53-bis ord. penit.

9 Article n° 69(8) ord. penit.

10 Article n° 11(2) ord. penit.

11 Article n° 69(8) ord. penit.

12 Article n° 17(2) ord. penit.

13 Article n° 18(8) ord. penit.

14 Article n° 53(2) and n° 54(3) Executive Regulations(Regolamento esecutivo), from now on Reg. esec.

15 Article n°20(5) Reg. esec.

16 Article n° 69 ord. penit.

17 Article n° 331(1) Code of Criminal Procedure, from now on C.C.P.

18 Article n° 46 Reg. esec. and articles n° 21(4) and n° 69(5) ord. penit.

19 Article n° 69(5) ord. penit.

20 There is not even a minor treatment planning as other legal systems regulate; for example the German rules provide for seven areas which cannot be ignored in the treatment programming (See § 7, Absatz 2, Strafvollzugsgesetz, 16 March 1976). Another interesting experience is the Integrated Prison Regime (IPR) in Western Australia. This initiative is a major change strategy being implemented by Prisons Service. IPR seeks to establish the regime as the "glue" which binds together and which provides reinforcement of the many different activities and initiatives within the prison that seek to provide particular outcomes for prisoners. Rehabilitation occurs through unit management, via programs and initiatives such as case management, therapeutic interventions including cognitive skills, educational and vocational training and improved employment opportunities. See http://support.csa.com.

21 Articles n° 51-bis and n° 51-ter ord. penit.

22 Article n° 47(8) ord. penit.

23 Article n° 47(4) ord. penit.

24 Article n° 679 C.C.P. according to article n° 69(3) and 69 (4) ord. penit.

25 Article n° 47 ord. Penit.

26 Article n° 94 Presidential Decree D.P.R. 309/1990.

27 Article n° 50 ord. Penit.

28 Article n° 47-ter ord. Penit.

29 Article n° 683 C.C.P. and article n° 178 Criminal Code, from now on C.C. We have to specify what «Rehabilitation Order» is for the Italian legal system. It is similar to a Supervision Order or to a Community Rehalibitation Order (provided for a specific age range: young people aged 16-17), both regulated by «common law» legal system. The Italian Rehabilitation Order is an institution by which all legal consequences of conviction are cancelled if sentenced have paid legal costs and victim compensation, in addition to showing their reformation. It is similar to the Discharge of a bankrupt.

30 Article n° 47-bis ord. penit.

31 Article n° 684(1) C.C.P. and articles n° 146 and n° 147 C.C.

32 Article 14-ter ord. penit.

33 Articles n° 30 and n° 30-ter, and n° 52 and n° 53 ord. penit.

34 Article n° 53-bis ord. penit.

35 Article n° 680 C.C.P. and article n° 70(2) ord. penit.

36 To tell the truth, the judges in hearing are three (the President and two judges) more often than not, because in a same day the court discusses more cases, each one set down to a Surveillance Judge.

37 From now on C.S.M.

38 The circular of C.S.M. dated 19 February 2004, "Appointment and Ratification Criteria of the experts at Surveillance Court for three-year period 2005-2007", states that as an expert it doesn't necessarily need to have a degree, but the further attribute of "professional" doesn't makes, in fact, the attainment being ignored". See http://www.csm.it.

39 In the United States politicians hold press conference with victims' relatives to announce provision for minimum compulsory penalties. Acts passed are called after the victims' name: Megan's Law, Jenna's Law, Brady's Bill. In the United Kingdom victims are invited as speakers to conventions arranged by both political parties: Conservatives and Labour have uphold "Victims Charter". For more about this subject, see Garland (2004).

40 Viano claims that there is a strong connection between the victim movement and the powerful conservative forces that have dominated American life and the shaping of the criminal justice agenda during the 1980s. Wondering whether balancing the scales of justice is due to genuine concern about victims rights or to genuine cooptation, he concludes that "The importance and popularity that victim-related issues enjoy today is due in great part not so much to a reawakening of compassion, decency and concern for fellow human beings but rather to the prevalence of conservative ideology in the 1980s" (Viano, 1987: 443).

41 For example, the journal "Crime & Delinquency" has dedicated an interesting special issue to criminal victimization and crime in 1987. Cf. Lurigio A. J., (Ed.). (1987), Criminal Victimization and Crime. Crime & delinquency, 33 (4).

42 This report deals with seventeen industrialized countries (Australia, Belgium, Canada, Catalonia, Denmark, England and Wales, Finland, France, Japan, the Netherlands, Northern Ireland, Poland, Portugal, Sweden, Switzerland, USA) and interviews were mainly conducted by telephone (with samples selected through variants of random digit dialing). The overall response rate in the 17 countries was 64%. Samples ware usually of 2,000 people. Each participating country paid for its own fieldwork. The results in this report relate mainly to respondents' experience of crime in 1999. Those interviewed were asked about crimes they had experienced (car-related crime, motorcycle theft, bicycle theft, burglary and theft of

personal property, contact crime, robbery, sexual incidents, assault and threats) whether or not reported to the police.

43 See http://www.worldsocietyofvictimology.org.

44 On this point, Fielding writes: "Formal models of occupational socialization, which commonly separate processual and structural influences on individuals, divert attention from the active inter-relation of these elements, and mask the world they seek to describe by neglecting matters of situated, local and social organization. To gain analytic purchase on police practice one must distinguish between the police organization and the police occupation; the former is the formal institutional apparatus whose 'license' is the achievement of specified objectives, while the latter is the complex of formal and informal practices sanctioned under the organization's 'mandate'. The 'occupational culture' is counterposed to organizational demands, referring to the informal culture of members in contrast to the formal organization" (Fielding, 1984: 568-9).

45 It was a landmark decision of the United States Supreme Court which overturned earlier rulings going back to Plessy v. Ferguson in 1896, by declaring that state laws that established separate public schools for black and white students denied black children equal educational opportunities. See http://www.nationalcenter.org/brown.html.

46 Frank M. Boolsen was a Professor of Police Science and Administration at Fresno State College, Fresno, California.

47 On this point the debate is still open. Cf. Joseph A. Schafer and Thomas C. Castellano who examined the contention whether professional training is analogous to learning experiences obtained in the college classroom. They explored how Criminal justice educators view this issue in the context of police training (2005).

48 Students selected received a stipend covering living expenses and a travel allowance.

49 For information, http://www.cjed.com.

50 For information, http://www.acjs.org/.

51 See http://www.csm.it/documenti/ or http://www.csm.it/circolari/.

52 The educational programs of the French École Nationale de la Magistrature pay a great attention to various aspects, both those technical and juridical, and those aiming to a cultural training of judges, meant in a broad sense. In fact, some E.N.M. documents define judges as "social workers" who have to understand implications of their decisions to direct their actions to the achievement of the law purposes. It is no surprise to us that training programs include many activities "de réflexion sur le evolutions de la société contemporaine, de sensibilitation, et d'ouverture" (Quaderni del Consiglio Superiore della Magistratura, 1996: 49) among which we can remember foreign language, psychology, psychiatry, accountancy, juvenile delinquency, the analysis of the judicial intervention impact on the town center and the social and working reintegration of ex-convicts.

53 This is the first official document in which the educational planning is circumstantial and organized also on the base of data concerning the educational activity of a four-year period (2001-2004): the trend of the attendance at courses; scientific fields involved and the teaching methodology used.

54 For instance, we can quote the Victims Racket and Usury Fund, the Commissioner of the Fight against the Counterfeit, the O.C.S.E., the Ministry of the Environment, the Observatory for the protection of fundamental rights (Quaderni del Consiglio Superiore della Magistratura, 2008).

55 Plenary session 9th July 1996.

56 See http://www.csm.it/circolari/05111o_1.pdf.

57 See http://magistraturademocratica.it/files/brochure%20sito.pdf.

58 The EJTN acts within the scope of the Amsterdam Treaty of 2nd October 1997, the Tampere European Council meeting of 15th and 16th October 1999, the Hague Programme of 4th and 5th November 2004 and the European Commission Communication on judicial training of 29th June 2006, which set an ambitious goal for the EU: to build a genuine European area of justice, to promote awareness of legal systems and thus, to enhance understanding, confidence and cooperation between judges and prosecutors within the Member States. See http://www.appinter.csm.it/ejtn_dw/pdf/delibere/guida_EN.pdf.

59 For details, see http://www.appinter.csm.it/ejtn_dw/pdf/delibere/guida_EN.pdf.

60 The EJNT, which has been organizing the Program since 2006, now has a monopoly position for its implementation, as acknowledged by the European Commission (Decision of 11th July 2006).

61 Exchanges for a longer period (from 3 months to 1 year) at the Court of Justice of the European Communities and Eurojust will be continued, with the extension of this offer, for the first time in 2008, at the European Court of Human Rights. In the same way, individual judges and prosecutors or courts will be offered the opportunity to submit projects that could benefit from the Program's funds provided that they are in line with its objectives. See the EJTN website (http://www.ejtn.eu) which contains information about the members and the activities of the Network, about judicial systems in the EU Member States, as well as recent publications and links to the main national and European databases.

# Chapter 14
# Teaching Criminology to Police Officers:
## Bologna's Local Police Case

**Andrea Piselli**
*University of Bologna, Italy and Bologna Local Police, Italy*

## EXECUTIVE SUMMARY

*This article introduces the main division within the police corps in Italy and explains some historical reasons and their different task. Then it is exposed the recent change of the local police from political evolution of the State and new tasks established by law. This fast translation entailed a new training of policemen and in few years many changes occurred. While analyzing what happened in these years and which choices were made, it is argued that local police well adapted to new role with flexible cultural instruments. Main school were organized to satisfy the need of standard training, but corps independence allowed to realize single efficient projects particularly needed. Conclusion is the appreciation of free training method for police subjects.*

## ITALY'S POLICE CORPS

It is not easy to talk about Italy's Police because for some historical reasons there is in Italy a large number of different Police corps. Before beginning the study of a special case we must resume some notes about this situation. It is an ancient tradition coming from the early Roman Empire that led to this multiplicity. We may remember the traditional four police corps instituted in the age of the empire and recognize in them some characteristics that still survive. The *Praetoriani* were a kind of military police, directly depending from the emperor and employed for the defence of his person and in the state security; *Vigiles* were a police Corp composed by civilians with a military organization, with tasks of fire brigade and nightly patrol of the town; *Cohors urbana* was a military organized Corp made of civilians, of town police depending from city managers and employed to control the traffic in the streets and the markets; *Lictores* were civilians police officers representing and serving magistrates while administering justice. It is not difficult to recognize in these ancient corps some of the characteristics

DOI: 10.4018/978-1-60566-872-7.ch014

still surviving in modern police institutions: (1) the military vs civil nature; (2) the speciality of tasks; (3) the dependence from central vs local political power; (4) the relation with justice institutions. Reflection concerning Police is always focused in the solutions given to these points. We could say that political history of a country might be written according to the history of its police institutions. According to this premise, we may see along political history of Italy many police corps which replicate the same characters of the ones during the early roman empire. It is a series of military, civil, national, local, specialized corps which reflect the political institutions of the time: absolute monarchy, revolutions, commune, civil war etc.

Nowadays it seems that police corps variety and multiplicity reflect political complexity (or confusion?) so we have:

1. five national police corps: National Police (*Polizia di Stato)*[1], *Carabinieri*[2], Economic Police (*Guardia di Finanza)*[3], Penitentiary Police (*Polizia Penitenziaria)*[4], National Forestry Commission (*Corpo Forestale dello Stato)*[5];
2. about a hundred of country corps of Provincial Police (*Polizia Provinciale)*[6];
3. about a thousand of town corps of Municipal Police (*Polizia Municipale)*[7].

In some places in Italy the corps of Provincial Police have been fused together with those of Municipal Police of their country's towns realizing new corps of Local Police: this kind of experience is actually developed just in Lombardy Region.

The police service is so divided in five national agencies, depending from five different ministers, and specifically *Carabinieri* from Defense, National Police from Home Office, Economic Police from Treasury, Penitentiary Police from Justice and National Forestry Commission from Agriculture; beside there are many local agencies depending from city mayors or country governors. This kind of hierarchical relation with different political powers, both the central government and the local administration, is typical of Italy and answers to one of the questions we pointed before: answer to question (3) is that any political power in Italy owns its police Corp! About other questions we note that nowadays two of the national agencies, *Carabinieri* and Economic Police are military corps, while all the others are civilians, although under special rules. There has been a translation to civil police in Italy during the 80's, but we must remember that before 1981 all national police corps were military. This means that answering to question (1) in Italy there is both military and civil police. The particularity of task, which is question (2) is, as we may guess, a middle solution: all police corps are specialized in some disciplines, but all police corps have the power/right to pursuit any kind of crime. For example *Carabinieri* is the only Military Police agency, but they are deputed to pursuit all crimes, and actually specialized also in environmental crime, art, health etc., as well as Economic Police, that is the agency deputed to pursuit smuggling, but nowadays is also specialized in drugs, recycling, counterfeit and so on. Last question we pointed before, (4), concerning the relation with justice institution, is particularly problematic. All police corps depend from either political power and magistrates: this double nature of police is explained with the phrase "the double hat". In fact, according to constitutional principles, it is stated for magistrates only the power and duty to pursuit all crimes, and the duty for police to refer magistrates about all crimes. The problem of double hat is that one power (the political one) orders to police what to do, but another power (the justice one) is called to judge the action, and it is a national tradition that these two different powers do not agree very often! The balance of double dependence of police corps from both policy and justice is another character which distinguishes modern police.

There is a birthday of new local police: 1986, March 7 when law n° 65 at article n° 1 stated that "municipality exercises local police actions. For this duty it may create a service of Municipal Police". This new service in a few years will substitute the former *Vigili Urbani*, all around the nation[8]. A new law established also a formal equality of power between Municipal Police and other police corps, although only in the area of the municipality which the Corp belongs to (article n° 5 Law n° 65/1986). There has been then a translation to this new task of local police, where single steps should be examined. New court law Presidential Decree (D.P.R.) 1988 September 22, n° 447 at article n° 57 repeats investigation duty of local corps; new street law Legislative Decree (D. Lgs.) 1992 April 30, n° 285 at article n° 12 lists local police among street police services; all new laws usually talk about police services without distinction between existing corps. New power and duties, formally acquired over 22 years ago, could not transform some thousands of *Vigili* into local policemen in a little, and we may say that the wave of translation into modern police corps is still in progress, although it is actually discussed a complete revision of mother law 65/86 we talked above. Last step of this path we will consider is the Constitutional Law (L.Cost.) 2001 October 18, n° 3 which revised the article n° 117 of Italian Constitution. New federal purpose stated that local police service is ruled by Regions laws. About this we must note that first impression might be an illusion. In fact a change of the Constitution in a federal way should be interpreted as a loss of equality around the nation, but this is not true. Different development of political institutions all over the nation and a tradition of domestic self governance *already* obtained a thousand of different corps, each one image of a different city mayor, therefore the new duty stated by revised article of Constitution implies that local police service will now be standardized at least at region level.

## LOCAL POLICE ACADEMIES

The brief introduction above to Italy's police corps is needed for the definition of the problem we will study. What about police training? We saw there are five national corps, and these are constituted of 15,000 up to 100,000 officers each. These agencies provide training to members in national police academies, specialized schools etc. and in this way the training is standardized. But in this study we will concentrate on local police corps and here the situation is quite different. Local police corps enlist 1 to 6.000 officers each: the largest Corp is obviously the Municipal Police of Rome (capital city of Italy), but there are a lot of towns where only one policeman is enlisted. It does not exist in Italy a unique local police academy and different choices have been taken in different places. The relatively brief history of local police let us recognize how close is the evolution of police corps to political system. We may resume status of local police academies in this way:

- **Before 2001:** every police Corp is independent and provides training to his members. Inside bigger ones is created an instruction office and projected some training plan. It is often seen a satellite system where little corps (that are corps of little towns which enlist a few officers) send their officers to the closest city to train. In this way there is an advantage for both towns, as far as costs are concerned, and it is obtained a kind of informal standardization.
- **After 2001:** region council is called to decide general rules concerning service of local police, including training programs. There has been a different answer to this call, and we may resume three models:
    - some regions institute an *official local police academy*, directly depending from region itself (a public agency), which is deputed to release degrees for local police service in the region;

- some regions release a *license* to release credit or degree for local police service to private or public agencies: these are founded as private enterprises, syndicate services, societies of many municipalities etc;
- some regions *suggest* guidelines for local police training but do not impose a standard curriculum: this way is not really different as it was before 2001.

The result of these different solutions is, in the better case, a standardization of service, nonetheless a renewed attention to local police training.

## CASE STUDY: THE CITY OF BOLOGNA

We will now study a particular town of northern Italy: Bologna is the capital of Emilia-Romagna Region (one of largest Italy's regions), the municipality is around 400,000 inhabitants and the country nearly twice, it is one of the 10 largest towns in Italy. The Emilia-Romagna Region promulgated the Regional Law 2003 December 4, n° 24 about management of local police. This law establishes some standardization rules concerning vehicles, uniforms, weapons etc. and suggests the foundation of local police school, according to municipalities a financial contribution for police training. It looks like we were in the situation (3) before, and in fact actually the Municipal Police of Bologna, a great Corp of over 600 officers, has got an own study office which is deputed to plan and realize training. By the way in Emilia-Romagna Region was founded a Local Police School as a private enterprise but with many municipalities involved, comprehending Bologna, like in situation (2) above. After a short time the private school becomes a foundation and Regional Law 2007 September 28, n° 21 recognizes it as the official police academy for local police in the region. It is now realized a uniformity of training among all local corps of region because regional law establishes standard training and there is a school that offers it. Nonetheless if a great Corp is to obtain same standard training itself, it might be allowed to do it, and this is just the case of Bologna corp. Moreover, in Emilia-Romagna is widely diffused the activity of a local policemen syndicate (S.U.L.P.M.), which is quite different from general syndicates operating in Italy. It is known that insofar as syndicates are representative of great number of workers (like General Unions), they concentrate activity on general purposes concerning salary, holidays, health care, insurance etc. On the other side syndicates representing a particular and determined class of workers usually focus their action on specific and technical points such as equipment, training, operative plans etc. The S.U.L.P.M. syndicate study department uses to organize a lot of training days around the region, concerning different topics requested from members of syndicate, performed by syndicate members who are well known experts of the matter, free for syndicate members and opened to all police officers. Therefore training for local police officers in Bologna may be divided into some categories:

- official training realized inside the Corp, eventually integrated with;
- official training acquired by the local police school, which is now region police academy;
- semi-official training privately offered by syndicate but recognized by the Corp;
- semi-official training privately acquired and recognized by the Corp (i.e. University, other private schools etc.)

It is likely to be a confused situation we have depicted, with no completely certain training curriculum, possible duplication of study, need of personal interest to find proper training etc. but we may anticipate that this is actually the power of this method, as we will see later. For now it is important to point some characteristics of this solution:

- local police of Bologna is still attractive for some little towns of the country which send their officers to train;
- some teachers of the Corp become trainers for local police school and/or for syndicate;
- free access to training permits an exchange of experience and contacts with other officers of different police corps;
- semi-free organization of training allows to use existing resources with flexible organization;
- semi-free organization in a great cultural capital town as Bologna permits to local police to test new training solutions as a pioneer.

We may now give an example of the training structure as it really works. The town of XXX enlists few new officers and there is no resource to train them inside the local corp. The town may send the new enlisted to local police school (that is in the city of Modena, 35 km West of Bologna, almost the geographic center of region) to follow a basic course for local police, or send them to Bologna because that Corp is now offering an interesting program mainly concerning for example topics that are specially useful for the task new officers will be destined to (e.g. car crash investigation trained by metropolis experts might be very attractive for officers who will work in a little town but with busy traffic), or both. It is possible that if town XXX enlists officers and at the same time Bologna Corp does, those enlisted are sent to Bologna and train together with host a basic course in Bologna. The new relation between town XXX officers and training organization persists: officers met the largest Corp of region, the school, the teachers. While operating in their own town, officers may feel the need of training in a special topic or specialize a matter, so they can call local police school, syndicate teachers, Bologna Corp to ask for more training. On the other side syndicate, regional school and greater Corp are invited to plan and realize much more training than what is strictly needed for degree, insofar as they answer to request for refreshment, news study, new techniques, coming from operating officers. This sort of network between different organizations dealing the same matter looks like a valid solution to training question. There are some problems in this method and we will discuss it now. We already said there's need of interested and curious people to obtain best results, insofar it pretends a sort of initiative coming from single officers to search and find training offer. This seems a false problem, in two considerations. First, it is a well known fact that knowledge and study pretends curiosity and application, and this was already described by Plato in an amazing picture[9]. According to this, it is a cynical argument to recognize that this kind of training entails a selection of good students just as school does. All policemen attend to basic courses (because mandatory), best ones go on and specialize themselves. Second point leads to the most important technology that allows this method: the web. Nearly all police officers of the region are provided by municipality of an own e-mail and syndicate, local police school, police associations etc. edit web pages where they share information, the training days, seminars, conferences[10]. It is always possible to subscribe a mailing list and so to obtain news about training directly to own e-mail address. Therefore problem of initiative requested from officers is solved by the web. The only really existing trouble concerning this network training system concerns teachers and their emoluments: it is easy to imagine how it is difficult to rule this subject. We may think to a teacher enlisted in a major Corp *and* in a school *and* in a syndicate: how will the same lesson be paid in three different contests? But this is another matter and does not pertain to this study.

## TEACHING SOME TOPICS TO POLICE OFFICERS

We saw how much new political institutions and internet technology have changed local police training in a network of different resources; we will now examine what is police training in modern local police corps. We said above about translation occurred during the '80s from military to civil police, and at same time the birth of local (civil) police. This choice of civil police implied a change in training programs too. It is a military tradition a special attention to physical strength, discipline, weapons care, fighting technique, and the result is typical military organization of few thinking heads, many obedient executors, efficient and complete control. On the other hand civil corps usually prefer to create responsibility and self government in single officers, even if they have not skills in mass manoeuvre, habit in unique command line, stress resistance: the outcome is an army of "chaotic messy law professors". There is a problem about this and something in progress. Concerning national police corps, we see a change from the end of '90s: the suppression of military service and change of army into a professional Corp offered a pragmatic solution: army needs a lot of young people and few matures, police prefers mature. Nowadays to become (civilian) policemen you need to serve at least three years in the army before. This solution allows to preserve a civil attitude to self responsibility but on a substrate of military strength and discipline. It is not actually the same for local police, where civilians are enlisted in a civil police Corp without military experience. Maybe in future the same way of national corps will be followed, but nowadays we have civilians (former civilians) in a civil police corp. It is important to point this fact because it is related with another circumstance regarding police officers. Some national political evolutions involved a general indiscipline in Italian people (and guest foreigners too) together with a sort of supposed right to resist to police action, on the contrary police officers are often inquired for abuses. It is not a sociological clue that these two trends are probably related, but we will explain better using some example. Some people have been absolved in court recognizing the "right to escape" when guilty. This means: are you guilt? Try to escape: your guilty will not get worst! Some people have been absolved in court for insulting policemen with phrase like "go to @$$" because "they just invited the policeman: if he likes, he goes, if not he doesn't". Otherwise, although criminal law in Italy allows the use of weapons by police officers for self-defence and to win resistance to their action (articles n° 52 and n° 53 of Italian Criminal Code), it is the rule that every police officer who uses weapons (really few) will be inquired by magistrates for abuse, because "there was another way to obtain the same result without using the gun". All these facts pertain actual relation between citizen and national authority, magistrates and government and are a topic of Italy's political history. This is not the argument of present study, but we must consider it in a result: in Italy police officers are often victimized during the service, insulted, hit, injured, accused, sometimes processed. The loss of authority for police corps is a characteristic of modern social organization and this fact entails a series of problems: both the augmented request (under the principle that police is a service for citizen) and the less respect ("you cannot", "I have the right", "I shall tell the judge that") lead police officers to real fear of being victimized[11]. We will then discuss the topic of victimology in police training according to these premises.

## SPECIAL VICTIMOLOGY FOR LOCAL POLICE

We may recognize different meaning to "victimology":

- a science studying with a sociological method a specific subject (the victim);
- an empirical science providing a technical support to a certain kind of people (victims);
- an empirical art trying to prevent crimes by recognizing and defending probable victims;
- an art of manage victims to obtain best results in crime investigation.

All of these points entail some different tasks: (1) the search of scientific knowledge about a phenomenon, (2) the help to victimized people, (3) the social defence of population, (4) the investigation of crime. It is obvious that the results of each part allow progress of each other. Nevertheless it is really difficult a harmony among these parts, since they are often performed by different agencies: (1) is a typical university subject, (2) is a medicine and social service goal, (3) and (4) are usually police duties. Concerning our special case, the particular situation we have depicted before is:

- police officers are often victimized (historical reasons and civil status implications);
- there is request for increasing professional training and successful police action;
- there is a relatively free organization of training.

Adaptation of system is the use of c) power to resolve both a) and b) problems. Concerning point a) we may see two different ways. The first is a technical solution and pertains equipment and training against offence, the second one is a cultural solution and pertains training to conflict prevention. New equipment for local police means less lethal weapons like spray and batons, which are nowadays a standard for all police of the world yet not in Italy, and training for these instruments is increased with a recovery of lost time by training security positions, self-defense, weapon defense[12], body search technique and all forgotten topics… so military. This kind of training is usually performed in shooting range during gun exercises and instruments required are very simple, some PowerPoint® files with text, images and movies, an open area and a shooting range. What is needed more is experienced teachers with some skill: for example to insert a false cartridge in pupil's gun to create a malfunction while he is shooting and train his reaction to any accident under stress, or simulate body search on a teacher acting reaction (eventually playing accent/phrases of typical local suspects). The chance of free training allows the selection of teachers among experienced officers from patrol squad with no special procedures (and no regard to their rank). They could then project and manage proper exercises oriented to Corp needs. This would mean in a couple of years to train all local policemen of Bologna about skills preventing self-victimization, and would obtain a strange but useful result also in shooting efficacy: in year 2005 about 25% of officers had insufficient shooting report and had to repeat the lesson, while in year 2008 just 5% did. No doubt a successful training operation with a low cost[13]. It might be interesting to investigate relations between increasing self-assurance and attack efficacy, are those phenomena two sides of the same moon?

Concerning conflict prevention, we see a new program which is not curricular topic for police officers (at least not yet) and is an example of meeting between police Corp and cultural institutions we talked above. A municipality committee for women equality, where some female police officers participate, organized a seminar for female officers concerning communication techniques and conflict management. Teachers from psychology professionals, invited by an association, granted to some police officers a special training which was officially recognized by the corp. It is another kind of free training we may recognize in local police organization and specially related to actual needs. The greatest difficulty for female officers is due to massif immigration from Africa and Asia, regarding Italy from the '90s, of populations which have not yet imported cultural gender equality and do not easily recognize female's authority. This kind of problem is emerging if we analyze patrol composition in street by women. In Bologna female patrol service is granted from *Carabinieri* 1%, Economic Police 1%, National Police 5%, Municipal Police 40%, while other corps do not patrol. It means in the whole town nearly all police women in uniform directly in action are local police ones[14]. This seems to have a double meaning: one is that local police enlists many more women than other corps, which is true; second is that other police corps hide women from dangerous service, which is true also. In any case patrol service for women is much more dangerous nowadays and it needs a special careful training to fill a cultural gap. The experimental training in conflict management is an important step and represents a success for local training method[15].

What we said above pertains training preventing self-victimisation of police officers, but we also saw that there is an increasing request for police action and an institutional duty of population defence (from victimisation). This is another subject of local police action, in an interesting way, so we will examine two programs actually operating. The street law Legislative Decree (D.Lgs.) 1992 April 30, n° 285 at the article n° 230 establishes street safety as obligatory subject in all schools, and allows local police to join these programs. It is already ten years ago that local police became leader in this kind of training and we may say that almost all Bologna teenagers met an officer in their classroom teaching about street rules and incident prevention. This long experience leads to production of technologic support which is well appreciated by students. In particular standard instruments like panels, PowerPoint® and lessons are been integrated with a PC software projected and realized by the cooperation between software house and police officers[16]: rPat...entino® (even called "cinquanta special"). This software is look something like a video game where user is called to give answers concerning street law; it is useful to apprehend traffic rules, with help of time record, statistics on errors and self-correction. After completion of the game, students are ready to sustain driving license tests for little motorbikes. Inside the compact disk is also contained a series of lessons, the same one that police officers taught in school, and official quiz for driving license[17]. There is an extension of this street safety program which is actually tested by younger classes: the meeting with K9 units of local police, led by trained officers, to teach children how to behave with dogs[18]. This subject looks strictly connected with a social problem which is increasing in town, the great number of injures due to free dogs occurred in last years. It is a matter of fact that all over first six months of year 2008 nearly 180 people have been injured by dogs in town, and this fact needs its own explanation, which is not actual interest of the study[19]. Regarding the above said point (3) of different sense of victimology, we may recognize in this new program another special teaching offered by local police and actually pertaining a local problem, with clear task of reduction of victimisation among younger people, who are designed victims of this kind of offence.

Another project of prevention from victimisation began this year and it is something similar to what we saw about street laws. Drug law Presidential Decree (D.P.R.) 1990 October 9, n° 309 at articles n° 104 and n° 105 provides some lessons in all schools pertaining risks of drug use and abuse and allows school managers to provide these lessons also inviting experts from public administrations and health institutions. This frame of freedom let us present a double program concerning drug use prevention, in two ways. One destined to young students is a lesson explaining drug action, health risk and criminal pursuit. The second one is a lesson detailing different drug symptoms, use residua and traces and is addressed to school teachers and surveillance staff, to train about drug use detection inside the school. Both kind of lessons are characterized by little theory and lot of pragmatism. For students a few definitions explaining the drug circle and lots of images concerning car crashes, social disease of drug addicted (homeless, beggar, ill), prison etc. For professors almost only images of all kind of known drugs, mode of employ, transfer, dealing, physical signs and symptoms of use. All material was self-produced (photos from operation report) or downloaded by web pages, and shown together with real items coming from police operations, like paraphernalia, residues, boxes, tools etc. This project has been proposed to thirteen years students, two classes a time, for about two hours, and to teachers of high school during the periodic professors meeting, for about three hours. Both experiences have been appreciated from listeners and it has been already proposed to reply them next year [20].

We have surveyed the different teaching of victimology topics among local police and we may describe a system of action/reaction between victimisation problems occurring in the town, both to people and to officers, and the organization of technical answers from local police, according to legal instruments (like proposal of special laws concerning prevention), free teaching organizations and a little useful technology support. All these premises are necessary to obtain good results, and it's likely that the relation among these premises is much more successful than what would be expected. I mean that only in a system which allows personal initiative concerning training, officers who are really close to city troubles may project a reaction program with immediate efficacy, and this hypothesis could be the key to read the argument of training in local police.

## CRIMINOLOGY TOPICS

What we said above about the sense of victimology could be useful also for a division of branches in criminology, at least:

- social science concerning the subject "crime" (and criminals);
- pragmatic support to detect/prevent crime;
- technical investigation of crime (forensic science).

As usual (1) is a typical university subject, while (2) and (3) are police duties. It is worldwide known that a larger use of increasing technology and natural sciences discoveries have augmented the power of forensic science, largely shown by many tv programs. Forensic wave invested local police in different ways. The main task of local police has always been the street law and the traffic control. New technology solutions to prevent and detect this kind of crime comprehend intelligent traffic lights which detect forbidden transit with red light and take photos of car plates, with Photo-red® system, similar camera over all streets where only a limited access is allowed detect and take a photo of illicit transit. All procedures following are completely automated and the officers employed must only check and control computer working, or even resolve occurring problems. Those officers are trained in management of this specific software. This approach of automated detection of traffic crime is largely used by all local police corps of big Italian towns and it is now increasing its power with experimental programs of mobile systems to detect illicit parking, with Scout® machine[21]. The ancestor of all traffic control system, the *Autovelox*® detecting vehicles speed is still working on main roads. All of these solutions are characterized by the automated detection of crime, so that we may talk of a kind of automated police action, but we also have to note a persistent increasing empowerment of human police action thanks to technology. Speed detection by Tele-laser® mobile system allows patrol officers to pursuit street crime from an unexpected position with the same efficacy as the fixed machine does. Different alcohol-meter systems, easy to use and movable, allow police officers to detect drunk drivers immediately in street without medical referee. Useful portable cases containing few tools as Wood-light, lens etc. allow accurate analysis of suspect documents exhibited, and digital photo camera assists all police operations. We briefly referred to these tools as an example of what is natural increasing of police officer capacity according to technology progress. The training in technical machines use is usually very easy and informal, for two reasons: the first one is that these instruments are well produced and really easy-to-use; the second one is that progressive introduction of these tools allowed an informal transmission of knowledge among officers-users. This traditional training based on experience does not seem completely satisfying, because the simple use of machine does not grant efficacy. As a clear example of it we can see the counterfeit documents detection, where it is not sufficient to employ a Wood light to detect a false document, since most part of this kind of investigation pertains the deep knowledge of documents specs, format, etc. which is a subject to study and cannot be learn just looking someone else doing it. This need is well known and solution is, according to free training, the proposal of some technical seminars concerning specified topics, as we said above. So we have a double approach: one is buying a series of technical tools very useful for police duty; the other is to offer a lot of lessons concerning technical topics. It is obviously an ideal target that all police officers join all technical seminars and become masters in using all technical tools, in fact it usually doesn't happen, but the idea of giving instruments and offering skills seems the best possible solution. This is also argued by the fact that there is usually a good interest to seminars where new machines are bought by the Corp, and a diffused query to corps or syndicates for training about the related topics. The local police of Bologna has recently (last two years) offered such seminars: car crash and technical instruments, heavy trucks and electronic control, foreigners and counterfeit documents, mental disease and psychological techniques to approach nuts, shops control, investigation method and data-base use, drug abuse etc. All these seminars led by experienced Corp officers were organized using classrooms and computers inside Corp barracks and offered to officers during service and according to a program. Syndicate also offered a series of seminars concerning drugs enforcement, self-defence, motorbike control, car crash trial investigation, foreigners control etc. These lessons were organized after hours using classrooms and computers found by syndicate organization. We may see how similar are topics from different sources. This might look wrong in an economic evaluation but it's not. In fact all police topics, insofar as they are strictly related to evolving world and laws, different court sentences, increasing technology, renewed criminal techniques etc, they do *need* continuous refreshment and some kind of critical dialectic, and this is exactly what happens in this way.

Moreover we must talk about e-learning, that is a new project offered by municipality study office which has been attended by local police officers about privacy and data-base security, according to new privacy law Legislative Decree (D.Lgs.) 2003 June 30, n° 196. Lessons and drills were self performed online by all students with a specific software. Every student, using a personal password, was able to enter the program from his own work position to study lessons and resolving exercises. Software could control all operations comprehending a minimal time given to a single page, and the solutions of drills before allowing to open next chapter, something in the middle between a multilevel video game and a virtual teacher who guards too smart students! The success of this kind of training has been confirmed by the large number of students who hated it...

## EFFECTS OF TECHNOLOGY RESOURCES

We have seen how much modern technology, particularly network and informatics resources, has increased the power of training on police topics. The main characteristics of this method are software which allow easy learning, remote lessons and useful accessories computer related. We must now pay attention on how much this attitude returns a positive feed back on police service, which is the main task for local police. Everybody knows that digital revolution entailed a new concept of data-base, and that the internet protocol lets this information storage system available everywhere. This technology obviously empowers police service, and this is also a reason for another political conflict (concerning privacy of citizens etc.), but this is not our subject now. We deeply concentrate here on feed-back of digital revolution on police service, so let us go on with an example.

We may think back to 70's: if a police patrol needs to check some people, they must be taken to police office and the operations will involve a slow study of fingerprints by a technical officers with a lens, with a useful result limited to city report; a lot of phone calls to different offices like census or surveillance or insurance companies etc. where (if present) human employees would search into big paper archives. After a (very likely) long time there could have been found a nothing, but in any case at least one patrol and some other people would have lived a considerable lapse! This involves some other problems like the right of police to stop suspects for due controls just for a limited established time, and on the other hand the need to contain abuse against innocents. It seems that advent of computers and the internet resolves all these troubles: a patrol can usually perform a complete check of citizens, cars, documents directly in the place where they have been found in a few minutes just calling headquarter where a single officer with a computer is able to answer to all questions. In more complicated situations, the check of fingerprints is executed by a software[22] in a brief time. As an immediate consequence of this empowerment due to digital technology is an increasing activity of controls, which is absolutely confirmed by trends in criminal statistics. Next step is that increased police service power entails an enlarged duty for police corps: it is nowadays the rule that every police unit will pursuit at least one crime during a normal service, as long as they have instruments to do it[23]. This is another point of interest where an efficient use of new technology distinguishes the local police Corp of Bologna. We may resume the starting situation by stating a few points which mainly depend from historical and sociological reasons we said before:

- there is an increasing query for an efficient police action;
- police action must be realized with due accuracy, otherwise it will immediately fail;
- Italian court law establishes complicated procedures to pursuit crimes.

Solution to these premises is the development of specific technical software to support police action of officers, and this is the goal of *Core*®, *Verbatel*® and *Grandi Utenti*® computer software. *Grandi Utenti*® is a software which manages the procedures concerning street law, fines, judgement, payment etc. also comprehending the automated traffic fine system we talked about before. This software allows to manage many thousands of fines every year and is autonomous in production of statements, mail communications etc. *Verbatel*® is a specialized multipurpose software for police corps and is actually used in Bologna for car crash management: officers who investigate the accident can immediately produce the report online, and this can be integrated by different officers (for example later in office when witnesses come). When report is complete, it is automatically transformed in a single file comprehending everything pertains the accident, and directed to magistrates and insurance companies. *Core*® is a similar software pertaining criminal investigation, and its advantage is that, according to Italian court law which establishes that every single police action must be stated, it can generate every kind of statement concerning a suspect, leaving to officer just the completion of a few steps of procedure. This means that from a main frame the proceeding officer is able to choice the form he needs to fill and software presents it already completed in common parts (like suspect name, date of birth etc.), date-time indications, information already employed (like lawyer assigned to suspect etc.). More workstations may operate on the same file together, each seeing what the other is writing, thus allowing officers to work on same case although from different offices. The same software is also a useful data-base system of all statements produced with an efficient search engine which allows multiple query and supports long time investigations. This mass storage capacity must be explained: usually police data-base software records an abstract of police action, a little resume of what happened, and some more information like links where more notices can be found, notices that are stored on paper files and that consequently need an officer to be found. The Core® software, once it is correctly used, *creates* all statements online: they obviously have a paper copy which is stored as usual, but anyone who enters the software may read every statement concerning every single investigation. Empowerment allowed by this software is not completely explored yet, and it is already been found some difficulties in single parts, which are going to be corrected, but its potential capacity is absolutely wonderful, and well demonstrated. Actually it is been compared the time required to complete similar investigations (also acted by the same officers) using traditional instruments like text processors or pre-compiled forms hand filled, and the result is that we may need until 20 to 30% time faster using Core® software. This is not a scientific experiment but an experience report, for now there is not evidence of actual success of this kind of operative software, but the reasons described above about useful characteristics of the software allow to sustain its probable increasing use. Training in Core® use is nowadays empirically organized. The software is a part of Lotus® software which manages most part of Bologna local police actions, like e-mail, corp orders data-base, headquarters organization, radio telecommunications center records patrols display etc. This means that every officer lives his job in a Lotus® area and is acquainted with it. In this way a specific *Core*® training doesn't need a complete course, but a single lesson introducing its characteristics and possibilities; this lesson is given in little classrooms by computer tutors of the corp. The following step of training is given through the use of the software in daily activity. We have here another example of informal training given by a relatively free method of teaching, with easy organization and visible good effect.

## REFERENCES


Balloni, A. (Ed.). (2003). *Il vigile di quartiere a Milano.* Milano, Italy: Franco Angeli.

Forum italiano per la sicurezza urbana (2005). *Codice europeo di etica per la polizia.* Imola, Italy: Datacomp.

Francica, I., Del Percio, C., & Reina, M. (2001). *Bologna e i suoi vigili.* Bologna, Italy: Costa.

Gamberini, S., & Moro, S. (2008). *Ma le vigilesse sono più cattive?* Bologna, Italy: Avenue Media.


## WEBSITES

www.asaps.it

www.sulpm.it

www.vehicle-documents.it

www.polnews.it

www.poliziaregionale.it

www.scuolapolizialocale.it

## ENDNOTES

1 The National Police (*Polizia di Stato*) is the main police Corp, with politic authority and general power. It might be compared with a federal police in the U.S.A., like F.B.I., but with a large deployment in the towns.

2 *Carabinieri* is the second main police Corp, and the only Military Police, largely deployed in small towns such as in bigger ones.

3 The Economic Police (*Guardia di Finanza*) is a multipurpose police Corp, but with some special tasks such as drug enforcement, custom police, financial crimes, etc. It is similar to some U.S. federal agencies like I.R.S., A.T.F. or D.E.A.

4 The Penitentiary Police (*Polizia Penitenziaria*) is the national Corp deputed to surveillance of all kind of jail and prisoners transfer.

5 The National Forestry Commission (*Corpo Forestale dello Stato*) is the special national agency deputed to surveillance of forests and national parks, defence of protected animals and fire brigade in the country (while *Vigili del Fuoco* is the fire brigade deputed to town). It is similar to what Ranger corps are in the U.S.A.

6 The Provincial Police (*Polizia Provinciale*) is a local police Corp specially deputed to surveillance of hunting and fishing, and typical country duties.

7 The Municipal Police (*Polizia Municipale*) is the main Corp we will talk about. The name recalls the Metropolitan Police of the U.S.A.

8 For history of local police in Bologna, see Francica, Del Percio & Reina (2001).

9 We refer to Plato, *Symposium* (174 D-E): Agato asks Socrates to lay near him during the supper in the hope to obtain his wisdom, but Socrates replies that it is not possible to move knowledge as if it was water from a cup to another.

10 An example of these web sites is www.sulpm.it, www.vehicle-documents.it, www.asaps.it, www.polnews.it, www.poliziaregionale.it, www.egaf.it, all referred to syndicates, police associations and editors.

11 This is not the subject of this study but it is interesting to know that every year in Italy between 800 to 1,000 police officers are injured (i.e. with hospital report) in service and the trend is increasing. This is actually a new subject of interest for police association, see http://www.asaps.it/?url=showpage.php?id=17282&cat=17&sezione=Sbirri%20Pikkiati&pubblicazione=29.03.2008.

12 It might look crazy but in Italy a criminal tradition is to steel the gun to a policeman as a skill proof. This drill is consistent with police difficulty in legally using weapons against criminal offence for reasons we said above. The result is that one of main police officer's care is to protect himself from injury *and* his weapon from theft.

13 New deal of training concerning weapons and security manoeuvres was lead by my colleagues Giovanni Ercolino, Angelo Nanuzzi, Riccardo Ciocca, and me. It was a surprise to see the success obtained and the active participation of all officers in training, clearly representing a satisfied necessity!

14 Concerning this topic, with humour, Gamberini & Moro (2008).

15 I want to represent that this training was projected by my colleague Simonetta Moro,

who is doctor in Psychology and local police officer too, another clear example of low rank, well experienced officer who is valid resource emergent in a free training method.

[16] The father of the software is Prof. Mastri, teacher in a high school of Bologna.

[17] Main promoter of this great and successful program were my colleagues Giuliana Calzolari and Daniele Zaniboni (who is also a computer expert).

[18] This experience was possible thanks to interest of above said colleagues Simonetta Moro, and K9 leaders, Luca Venturi and Alessia Garagnani.

[19] We may just resume three points: citizens do not remember cultural rules of living with animals but it is increasing the number of dogs (comprehending large size or aggressive ones) owned by citizen for different reason; there is a return of the social phenomenon of homeless (young and adult) deviant people usually accompanied by dogs (in Italy called "punkabbestia"); the national laws concerning animal governance are not particularly harsh and only few local mayor ordinances have restricted rules with heavier punishments for offenders.

[20] This program was a project of mine and of the colleague Isabella Melloni, and probably it will be united with the bigger one on street law in a comprehensive proposal concerning city safety.

[21] It is actually used in experimental way in Bologna a unit tested by few officers trained by the producer.

[22] The famous Automatic Fingerprints Identification System (AFIS) which is actually worldwide standardized with Henry code system and nowadays could allow (although this is not yet) to link all national database in the first global database for police forces.

[23] This entails also an Italian own problem, that justice administration didn't empower similar instruments, depending on different reasons (the change of court law is a cultural question), and the result is that there is an infinite queue of forgotten trials opened by police corps that will never have a sentence and will finally fall.

[24] Concerning digital way of development we did not talk about the costs of modern police service. It is clear that digital equipment, new machinery and instruments are expensive, but the costs of technology must be calculated also in their economical cycle. An automated street control software fines much more offenders than a great number of human patrols, so that kind of software will earn the money (needed) to maintain itself and some other instruments used by patrols. That is to say that a part of the expenses in technology of Bologna municipality has been an investment and local police instruments are actually paid by other local police instruments!

# Chapter 15
# University Branches in Prison: The Italian Case

**Daniela Ronco**
*University of Turin, Italy*

## EXECUTIVE SUMMARY

*This chapter introduces the Italian experience about university in prison. Since ten years many faculties all over the country signed cooperation agreements with penitentiary administrations to pursue and realize the prisoners right to study at the highest levels. Prison management engage itself to warrant structural possibilities to study: quietly sections where prisoners can concentrate while preparing exams, entry license to professors and didactic materials, personnel engaged in monitoring detainees programs of rehabilitation through study. University carries out academic tutorship to support study careers and individual preparations to exams and degree. A bilateral connection links the two institutions: on the one hand, university forwards a service to warrant the prisoners' right to study. Prison, on the other hand, is an important matter of study for academics (particularly to specific branches: criminology, sociology of law, sociology of deviance, penal and penitentiary law, psychology). This paper offers a national survey about these experiences and concentrate about a specific case: the University of Turin inside the local prison, where Faculties of Law and Political Sciences forward, since 1998, a didactic project, with the involvement of professors and assistants in lectures and exams inside the prison. A specific section is reserved to a certain number of prisoners determined in carrying out a study program, till the degree. The aim is to examine how academic studies may be considered as a specific opportunity to put the rehabilitation ideal into practice, as the article 27 of the Italian Constitution asserts ("punishment must aim to re-education"). Education, combined with work, religion, leisure activity, sport and family contacts, is the means to pursue such function. The university involvement into these projects makes possible a better comprehension about life in prison and an active participation into implementation of detainees people's rights.*

DOI: 10.4018/978-1-60566-872-7.ch015

## ITALIAN LEGISLATION: PENITENTIARY TREATMENT AND RE-EDUCATION

Penitentiary treatment and re-education represent two key concepts of the legal language in the Italian penal system.

This system is regulated by law n. 354 of 1975 (Penitentiary System) and by the executive regulation n. 230 of 2000. Both of them express the text of the Constitution provided for by art. 27: "Penalties must aim to re-education of the convicted".

The term treatment appears in the Italian legislation with the "*Codice Rocco*" (the Italian Criminal Code) of 1931. It makes reference to everything concerns the prisoners system. "In the authoritative conception of the Minister of Justice Rocco, the accent essentially fell on the organizational dimension of the penitentiary administration and on the correlative requirements of discipline, with all the corollary of powers and prerogatives assigned to penitentiary organs for the exercise of the punitive power" (Grevi, 1981, p. 7).

The law reform of 1975, on the contrary, assumes a concept of treatment understood as the whole rights of detained persons: considering the normative level, there is a reversal of the traditional relation prisoner-institution. If, in the previous regulation, the legislator drew attention on organizational and disciplinary issues, and the ultimate purpose was the maintaining of order, the law of 1975 focuses on the detainee, through the arrangement of a series of obligations for the penitentiary administration. "Penitentiary treatment has to meet the special needs of each subject", states art. 13 of the Penitentiary System. "Towards convicted and interned it has to be carried out a re-educational treatment aiming at the social reintegration of them, also through contacts with the external world". The treatment is performed in accordance with a criterion of individualization concerning the specific conditions of the subjects". (art. 1, Penitentiary System).

This change of perspective is reflected on the operating plan of the treatment. "Abandoned the old logic of the de-personalization, as repercussion of an afflicting and mortifying philosophy of penalty, the legislator of 1975 definitely counts on the exploitation of the elements belonging to the detainee's personality, useful for his social readapting. To this purpose he built the whole discipline of the treatment in institute making sure that it gravitates on the same detainee: as an active protagonist and, at the same time, as the ultimate object of the penitentiary execution, with a re-educating perspective" (Grevi, 1981, p. 7). For this reason it is possible to talk about treatment as a *right* of the prisoner, instead of an obligation to comply with in a passive way. Hence, treatment results to be an *offer* of the institution and not anymore a command like the previous regulations provided for.

Essential features of treatment have to be, according to the Penitentiary System provisions, the *individualization* of the treatment and the *observation* of the prisoner. The first one concerns the modality with which treatment is realized: it is fundamental to adjust it to the peculiar characteristics and needs of the individual. This aim can be pursued through an observation activity consisting of a survey, mainly a sociological one, carried out by experts, and focusing on the family story, the processes of growth, the social relations of the subject and the positive and negative influences exerted by the environment.

Law identifies the elements of the treatment, i.e. the tools that penitentiary administration has to plan and to promote, in order to pursue the re-educational ideal.

"The treatment of condemned and interned is carried out making use of education, work, religion, cultural, amusing and sports activities, and facilitating opportune contacts with external world and the relationships with family" (art. 15 Penitentiary System). Subsequent articles regulate every single element. On the whole, what is immediately apparent is the total absence of afflicting features in the treatment activities, in conflict with past systems. The purpose of treatment results in a progressive prisoner re-socialization, hence it, instead of representing an additional sanction with respect to the loss of liberty, tends to weaken the penalty itself.

As already said, the ultimate purpose of the treatment is the re-education. Nevertheless the misguiding nature of prison has been highlighted: Goffman talks about *infantilization* and *self-mortification*, Sykes mentions the adhesion to prison *subculture*, Clemmer refers to phenomenon of *prisonization*, to cite some classics. These processes, following the individuals from the entry into prison and for all the period of detention, are a very considerable obstacle to the ultimate aim of penalty provided for by the modern constitution, the re-educational one.

The failure of the re-socializing ideal of prison seems to be confirmed, on an empirical level, by the data pertinent to recidivism rates. Although researches on the topic are little developed in Italy, the few and authoritative ones carried out till now show that the recidivism rate of people having served a prison sentence settles around 70%, in comparison with recidivism rates much lower in case of persons subjected to alternative measures (around 20%)[1]. A similar trend is noticed in the United States: according to the Bureau of Justice Statistics data, in 2007 parolees returned to incarceration were 15.5%, while nearly 1 in 5 probationers who exited from supervision in 2006 were incarcerated[2]. Nevertheless, the actual measurement of recidivism is not so simple and determining the success and failure of community corrections in comparison to imprisonment is not an easy task (see Stevens, 2006; Petersilia, 2002; Clear-Dammer, 2000).

To this regard it should be specified that the comparison between the recidivism of persons detained and the one of persons benefiting from an alternative measure seems to be invalidated by the fact that subjects obtain an alternative measure after a period of scientific observation of personality, ending with a positive prognosis on their reintegration. Moreover, the possibility to commit a crime that will not be brought to light results to be much more higher outside the prison walls rather than inside, due to the controls diffusely carried out in view of the Bentham's Panopticon. Thus it seems to be natural the chance to ascertain recidivism rates lower in people serving a sentence outside the prison. Nevertheless the numerical discrepancy turns out to be too high to be explained exclusively through these elements.

The misguiding character of prison seems thus confirmed by the analysis of recidivist behaviors. In this view prison carries out a de-socializing function, in contrast with the idea of re-education. To contrast these effects of prison it is necessary to act on the single components (Dolcini, 1981, p. 62): first of all it is necessary to limit the process of infantilization, making the widest possible room to the individual's freedom to choose how to behave so to assure him the keeping of his own willingness. Secondly it is necessary to increase the relations between the prisoner and the free society: this is the only instrument to limit the grasp of the prison subculture on the individual's morality. The forming of the subculture in prison is the direct consequence of the deprivation cited by Goffman (1961), understood as the mechanism of one's identity loss that inexorably threatens the person entering into prison. To keep an identity the prisoner becomes part of the *subculture*, often for lack of alternatives. Thus, the broadening of relations with the external world and with the culture of various social groups can be an useful tool to oppose the individual's adhesion to subculture.

Re-education is a concept with very weak borders, it can be variously understood from a maximum to a minimum of moral contents. The alternative is between considering re-education as the acquisition of a new morality, that is to say the change of the offender's behavior in comparison with the value of goods protected by the juridical system, and considering it as a simple good external conduct, that means the respect of penal laws from the individual, aside from his internal morality (Dolcini, 1981).

In the present Italian system, it seems that the second hypothesis has to be pursued, as the Italian Constitution safeguards the freedom of thought and it does not authorize the State to order a certain mentality by no means, neither the cultural pluralism typical of any democratic society, allows to affirm the idea of a model citizen. According to the law, re-education thus is the acquisition of the capacity to live in the society respecting its laws (Dolcini, 1981), aside from any type of manipulation of the prisoner's personality.

## FROM RE-EDUCATION TO TRAINING IN PRISON

If the concept of re-education presents ambiguities and difficulty in the realization, its abandon risks to imply the affirmation of a merely punitive ideal (with its corollaries of neutralization and deterrence). On this subject Baratta (1994) suggests to consider the re-socialization as a purpose to be realized not *through* prison, but *despite and against* it, that is to say opposing the de-socializing elements of prison.

In this sense the elements of treatment, among which the study at university level inside penal institutions, have not to be necessarily intended depending on re-educating purposes, but as means to contrast the de-socializing effects that the entry into prison and the features typical of a secluded life imply.

On this subject Migliori (2007) suggests a change of mind about the treatment activity in the first place from the terminological point of view: the *scientific observation of personality* may become an *observation and formative planning*, while the *re-educating treatment* can become *formative offer*.

The overcoming of the correctional perspective and of its medical and disciplinary reflexes implies an ever growing attention to individualization. This means that the modalities through which the observation is developing have to change, in the direction of a greater attention to the formative aspect, to the individual needs, to the bargaining of the treatment program.

Similarly the penitentiary system has to commit itself more in the offer of formative opportunities. The observation shall end not through a *treatment agreement* (that emphasizes the aspect of the prisoner duty rather than his right, often being the result of standardized treatment proposals) but through a *formative contract*, which is the result of the bargaining and of a greater and more conscious interaction between prisoner and penitentiary administration. The trend of the treatment, in fact, seems to be the aim of objectifying the individual's problems and the respective causes. On the contrary the idea of the education implies the ordering of the approaches and the educational methods, through a move from logic to a greater open-mindedness to innovations coming from various cultural and social contexts, experimented in different areas.

In this sense the teaching given by the university professors inside prisons represent an interesting example of realization of a formative offer according to the above mentioned modalities. In the first place for the element of spontaneity typical of the participation; secondly because this kind of education is organized through external resources and criteria of accomplishment. If the university formative intervention is carried out by the proper institutions, the users convince themselves that an ordinary context is developing also inside the prison and the quality settles on ordinary levels. In fact education permits to obviate, even if only in a very low part, to the lack of communication typical of prison: in the industrialized countries mass media represent an integral part of the individual's every day life and they create an effect of community (Germano, 2001, p. 121), just because it puts in common the life style of everybody. The impossibility to communicate creates in the prisoner a sense of extraneousness with respect to the passing of every day life, which can lead to demoralization, resignation, frustration, uselessness sensation and loss of stimuli. Education in prison has to be intended as the attempt to prevent all these feelings, as the tool to warrant the flow of information that allows to the individual to feel like every other member of the society. In the age of globalization and of the voyage myth the worst penalty is *to be impeded in one's movement* and the prison becomes a *factory of immobility* (Bauman, 1998); the entrance of the culture in prison can be a sort of antidote to frustration that immobility and extraneousness cause in the individual.

"Both work and school are the few internal activities allowing a qualitative enlargement of the internal social relations with other prisoners and sometimes also external with civil professors, avoiding that the subject passes his days always in cell, with time beaten by the forced rhythms of the division. This broadening of social relations contributes to limit the deterioration of lucidity and of project capacity of the detainee" (Berzano, 1994, p. 126).

Education is a prisoner's personal resource that may contribute to live the experience of prison as an interlude, in the case the prisoner keeps contacts with the social network; in any case education may produce a prisoner's mobilization inside the prison, if he has no favorable contacts outside, but, also thanks to the admittance to education, he has significant capabilities and abilities (Berzano, 1994). In both cases (prison as an interlude or as internal mobilization), the prisoner having personal resources is able to avoid that prison leads to exclusion. Education is part of one of variables (*service*) that, according to Dilulio (1987) have to be considered to determine the quality of the prison life; thus, besides being an element of the treatment, it permits to live the prison experience in a less traumatic way.

## THE RIGHT TO THE UNIVERSITY STUDY IN PRISON ACCORDING TO THE ITALIAN LEGISLATION

The rules regulating the education in prison in Italy are provided for in Law n. 354 of 1975 (art. 19) and in Presidential Decree (D.P.R.) n. 230 of 2000, "*Regolamento ordinamento penitenziario*" (articles 41-46)[3].

The most important novelty brought in by the reform law of 1975 is that the education as a duty (as provided for in the previous "Codice Rocco", that is the Italian Criminal Code) becomes in the proper sense a *right*. In this sense two elements distinguishing the preceding formulation fail: on the one hand the basic idea that crime springs from the lack of religious pity, the lack of culture, the ignorance, so that in order to readapt the criminal to the society reducing therefore the impact of crime it is necessary to remove these factors (Fassone, 1981, p. 133-134).

Secondly the afflictive character of the education itself fails: the activity of study is deprived of any expiatory potential, it becomes an instrument to prevent the de-socializing effects of a long detention. "The school has to represent a communicative opportunity, aimed at restoring the balance among different rhythms of the penitentiary existence with respect to the social one" (Germano, 2001, p. 124). It represents therefore a bridge that prepares the prisoner to re-enter in the society after a period of exclusion.

The whole structure of the Penitentiary System reveals this change from duty to right.

Art. 19 of law 345/75 attributes the duty to organize courses of compulsory education and vocational training to the penitentiary administrations, and it provides for the possibility to found schools of secondary education inside the penitentiary Institutes and to favor the fulfillment of university studies. It is not mentioned the duty for the prisoner to participate at school activities, he can only be stimulated to participate by the prison management, as reaffirmed by art. 41 of regulation of 2000: "the prison management make sure adequate information about the carrying out of school courses is given to prisoners and to internees; they also encourage the largest participation". The same is valid for the vocational training courses.

The regulation of 2000 introduces a series of considerable clarifications. First of all it provides for the involvement of external figures in the education field. The "Codice Rocco" provided that education was given by persons belonging, with other titles, to the prison institution (the prison management, the chaplain, and so on); with the new regulations there is the involvement of bodies and persons external to the institution: the Ministry of Education, the Region, the head offices of school institutes, the academic authorities, as well as the voluntary contribution of qualified persons (art. 41 and 43, D.P.R. 230/2000). Among these figures, teachers with a specific professional qualification, certainly more suitable for warranting a diversified and accurate instruction, play a leading role. The opening of prison to the external society reflects the legislator's intention to voice the pluralism typical of the democratic State, as well as the need to extend education to spheres not concerning only the agrarian one, as it occurred in the first half of 20th century, offering a more careful and complete service.

Secondly, even if education is not a duty for the prisoner, the penitentiary administration is obliged anyhow to guarantee for the possibility to participate in a continuative way, as provided by art. 41 of the regulation: "the prison management make sure that the course timetable are compatible with the participation of persons already engaged in working activity or in other activities organized by the institute. If it is possible, transfers of detainees and interned engaged in school activities to other institutes have to be avoided, even though they are motivated by exigencies of displacement, and any intervention that can interrupt the participation to these activities have to be avoided too [...]. If a transfer is planned, it is carried out in an institute assuring the didactic continuity to the transferred person". This is valid, once again, also for the vocational training courses (art. 42).

Art. 45 of the regulation finally provides a series of benefices of economic nature to assign to prisoners following education courses: an hourly benefit is established for those who follow vocational training courses, a daily one for those who follow courses of secondary education, a refund of taxes and of expenses for books at the end of the course, as well as production bonus for those who live in straitened circumstances.

It is a question of a series of incentives with which the legislator wanted to create the conditions for a wide participation of prisoners to educational activities. In this way it would be possible to guarantee the individual freedom of choice and to realize a sort of assumption of responsibilities of the prisoner aimed at protecting him from the risks of *infantilization*.

University in prison represents a mixture between school education and cultural training. The position of the matriculated prisoner (regulated by art. 44 of D.P.R. 230/2000), in fact, is in some ways assimilated to the position of the one who attends a secondary school: art. 45, for example, assigns the refund of expenses for taxes and books to prisoners living in straitened circumstances, both to those attending a secondary school and to those matriculated. Not only the economic benefits but also the exemption from the obligation of work concern all the students, the university ones too, as provided for by art. 44 ("the ones who follow university courses may be exempted from work, at their request, in the light of the diligence and profit shown").

The modality of the course of the university studies bring them closer to the concept of cultural training. In particular, the element related to the self-management of study, peculiar feature of the cultural training, diverges from the organization of school studies through the relation teacher-detainee. Art. 44 provides that "the prisoners and the interned university students are assigned, where possible, in rooms and divisions suitable for the carrying out of the study, offering them proper common rooms. Students can be authorized to keep in their own cell and in the other study rooms the books, publications and all the didactic instruments necessary to their study". In this way, the condition of quiet to study or in collaboration with fellow students is assured.

## THE UNIVERSITY BRANCHES IN PRISON ("POLI UNIVERSITARI IN CARCERE")

According to data furnished by the Ministry of Justice, the university branches active in the Italian prisons at the moment amount to 15, in particular: Alessandria, Bologna, Brescia, Cagliari, Catania, Catanzaro, Lecce, Milan, Padova, Pescara, Prato, Reggio Emilia, Rome, Turin.

Some of them are long-standing (in the prison of Turin the university branch is active since 1998, in Prato since 2000), some others of more recent date or on the way to institutionalization, but, in any case, it is a question of a growing phenomenon over the last few years, which is developing all over the Italian territory.

The formal tool for the establishment of a university branch in prison is generally the protocol of agreement: an agreement usually signed by University and Penitentiary Institutes or Regional Department of the Penitentiary Administration and, depending on the circumstances, Surveillance Magistracy (*Magistratura di Sorveglianza*)[4], Local Authorities, no-profit cooperatives, no profit organizations, foundations, and so on.

In many cases there are proper divisions of penitentiary institutes exclusively destined to prisoner students; in other cases the possibility of putting them together is studied, without formally providing for a proper division. In any case the basic idea is to guarantee conditions suitable for study, beginning from the structural point of view. Common rooms to study in group as well, possibility to keep in the cell computers which are personal or furnished by universities or by penitentiary institutes.

University branches in prison get to the root of two vice versa insurmountable problems for the prisoner students: the cost of the studies and the bureaucratic relations with university, almost not manageable from inside the prison.

In some cases the engagement of the university in prison is fulfilled through a teaching method telecasted. This is the case, for example, of the district penitentiary of Rebibbia (Rome), where, beginning from 2006, a pilot scheme has been started, entitled: "University in prison"[5], owing to a protocol of agreement between the Ombudsman of the persons subjected to restrictive measures of the personal freedom[6], the district penitentiary of Rebibbia New Complex, Fastweb, the University of Tor Vergata (Rome) and Laziodisu[7]. As cited by the protocol of agreement, the conditions of this accord lie in two guidelines: the undoubted utility that also prisoners have the possibility to be admitted to university studies, overcoming the obvious limitations deriving from their status, and the fact that each subject agreeing to the protocol of agreement has shown interest in the carrying out of the pilot scheme "University in prison". The aim is to promote the right to study of detained citizens through a computer platform that is able to connect in real time the prison with the university.

A last element is that prisoners show the wish to matriculate and *to attend lectures*, making use of the computer platform.

The agreement clarifies that the Ombudsman commits himself to serve as a connecting element between the parties and the prisoners who enrolled on education classes. Laziodisu commits itself to give its support throughout all the project (besides, with the purchase of books and other indispensable means for study). The Tor Vergata

University is available to get the possibility of virtual participation of prisoners to lectures effective and to assure the tutoring with subsequent possibility of interaction between professors and imprisoned students. The penitentiary district of Rebibbia commits itself to single out equipped classrooms suitable for the lectures and to allow the participation of detainees to the degree courses they have chosen.

A particularly revealing element concerns the commitment of the Penitentiary Administration Department to favor, with its directives and programmatic instructions, not only the carrying out of the project, but also the removal of incidental obstacles and the use of potentialities resulting from this experience for the promotion and circulation of similar experiences in other Italian regions.

The Faculties involved, at experimental stage, are Literature, Economics and Law Faculty.

In the academic year 2007/2008 the second year of experimentation has been accomplished.

In real terms, the project has been carried out through distance learning and tutoring actions with modalities that consent to detained students to regularly enjoy university services in the same way as their colleagues.

Each detainee has at his disposal books for study and for the preparation of the exams. The didactic activities take place following fundamentally two phases. In the first place lectures are directly filmed in the classrooms of the University Tor Vergata, while afterwards they are transferred in the platform of teleteaching and made available to detained students who can examine them in two special multimedia classrooms equipped with computer, acoustic cases and TV projectors (a classroom is reserved to common prisoners, the other one to prisoners in high security measures). In the faculties involved, on the contrary, there are computerized tutoring positions, activities that unlike lectures (registered and thus available also in subsequent moments) are carried out through videoconferences system. These meetings are thus scheduled at the beginning of the academic year, in concert with the Penitentiary Administration. Besides the tutoring in videoconference there are forms of tutoring (especially through a guidance at the moment of entry for the arrangement of the plan of studies) and of administrative tutoring, which is realized through the connection between the didactic problems and the bureaucratic- administrative issues (admission, evaluation of previous educational qualifications, administrative conduct of exams and so on).

In the first two years of experimentation 40 students have been involved.

A further, recent, model of contact between University and prison is formed by information counters inside prison, addressed to prisoners and often managed through the collaboration of university students. Information counters are present in various institutes since long (Milano Bollate, Florence, Bologna).

There is a starting project structured at the prison of Verona that provides for a first phase of lectures and seminars concerning the world of punishment, addressed to university students, some of them could, in a second phase and after a careful selection, pursue the knowledge of punishment through training to do at the information counter inside the prison, among the different possibilities offered. If this project seems to lie outside the mere didactic activity inside the Italian prisons, it represents nevertheless one of the approach signals between two realities, the prison and the university one, that till a few years ago had only rare occasions of contact.

## CASE STUDY: THE UNIVERSITY BRANCH INSIDE THE TURIN PRISON

### Origin and Objectives

On the 27 July 1998 the agreement protocol among the University of Turin, the Tribunal and the regional Department of the penitentiary administration for the constitution of the university section in prison *Le Vallette* in Turin has been formally signed. It is a question of formalizing the relations between university and the Turin prisons started during the eighties. These are the years during which the presence of a high number of students who enroll on education classes induces the Faculty of Political Science first (and then the Law Faculty) to take an interest in prison. The incentive comes especially from the so called "homogeneous area" (*area omogenea)*, that is to say a group of detainees for crimes of terrorism, dissociated, who benefit from an *ad hoc* treatment, in a proper division of the prison (Berzano, 1994, p. 47). Having left their studies they wish to continue them in prison and they mostly matriculate to the Faculty of Political Science that decides to set up a Commission specifically dealing with this subject, in order to warrant the prisoner's right to study. "On the one hand it was a question of organizing the complex procedure that allows the prisoner student to meet professors in prison and to pass examinations, on the other hand it was a matter of establishing a relation of reciprocal acquaintance with the Surveillance Magistracy and the prison management in order not only to benefit from an informal acknowledgment, but also to play a valued role in the re-socialization of the prisoner. It was important to understand if, beyond the answer to the specific request of prisoners-students, the prison universe as a whole expected and what from the University, in particular from the Faculty of Political Science" (Marucco, 1994, p. 15).

The Commission, made up of some professors of Political Science, to which some professors of Law joined afterwards, was established in 1984 and during the ensuing years it carries out a series of seminars inside the prison *Le Nuove*, addressed not only to university students, but to the whole prison population.

The first seminar is about the "Reform of the family Law and crimes against the sexual freedom". Another seminar, conducted by Nicola Tranfaglia, about the stories of life and militancy of eighteen members of the homogeneous area; another, conducted by Luisa Passerini, only with the women of the homogenous area, about "feminine identity and political violence".

These first seminars involve almost exclusively the prisoners members of the homogenous area that assembled, at that time, about twenty prisoners for crimes of terrorism, dissociated, who enjoy an ad hoc treatment, in a special division of the prison, in accordance with the directives given by the General prison management of penal institutes. The lack of participation as far as the rest of the prison population is concerned was mainly due to the distance between the argument dealt and the more urgent and dramatic problems characterizing the everyday life of a big metropolitan prison such as the one of Turin: on the one hand the problem of health and of the medical assistance, on the other hand the problem of work inside and outside the prison. For this reason the idea to organize a seminar on the work problem inside *Le Nuove* arose, aimed at guarantying, through the presence of hundred of prisoners, a proportional delegation of all the prison divisions, instead of the only division (largely minority) reserved to the homogenous area. This seminar represented, as pointed out in the last paragraph, an important point of contact between university and imprisoned population. It was carried out between 1988 and 1991 and it took place through weekly meetings between a research group consisting of professors of Political Science Faculty and prisoners. At first professors gave lessons about the subject "prison-work", following different approaches: historical, juridical, economic and sociological. A considerable number of prisoners took part in these meetings. In a second phase, on the contrary, a restricted group of prisoners worked with the group of professors to prepare a questionnaire that was afterwards given to the rest of the prison population by the prisoners themselves. Then there was the phase devoted to the elaboration of collected data and to the draft of the final report.

It was envisaged a subsequent phase of official presentation of collected data to the social forces and to the labor market. Nevertheless this phase was not carried out. Different factors contributed to this result: the transfer of the prison from *Le Nuove* to *Le Vallette* between 1988 and 1989, the fire in the feminine part of *Le Vallette* in June of 1989, a certain difficulty in cooperation and meeting of interests among various penitentiary institutions (Prison management, Surveillance Court [*Tribunale di Sorveglianza]* and Social Service Center for Adults), but above all a substantial indifference to the problem from company associations. Seminars thus represent the tool with which university approaches the prison context during the eighties, and some of them, as it has been seen, involve not only the matriculated prisoners, but the whole prison population, objective demanded by the same prisoners of the homogenous area to the Commission. They ask to university to play a function of cultural activity in prison through initiatives involving all the prisoners.

The peculiar element of this experience is represented by the fact that all the parties involved in the research on the work in prison have been directly produced by prisoners, who have not simply been the passive objects of the research; in this sense we can talk about a downright auto-survey.

The activation permitted to prisoners (at least for the whole period of the research) to turn their passivity into participation, in other words in progressive ability *to take up their life again* in spite of the thousand and one limits imposed by the current conception of the penalty in our country.

This conception adds various and further afflictive and restrictive mechanisms of the personality to the one that should be the only characteristic of the penalty, in other words the *simple* deprivation of liberty (Nicolotti, 1994).

The presence of university in prison (symbolized by professors) may satisfy therefore the double purpose to warrant the right to university study and bring initiatives addressed to the greatest possible number of prisoners inside the prison.

Beginning from the nineties, it emerges the prospect of institutionalizing the presence of professors, to render it a continuative one. The first objective of the establishment of a university section in prison can be defined, thus, as the formalization of relations between university and prison.

Among the purposes of the branch creation there is also the challenge the university faces with itself with respect to its involvement in innovative didactic activities and in quite precarious teaching conditions. University is enriched by the experience of the section for two reasons: in the first place because it permits to the university to know the prison from close up, institution that it studies by itself; from the didactic point of view it permits to study and try new methods of teaching addressed to students far from university centers, thus it introduces innovations concerning the deferred didactic, the self- learning, and so on.

The establishment of the university branch gives also an answer to the need to overcome some organizational difficulties of the penitentiary institutions: in each prison there are classrooms used for the teaching, daily attended by university teachers, and prisoners are accompanied from their cell to these classrooms by prison guards to follow lectures. Initiatives of this kind often are not carried out owing to high prices of the necessary personnel to accompany prisoners and control them during lectures.

## Structure and Organization

The "Polo universitario" consists of a university division inside the prison district "Lorusso e Cutugno" of Turin (ex *Le Vallette*).

The Faculties involved are Political Science and Law.

The project is supported by the *Compagnia di San Paolo* that finances the payment of the university taxes of students, the purchase of books and of educational materials, one unit of personnel for the coordination of the didactics.

The division is formed by 22 single cells, opened from 7.00 till 21.00, plus a classroom of about 20 square meters, two classrooms for meetings, a classrooms with some computers supplied by university.

Students can keep private computer in their cell.

The two Faculties organize every year the courses relative to the plan of studies envisaged: university teachers and researchers carry out 7/8 lectures (each one from two to three hours) directly in the division; the examinations are taken in the division too.

About 40 university teachers (belonging to the two Faculties of Political Science and Law) are engaged: they are assisted by the same numbers of assistant lecturers and collaborators and by a tutor who deals with the organizational and didactic coordination.

The opened courses are the following ones: a three-year Degree in Political Science; a three-year Degree in Juridical Science; a Master's Degree in Political Science.

In the period October 2005 – October 2006 the university has realized a project of civil service entitled "The University at the service of a new citizenship": four volunteers carried out an activity of didactic support at the university branch in prison. The project has been repeated in the period October 2007 – October 2008, with other four volunteers. During the realization of the two projects the volunteers involved, besides carrying out an activity of mere didactic tutoring, have contributed to the realization of a wider cultural activity, among which, for example, a project of discussion after some films on the issue of diversity, analyzed following different views: juridical, sociological, anthropological, media and so on. This activity has been carried out through the projection of film with a fixed theme preceded by meetings with experts of the themes at issue, often university teachers involved on that occasion.

The realization of this project, besides the intrinsic cultural value it represented, is an example of a trend the university seems to pursue: the broadening of the cultural offer that goes beyond the courses institutionally provided for in the single plans of study, as well as the involvement of experts called for bringing in arguments as a basis for subsequent discussions, in accordance with the more profound spirit of academic study. In this way, what is meant to be developed is a cultural debate representing a wide-ranging work, that lies outside the simple education from teacher to student.

Another meaningful tendency concerns the commitment of the university, in concert with the penitentiary administration and the local authorities, in creating paths of working insertion for the students graduated in prison. In this regard, in December 2007, an agreement among University, Prison District, the municipality district of Turin, the *Compagnia di San Paolo*, has been signed. This agreement provides for the sharing of the respective competences in order to offer a concrete opportunity for those prisoner students who need a support through preparatory paths for the reintegration into the world of work, to continue the studies and to reach the indispensable autonomy aimed at achieving an effective social reintegration. Under this perspective the signer subjects, combining their own different competences, have set up an experimental project for the activation of formative training to support a working insertion permitting the university attendance as well.

This project involved, at the experimental stage for the academic year 2007/2008, four prisoners students matriculated to the Master's Degree, having the requirements to be admitted to alternative measures or to be started off on external work (ex art. 21 law 26.7.1975 n. 354).

In particular the Head Office of the Prison District identified, among the prisoner students matriculated to degree courses, those persons having the requirements to demand alternative measures or the start to external work, and it performed the practices for their achievement.

The Division Work, vocational training and economic development of the municipal district of Turin, identified the business resources where it is possible to carry out training; the *Compagnia di San Paolo* provided for the start of training (ex art. 18 Law 196/1997), for the payment of remunerated stage and for monitoring of paths in the firm; the University of Turin continues to carry out a support of tutoring for the examinations of the Master's Degree students inside the Prison District and identified an external referent, permitting to the students included in the project to follow specialized courses outside the prison.

The Ombudsman of the prisoners rights promotes the realization of the projects, facilitating the integration with those resources already present on the civic territory.

As mentioned in the Protocol of agreement, the common purpose is to try and experiment a *sharing* of resources and competences, committing oneself to collaborate so that everybody consider prison and citizens living there as a place belonging to the town, at cultural level too.

If the facilitation in the admittance to university studies inside a total institution represents in itself a value to pursue and to implement, the transposition of the acquired competences during the course of study in a formative training seems to represent the point of junction between university purposes and needs of re-socialization. If the aims of the penitentiary institution include the restoration to the society of an individual who presents minor possibilities to commit a crime, the possibility to enter into working experiences in a certain measure congruent with the course of study seems to pursue this purpose.

## Numbers of Subjects Involved

Since 1998, when the university branch has been established inside the prison of Turin, the total number of enrolled is equal to 71 persons. Most of them (equal to 67.6%) decided to matriculate to Political Science, while 32.4% chose Law.

As indicated in Table 1, the number of women is very small: 2 on a total of 71 persons. In this regard it is important to stress that the average percentage of women detained at the prison district of Turin settles down on 3-5% of the whole imprisoned population (showing a percentage not different from the national average). Moreover, taking into account the variable related to the "level of education" of the detained population, the percentage of persons having a middle school certificate, required for the admittance to university studies, settles down on 4-5%. These numbers explain the very limited admittance of women to this kind of studies.

In the case of the university branch of Turin the only two matriculated women could formally enter "Polo Universitario", with all the correlative supports in terms of taxes and possibility to consult books and teaching equipment, as well as tutor support. Nevertheless, being the university division situated in a male section, and being impossible any contacts among sexes, the women could not benefit from university lectures given by teachers, peculiar element of the project.

Analyzing the variable concerning the area of provenance of the prisoners who enrolled on educational classes, it is possible to note that most students are of Italian nationality, with a fair percentage of students coming from Center & South America and from North Africa.

*Table 1. Students number and gender*

| | | Faculty | | |
|---|---|---|---|---|
| | | Political Science | Law | Total |
| Gender | Male | 48<br>67.6% | 21<br>29.6% | 69<br>97.2% |
| | Female | 0<br>.0% | 2<br>2.8% | 2<br>2.8% |
| Total | | 48<br>67.6% | 23<br>32.4% | 71<br>100.0% |

*Table 2. Nationality*

| | | Faculty | | |
|---|---|---|---|---|
| | | Political Science | Law | Total |
| Nationality | Italy | 32<br>45.1% | 17<br>23.9% | 49<br>69.0% |
| | Center & Eastern Europe | 3<br>4.2% | 0<br>.0% | 3<br>4.2% |
| | North Africa | 7<br>9.9% | 1<br>1.4% | 8<br>11.3% |
| | Middle East | 1<br>1.4% | 0<br>.0% | 1<br>1.4% |
| | North America | 0<br>.0% | 1<br>1.4% | 1<br>1.4% |
| | Center & South America | 5<br>7.0% | 4<br>5.6% | 9<br>12.7% |
| Total | | 48<br>67.6% | 23<br>32.4% | 71<br>100.0% |

The percentage of foreign students (31%) results much higher than the national average of the university students. According to Istat (Italian National Institute of Statistics) data concerning 2007 the foreign university students would constitute the 2.63% of the total of university students in Italy[8].

This difference can be explained analyzing the composition of the imprisoned population in Italy.

Up to June 30, 2008, the foreigners in prison represent the 37.45% of the total of detainees, with respect to a presence of resident foreigners (according to Istat data) equivalent to 4.7% (percentage certainly underestimated by the presence of foreigners not resident, but meaningfully inferior to presences in prison). The datum about the nationality confirms the over-representation of the foreign population in prison[9].

Analyzing the variable age of the detained students (in this respect it has to be stressed that we have considered the age concerning the arrival at the university section), it is possible to point out that most of them are between 28 and 47 years old (75.7% of the total of arrivals).

In this regard an important difference stands out with respect to the average of university students who, generally, matriculate immediately after the end of the advanced studies, that is between 18 and 20 years old[10].

This datum, combined with the higher percentage of foreign students compared to the ordinary contexts, implies a first factor to take into account as regards the modalities with which teachers carry out their didactic activity. They can not disregard two elements: first of all the fact that the audience can have since long interrupted the studies; secondly the fact that a considerable percentage of listeners has a cultural background different from the one of Italian students. This implies, for instance, the need not to take knowledge for granted, for example in the case of historical or juridical teaching.

It is important to point out the testimony of a teacher: "in December 1998, at the presentation of the course we faced a *class* certainly very different from ours, usually, of nineteen-twenty-year-old, boys and girls. Mature men – with the exception of a young non-European – serious

*Table 3. Age*

| | | Faculty | | |
|---|---|---|---|---|
| | | Political Science | Law | Total |
| Age | 18-27 | 7<br>10.0% | 2<br>2.9% | 9<br>12.9% |
| | 28-37 | 20<br>28.6% | 7<br>10.0% | 27<br>38.6% |
| | 38-47 | 17<br>24.3% | 9<br>12.9% | 26<br>37.1% |
| | 48-57 | 2<br>2.9% | 5<br>7.1% | 7<br>10.0% |
| | 58-67 | 1<br>1.4% | 0<br>.0% | 1<br>1.4% |
| Total | | 47<br>67.1% | 23<br>32.9% | 70<br>100.0% |

and with a great desire to talk about vaguely political and general topics. Everyone, with the above mentioned exception, had at least 10-15 years passed from the achievement of the school leaving certificate. We teachers did not know if they had in past and still they have cognitive and cultural interests, what real knowledge they had. The certain datum is that most of them had not the habit to read daily information or cultural readings" (Bravo, 2000).

Let's proceed analyzing the results, measured through a series of indicators, including the number of graduated, the situation of students (regular or undergraduate who had failed to get as degree in the minimum time prescribed), possible abandons, the number of enrolments.

Up to November 2008 the graduated were 13.

Among these, ten obtained a three-year Degree in Political Science, one obtained at first a three-year Degree and afterwards a Master's Degree in Political Science (for a total of 5 years of study), while two obtained a degree named "old system" (quadrennial) in Law.

For a combined analysis of university objectives (investing resources so that the largest possible number of students obtain a degree) and of constitutional objectives of the penitentiary system (to contribute to the re-socialization of the largest possible number of detainees), it is necessary not to limit one's analyzing of graduate's number. Indeed it is important to try an evaluation of study paths

*Table 4. Graduated*

| | | Faculty | | |
|---|---|---|---|---|
| | | Political Science | Law | Total |
| Graduate | 3 year Degree | 10<br>76.9% | 0<br>.0% | 10<br>76.9% |
| | Master Degree | 1<br>7.7% | 0<br>.0% | 1<br>7.7% |
| | 4 year Degree | 0<br>.0% | 2<br>15.4% | 2<br>15.4% |
| Total | | 11<br>84.6% | 2<br>15.4% | 13<br>100.0% |

of those people who, for different reasons, come out of university branch at a certain moment of their university career.

The coming out reasons, first of all, can be different: the end of the penalty, the access to an alternative measure, the transfer to other divisions of the institute or to other institutes (on request of the individual or, more frequently, for disciplinary reasons), the drop of studies.

It has been carried out an analysis of the percentage of persons continuing studies in correlation with the coming out reasons.

First of all, the main coming out reasons are due to transfer (30% of cases) and, then, end of the penalty (25%) and access to alternative measures (21.7%).

In general, among all the people come out, the 76.7% interrupted the studies, while the 23.3% continue with their studies. The 76.7% of interruptions is deduced by the fact that, even if there are no news about people coming out from the university branch before the degree, the administrative offices do not register renunciation to studies (indispensable to matriculate to other university faculties in Italy) nor exams passed. This permits to infer that these persons interrupted their study path, in Italy at least, since it is not possible to know if a new path has been undertaken in another country.

Table 6 draws on the previous one, considering the percentages of those who continue or not the studies with respect to the reasons of the coming out from the section. Among those who come out for end of penalty, for instance, the 20% keep on with their studies, the 80% not. The table permits to cast light on the fact that a better chance in continuing studies concerns those who come out with an alternative measure (38.5% of cases) and, secondly, those who have been transferred (33.3%) and, finally, those who are going out for end of penalty (20%).

In general it is possible to assume that the coming out for end of penalty may imply a priority reversal because often it becomes essential to drop

*Table 5. Keeping going studies elsewhere*

| | | Does they continue to study? | | |
|---|---|---|---|---|
| | | Yes | No | Total |
| Coming out reasons | End of penalty | 3<br>5.0% | 12<br>20.0% | 15<br>25.0% |
| | Alternative measures | 5<br>8.3% | 8<br>13.3% | 13<br>21.7% |
| | Transfer | 6<br>10.0% | 12<br>20.0% | 18<br>30.0% |
| | Drop-out | 0<br>.0% | 3<br>5.0% | 3<br>5.0% |
| | Not available | 0<br>.0% | 11<br>18.3% | 11<br>18.3% |
| Total | | 14<br>23.3% | 46<br>76.7% | 60<br>100.0% |

*Table 6. Coming out reasons and prosecution to study*

| | | Do they continue to study? | | |
|---|---|---|---|---|
| | | Yes | No | Total |
| Coming out reasons | End of penalty | 3<br>20.0% | 12<br>80.0% | 15<br>100.0% |
| | Alternative measures | 5<br>38.5% | 8<br>61.5% | 13<br>100.0% |
| | Transfer | 6<br>33.3% | 12<br>66.7% | 18<br>100.0% |
| | Drop-out | 0<br>.0% | 3<br>100.0% | 3<br>100.0% |
| | Not available | 0<br>.0% | 11<br>100.0% | 11<br>100.0% |
| Total | | 14<br>23.3% | 46<br>76.7% | 60<br>100.0% |

the studies in view of the research or the carrying out of a working occupation. This frequently occurs also in the case of access to alternative measures. Nevertheless, the activation of ad hoc formative training for students detained at the university section (see the preceding paragraph) implied the acknowledgment of alternative measures on the basis of programs explicitly providing for the continuation of studies, along with part-time working activities.

Finally, the quite high percentage of keeping going studies from those who has been transferred to other divisions of the institute or to other institutes, seems to be linked to the nationwide diffusion of the possibility to act the right to university study (see paragraph "The university branches in prison").

The numbers result however too low to give further evidence of the aforementioned affirmations, that have therefore to be read as hypothesis to be empirically verified, maybe through the correlation among the data concerning the nationwide different projects, and especially through qualitative researches.

The analysis of the number of people arrived to the university section in each year shows a tendency ascending at first (between 1998 and 2002). In these years the number of new subjects who enrolled on educational classes progressively grows from 6 to 13, and then it starts to decrease (between 2003 and 2008), settling finally down on 2 enrolled people in 2007 and 2008.

Figure 1 shows what it has been said more clearly.

The progressive increase of registered members between 1998 and 2002 seems to be connected to the strengthening of the experience and to the progressive widening of the possible users' knowledge about the possibility to enter into this path.

The subsequent decrease of registered members between 2003 and 2008, on the contrary, seems to be connected with the birth of other university branches in prison nationwide, or to the more general tendency concerning the strengthening of the affirmation of the right to university study inside penal institutions. This fact, whereas it has not led to the establishment of true university sections, seems to have affirmed the right to the

*Table 7. Enrollment year*

| | | Faculty | | |
|---|---|---|---|---|
| | | Political Science | Law | Total |
| Enroll-ment year | 1998-99 | 3<br>4.2% | 3<br>4.2% | 6<br>8.5% |
| | 1999-00 | 4<br>5.6% | 3<br>4.2% | 7<br>9.9% |
| | 2000-01 | 6<br>8.5% | 2<br>2.8% | 8<br>11.3% |
| | 2001-02 | 10<br>14.1% | 3<br>4.2% | 13<br>18.3% |
| | 2002-03 | 6<br>8.5% | 7<br>9.9% | 13<br>18.3% |
| | 2003-04 | 7<br>9.9% | 0<br>.0% | 7<br>9.9% |
| | 2004-05 | 3<br>4.2% | 2<br>2.8% | 5<br>7.0% |
| | 2005-06 | 4<br>5.6% | 1<br>1.4% | 5<br>7.0% |
| | 2006-07 | 2<br>2.8% | 1<br>1.4% | 3<br>4.2% |
| | 2007-08 | 1<br>1.4% | 1<br>1.4% | 2<br>2.8% |
| | 2008-09 | 2<br>2.8% | 0<br>.0% | 2<br>2.8% |
| Total | | 48<br>67.6% | 23<br>32.4% | 71<br>100.0% |

support for university study in the larger part of the territory.

Both as for the penitentiary administration and as for detainees inclined to matriculate there is the awareness about the necessity of guarantying on the one hand and of having assured on the other hand the right to study.

Finally a look at the state of studies of people involved shows a rather high percentage of students who have not passed their exams within the prescribed period, both with respect to students of a three-year degree (13 out of 20 matriculated) and with respect to the students of Master's degree (4 out of 5 matriculated)[11]. Moreover, considering the datum related the remissive persons (53.5% of the total) it is possible to infer a rather high percentage of *failures* or in any case of difficulties in completing the studies in accordance with ordinary times.

Among the possible factors explaining the reasons of these difficulties, it has to be mentioned the question related to the end of penalty (or alternative measure) that, in many cases, can imply the necessity of abandoning studies to devote oneself to a working activity. Secondly, it has

*Figure 1. Number of incoming per year.*

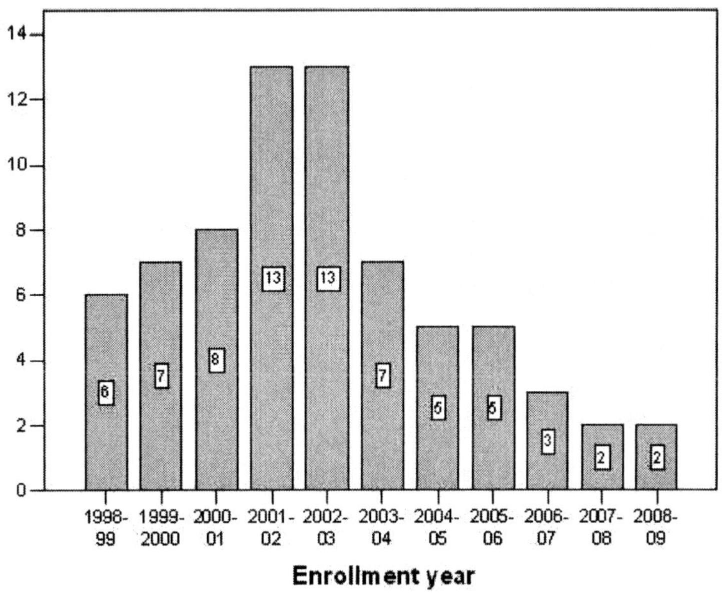

*Table 8. Situation of study*

| | Frequency | % |
|---|---|---|
| Graduate | 8 | 11.3 |
| First year T.Y.D. | 2 | 2.8 |
| Second year T.Y.D. | 1 | 1.4 |
| Third year T.Y.D. | 4 | 5.6 |
| Out of date T.Y.D. | 13 | 18.3 |
| Second year M.D. | 1 | 1.4 |
| Out of date M.D. | 4 | 5.6 |
| Drop-out | 38 | 53.5 |
| Total | 71 | 100.0 |

* T.Y.D. = Three years Degree
* M.D. = Master's Degree

not to be disregarded the fact that in the case of foreign students, generally the subsequent stage to the prison sentence is formed by the expulsion (or in any case by the stay clandestinely on the territory) and thus by the objective impossibility to continue on the undertaken way. Besides, the high number of students who have not passed their exams within the prescribed period can be linked to the length of the punishment to serve. In front of remaining punishment of a consistent numbers of years it seems reasonable to suppose that anyone may assess the opportunity to spread the exams during this period. It is necessary to avoid the risk of arriving to the degree before the possibility to exit and, consequently, obliged to be transferred to a common division, with an undeniable loss of a series of favorable conditions implied in the stay within the university section.

## UNIVERSITY AND PRISON: A BI-UNIVOCAL RELATIONSHIP

An experiment, consolidated by now, as a university branch in prison, represents a significant model of meeting of interests between two complex institutions, in addition to the interests of single members of those institutions.

On the one hand, there are the needs of imprisoned students. A continuous and constant entry of professors and researches certainly favor their study path, in terms of enhancement of human relations and in terms of a simpler access to resources. On the other hand, there are the teachers. Considered separately, each involved teacher may answer to his different exigencies or ambitions: to test himself in a way of teaching peculiar for different aspects, to reply to ethical imperatives of equality towards the highest levels of knowledge, to observe a reality hardly accessible, especially if it concerns scholars of the penalty discipline, of the complex organizations, of the political and social institutions (and particularly the Faculties of Political Science and of Law result quite interested in this sense). This didactic activity may therefore show itself a resource for the research.

To analyze the institutional needs, both prison and university can take sure advantages from the diligence spent in such an activity, in terms of visibility and in the forefront of offered services.

Nevertheless it is necessary to consider that this is feasible only through an outstanding commitment from both parties, especially in terms of loosening related to a series of structural rigidity characterizing mostly the prison, but, to a lesser extent, the university too.

This latter, in particular, has a lot to learn from this experience: on the one hand, it can directly know the prison and reflect upon this reality scientifically studied and governed. On the other hand, on the didactic level, it is led to progress in the creation and experimentation of methods and means of education addressed to students far from university centres (Marucco, 2000, p. 50). The experience of the university branch in prison has been useful not only to the opening of the prison towards the external world, but also in the opposite direction. It has actually marked a greater sensitiveness from the University towards the problems of the prison and the role played in respect of citizens paying their debt to the society. This initiative has been of great help to several professors who, with their fund of unavoidable prejudices, went to prison and were surprised of the world they found. Probably it is possible to learn much more about punishment and justice considering the emotive impact given by the entry in prison than reading many books. The university branch has been of great help also to open a small scope of knowledge about a reality that, even if it is often in the spotlight of the public opinion, remains still unknown for the outsiders.

The experience of the university sections, to be inserted in the activities of the prison, represents an example of excellence within the context of such activities, for the necessary efforts made by all the subjects involved (promoting bodies, single persons engaged in the carrying out of the project, the prisoner students who benefit from this opportunity).

These experiences deserve the right enhancement, also in terms of social awareness through a wide promotion that can spread the knowledge of these projects, in order to export the consolidated models. It seems useful as well to compare experiences, in sight of a reciprocal enrichment and in order to share good practices and solution of contingent problems.

It is important to avert that a project, as the university section, becomes a buttonhole flower that the single institute parades on the occasion of public meetings, without making it a tool of cultural increase, in the broadest sense of the word, relative not only to the section directly interested in the project, but also as an incentive for the promotion of treatment activities involving all the institute. Something that is similar to the atmosphere breathable in the eighties in the prison of Turin, where the homogenous areas promoted a demand for support of the university not only with respect to studies, but also in sight of a more careful and widespread interest on the part of the academic world inside the prison (see Paragraph "Origins and objectives"). All this with a kind of recall to values, rather than a mere utilitarian purpose which is the support to studies.

This aim seems to be indirectly pursued just through the entry into prison of university personnel. Entering and observing from the inside a reality generally studied on books or inevitably marked by the collective imagination bound to the common sense, often transmitted by media, is an occasion to develop a wider sensitiveness from the university towards the problems of prison and the role it has to play within this reality.

Beside the emotive impact and the awareness that grows with the increase of entries into prison, there is also a social group consciousness about the importance of the intervention at different levels, through the planning of interventions addressed also to subjects culturally less equipped, so that the general level of culture raises as a reaction to the spread of prison *subculture*. Moreover it seems to be important that, thanks to the experience of the *prison university pole*, the university really becomes a bi-directional communicative bridge: not only bringing inside the prison a wide slice of social reality precluded to the prisoner, but also carrying out an activity on the prison issues towards the external society (through seminars and conferences, the running and presentation of researches, the strengthening of relations with local authorities, and so on).

In conclusion it seems important to analyze other two questions. The first one concerns the necessity to go on with the experience, not only to strengthen in the time a didactic structure, but also as interest in individualized paths also after the exit from prison, especially during the phase of the alternative measures. It is fundamental that the activity of didactic support remains also during the difficult passage to the alternative measures; in this situation the need of a collaboration between university and operators of the prison arises again.

The second question that has to be underlined concerns the need of a constant and careful activity of monitoring, that, on the one hand, offers a picture about the single local experiences and, on the other hand, gives an overview on what occurs nationwide, through a comparison among various contexts, also in view of a subsequent look at the international situation. This activity permits to obtain instruments to operate in a more conscious and effective way and, besides, to reduce the risk of leveling and loss of stimulus typical of people engaged in a certain activity for a long time.

Also a sector of *excellence* as the one of university sections seems to run the risk implied in all the activities carried out inside the prison, to change into routine, to lose the motivational burst.

Useful means to protect against the risk of leveling seem to be the preservation of a vivid and deep cultural debate and the refining of new operational modalities depending on fortuitous circumstances, through a process of circulation of ideas.

## REFERENCES

Baratta, A. (1994). Reintegrazione sociale. Ridefinizione del concetto ed elementi di operazionalizzazione. *Dei delitti e delle pene, 3*, 137-150.

Barman, Z. (2001). *Dentro la globalizzazione. Le conseguenze sulle persone*. Bari, Italy: Editori Laterza.

Berzano, L. (Ed.). (1994). *La pena del non lavoro*. Milano, Italy: Franco Angeli.

Berzano, L., Buffa, P., & Ziccone, E. (2001). L'università in carcere. *Le Due Città, 2*(7-8), 12–17.

Bravo, G. M. (2000). Intervento. In A. Chiribiri (Ed.), *Carcere e società: il ruolo della cultura universitaria. Atti del seminario, 4 ottobre 1999* (pp. 115-121). Torino, Italy: Editrice Tirrenia Stampatori.

Chiribiri, A. (Ed.). (2000). *Carcere e società: il ruolo della cultura universitaria. Atti del seminario, 4 ottobre 1999*. Torino, Italy: Editrice Tirrenia Stampatori.

Clear, T. R., & Dammer, H. R. (2000). *The Offender in the Community*. Belmont, USA: Wadsworth.

Clemmer, D. (1941). *The Prison Community*. Boston: The Christopher Publishing House.

DiIulio, J. J. (1987). *Governing Prisons. A Comparative Study of Correctional Management*. New York: Free Press.

Dolcini, E. (1981). La rieducazione del condannato tra mito e realtà. In V. Grevi (Ed.), *Diritti dei detenuti e trattamento penitenziario* (pp. 55-97). Bologna, Italy: Zanichelli.

Fassone, E. (1981). Religione e istruzione nel quadro del trattamento. In V. Grevi (Ed.), *Diritti dei detenuti e trattamento penitenziario* (pp. 120-142). Bologna, Italy: Zanichelli.

Frudà, L. (Ed.). (2006). *Alternative al carcere. Percorsi, attori e reti sociali nell'esecuzione penale esterna*. Milano, Italy: Franco Angeli.

Germano, I. (2001). Scuola e carcere, sottoinsiemi comunicativi. In R. Mancuso (Ed.), *Scuola e carcere. Educazione, organizzazione e processi comunicativi*. (pp. 101-132). Milano, Italy: Franco Angeli.

Glaze, L. E., & Bonczar, T. (2007). Probation and Parole in the United States, 2007, Statistical Tables. *Bureau of Justice Statistics Bulletin*, from http://www.ojp.usdoj.gov/bjs/pub/pdf/ppus06.htm.

Glaze, L. E., & Bonczar, T. (2008). Probation and Parole in the United States, 2007, Statistical Tables. *Bureau of Justice Statistics Bulletin*, from http://www.ojp.usdoj.gov/bjs/pub/pdf/ppus07st.pdf.

Goffman, E. (1961). *Asylums. Essays on the social situation of mental patients and other inmates.* New York: Random House.

Grevi, V. (Ed.). (1981). *Diritti dei detenuti e trattamento penitenziario.* Bologna, Italy: Zanichelli.

Leopardi, F. (2007). Le misure alternative alla detenzione tra reinserimento sociale e abbattimento della recidiva. *Rassegna penitenziaria e criminologica, 2*, 7-26.

Mancuso, R. (Ed.). (2001). *Scuola e carcere. Educazione, organizzazione e processi comunicativi.* Milano, Italy: Franco Angeli.

Marucco, D. (1994). Introduzione. In L. Berzano (Ed.), *La pena del non lavoro* (pp.15-16). Milano, Italy: Franco Angeli.

Marucco, D. (2000). Il diritto allo studio dei detenuti come impegno culturale e sociale. In A. Chiribiri (Ed.), *Carcere e società: il ruolo della cultura universitaria* (pp. 49-52). Torino, Italy: Editrice Tirrenia Stampatori.

Migliori, S. (2007). *Carcere, esclusione sociale, diritto alla formazione.* Roma, Italy: Carocci Faber.

Mosconi, G. (1998). *Dentro il carcere, oltre la pena.* Padova, Italy: Cedam.

Nicolotti, L. (1994). Carcere e lavoro: il seminario e la ricerca. In L. Berzano L (Ed.), *La pena del non lavoro* (pp. 47-77). Milano, Italy: Franco Angeli.

Palma, M. (2000). La cultura della legalità e l'esercizio dei diritti in carcere. In A. Chiribiri (Ed.), *Carcere e società: il ruolo della cultura universitaria* (pp. 89-93). Torino, Italy: Editrice Tirrenia Stampatori.

Petersilia, J. (2002). *Reforming Probation and Parole in 21st Century.* Lanham, USA: American Correctional Association.

Santoro, E., & Tucci, R. (2004). *L'incidenza dell'affidamento sulla recidiva: prime indicazioni e problemi per una ricerca sistematica, rapporto finale del progetto Misura.* Regione Toscana, Italy.

Stevens, D. (2006). *Community Corrections. An applied approach.* Upper Saddle River, NJ: Prentice Hall.

Sykes, G. M. (1958). *The Society of Captives. A study of a Maximum Security Prison.* Princeton, NJ: Princeton University Press.

## ENDNOTES

1 For an analysis of recidivism rates in case of persons subjected to alternative measures, in comparison to the recidivism rate of people having served a prison sentence, see: Leopardi, F. (2007). Le misure alternative alla detenzione tra reinserimento sociale e abbattimento della recidiva. *Rassegna penitenziaria e criminologica*, Ministero della Giustizia, Rome, 2, 7-26; Santoro, E., & Tucci, R. (2004). *L'incidenza dell'affidamento sulla recidiva: prime indicazioni e problemi per una ricerca sistematica, rapporto finale del progetto Misura*, Regione Toscana, Italy.

2 For more detailed data, see: Glaze, L.E., & Bonczar, T. (2008). Probation and Parole in the United States, 2007, Statistical Tables. *Bureau of Justice Statistics Bulletin*, from http://www.ojp.usdoj.gov/bjs/pub/pdf/ppus07st.pdf and Glaze, L.E., & Bonczar, T. (2007). Probation and Parole in the United States, 2006. *Bureau of Justice Statistics Bulletin*, from http://www.ojp.usdoj.gov/bjs/pub/pdf/ppus06.htm.

3 Regulations of the Penitentiary System

4 The Surveillance Magistracy (*Magistratura di Sorveglianza)* is the part of the judicial system dealing with control over the penal enforcement.

[5] The complete text of the protocol of agreement is available on the Web site: http://www.ristretti.it/areestudio/affetti/inchieste/teledidattica_rebibbia.pdf.

[6] The Ombudsman is called in Italy "Garante dei diritti delle persone detenute o private della libertà personale".

[7] Laziodisu is a Local Authority for the right to university study in the Italian Lazio's Region (see: www.laziodisu.it).

[8] These data are taken from the Istat (the National Institute of Statistics) Web site, see in particular http://www.istat.it/lavoro/sistema_istruzione/tavoleuniversitario.html.

[9] This datum should be analysed through empirical researches about the criminalization of foreigners, but this is not the aim of the present work. See: Mosconi, G., & Padovan, D. (Ed). (2005). *La fabbrica dei delinquenti. Processo penale e meccanismi sociali di costruzione del condannato*. Torino, Italy: L'Harmattan Italia; Barbagli, M. (2002). *Immigrazione e reati in Italia* Bologna, Italy: Il Mulino; Dal Lago, A. (1999). *Non persone*. Milano, Italy: Feltrinelli; Cottino, A., & Sarzotti, C. (1995). *Diritto, uguaglianza e giustizia penale*. Torino, Italy: L'Harmattan Italia.

[10] According to the CENSVU (National Committee for University System Evaluation) data, the matriculated 21 years old or younger are about 80% of the total amount of matriculated per year (*Ottavo Rapporto sullo Stato del Sistema Universitario*, Rilevazione Nuclei 2007, from http://www.cnsvu.it/_library/downloadfile.asp?id =11624)

[11] According to the CENVSU data, the students who have not passed their examinations within the prescribed period are the 42.3% of the total amount of Italian university students.

# Compilation of References


AA. VV. (1995). *Il dilemma dell'Islam. Politica e movimenti islamisti nel mondo arabo contemporaneo.* Milano, Italy: Franco Angeli.

AA. VV. (2002). *Erased in a moment: Suicide bombing attacks against Israeli civilians.* New York: Human Rights Watch.

AA. VV. (2002). *Suicide, martyrdrom, terrorist attacks, or homicide – a debate in Arab media.* Germany: Middle East Media Research Institute (MEMRI).

AA. VV. (2003). *The profile of the suicide bomber. An ICT Research project.* USA: ICT.

AA.VV. (1998). La tutela della sicurezza nel settore economico. Il ruolo dell'intelligence. *Per aspera ad veritatem, 12*, 783-796.

AA.VV. (1999). Intelligence e analisi strategica. *Per aspera ad veritatem, 14*, 447-498.

AA.VV. (2000). Intelligence e statistica. *Per aspera ad veritatem, 16*, 21-54.

AA.VV. (2001). La comunicazione istituzionale e la comunicazione dell'intelligence. *Per aspera ad veritatem, 20*, 449-476.

AA.VV. (2003). Fondamento, fondamentalismo: uno sguardo dal profondo. *Rivista di psicologia analitica, 15*(67), 111-167.

AA.VV. (2004). Progetto Jihad. *Limes*, Gruppo Editoriale L'Espresso, 1/2004.

Aarons, G. (2005). Measuring provider attitudes toward evidence-based practice: consideration of organizational context and individual differences. *Child and Adolescent Psychiatric Clinics of North America, 14*, 255–271. doi:10.1016/j.chc.2004.04.008

Academic Credit for police training. *Journal of Criminal Justice Education, 16*(2), 300-317.

Acquaviva, S., & Pace, E. (1996). *Sociologia delle religioni. Problemi e prospettive.* Roma, Italy: La Nuova Italiana Scientifica.

Alexiadis, St. (2001). *Penology.* Athens-Thessaloniki: Sakkoulas Publ. S.A., (in Greek).

Alexiadis, St. (2004). *Criminology.* Athens-Thessaloniki: Sakkoulas Publ. S.A., (in Greek).

Alexiadis, St. (2008). The Criminology from yesterday to tomorrow. In *Essays in honour of Anna Benaki-Psarouda, Penal Sciences-Theory and practice* (pp. 1169-1184). Athens-Komotini: A.Sakkoulas Publ. (in Greek).

Alvarez, K., Kenny, M. C., Donohue, B., & Carpin, K. (2004). Why are professionals failing to initiate mandated reports of child maltreatment, and are there any empirically based programs to assist professionals in the reporting process? *Aggression and Violent Behavior, 9*, 563–578. doi:10.1016/j.avb.2003.07.001

Amadori, A. (2002). *Bin Laden. Chi è, cosa vuole, come comunica il profeta del terrore.* Milano, Italy: Libri Scheiwiller.

American Psychological Association Child Abuse and Neglect Working Group. (1996). *A guide for including information on child abuse and neglect in graduate and professional education and training.* Washington, DC: American Psychological Association.

Anagnostakis, S. (1964). *Bibliography of criminological and penal studies in Greece* (1830-1964). Athens: Center of Criminological Research (in Greek).

Andrew, C. (1997). L'intelligence in un mondo multipolare, *Per aspera ad veritatem, 8*, 307-328.

Andrew, C. (2001). L'intelligence nel XXI secolo, *Per aspera ad veritatem, 20*, 437-448.

Angelini, F., & Centonze, S. (2002). *Numero Verde contro la tratta. L'esperienza dell'Emilia Romagna.* Ravenna, Italy: Regione Emilia-Romagna & Cooperativa Sociale il Mappamondo.

Antonelli, C. (1984). *Cambiamento tecnologico e impresa multinazionale: il ruolo delle reti telematiche nelle strategie globali.* Milano, Italy: FrancoAngeli.

Aprile, E. (2007). *La competenza penale del Giudice di Pace.* Milano, Italy: Giuffrè.

Apruzzese, A. (2007). Dal computer crime al computer-related crime (Electronic version). *Rivista di Criminologia, Vittimologia e Sicurezza, I*(1), January-April, 55-60. Retrieved from http://www.vittimologia.it/rivista.

Aruffo, A. (1995). *Il Mondo islamico. Movimenti Stati e rivoluzioni da Maometto ad oggi.* Roma, Italy: Datanews.

Aruffo, A. (2002). *L'islamismo militante. Dal Maghreb all'Asia Centrale.* Roma, Italy: Datanews.

Associazione Nazionale Magistrati [ANM] (2003, March 23). *Magistrati e la sfida della professionalità*, from http://www.associazionenazionalemagistrati.it/public/File/Convegni/proposta.doc.

Astrinakis, A., & Stylianoudi, L. (Eds.). (1996). Heavy metal, rockabilly fanatic fans. *Juvenile cultures and subcultures in western Attica.* Athens: Ellinika Grammata, (in Greek).

Atran, S. (2003). Genesis of suicide terrorism. *Science, 299*, 1534–1539. doi:10.1126/science.1078854

Baldi, F. *(2000).* Manuale del giudice di pace. Tutti i reati di competenza del giudice di pace, con ricchi richiami di dottrina e giurisprudenza; il nuovo processo ed il nuovo sistema sanzionatorio introdotti dal D.lgs. 28 agosto 2000, n. 274. *Milano, Italy: Giuffrè.*

Balloni, A. & Bisi, R. (1993). Le tecniche complesse di indagine nelle tossicodipendenze. *Giovani realtà*, XIII(46), 65-78.

Balloni, A. (1983). *Criminologia in prospettiva.* Bologna, Italy: Clueb.

Balloni, A. (1999). Psichiatria forense. In P. Pancheri, G.B. Cassano (Eds.), *Trattato italiano di psichiatria* (pp.3899-3931). Milano, Italy: Masson.

Balloni, A. (2004). *Criminologia e psicopatologia. Analisi di 110 perizie psichiatriche.* Bologna, Italy: Pàtron.

Balloni, A. (Ed.). (1989). *Vittime, crimine e difesa sociale.* Bologna, Italy: Clueb.

Balloni, A. (Ed.). (1998). *Criminologia e sicurezza.* Milano, Italy: Franco Angeli.

Balloni, A. (Ed.). (2003). *Il vigile di quartiere a Milano.* Milano, Italy: Franco Angeli.

Balloni, A. (Ed.). (2006). *Cittadinanza responsabile e tutela della vittima.* Bologna, Italy: Clueb.

Balloni, A., & Bisi, R. (2004). The evolution of Victimology: a view over Italy and and Europe throught Research. *International Persepectives in Victimology, I*(1), Tokiwa International Victimology Institute Journal.

Balloni, A., & Bisi, R. (Eds.). (1996). *Dalla criminologia alla security.* Bologna, Italy: Clueb.

Balloni, A., & Bisi, R. (Eds.). (1998). *Criminologia applicata per l'investigazione e la sicurezza.* Milano, Italy: Franco Angeli.

Balloni, A., & Bisi, R. (Eds.). (2008). Processi di vittimizzazione e reti di sostegno alle vittime. *Rivista "Salute e Società", VII*(1). Milano, Italy: Franco Angeli.

Balloni, A., & Sette, R. (Eds.). (2000). *Didattica in criminologia applicata. Formazione degli operatori della sicurezza e del controllo sociale*, Bologna, Italy: Clueb.

Balloni, A., & Viano, E. (Eds.). (1989). *IV Congresso Mondiale di vittimologia. Atti della giornata bolognese*. Bologna, Italy: Clueb.

Balloni, A., Mosconi, G., & Prina, F. (Eds.). (2004). *Cultura giuridica e attori della giustizia penale*. Milano, Italy: Franco Angeli.

Bandini, T. (2003). *Criminologia, il contributo della ricerca alla conoscenza del crimine e della reazione sociale*. Milano, Italy: Giuffrè.

Baratta, A. (1994). Reintegrazione sociale. Ridefinizione del concetto ed elementi di operazionalizzazione. *Dei delitti e delle pene, 3*, 137-150.

Barbagli, M., & Gatti, U. (2005). *Prevenire la criminalità*, Bologna, Italy: il Mulino.

Barbagli, M., & Sabbadini, L. (1999). *La sicurezza dei cittadini*. Bologna, Italy: il Mulino.

Barman, Z. (2001). *Dentro la globalizzazione. Le conseguenze sulle persone*. Bari, Italy: Editori Laterza.

Bauman, Z. (2000). *La solitudine del cittadino globale*. Milano, Italy: Feltrinelli.

Bauman, Z. (2005). *La fiducia e la paura nella città*. Milano, Italy: Mondatori.

Baumann, B. L., Kolko, D. J., Collins, K., & Herschell, A. D. (2006). Understanding practitioners' characteristics and perspectives prior to the dissemination of an evidence-based intervention. *Child Abuse & Neglect, 30*, 771–787. doi:10.1016/j.chiabu.2006.01.002

Becker, H. S. (1963). *Outsiders*. Paris, France: A.M. Métailié.

Becker, H. S. (1963). *Outsiders: Studies in the Sociology of Deviance*. New York: Free Press.

Benedetti, A. (2004). *Decisione e persuasione per l'intelligence (e la politica)*. Genova, Italy: Erga.

Benedetti, A. (2004). *L'osservazione per l'intelligence e l'indagine*. Genova, Italy: Erga.

Berardino, F. (1997). Modalità e strumenti dell'attività di informazione e sicurezza tra legittimità ed illegalità. *Per aspera ad veritatem, 9*, 697-706.

Berliner, L., & Elliott, D. (2002). Sexual abuse of children in the field of child maltreatment. In J. Myers, L. Berliner, J. Myers, et al (Ed.), *The APSAC Handbook on Child Maltreatment* (55-78). London: Sage.

Bernstein, B. (1971). *Class, Codes and Control*. London: Routledge & Kegan Paul.

Bertaccini, D. (2006). *Modelli e strategie di polizia nelle società di sicurezza*. Roma: Italy: Carocci.

Berzano, L. (Ed.). (1994). *La pena del non lavoro*. Milano, Italy: Franco Angeli.

Berzano, L., & Prina, F. (2004). *Sociologia della devianza*. Roma, Italy: Carocci.

Berzano, L., Buffa, P., & Ziccone, E. (2001). L'università in carcere. *Le Due Città, 2*(7-8), 12–17.

Bessette, J. M. (1982). *Sociologie du crime*. Paris: PUF.

Bettetini, G., & Colombo, F. (1996). *Dall'alfabeto alle reti*. Roma, Italy: SEAM.

Bianchini, E. (2008). Processi di vittimizzazione e competenze penali del giudice di pace. In A. Balloni, & R. Bisi (Eds.), *Processi di vittimizzazione e reti di sostegno alle vittime* (pp. 27-29). Milano, Italy: Franco Angeli.

Bisi, R. (1992). *Grafologia e strutturalismo. Analisi e prospettive*. Bologna, Italy: Clueb.

Bisi, R. (1996). Vittime, vittimologia e società. In R. Bisi, & P. Faccioli (Ed), *Con gli occhi della vittima*. Milano, Italy: Franco Angeli.

Bisi, R. (1999). Teaching and professional training in criminology. *European Journal of Crime Criminal Law and Criminal Justice, 7*(2), 103–129. doi:10.1163/15718179920518763

Bisi, R. (2002). La psicodiagnostica in criminologia: orientamenti e prospettive. In G. Mucciarelli, R. Chattat, G. Celani (Eds.), *Teoria e pratica dei test* (pp. 507-527). Padova, Italy: Piccin.

Bisi, R. (Ed.). (2004). *Vittimologia. Dinamiche relazionali tra vittimizzazione e mediazione*. Milano, Italy: Franco Angeli.

Bisi, R. (Ed.). (2006). *Scena del crimine e profili investigativi. Quale tutela per le vittime?* Milano, Italy: Franco Angeli.

Bisi, R., & Faccioli, P. (Eds.). (1996). *Con gli occhi della vittima: approccio interdisciplinare alla vittimologia.* Milano, Italy: Franco Angeli.

Bisi, R., & Sette, R. (2002). Victimes de tragédies en Italie. Ombres et lumières d'une réalité oubliée. *Revue Francophone du Stress et du Trauma, 2*(1).

Bisi, R., & Sette, R. (2006). Trasformazioni sociali e nuove esigenze di formazione professionale. In A. Febbrajo, A. La Spina, & M. Raiteri, (Ed.), *Cultura giuridica e politiche pubbliche in Italia,* (pp. 553-568). Milano, Italy: Giuffrè.

Bohm, E. (1969). *Manuale di psicodiagnostica di Rorschach.* Firenze, Italy: Giunti-Barbèra.

Bosinelli, M. (Ed.). (1982). *Metodi in psicologia clinica.* Bologna, Italy: il Mulino.

Botash, A. S. (2003). From curriculum to practice: Implementation of the child abuse curriculum. *Child Maltreatment, 8*(4), 239–241. doi:10.1177/1077559503257960

Braithwaite, J. (1989). *Crime, Shame and Reintegration.* New York: Cambridge University Press.

Bravo, G. M. (2000). Intervento. In A. Chiribiri (Ed.), *Carcere e società: il ruolo della cultura universitaria. Atti del seminario, 4 ottobre 1999* (pp. 115-121). Torino, Italy: Editrice Tirrenia Stampatori.

Brosig, C., & Kalichman, S. (1992). Clinicians' reporting of suspected child abuse: A review of the empirical literature. *Clinical Psychology Review, 12,* 155–168. doi:10.1016/0272-7358(92)90112-L

*Brown v. Board of Education.* 1954.349 U.S. 294 from http://www.nationalcenter.org/brown.html

Bufkin, J. (2004). Criminology/criminal justice master's programs in the United States: Searching for commonalities. *Journal of Criminal Justice Education, 15*(2), 239–262. doi:10.1080/10511250400085971

Burrogh, P. A. (1986). *Principles of geographical information systems for land resource assessment.* Oxford, U.K: Clarendon Press.

Button, D. M., & Payne, B. K. (2008). Training child protective services workers about domestic violence: Needs, strategies, and barriers. *Children and Youth Services Review.* doi:.doi:10.1016/j.childyouth.2008.08.011

Caffo, E. (2003). *Consulenza telefonica e relazione d'aiuto. La qualità dell'ascolto e dell'intervento con i bambini e gli adolescenti.* Milano, Italy: McGraw-Hill.

Caffo, E., & Forresi, B. (2005). L'abuso all'infanzia e all'adolescenza: prospettiva storica e questioni aperte. In M.L. De Natale (Ed.), *Pedagogisti per la giustizia* (795-818). Milano, Italy: Vita e Pensiero.

Caffo, E., Ghiringhelli, B., & Forresi, B. (2007). Minori stranieri vittime di abuso: quale ruolo per il pediatra? In G. R. Burgio, S. Bertelloni (Eds.), *Una pediatria per la società che cambia* (pp. 279-288). Milano, Italy: Edizioni Tecniche Nuove.

Caffo, E., Strik Lievers, L., & Forresi, B. (2006). Child abuse and neglect, a mental health perspective. In M.E, Garralda, M. Flamant (Eds.), *Working with children and adolescents: an evidence based approach to risk and resilience* (pp. 95-128). Oxford, UK: Aronson, an imprint of Rowmans and Littlefield publishers.

Caligiuri, M. (2000). Intelligence: un problema di comunicazione istituzionale?. *Per aspera ad veritatem, 16,* 57-80.

Caligiuri, M. (2003). Università e intelligence. Un punto di vista italiano. *Per aspera ad veritatem, 25,* 85-119.

Canetti, E. (1981). *Massa e potere.* Milano, Italy: Adelphi.

Carte, G. E., & Carte, E. H. (1975). *Police Reform in the United States: The Era of August Vollmer, 1905-1932.* Berkeley, CA: University of California Press.

Carter, Y. H., Bannon, M. J., Limbert, C., Docherty, A., & Barlow, J. (2006). Improving child protection: a systematic review of training and procedural interventions. *Archives of Disease in Childhood*, *91*(9), 740–743. doi:10.1136/adc.2005.092007

Caso, L., & Josi, E. (2006). Lo psicologo criminologo come giudice esperto: riflessioni sul tribunale di sorveglianza. In G. De Leo, & P. Patrizi, (Ed.), *Lo psicologo criminologo* (pp. 339-368). Milano, Itlay: Giuffrè. Consiglio Superiore della Magistratura [CSM] (n.d.). Retrieved from http://www.csm.it/circolari/ & http://www.csm.it/documenti/.

Cavalletti, A. (2005). *La città biopolitica – Mitologie della sicurezza.* Milano, Italy: Mondadori.

Ceccarelli, G. (1998). *Psicologia e grafologia: quale rapporto?* Milano, Italy: Angeli.

Ceci, S. J., & Bruck, M. (1993). The suggestibility of the child witness: A hystorical review and synthesis. *Psychological Bulletin*, *113*, 403–440. doi:10.1037/0033-2909.113.3.403

Cernetti, S., & Spriano, M. (2006). *La sentenza penale del giudice di pace.* Torino, Italy: G. Giappichelli.

Cesareo, V. (1979). *Socializzazione e controllo sociale.* Milano, Italy: FrancoAngeli.

Champion, K., Shipman, K., Bonner, B. L., Hensley, L., & Howe, A. C. (2003). Child maltreatment training doctoral programs in clinical, counseling, and school psychology: Where do we go from here? *Child Maltreatment*, *8*(3), 211–217. doi:10.1177/1077559503254139

Chiavario, M., & Marzaduri, E. (Eds.). (2002), *Giudice di pace e processo penale. Commento al D. lgs. 28 agosto 2000 n. 274 e alle successive modifiche.* Torino, Italy: UTET.

Chiribiri, A. (Ed.). (2000). *Carcere e società: il ruolo della cultura universitaria. Atti del seminario, 4 ottobre 1999.* Torino, Italy: Editrice Tirrenia Stampatori.

Christian, C. W. (2008). Professional education in child abuse and neglect. *Pediatrics*, *112*(1), 13–17. doi:10.1542/peds.2008-0715f

Cimini, B. R. (2006). Il contrasto della criminalità informatica. In AA.VV., *Diritto penale europeo e ordinamento italiano.* Milano, Italy: Giuffrè.

Cipolla, C. (Ed.). (2003). *Il ciclo metodologico della ricerca sociale.* Milano, Italy: Franco Angeli.

Clarke, R. V. (1992). *Situational crime prevention. Successful case studies.* New York: Harrow.

Clarke, R. V., & Felson, M. (Eds.). (1993). *Routine activities and crime prevention.* New Brunswick, NJ: Transaction.

Clarke, R. V., & Felson, M. (Eds.). (1993). *Routine activity and rational choice.* New York: Transaction Books.

Clear, T. R., & Dammer, H. R. (2000). *The Offender in the Community.* Belmont, USA: Wadsworth.

Clemmer, D. (1941). *The Prison Community.* Boston: The Christopher Publishing House.

Cohen, A. K. (1955). *Delinquent Boys. The Culture of the Gang.* New York: Free Press.

Cohen, D. J., & Caffo, E. (1998). Developmental Psychopathology: a framework for planning child mental health. *Epidemiologia e Psichiatria Sociale*, *7*, 156–160.

Cohen, J. A., Berliner, L., & Mannarino, A. P. (2003). Psychosocial and pharmacological intervention for child crime victims. *Journal of Traumatic Stress*, *16*(2), 175–186. doi:10.1023/A:1022851324044

Cohen, L. E., & Felson, M. (1979). Social Change and Crime Rate Trends: A Routine Activities Approach. *American Sociological Review*, *44*, 588–607. doi:10.2307/2094589

Cohen, S., & Scull, A. T. (1983). *Social Control and State: Historical and Comparate Essays*, Oxford: Robertson.

Cooper, A. (1999). *Disagio tecnologico.* Milano, Italy: Apogeo.

Corbetta, P. (1999). *Metodologia e tecniche della ricerca sociale.* Bologna, Italy: il Mulino.

Corso, C., & Trifirò, A. (2003).... *E siamo partite! Migrazione, tratta e prostituzione straniera in Italia.* Firenze: Giunti Gruppo Editoriale.

Cottrell, D., Lucey, D., Porter, I., & Walker, D. (2000). Joint working between child and adolescent mental health services and the department of social services: The Leeds model. *Clinical Child Psychology and Psychiatry*, *5*(4), 481–489. doi:10.1177/1359104500005004003

Coulouris, N. (2008). The role of the criminologist in the prison: known secrets and true lies. In S. Vidali & P. Zagoura (Eds.). *Consultative and prison*. (pp.141-168). Athens-Komotini: A.Sakkoulas Publ. (in Greek).

Courakis, N. (2000). The K. Gardikas' contribution in criminological science. In C.D. Spinellis (Ed.), *K. Gardikas the founder of Criminology in Greece* (pp.37-45). Athens-Komotini: A.Sakkoulas Publ. (in Greek).

Courakis, N. (2005). *Penal repression*. Athens- Komotini: A.Sakkoulas Publ. (in Greek).

Courakis, N. (2006). *In order to feel safe in a society with active citizen*. Athens-Komotini: A.Sakkoulas Publ. (in Greek).

Courakis, N. (2008). After prison care: The main condition for the decrease of the recidivism as well as for a humanitarian criminal policy. [Penal Speech]. *Poenikos Logos*, *2*, 253–257.

Courakis, N. (2008). Crime and Criminology through the perspective of 2020. *Youths, crime and society*, *1*, 20-23 (in Greek).

Courakis, N. (n.d.). *The Laboratory of penal and criminological research of the Athens University*. Retrieved from http://www.law.uoa.gr/crime-research/ergastirio.htm (in Greek).

Darlington, Y., Feeney, J. A., & Rixon, K. (2005). Interagency collaboration between child protection and mental health services: practice, attitude and barriers. *Child Abuse & Neglect*, *29*(10), 1085–1098. doi:10.1016/j.chiabu.2005.04.005

Daskalakis, E. (1985). *The Criminology of social reaction*. Athens-Komotini: A.Sakkoulas Publ. (in Greek).

Daskalakis, E. (1985). *The treatment of the offender*. Athens-Komotini: A.Sakkoulas Publ. (in Greek).

Daskalakis, E., et al. (Eds.). (1983). *The administration of penal justice in Greece*. Athens: National Centers of Social Research (in Greek).

Davey, R. I., & Hill, J. (1995). A study of the variability of training and beliefs among professionals who interview children to investigate suspected sexual abuse. *Child Abuse & Neglect*, *19*(8), 933–942. doi:10.1016/0145-2134(95)00055-D

De Leo, G., & Patrizi, P. (Eds.). (2006). *Lo psicologo criminologo*. Milano, Italy: Giuffrè.

Debuyst, C. (1990). Présentation et justification du thème. In AA.VV., *Acteur social et délinquance Hommage à Christian Debuyst* (pp. 21-23). Liège-Bruxelles, Belgium: Pierre Mardaga Editeur.

Della Casa, F. (1998). *La magistratura di sorveglianza. Organizzazione, competenze, procedure*. Torino, Itlay: Giappichelli.

Department of UK Health. (1999). *The NHS plan*. London, UK: The Stationery Office.

Der Pan, P. J., Chang, S., & Lin, C. (2007). Correctional officers' perceptions of the competency-based counseling training program in Taiwan. *International Journal of Offender Therapy and Comparative Criminology*, *51*(5), 523–540. doi:10.1177/0306624X06294134

*DESTATIS* (Statistisches Bundesamt Deutschland) (2007). Fast 70% der Bevölkerung ab 10 Jahren nutzen das Internet. *Pressemitteilung Nr. 486*. URL: http://www.destatis.de/jetspeed/portal/cms/Sites/destatis/Internet/DE/Presse/pm/2007/11/PD07__486__63931,templateId=renderPrint.psml (27.02.2009).

Di Tullio, B. (1975). *Principi di criminologia generale e clinica con note di psicopatologia sociale* (5th ed.). Roma, Italy: Lombardo Editore.

DiIulio, J. J. (1987). *Governing Prisons. A Comparative Study of Correctional Management*. New York: Free Press.

Dolcini, E. (1981). La rieducazione del condannato tra mito e realtà. In V. Grevi (Ed.), *Diritti dei detenuti e trattamento penitenziario* (pp. 55-97). Bologna, Italy: Zanichelli.

Donadel, C., & Martini, E. R. (2005). *La prostituzione invisibile*. Ravenna, Italy: Regione Emilia-Romagna, Grafiche Morandi.

Donohue, B., Carpin, K. M., Alvarez, K. M., Ellwood, A., & Jones, R. W. (2002). A standardized method of diplomatically and effectively reporting child abuse to state authorities: A controlled evaluation. *Behavior Modification, 26*(5), 686–701. doi:10.1177/014544502236657

Dubin, R. (1959). Deviant Behavior and Social Structure: Continuities in Social Theory. *American Sociological Review, 24*, 147–164. doi:10.2307/2089426

Durkheim, E. (1963). *Le regole del metodo sociologico.* Milano, Italy: Edizioni di Comunità.

Durkheim, E. (1983). *Les Règles de la Méthode sociologique.* Paris: PUF.

Durkheim, E. (1985). *Le suicide.* Paris: PUF.

Durkheim, E. (1986). *De la division du travail social.* Paris: PUF.

Durkheim, E. (1991). *Il suicidio. Studio di sociologia.* Milano, Italy: Rizzoli Libri.

Engels, F. (1972). *La situazione della classe operaia in Inghilterra.* Roma, Italy: Editori Riuniti.

Engeström, Y. (1987). *Learning by Expanding. An Activity Theoretical Approach to Development Research.* Helsinki, Finland: Orienta-Konsultint.

Enguéléguélé, S. (1998). *Les politiques pénales (1958-1995).* Paris: l'Harmattan.

Etienne, B. (2001). *L'islamismo radicale.* Milano, Italy: Rizzoli Libri.

Evans, E., Hawton, K., & Rodham, K. (2005). Suicidal phenomena and abuse in adolescents: a review of epidemiological studies. *Child Abuse & Neglect, 29*, 45–58. doi:10.1016/j.chiabu.2004.06.014

Faget, J., & Wyvekens, A. (1999). Bilan de la recherche sur le crime et la justice en France de 1990 à 1998. Van Outrive, L., & Robert, Ph. (Eds). *Crime et justice en Europe depuis 1990,* (pp. 147-172). Paris: L'Harmattan.

Fallace, P. (2000). *La psicologia di Internet.* Milano, Italy: Raffaello Cortina.

Farsedakis, J. (1984). *Criminal investigation, human rights and criminogenesis.* Athens: Nomiki Vivliothiki (in Greek).

Farsedakis, J. (1990). *The criminological thought. From the antiquity until our days.* Vol A'. Athens: Nomiki Vivliothiki (in Greek).

Farsedakis, J. (1991). Introductory note. In *Offering in memory to Elias Daskalakis.* Athens: Panteion University, (in Greek).

Farsedakis, J. (1996). *Elements of Criminology.* Athens: Nomiki Vivliothiki (in Greek).

Farsedakis, J. (2000). Introduction. In I. Daskalaki et al.(Eds.). *Offenders and victims in the threshold of 21th century.* Athens: National Centers of Social Research (in Greek).

Farsedakis, J. (2003). For advancement of Criminology, Prerequisities and demands. In *Essays in Honour of Alice Yotopoulos-Marangopoulos. Human rights-Crime-Criminal Policy* (357-366). Athens-Brussels: Nomiki Vivliothiki-Bruylant.

Farsedakis, J. (2007). The state of penal justice in Greece. In Str. Georgoulas (Ed.), *Criminology in Greece today, Volume in honor of Professor St. Alexiadis* (pp.72-76). Athens: Center of military unit's distraction (in Greek).

Farsedakis, J. (2008a). Criminology and human rights. In *Essays in honor of Anna Benaki-Psarouda, Penal Sciences-Theory and practice* (pp.1141-1148). Athens-Komotini: A.Sakkoulas Publ. (in Greek).

FarsedakisJ. (2008b): www.theartofcrime.gr, v.8.

Fassone, E. (1981). Religione e istruzione nel quadro del trattamento. In V. Grevi (Ed.), *Diritti dei detenuti e trattamento penitenziario* (pp. 120-142). Bologna, Italy: Zanichelli.

Faugeron, C. (1991a). La production de l'ordre et le contrôle pénal. Bilan de la recherche en France depuis 1980. *Déviance et Société, 15*(1), 51–91.

Faugeron, C. (1991b). De la Libération à la guerre d'Algérie: l'espoir d'une réforme pénitentiaire. Petit, J.-G. (Ed.). *Histoire des galères, bagnes, prisons.* Toulouse: Privat, 289-317.

Felitti, V. J. (1991). Long-term medical consequences of incest, rape, and molestation. *Southern Medical Journal, 84*, 328–331.

Feltes, T. (2005 c). *Studiengänge im deutschsprachigen und nichtdeutsprachigen Bereich.* URL: http://www.kriminologie.com/studiengaenge.html (27.02.2009).

Feltes, T. (2005a). Kriminologie als interdisziplinäre Wissenschaftspraxis – wie der Masterstudiengang „Kriminologie und Polizeiwissenschaft" an der juristischen Fakultät der Ruhr-Universität Bochum eine Brücke zwischen Theorie und Praxis schaffen will. *Bewährungshilfe, 52* (4), 359-369. URL: http://www.thomasfeltes.de/pdf/veroeffentlichungen/Bewaehrungshilfe_MA_Studiengang.pdf, p. 1-14 (27.02.2009)

Feltes, T. (2005b). *Stand eines Masterstudienganges „Kriminologie und Polizeiwissenschaft" an der Ruhr Universität.* URL: http://www.kriminologie.com/neues.htm (27.02.2009).

Feltes, T. (2008). Kriminologie und Polizeiwissenschaft im Verbund: Erste Erfahrungen mit dem Masterstudiengang „Kriminologie und Polizeiwissenschaft". In H.-G. Jaschke (Ed.), *Polizeiwissenschaft an der Polizei-Führungsakademie und der Deutschen Hochschule der Polizei – Eine Zwischenbilanz,* 142-163. URL:http://www.thomasfeltes.de/pdf/veroeffentlichungen/2007_Feltes_Beitrag_fuer_Jaschke_Endversion_1.pdf, p.1-14 (27.02.2009).

Feltes, T., & Feldmann-Hahn, F. (2008). Kriminologie aus der Ferne - Der weiterbildende Masterstudiengang setzt auf Blended-Learning. *Rubens, 15*(127), 5.

Fergusson, D. M., & Mullen, P. E. (1999). *Childhood sexual abuse: An evidence based perspective.* Thousand Oaks, CA: Sage Publications.

Ferrajoli, L. (2000). *Diritto e ragione. Teorie del garantismo penale.* Roma-Bari, Italy: Laterza.

Ferrario, B., & De Stefanis, C. (1995). *Procedimenti e provvedimenti della magistratura di sorveglianza.* Padova, Italy: CEDAM.

Ferri, E. (1981). Il tirocinio degli uditori giudiziari nella realtà normativa della Repubblica Italiana. Consiglio Superiore Magistratura [Special Issue]. *Il magistrato. Dal reclutamento alla formazione professionale. Esperienze in Italia e nel mondo* (pp. 15-30).

Ferrua, P. (2005). *Il 'giusto processo'.* Bologna, Italy: Zanichelli.

Fielding, N. (1984). Police socialization and police competence. *The British Journal of Sociology, XXXV*(4), 568–590. doi:10.2307/590435

Finkelhor, D. (1993). Epidemiological factors in the clinical identification of child sexual abuse. *Child Abuse & Neglect, 17*, 67–70. doi:10.1016/0145-2134(93)90009-T

Fiorani Piacentini, V. (2003). *Islam - Logica della fede e logica della conflittualità.* Milano, Italy: FrancoAngeli.

Flor, R. (2008). Art. 615 ter c.p.: natura e funzioni delle misure di sicurezza, consumazione del reato e bene giuridico protetto. *Rivista italiana di diritto e procedura penale,* 106.

Forresi, B. (2003). Un nuovo approccio alla relazione d'aiuto: la psicopatologia dello sviluppo. In E. Caffo (Ed.), *Consulenza telefonica relazione d'aiuto. La qualità dell'ascolto e dell'intervento con i bambini e gli adolescenti* (pp. 53-70). Milano, Italy: McGraw-Hill.

Forum italiano per la sicurezza urbana (2005). *Codice europeo di etica per la polizia.* Imola, Italy: Datacomp.

Foucault, M. (1974). *Surveiller et punir. Naissance de la prison.* Paris: Gallimard.

Fowler, P., Hannigan, B., & Northway, R. (2000). Community nurses and social workers learning together: A report of an interprofessional education initiative in South Wales. *Health & Social Care in the Community, 8*(3), 186–191. doi:10.1046/j.1365-2524.2000.00241.x

Francica, I., Del Percio, C., & Reina, M. (2001). *Bologna e i suoi vigili.* Bologna, Italy: Costa.

Frudà, L. (Ed.). (2006). *Alternative al carcere. Percorsi, attori e reti sociali nell'esecuzione penale esterna.* Milano, Italy: Franco Angeli.

Gallmeier, T., & Bonner, B. (1992). University-based interdisciplinary training in child abuse and neglect. *Child Abuse & Neglect, 16*, 513–521. doi:10.1016/0145-2134(92)90067-2

Gamberini, S., & Moro, S. (2008). *Ma le vigilesse sono più cattive?* Bologna, Italy: Avenue Media.

Gannon, J. (2001). Il ruolo dei servizi di intelligence in un mondo globalizzato. *Per aspera ad veritatem, 20*, 493-508.

Gardiner, J. (2000). *Literature review on models of coordination and integration of service delivery.* Perth, Australia: Women's Policy Office, Domestic Violence Prevention Unit.

Garland, D. (2001). *La cultura del controllo.* Milano, Italy: Il Saggiatore.

Garland, D. (2004). *La cultura del controllo. Crimine e ordine sociale nel mondo contemporaneo.* Milano, Italy: Il Saggiatore (original title: *The Culture of Control.* Oxford, UK: Oxford University Press, 2001).

Gatti, U., & Barbagli, M. (2005). *Prevenire la criminalità.* Bologna, Italy: il Mulino.

Gennaro, G. (1993). *Manuale di sociologia della devianza.* Milano: FrancoAngeli.

Germani, L. S. (Ed.). (2001). *L'Intelligence nel XXI secolo.* Roma, Italy: Quaderni del Centro Studi Gino Germani.

Germano, I. (2001). Scuola e carcere, sottoinsiemi comunicativi. In R. Mancuso (Ed.), *Scuola e carcere. Educazione, organizzazione e processi comunicativi.* (pp. 101-132). Milano, Italy: Franco Angeli.

Giambelluca, F. C., Parisi, S., & Pes, P. (1995). *L'interpretazione psicoanalitica del Rorschach. Modello dinamico strutturale.* Roma: Edizioni Kappa.

Gisese, A., Thomas, M., Dubovsky, S., & Hilty, S. (1998). The impact of a history of childhood abuse on hospital outcome of affective episodes. *Psychiatric Services (Washington, D.C.), 49*, 77–81.

Glaze, L. E., & Bonczar, T. (2007). Probation and Parole in the United States, 2007, Statistical Tables. *Bureau of Justice Statistics Bulletin*, from http://www.ojp.usdoj.gov/bjs/pub/pdf/ppus06.htm.

Glaze, L. E., & Bonczar, T. (2008). Probation and Parole in the United States, 2007, Statistical Tables. *Bureau of Justice Statistics Bulletin*, from http://www.ojp.usdoj.gov/bjs/pub/pdf/ppus07st.pdf.

Goad, J. (2008). Understanding roles and improving reporting and response relationships across professional boundaries. *Pediatrics, 122*(1), 6–9. doi:10.1542/peds.2008-0715d

Goffman, E. (1956). *The Presentation of Self in Everyday Life.* New York: Anchor Books. Goffredson, M.R., & Hirschi, T. (1990). *A General Theory of Crime.* Stanford, CA: Stanford University Press.

Goffman, E. (1961). *Asylums. Essays on the social situation of mental patients and other inmates.* New York: Random House.

Goffman, E. (1969). *La vita quotidiana come rappresentazione.* Bologna, Italy: il Mulino.

Goffman, E. (1988). *L'interazione strategica.* Bologna, Italy: il Mulino.

Goldstein, H. (1979). Improving policy: a problem oriented approach. *Crime and Delinquency, 25*(2), 236–258. doi:10.1177/001112877902500207

Grevi, V. (Ed.). (1981). *Diritti dei detenuti e trattamento penitenziario.* Bologna, Italy: Zanichelli.

Guerrero, L. K., et al. (1999). *The Nonverbal Communication Reader: Classic and Contemporary Readings.* Illinois: Waveland Press.

Guevara, E. (1996). *Opere scelte 1. L'azione armata.* Milano, Italy: Baldini&Castoldi.

Guidicini, P. (1995). *Questionari, Interviste, Storie di vita: come costruire gli strumenti, raccogliere le informazioni ed elaborare i dati.* Milano, Italy: Franco Angeli.

Guidicini, P. (Ed.). (1991). *Nuovo manuale della ricerca sociologica.* Milano, Italy: Franco Angeli.

Gulotta, G. (1976). *La vittima.* Milano, Italy: Giuffré.

Habermas, J. (1974). *Storia e critica dell'opinione pubblica.* Roma-Bari, Italy: Laterza.

Habermas, J. (1980). *Teoria dell'agire comunicativo.* Bologna, Italy: Il Mulino.

Hagan, J. (1989). *Structural Criminology.* New York: Rutgers University Press.

Henggeler, S. W., Schoenwald, S. K., Rowland, M. D., & Cunningham, P. B. (2002). Serious emotional disturbance in children and adolescents. *Multisystemic Therapy.* London, UK: Guilford Press.

Hetherington, R., Baistow, K., Katz, I., Mesie, J., & Trowell, J. (2002). *The welfare of children with mentally ill parents: Learning from inter-country comparisons.* Chichester, UK: John Wiley & Sons.

Hibbard, R. A., Serwint, J., & Connolly, M. (1987). Educational program on evaluation of alleged sexual abuse victims. *Child Abuse & Neglect, 11*(4), 513–519. doi:10.1016/0145-2134(87)90077-9

Hirschi, T. (1969). *Causes of Delinquency.* Berkeley, CA: University of California Press.

Horwath, J., & Morrison, T. (2007). Collaboration, integration and change in children's services: Critical issues and key ingredients. *Child Abuse & Neglect, 31,* 55–69. doi:10.1016/j.chiabu.2006.01.007

Hudson, B. (2002). Interprofessionality in health and social care: The Achilles' heel of partnership? *Journal of Interprofessional Care, 16*(1), 7–17. doi:10.1080/13561820220104122

Hyman, H. H. (1969). *Political Socialization. A Study in the Psychology of Political Behavior.* New York: Free Press.

Idem, XXIX Congresso. (2008). *Un impegno per un'Europa dei diritti.* Retrieved from http://www.movimentoperlagiustizia.org/filedload/opuscolocongresso1.pdf.

Ingrassia, G. (1990). *Comunicazione sociale: crimine e devianza nel post-moderno informatico.* Torino, Italy: Giappichelli Editore.

International Perspectives in Victimology (2004). *Tokiwa International Victimology Institute Journal, 1*(1).

Jacobelli, J. (Ed.). (1996). *Dall'analogico al digitale.* Bari, Italy: Laterza.

Jaudes, P. K., & Martone, M.(1002). The importance of interdisciplinary evaluations of alleged sexual abuse cases. *Pediatrics, 89,* 1164–1168.

Jean, C. (2001). *Guerra, strategia e sicurezza.* Bari, Italy: Laterza.

Jean, C. (2004). *Geopolitica del ventunesimo secolo.* Bari, Italy: Laterza.

Johnson, L. J., Zorn, D., Kai Yung Tam, B., LaMontagne, M., & Johnson, S. A. (2003). Stakeholders' views of factors that impact successful interagency collaboration. *Exceptional Children, 69*(2), 195–209.

Johnson, P., Wistow, G., Schulz, R., & Hardy, B. (2003). Interagency and interprofessional collaboration in community care: The interdependence of structures and values. *Journal of Interprofessional Care, 17*(1), 69–83. doi:10.1080/1356182021000044166

Johnstone, D. B. (1990). Looking at New Links: New Models of Transfer and Articulation between Two-Year and Four-Year Campuses. *Journal of Criminal Justice Education, 1,* 51–57. doi:10.1080/10511259000082051

Juergensmeyer, M. (1993). *The new Cold War? Religious nationalism confronts the secular state.* Berkeley, CA: University of California Press.

Juergensmeyer, M. (2003). *Terroristi in nome di Dio.* Bari, Italy: Laterza.

Kahn, D. (1996). *The Codebreakers: The Comprehensive History of Secret Communication from Ancient Times to the Internet.* New York: Scribner.

Kaluszynski, M. (1994). Identités professionnelles, identités politiques: médecins et juristes face au crime au tournant du 19è et du 20è siècle. In L. Mucchielli, (Ed.), *Histoire de la criminologie française,* (pp. 215-235). Paris: L'Harmattan.

Kaplan, S. J., Pelcovitz, D., & Labruna, V. (1999). Child and Adolescent Abuse and Neglect Research: A Review of the Past 10 Years. Part I: Physical and Emotional Abuse and Neglect. *Journal of the American Academy of Child and Adolescent Psychiatry, 8*(10), 1214–1222.

Karli, P. (1987). *L'homme agressif.* Paris: O. Jacob.

Katz, J. (1988). *Seduction of Crime: Moral and Sensual Attractions in Doing Evil.* New York: Basic Books.

Kendall-Tackett, K. A. (2000). Physiological correlates of childhood abuse: chronic hyperarousal in PTSD, depression and irritable bowel syndrome. *Child Abuse & Neglect, 24,* 799–810. doi:10.1016/S0145-2134(00)00136-8

Kendall-Tackett, K. A., Marshall, R., & Ness, K. E. (2000). Victimization, healthcare use, and health maintenance. *Family Violence & Sexual Assault Bulletin, 16,* 18–21.

Kendall-Tackett, K. A., Williams, L. M., & Finkelhor, D. (1993). Impact of sexual abuse on children: a review and synthesis of recent empirical studies. *Psychological Bulletin, 113,* 164–180. doi:10.1037/0033-2909.113.1.164

Kenny, M. C. (2001). Child abuse reporting: Teachers' perceived deterrents. *Child Abuse & Neglect, 25,* 81–92. doi:10.1016/S0145-2134(00)00218-0

Kenny, M. C. (2007). Web-based training in child maltreatment for future mandated reporters. *Child Abuse & Neglect, 31,* 671–678. doi:10.1016/j.chiabu.2006.12.008

Klages, L. (1928). *Die Grundlagen der Charakterkunde.* Leipzig, Germany: Johann Ambrosius Barth.

*KMK* (Kultusministerkonferenz) (200372008). Ländergemeinsame Strukturvorgaben gemäß § 9 Abs. 2 HRG für die Akkreditierung von Bachelor- und Masterstudiengängen (Beschluss der Kultusministerkonferenz vom 10.10.2003 i.d.F. vom 18.09.2008). URL: http://www.akkreditierungsrat.de/fileadmin/Seiteninhalte/Dokumente/kmk/KMK_LaendergemeinsameStrukturvorgaben.pdf (27.02.2009)

Knapp, M. L., & Judith, A. H. (1996). *Nonverbal Communication in Human Interaction.* Orlando: Harcourt College Publishers.

Krug, E. G. (Ed.). (2002). *World Report on Violence and Health: Summary.* Geneva, Switzerland: World Health Organization.

Kuhn, T. (1972). *La structure des révolutions scientifiques.* Paris: Flammarion.

Laborit, H. (1970). *L'agressivité détournée.* Paris: UGE.

Lambropoulou, E. (2003). The teaching of Criminology in Greece and the contemporary criminological research. *Poeniki Dikaiosyni (Penal Justice),* vo. 7, 833-839 (in Greek).

Lambropoulou, E. (2005). Crime, Criminal Justice and Criminology in Greece. *European Journal of Criminology, 2*(2), 211–247. doi:10.1177/1477370805051274

Lambropoulou, E. (2008). About corruption and anti-corruption. In *Essays in honor of Anna Benaki-Psarouda, Penal Sciences-Theory and practice* (pp.1274-1303). Athens-Komotini: A.Sakkoulas Publ. (in Greek).

Lana, M. (2004). *Il testo nel computer.* Torino, Italy: Bollati Boringhieri.

Lardner, R. (1992). Factors affecting police/social work inter-agency co-operation in a child protection unit. *The Police Journal, 65,* 213–228.

Lazenblattt, A., & Freeman, R. (2006). Recognising and reporting child physical abuse: a survey of primary health care professionals. *Journal of Advanced Nursing, 56*(3), 227–236. doi:10.1111/j.1365-2648.2006.04030.x

Leathers, D. G. (1996). *Successful Nonverbal Communication: Principles and Applications.* Boston: Allyn & Bacon.

Léauté, J. (1972). *Criminologie et Science Pénintentiaire.* Paris: PUF.

Lefaucheur, N. (1994). Psychiatrie infantile et délinquance juvénile. L. Mucchielli, (Ed.), *Histoire de la criminologie française,* (pp. 313-332). Paris: L'Harmattan.

Lemert, E. M. (1967). *Human Deviance, Social Problems and Social Control.* Englewood Cliffs, NJ: Prentice-Hall.

Leonard, V. A. (1950). Current notes. *Journal ofCriminal Law and Criminology*, Jul/Aug(41), 201-2.

Leopardi, F. (2007). Le misure alternative alla detenzione tra reinserimento sociale e abbattimento della recidiva. *Rassegna penitenziaria e criminologica, 2*, 7-26.

Lepri, G. L., & Genovese, M. R. (2003). La formazione nel corso della pratica professionale: costruzione e sviluppo di gruppi operativi integrati. In P. Patrizi, M.S. Di Tullio D'Elisiis, B. Del Vecchio (Ed.), *Strategie della formazione,* (pp. 145-163). Roma, Italy: Carocci.

Leroi-Gourhan, A. (1963-1964). *Le geste et la parole*. 2 tomes. Paris: Albin Michel.

Levasseur, G. (1991). L'influence de Marc Ancel sur la législation répressive française contemporaine. *Revue de science criminelle et de droit pénal comparé, 1*, 9-24.

Levitan, R., Parikh, S., Lesage, A., Hegadoren, K. M., Adams, M., Kennedy, S. H., & Goering, P. N. (1998). Major depression in individuals with a history of childhood physical or sexual abuse: relationship to neurovegetative. *The American Journal of Psychiatry*, *155*, 1746–1752.

Löschper, G. (1986). Kriminologie als selbständiges, interdisziplinäres Hochschulstudium: Internationales Symposium vom 8. - 10. Mai 1986. Pfaffenweiler, Centaurus-Verlagsgesellschaft.

Losito, G. (1993). *L'analisi del contenuto nella ricerca sociale.* Milano, Italy: Franco Angeli.

Luparia, L., & Ziccardi, G. (2007). *Investigazione penale e tecnologia informatica.* Milano, Italy: Giuffrè.

Lurigio, A. J. (Ed.). (1987). Criminal Victimization and Crime [Special issue]. *Crime and Delinquency*, *33*(4).

MacIver, R. M., & Page, C. H. (1957). *Society: An Introductory Analisysis.* London: MacMillan. Mantovani, G. (1995). *Comunicazione e identità. Dalle situazioni quotidiane agli ambienti virtuali.* Bologna, Italy: il Mulino.

Magganas, A. & Lazos, Gr. (1997). *Social values of delinquents and non-delinquents*. Athens: Panteion Univiersity of Social and Political Sciences (in Greek).

Magganas, A. (2004). *The criminal phenomenon in the practice*. Athens: Nomiki Viliothiki (in Greek).

Magganas, A. (Ed.). (2003). Human rights-Crime-Criminal Policy. In *Essays in Honour of Alice Yotopoulos-Marangopoulos*. Athens-Brussels: Nomiki Vivliothiki-Bruylant.

Mancuso, R. (Ed.). (2001). *Scuola e carcere. Educazione, organizzazione e processi comunicativi*. Milano, Italy: Franco Angeli.

Mantovani, G. (1995). *L'interazione uomo computer.* Bologna, Italy: il Mulino.

Marcel, J.-C., & Mucchielli, L. (2006). André Davidovitch ou le deuxième âge de la sociologie criminelle en France. *L'Annee Sociologique*, *56*(1), 83–117. doi:10.3917/anso.061.0083

Marcuse, H. (1968). *L'homme unidimensionnel.* Paris: Minuit

Margara, A. (1995). L'evoluzione della normativa e la situazione penitenziaria dopo la riforma del 1986. In Quaderni del Consiglio Superiore della Magistratura [Special Issue]. *La magistratura di sorveglianza* (pp. 94-117).

Marino, M. R. (1995). La magistratura di sorveglianza e l'esecuzione della pena. Le rispettive funzioni, le conseguenti problematiche. In Quaderni del Consiglio Superiore della Magistratura [Special Issue]. *La magistratura di sorveglianza* (pp. 449-460).

Marotta, G. (2004). *Teorie criminologiche. Da Beccaria al postmoderno*. Milano, Italy: Led.

Marotta, G. (Ed.). (2004). *Tecnologie dell'informazione e comportamenti devianti*. Milano, Italy: Led.

Marotta, G. (Ed.). (2004). *Temi di criminologia.* Milano, Italy: Led.

Marucco, D. (1994). Introduzione. In L. Berzano (Ed.), *La pena del non lavoro* (pp.15-16). Milano, Italy: Franco Angeli.

Marucco, D. (2000). Il diritto allo studio dei detenuti come impegno culturale e sociale. In A. Chiribiri (Ed.), *Carcere e società: il ruolo della cultura universitaria* (pp. 49-52). Torino, Italy: Editrice Tirrenia Stampatori.

Marzaduri, E. (2002). L'attribuzione di competenze penali al giudice di pace: un primo passo verso un sistema penale della conciliazione? In M. Chiavario, & E. Marzaduri (Eds.), *Giudice di pace e processo penale. Commento al D. lgs. 28 agosto 2000 n. 274 e alle successive modifiche* (pp. 17-19). Torino, Italy: UTET.

Mattevi, E., Panizzo, F., & Pongiluppi, C. (2007). I reati di competenza del giudice di pace. *Il giudice di pace, Quaderni, 8.* Milano, Italy: Ipsoa.

Matza, D. (1964). *Delinquency and Drift.* New York: John Wiley.

Mauss, M. (1966). *Sociologie et anthropologie.* Paris: PUF.

Mavris, M. (2008). Probation officers' service- An institution under "probation". In *Essays in honour of Anna Benaki-Psarouda, Penal Sciences-Theory and practice* (pp.1305-1335). Athens-Komotini: A.Sakkoulas Publ. (in Greek).

Mazza, F.A., & Caruso, R, (2006). Giudice penale di pace protagonista fra conciliazione e giurisdizione. *Diritto e giustizia, 1,* 58-76.

Mazzoli, G. (1998). *Profili sociali della comunicazione e nuove tecnologie.* Milano, Italy: Franco Angeli.

McCarty, C. (2008). Doing the right thing: a primary care paediatrician's perspective on child abuse reporting. *Pediatrics, 122*(1), 21–24. doi:10.1542/peds.2008-0715h

Melossi, D. (2002). *Stato, controllo sociale, devianza.* Milano, Italy: Bruno Mondatori.

Meloy, S. R., Hansen, L. T., & Weiner, I. B. (1997). Authority of the Rorschach: Legal Citations During the Past 50 years. *Journal of Personality Assessment, 69*(1), 52–62. doi:10.1207/s15327752jpa6901_3

Merton, R. K. (1938). Social Structure and Anomia. *American Sociological Review, III*(5), 672–682. doi:10.2307/2084686

Merton, R. K. (1965). *Eléments de théorie et de méthode sociologique.* Paris: Plon.

Mestitz, A. (1990). *Selezione e formazione professionale dei magistrate e degli avvocati in Francia.* Padova, Italy: CEDAM.

Migani, M., & Salerno, G. (2008). *Manuale ArcGis.* Palermo, Italy: Dario Flaccovio editore.

Migliori, S. (2007). *Carcere, esclusione sociale, diritto alla formazione.* Roma, Italy: Carocci Faber.

Milanesi, E., & Naldi, A. (2001). *Cantando sotto la pioggia. Insicurezza e sicurezza urbana,* Milano, Italy: FrancoAngeli.

Miller, D. A., McClusky-Fawcett, K., & Irving, L. M. (1993). The relationship between childhood sexual abuse and subsequent onset of bulimia nervosa. *Child Abuse & Neglect, 17,* 305–314. doi:10.1016/0145-2134(93)90050-F

Mogorovich, P., & Mussio, P. (1998). *Automazione del Sistema Informativo territoriale. Elaborazione Automatica dei Dati Geografici* (Vol 2). Milano, Italy: Masson.

Monzini, P. (2002). *Prostituzione, tratta e sfruttamento.* Roma: Donzelli Editore.

Morris, D. B. (1995). *The Meaning of Human Gestures.* New York: Crown Pub.

Mosconi, G. (1998). *Dentro il carcere, oltre la pena.* Padova, Italy: Cedam.

Mucchielli, L. (1994). Hérédité et " Milieu social ": le faux antagonisme franco-italien. La place de Lacassagne dans l'histoire de la criminologie. L. Mucchielli, (Ed.),

*Histoire de la criminologie française* (pp. 189-214). Paris: L'Harmattan.

Mucchielli, L. (1994). Le sens du crime. Histoire des (r) apports de la psychanalyse à la criminologie. L. Mucchielli, (Ed.), *Histoire de la criminologie française,* (pp.351-409). Paris: L'Harmattan.

Mucchielli, L. (1997). Une sociologie militante du contrôle social. Naissance du projet et formation de l'équipe francophone, des origines au milieu des années quatre-vingt. *Déviance et Société, 21*(1), 7–45.

Mucchielli, L. (1998). *La découverte du social. Naissance de la sociologie en France (1870-1914).* Paris: La Découverte.

Mucchielli, L. (1999). Les champs de la sociologie pénale. Vingt ans de recherches et de débats dans " Déviance et société ". *Déviance et Société, 23*(1), 3–40.

Mucchielli, L. (1999). Quelques interrogations épistémologiques sur la psychiatrie criminologique française, *Revue internationale de criminologie et de police scientifique et technique, 4*, 461-487.

Mucchielli, L. (2004). L'impossible constitution d'une discipline criminologique en France. Cadres institutionnels, enjeux normatifs et développements de la recherche des années 1880 à nos jours. *Criminologie, 37*(1), 13–42.

Mucchielli, L. (2006). Criminology, hygienism and eugenics in France (1870-1914): the medical debates on the elimination of"incorrigible" criminals. Becker, P. & Wetzell, R. (Eds.). *Criminals and their scientists. The history of Criminology in International Perspective*,(pp. 207-230. Cambridge, UK: Cambridge University Press.

Mucchielli, L. (2008). Une " nouvelle criminologie " française ? Pourquoi ? Pour qui ?, *Revue de science criminelle et de droit pénal comparé, 4*, 795-803.

Mucchielli, L., & Marcel, J.-C. (2002). La sociologie du crime en France depuis 1945. Mucchielli, L., & Robert, Ph. (Eds.). *Crime et sécurité: l'état des savoirs*, (pp. 53-63). Paris: La Découverte.

Murray, C. (1995). Interrogating justice: Research on race and gender bias in the South African Court system. *International Journal of Discrimination and the Law, 1*(1), 29–38.

Nappi, A. (2004). *La procedura penale per il giudice di pace.* Milano, Italy: Giuffrè.

Nicolotti, L. (1994). Carcere e lavoro: il seminario e la ricerca. In L. Berzano L (Ed.), *La pena del non lavoro* (pp. 47-77). Milano, Italy: Franco Angeli.

Norman, D. (1990). *La caffettiera del masochista: psicopatologia degli oggetti quotidiani.* Firenze, Italy: Giunti.

Norman, D. (1998). *The invisibile computer.* Cambridge, MA: MIT Press.

Ostrom, E., & Whitaker, G. (1973). Does Local and Community Control Make a Difference? *American Journal of Political Science, 17*, 48–76. doi:10.2307/2110474

Owston, R. O. (1997). The World Wide Web: A technology to enhance teaching and learning. *Educational Researcher, 26*(2), 27–33.

Pace, E. (1999). *Sociologia dell'Islam. Fenomeni religiosi e logiche sociali.* Roma, Italy: Carocci Editore.

Palaferri, N. (2001). *Dizionario grafologico morettiano.* Urbino, Italy: Libreria "G. Moretti".

Palma, M. (2000). La cultura della legalità e l'esercizio dei diritti in carcere. In A. Chiribiri (Ed.), *Carcere e società: il ruolo della cultura universitaria* (pp. 89-93). Torino, Italy: Editrice Tirrenia Stampatori.

Palusci, V. J., & McHugh, T. M. (1995). Interdisciplinary training in the evaluation of child sexual abuse. *Child Abuse & Neglect, 19*(9), 1031–1038. doi:10.1016/0145-2134(95)00065-G

Panoussis, Y. (1988). *The "requested" in Criminology.* Athens-Komotini: A.Sakkoulas Publ. (in Greek).

Panoussis, Y. (1994). Teaching Criminology in Greece. *Eurocriminology, 7*, 111–118.

Panoussis, Y. (2008). Central Scientific Council of Prisons. In S. Vidali & P. Zagoura (Eds.). *Consultative and prison*, (pp.121-140). Athens-Komotini: A.Sakkoulas Publ. (in Greek).

Panoussis, Y. (2008). What is criminology? First plan of an answer. *Youths, crime and society, 1*, 13-19, (in Greek).

Panteion University of Social and Political Sciences (2003). *University Guide*. Academic year 2002-2003.

Panteios Higher School of Political Sciences (1957). *Twentyfive years seniority-Eikosipentaetiris, 1930-1955*, (in Greek).

Paolucci, E., Genuis, M., & Violato, C. (2001). A meta-analysis of the published research on the effects of child sexual abuse. *The Journal of Psychology, 135*, 17–36.

Papathanassopoulos, E. (2006). Remarks-Brief presentation of basic points of the presidential decree 195/06 about the organisation and the function of the services of probation officers. [Penal speech]. *Poenikos Logos, 3*, 1069–1084.

Park, R. E., Burgess, E. W., & McKenzie, R. D. (Eds.). (1925). *The City.* Chicago: University of Chicago Press.

Parsons, T. (1965). *Il sistema sociale.* Milano, Italy: Edizioni di Comunità.

Patrizi, P. (1996). *Psicologia giuridico penale*. Milano, Italy: Giuffrè.

Patterson, G. T. (2004). Evaluating the effects of child abuse training on the attitudes, knowledge, and skills of police recruits. *Research on Social Work Practice, 14*(4), 273–280. doi:10.1177/1049731503262390

Pavarini, M. (1995). L'articolazione del sistema punitive: novità e prospettive. In Quaderni del Consiglio Superiore della Magistratura [Special Issue]. *La magistratura di sorveglianza* (pp. 43-65).

Pavone, M. (2005). *Le nuove competenze del Giudice di Pace.* Matelica, Italy: Halley.

Pence, D., & Wilson, C. (1994). *Team Investigation of Child Sexual Abuse: The Uneasy Alliance*. London, UK: Sage.

Perri, P. (2008). Profili informatico-giuridici della diffusione, mediante strumenti telematici, di materiale pedopornografico. *Cassazione penale*, 3466.

Petersilia, J. (2002). *Reforming Probation and Parole in 21st Century.* Lanham, USA: American Correctional Association.

Pether, P. (2005). Negotiating the structure of violence; or, on not inventing "The Sullivans". *Social Semiotics, 15*(1), 5–28. doi:10.1080/10350330500059080

Piccialli, P., & Aghina, E. (Eds.). (2001). *Il procedimento penale davanti al giudice di pace. Manuale teorico-pratico per gli operatori giudiziari.* Napoli, Italy: Edizioni Giuridiche Simone.

Pick, D. (1989). *Faces of Degeneration. A European Disorder, c.1848-c.1918.* Cambridge, UK: Cambridge University Press.

Picotti, L. (2004). Sistematica dei reati informatici, tecniche di formulazione legislativa e beni giuridici tutelati. In L. Picotti (Ed.). *Il diritto penale dell'informatica nell'epoca di Internet.* Padova, Italy: Cedam.

Picotti, L. (2008). Ratifica della Convenzione Cybercrime e nuovi strumenti di contrasto contro la criminalità informatica e non solo. *Diritto dell'internet*, 437.

Pietsch, J., & Short, L. (1998).*Working together in families in which a parent has a mental illness: Developing 'best practice' for service provision and interagency collaboration.* Melbourne, Australia: Mental Health Research Institute.

Pinatel, J. (1957). Les données du problème de l'enseignement de la criminologie. *Revue de science criminelle et de droit pénal comparé*, 411-421.

Platt, T. (1982). Crime and Punishment in the United States: Immediate and Long-term Reforms from a Marxist Perspective. *Crime and Social Justice, 18*, 38–45.

Poncioni, P. (2005). The professional police model and the professional formation of the future polireme in the Police Academies of Rio de Janeiro State. *Sociedade e Estado, 20*(3), 585–610. doi:10.1590/S0102-69922005000300005

Portigliatti Barbos, M., & Marini, G. (1964). *La capacità di intendere e di volere nel sistema penale italiano.* Milano, Italy: Giuffrè.

Powell, M. B., Fisher, R. P., & Hughes Scholes, C. H. (2008). The effect of using trained versus untrained adult respondents in simulated practice interviews about child abuse. *Child Abuse & Neglect*, *32*(11), 1007–1016. doi:10.1016/j.chiabu.2008.05.005

Rankin, J. A. (1995). *Body Language in Negotiations and Sales*. Springfield: Rankin File.

Rapetto, U., & Di Nunzio, R. (2001). *Le nuove guerre*. Milano, Italy: BUR.

Rapetto, U., & Di Nunzio, R. (2002). *Atlante delle spie*. Milano, Italy: Rizzoli.

Rasmussen, J. (1981). *Skill, Rules, Knowledge; Signals signs and symbols*. New York: Plenum Press.

Raymond, S. G., & Bornstein, S. J. (1988). Examen psychologique et médico-psycologique judiciaire. *Encycl. Méd. Chir. Psychiatrie*, *37903*(A10), 11–19.

Reder, P., & Duncan, S. (2003). Understanding communication in child protection networks. *Child Abuse Review*, *12*, 82–100. doi:10.1002/car.787

Reiniger, A., Robinson, E., & McHugh, M. (1995). Mandated training of professionals: A means for improving reporting of child abuse. *Child Abuse & Neglect*, *19*, 63–69. doi:10.1016/0145-2134(94)00105-4

Renneville, M. (1995). Alexandre Lacassagne. Un médecin-anthropologue face à la criminalité. *Gradhiva*, *17*, 127–140.

Renneville, M. (1997). *La médecine du crime. Essai sur l'émergence d'un regard médical sur la criminalité en France (1785-1885)*. Lille: Presses Universitaires du Septentrion.

Renouard, J.-M., Pradel, J., & Boucher, N. (1992). *La recherche française dans le champ pénal. Bilan et synthèse*. Paris: CEDAS.

*Riflessioni, proposte ed approfondimenti* (XXIX Congress of *Associazione Nazionale Magistrati*, 2008, June 6-8), from http://www.movimentoperlagiustizia.org/filedload/opuscolocongresso1.pdf

Rizzo, C., & Ferracuti, F. (1958). Impiego del test di Rorschach in criminologia clinica. *Comunicazione presentata al IV Congresso internazionale Rorschach*. Bruxelles, Belgium. 1st - 4th August.

Roché, S. (1998). *Sociologie politique de l'insécurité*, Paris: Puf.

Rodgers, J. (1994). Collaboration among health professionals. *Nursing Standard*, *9*(6), 25–26.

Rogers, J. R. (2003). Sexual abuse and suicide: Why we may not know what we think we know. *Archives of Suicide Research*, *7*, 83–91. doi:10.1080/13811110301564

Rossiaud, J. (1995). *La prostituzione nel Medioevo*. Roma: Laterza Editore.

Santinello, M., Gonzi, P., & Scacchi, L. (1998). *Le paure della criminalità: aspetti psicosociali di comunità*. Milano, Italy: Giuffrè.

Santoro, E., & Tucci, R. (2004). *L'incidenza dell'affidamento sulla recidiva: prime indicazioni e problemi per una ricerca sistematica, rapporto finale del progetto Misura*. Regione Toscana, Italy.

Saponaro, A. (2004). *Vittimologia. Origini, concetti, tematiche*. Milano, Italy: Giuffrè.

Sarzotti, C. (2006). *Cultura giuridica e culture della pena. I discorsi inaugurali dell'anno giudiziario dei procuratori Generali*. Torino, Italy: L'Harmattan Italia.

Schafer, J. A., & Castellano, T. C. (2005). Academie versus academy: Faculty views on awarding academic credits for police training. *Journal of Criminal Justice Education*, *16*(2), 300–317. doi:10.1080/10511250500082229

Schafer, S. (1975). The proper role of a victim-compensation system. *Crime and Delinquency*, *21*(1), 45–49. doi:10.1177/001112877502100106

Schwendinger, H., & Schwendinger, J. (1985). *Adolescent Subcultures and Delinquency*. New York: Praeger.

Schwind, H. D. (2007). *Kriminologie. Eine praxisorientierte Einführung mit Beispielen*. 17. Edition, Heidelberg, Kriminalistik Verlag.

Scopinaro, L. (2007). Furto di dati e frode informatica. *Rivista italiana di diritto e procedura penale*, 363.

Scott, D. (1997). Inter-agency conflict: An ethnographic study. *Child & Family Social Work*, *2*, 73–80. doi:10.1046/j.1365-2206.1997.00048.x

Scribner, S. (1985). Knowledge at work. *Anthropology & Education Quarterly*, *16*(3), 199–231. doi:10.1525/aeq.1985.16.3.05x1486d

Selmini, R. (Ed.). (2004). *La sicurezza urbana*. Bologna, Italy: il Mulino.

Selmini, R., & Braccasi, C. (Eds.). (2005). *Sicurezza urbana e ruolo della polizia locale*. Bologna, Italy: Maggioli.

Semerari, A., & Citterio, C. (1975). *Medicina criminologica e psichiatria forense*. Milano, Italy: Vallardi.

Sette, R. (1999). *L'insegnamento della criminologia nelle Università e in altre istituzioni*. Bologna, Italy: CLUEB.

Sette, R. (2003). Sicurezza urbana e centri di victim support. In A. Balloni (Ed.), *Il vigile di quartiere a Milano* (pp. 80-81). Milano, Italy: Franco Angeli.

Sette, R. (2008). *Controllo sociale e prevenzione. Un approccio criminologico*, Bologna, Italy: Clueb.

Sette, R., & Vezzadini, S. (2008), Quale sostegno per quali vittime? tavola rotonda con: Augusto Balloni, Gemma Marotta, Monica Raiteri, Raluca Simion, Emilio Viano. In A. Balloni A., & R. Bisi (Eds.), *Processi di vittimizzazione e reti di sostegno alle vittime* (pp. 89-118). Milano, Italy: Franco Angeli.

Shaw, C. R., & McKay, H. D. (1942). *Juvenile Delinquency in Urban Areas*. Chiacago: University of Chicago Press.

Shaw, E.(1979). Agenda Setting and Mass Communication Theory. *Gazette International Journal for Mass Communication Studies, XXV*(2).

Sicurella, S. (2008). Processi di vittimizzazione e centri di ascolto alle vittime. In A. Balloni, & R. Bisi (Eds.), *Processi di vittimizzazione e reti di sostegno alle vittime* (pp.73-87). Milano, Italy: Franco Angeli.

Simon, H. A., Smithburg, D. W., & Thompson, V. A. (1961). *Public Administration*. New York: Knopf.

Soubiran-Paillet, F. (2000). Juristes et sociologues français d'après-guerre: une rencontre sans lendemain. *Genèses*, *41*, 125–142. doi:10.3406/genes.2000.1653

Spinellis, C. D. (1995). Center for penal and criminological research, Section of penal sciences, University of Athens. *European Journal on Criminal Policy and Research*, 100–103. doi:10.1007/BF02243137

Spinellis, C. D. (1997). *Crime in Greece in perspective*. Athens-Komotini: A.Sakkoulas Publ.

Spinellis, C. D. (2000). Memories from the teacher K. G. Gardikas or the Criminology, the penology and the Criminalistic from yesterday in our days. In C.D. Spinellis (Ed.). *K. Gardikas the founder of Criminology in Greece* (pp.47-67). Athens-Komotini: A.Sakkoulas Publ. (in Greek).

Spinellis, C. D. (2005). *Criminology, Contemporary and older trends*. Athens-Komotini: A.Sakkoulas Publ., (in Greek). Papathéodorou, Th. & Mary, Ph. (Eds.). (2006). *Mutations des politiques criminelles en Europe*. Athènes: Éditions Papazissis.

Stella, F. (2003). *Giustizia e modernità. La protezione dell'innocente e la tutela delle vittime*. Milano, Italy: Giuffrè.

Stevens, D. (2006). *Community Corrections. An applied approach*. Upper Saddle River, NJ: Prentice Hall.

Sutherland, E. H. (1949). *White Collar Crime*. New York: Holt.

Sutherland, E. H., & Cressey, D. R. (1966). *Principes de criminologie*. Paris: Cujas.

Sykes, G. M. (1958). *The Society of Captives. A study of a Maximum Security Prison*. Princeton, NJ: Princeton University Press.

Sykes, G. M., & Matza, D. (1957). Techniques of Neutralization: A Theory of Delinquency. *American Sociological Review*, *22*, 664–670. doi:10.2307/2089195

Taylor, I., Walton, P., & Young, J. (1973). *The New Criminology: For a Social Theory of Deviance*. London: Routledge & Kegan.

Taylor, I., Walton, P., & Young, J. (1975). *Criminologia sotto accusa*. Firenze, Italy: Guaraldi.

Taylor, R. B. (2001). *Breaking away from broken windows*. Boulder, CO: Westview Press.

Tétard, F. (1985). " Délinquance juvénile ": stratégie, concept ou discipline? Collectif. *Problèmes de la jeunesse, marginalité et délinquance juvénile* (Vol. 2, pp. 125-147). Vaucresson: CFR-ES.

The National Advisory Mental Health Council Workgroup on Child and Adolescent Mental Health Intervention Development and Deployment. (2001). *Blueprint for change: research on child and adolescent mental health*. Washington, DC: The National Advisory Mental Health Council Workgroup on Child and Adolescent Mental Health Intervention Development and Deployment.

Thomas, W. (1966). *On Social Organization and Social Personality*. Chicago: University of Chicago Press.

Thompson, K. (1998). *Moral panics*. London: Routledge.

Turk, A. T. (1966). Conflict and Criminality. *American Sociological Review*, 338–352. doi:10.2307/2090822

Turk, A. T. (1969). *Criminality and Legal Order*. Chicago: Rand McNally.

Turnaturi, G. (1991). *Associati per amore: l'etica degli affetti e delle relazioni quotidiane*. Milano, Italy: Feltrinelli.

Tye, C., & Precey, G. (1999). Building bridges: The interface between adult mental health and child protection. *Child Abuse Review*, *8*, 164–171. doi:10.1002/(SICI)1099-0852(199905/06)8:3<164::AID-CAR556>3.0.CO;2-G

Vaciago, G., & Giordano, M. T. (2007). La qualificazione giuridica del phishing in una delle sue prime applicazioni giurisprudenziali. *Diritto dell'Internet*, 62.

Van Kesteren, J., Mayhew, P., & Nieuwbeerta, P. (2000). *Criminal Victimization in Seventeen industrialized Countries*. The Hague, the Netherlands: Wetenschappelijk Onderzoek – en Documentatiecentrum.

Veilt, P. (1994). La géographie sociale du crime et la pratique réformatrice d'Henri Joly. In L. Mucchielli, (Ed.). *Histoire de la criminologie française*, (pp. 269-285). Paris: L'Harmattan.

Venafro, E., & Piemontese, C. (2004). *Ruolo e tutela della vittima in diritto penale*. Torino, Italy: Giappichelli Editore.

Vetere, E., & David, P. R. (2005). *Victims of Crime and Abuse of Power (Bangkok, 18-25 April 2005): Festschrift In Honour of Irene Melup*. New York, NY: United Nations.

Vezzadini, S. (2006). *La vittima di reato tra negazione e riconoscimento*. Bologna, Italy: Clueb.

Vezzadini, S. (2006). Profilo geografico e crime mapping. Il contributo della criminologia ambientale allo studio del delitto. In R. Bisi (Ed.), *Scena del crimine e profili investigativi. Quale tutela per le vittime?* (pp. 83-94). Milano, Italy: Franco Angeli.

Viano, E. (1987). Victim's rights and the Constitution: reflections on a bicentennial. *Crime and Delinquency*, *33*(4), 438–451. doi:10.1177/0011128787033004002

Viano, E. (1989). *Crime and Its Victims: international research and public policy issues*. New York, NY: Hemisphere Publishing Corporation.

Vichnieswky, L. (1995). Le misure alternative nei paesi CEE con particolare riferimento alla legislazione francese. In Quaderni del Consiglio Superiore della Magistratura [Special Issue]. *La magistratura di sorveglianza* (pp. 527-585).

Volpe, R. (1981). The development and evaluation of a training program for school-based profession- als dealing with child abuse. *Child Abuse & Neglect*, *5*, 103–110. doi:10.1016/0145-2134(81)90027-2

Vulpiani, D. (2007). La nuova criminalità informatica. Evoluzione del fenomeno e strategie di contrasto (Electronic version). *Rivista di Criminologia, Vittimologia e Sicurezza*, *I*(1), January-April, 46-54. Retrieved from http://www.vittimologia.it/rivista.

Wainwright, G. R. (2000). *Teach Yourself Body Language*. Columbus: McGraw-Hill.

Walter, U. M., & Petr, C. (2000). A template for family-centered interagency collaboration. Families in society. *Families in Society*, *8*(5), 494–503.

Walzer, D. (1977). Citizen contact and legal support system. *Social Science Quarterly*, 3–14.

Ward, R. H., & Webb, V. J. (1984). *Quest for quality*. New York: University Publications.

Werner, J., & Werner, M. C. (2008). Child sexual abuse in clinical and forensic psychiatry: a review of recent literature. *Current Opinion in Psychiatry*, *21*(5), 499–504. doi:10.1097/YCO.0b013e328305e4b0

Wertham, F. (1949). *The show of violence*. New York, NY: Doubleday.

Wilkins, L. T. (1965). *Social Deviance: Social Policy, Action and Research*. Englewood Cliffs, NJ: Prentice-Hall.

Williams, F. P., & McShane, M. D. (2002). *Devianza e criminalità*. Bologna, Italy: il Mulino.

Williamson, V. (2001). The potential of project status to support partnerships. In S. Balloch & M. Taylor (Ed.), *Partnership working: Policy and practice* (pp. 117–141). Bristol, UK: Polity Press.

Yin, P. P. (1985). *Victimization and the aged*. Springfield, IL: Chas C. Thomas.

Yotopoulos-Marangopoulos, A. (1981). La criminologie en Grèce. In *Actas del XXIX Curso International de Criminologie* (pp.104-127). Spain: Fundacion Bartolomé de Carranza.

Zagoura, P. (2008). Consultative in minor delinquents and inmates. In S. Vidali & P. Zagoura (Eds.), *Consultative andprison*, (pp. 171-117). Athens-Komotini: A.Sakkoulas Publ. (in Greek).

Zani, B. (Ed.). (2003). *Sentirsi in/sicuri in città*. Bologna, Italy: il Mulino.

Zaniboni, A. (2004). *Magistratura di sorveglianza o tribunale della pena?* from http://www.sestaopera.it/home/CORSO_VOLONTARI/4_art.Zaniboni_Dignitas2004_MagistrSorv.pdf.

Zarafonitou, Ch. & Courakis, N. (2009). *Unsafety, punitivity and criminal policy.*, Athens-Komotini: A.Sakkoulas publisher (in Greek).

Zarafonitou, Ch. (2002). *The fear of crime. A criminological approach and inquiry based on an empirical study of the phenomenon within the city of Athens*. Athens-Komotini: European Studies in Law, A.Sakkoulas Publisher (in Greek and in English).

Zarafonitou, Ch. (2006). Criminological approaches of fear of crime and (in)security. [in Greek]. *Poeniki Dikaiosyni*, *8-9*, 1031–1039.

Zarafonitou, Ch. (2006). La peur du crime parmi les immigrés et leurs attitudes face aux institutions de la justice pénale. In Th. Papathéodorou & Ph.Mary (Eds.), *Mutations des politiques criminelles en Europe* (pp. 91-138). Athènes: Éditions Papazissis.

Zarafonitou, Ch. (2009). Fear of crime in contemporary Greece. In L. K. Cheliotis & S. Xenakis (Eds.). *Crime and Punishment in Contemporary Greece: International Comparative Perspectives*. Oxford: Peter Lang AG (forthcoming).

Zelenko, M. A., Huffman, L., Lock, J., Kennedy, O., & Steiner, H. (2001). Poor adolescent expectant mothers: can we assess their potential for child abuse? *Adolesc Health*, *29*, 271–278. doi:10.1016/S1054-139X(01)00272-5

Zlotnick, C., Mattia, J., & Zimmerman, M. (2001). Clinical features of survivors of sexual abuse with major depression. *Child Abuse & Neglect*, *25*(3), 357–367. doi:10.1016/S0145-2134(00)00251-9

# About the Contributors

**Raffaella Sette**, PhD in criminology, is senior researcher within the Department of Sociology of the University of Bologna (Italy) and she teaches "Criminal sociology" within the Faculty of Political Sciences and "Criminology" within the Faculty of Psychology. She is author of a large number of articles and essays concerning the sociology of the deviance, the criminology and the victimology. She is coordinator of the Editorial Board of the *Criminology, Victimology and Security Journal*, and since 2002, she is expert member of the Court of Surveillance of Bologna (Italy).

* * *

**Arije Antinori** is sociologist and geopolitical analyst. He is got a $2^{nd}$ level specializing Master (Hons) Degree on Criminal Investigation: Theory and Methods. Currently he is Ph.D. student in Criminology at University of Bologna linked to "Sapienza" University of Rome, Italy. He's Assistant Lecturer in Criminology and Social-Change Analysis. He's author of essays about cyber terrorism, terrorism & media, ICT intelligence, and develops project concerning: organized crime & terrorism in urban areas, emergency management, and critical infrastructure protection, at Observatory for National Security - Center for High Studies of Defence. He serves as Police Officer in Italian National Police.

**Antonio Apruzzese** is the executive of the Emilia-Romagna Region Postal and Communication Police, Italian National Police in Bologna. After a ten-year experience in the Criminal Investigation Department, he coordinates the operational activities of the Italian National Police engaged in countering the cyber crimes, the online pedophilia and the protection of the Communication.

**Augusto Balloni** graduated at Bologna University in medicine and surgery and he specialized in clinical mental diseases and in Legal and Insurance Medicine. Since 1970 he has been teaching specialization courses of Legal Medicine and Psychology at Bologna University. Since 1970 he has been teaching Criminology at the Faculty of Political Sciences of Bologna University. Since December 1983 he is full professor. Since 1992 he has been Director of the Research Interdepartemental Center of Victimology and Security (C.I.R.Vi.S) of Bologna University. He is a member of the Italian Society of Psychiatry, of the Italian Society of Criminology, of the Italian Society of Sociology and the International Society of Victimology. He is a member of ASIS (American Society for Industrial Security) and an honorary member of the Mexican Society of Criminology. He is the President of the Italian Society of Victimology (S.I.V.), he is a member of the board of governors of the International Society of Criminology. He is the editor-in-chief of the Rivista di Criminologia, Vittimologia e Sicurezza (Criminology, Victimology and

Security Journal). He is the author of more than 150 publications including books, essays, articles and outcomes researches reports related to legal and social Medicine, to forensic and clinic Psychiatrics, to Psychology and above all to Criminology.

**Elena Bianchini** has a degree in Political Sciences (curriculum: Social Sciences), obtained on the 20.01.2006 at the faculty of Political Sciences at the University of Bologna "Alma Mater Studiorum" (Italy). Thesis in criminology: "Conflicts and Justice of the Peace. A victimological and criminological analysis". On the 1st November 2006 she had one year contract at the University of Bologna "Alma Mater Studiorum", that consists of a research in criminology named: "Justice of the Peace, Criminal Jurisdiction and relationship between author and victim: a criminological and social-victimological analysis". On the 1st November 2007 she had resigned one year contract at the University of Bologna "Alma Mater Studiorum". Now she is enrolled for the 1st year of Ph.D. in Sociology at the University of Bologna "Alma Mater Studiorum".

**Roberta Bisi**, graduated in Political Sciences in 1982, Ph. D. in Criminology in 1989. She has been enrolled in the Psychologists' Association List of Emilia-Romagna since 1993- ex.art.33 Law 18 Feb.1989, n.56. Since 2001, she is Full Professor in Criminology and Sociology of Law, of Deviance and Social Change at the Faculty of Political Sciences "Roberto Ruffilli", University of Bologna (Italy). She is a member of the Boards of Ph.D. in Criminology and in Sociology (Department of Sociology) and among other activities in the field of victimology she uses to train social control and security operators. In January 2008 and in January 2009 she was visiting professor at Toulouse University, Faculty of Political Science. She is the chief of the Editorial Board of the Rivista di Criminologia, Vittimologia e Sicurezza (The Criminology, Victimology and Security Journal). She is the Vice Chairman of the Board of the Italian Society of Victimology. She is an honorary member of the Mexican Society of Criminology. She is the author of a great number of works, papers, articles, books. Some of them deal with the contribution of the Classics to the foundation of criminology and victimology sciences.

**Jean-Michel Bessette**, State PhD ès Lettres and Human Sciences (Paris V - Sorbonne University), Ph.D. in Sociology, University professor, currently head of the department of Sociology and Anthropology at the University of Franche-Comté (France). He also is a trustee for the French Association of Criminology and a member of the jury for the Gabriel Tarde Award (French award in criminology, delivered by the Department of Law).

**Ernesto Caffo** is Professor of Child Psychiatry at the University of Modena and Reggio Emilia (Italy) and Past-President of the European Society for Child and Adolescent Psychiatry (ESCAP). He is the President of Telefono Azzurro – an Italian child line – as well as the President of Child Foundation (Italy) and of Childrenfirst Foundation (New York). He is the Director of a post-graduated University-based training course on child abuse at the University of Modena and Reggio Emilia. He is also the Director of two Centers for diagnosis and treatment of abused children, located in Rome and in Treviso. He is the author of several books and articles on child and adolescent psychiatry, autism, child abuse and children's rights.

**Giovanna Fanci** is Ph.D. in "Sociology of Legal and Political Institutions and Analysis of Administrative Apparatus" at Faculty of Law, University of Macerata (Italy), and expert at Surveillance Court *(Tribunale di Sorveglianza)* in Ancona (Italy).

**Felix Feldmann-Hahn** studied law at the Ruhr-University of Bochum (Germany) between 2003 and 2008. During this time he started working at the chair of Criminology, Police Science and Criminal Policy of Professor Dr. Thomas Feltes M.A. as a student assistant. After his graduation he stayed at the chair and is currently research assistant within the master's program in Criminology and Police Science in which he gives lectures as well (Module 9/2a – Academic Writing and Working). Besides this work he is writing on his PhD-thesis dealing with unreported crime in Germany. His research interests focus (moreover) on criminal geography and criminal law.

**Barbara Forresi** is clinical psychologist. She received her Ph.D. from the University of Modena and Reggio Emilia (Italy). Her clinical and research interests are in developmental psychopathology, child abuse and psychological impact of traumatic events on children and adolescent.

**Gian Luigi Lepri** is forensic psychologist and psychoterapist. He is Training Manager of *Telefono Azzurro* (an Italian child line). His clinical and research interests are in social psychology, child abuse and inter-agency relationships and training.

**Laurent Mucchielli** is senior research fellow at CNRS (the national center for scientific research) and the Director of the CESDIP (Center of sociological researches on law and penal institutions) - Saint-Quentin-en-Yvelines (France). He teaches sociology and political sciences at the University of Versailles-Saint-Quentin. He is a member of the Editorial Board of the french-speaking international review *Déviance et Société*, as well as the coeditor of the new French scientific journal *Sociologie*. He is the author of several books and articles on sociology of deviance and violence, political sociology of security, history of social sciences and sociology of urban riots.

**Daniela Passaro** (1983) is a journalist and the recipient of an M.A. in "Institutional and Corporate Communication" from the Suor Orsola Benincasa University in Naples. Since February 2009, she is a member of the Italian Society of Victimology (SIV). She is aresearch assistant inStrategic Management and Strategic Communication for public, private and non-profit associations of Naples. Currently, she's also a journalist of the magazine "I'M" edited by Maurizio Aiello and responsible of the web portal www.tuttocomunicazione.it.

**Andrea Piselli** is 37 years old. Studies: scientific high school, Degree in both Philosophy and Sociology, actually ending a Ph.D. in Criminology. Graduated at armoured school, served in the Army as tank officer for three years (1994-1997), also employed in public security in south of Italy during the anti-mafia operations. Then experienced two years in both airport security, when new private services began operating in Italy (2000-2002), and private investigation. During last six years (2003-2008) employed as Bologna Local Police officer in drug enforcement, street control, investigation, forensic and training. Practices in explosives and demolitions.

**Silvia Ricci Lucchi** was born in Castel San Pietro Terme (1980) and lives in Imola (Bologna), Italy. Since 2006, she has worked as an educational therapist in a psychiatric community. In 2002 she obtains a diploma as cameraman at the "School for Cinema, Television and New Media" in Milan. In 2006 she graduates from Bologna University in "Sociology and Criminal Sciences for Security". At the same university, she is currently pursuing a Master's Degree in "Occupation, Market Environment, Social

Politics and Social Services". During the academic years 2007-2008 and 2008-2009 she is acting as a tutor on a course (Criminology 3) within the context of a 3-year degree in "Sociology and Criminal Sciences for Security" at Bologna University.

**Rosaria Romano** graduated in arts, majoring in philosophy and psychology at the Naples University, Federico II, where she has worked in Philosophy of Education department as a lecturer and researcher. She later won a master's scholarship at the Milano Politecnico to qualify as an EPeL (master in e-learning processes and course design), and went on to work for a number of universities, both giving and designing on-line courses. She also works as a gestalt counselor and with youth at risk, in particular she has worked in the highest risk areas of the Neapolitan hinterland, in juvenile delinquency rehabilitation programs , reintegrating young offenders into mainstream society. Currently she is researching into questions of social unease, and phenomena of criminality and of deviance.

**Daniela Ronco** is a Ph.D. student in Philosophy of Law and Sociology of Law at the University of Turin, Italy. Since 2005 she collaborates to the Sociology of Law professorship, Faculty of Law, University of Turin. Since 2003 she's engaged in the didactic support to the university centre for detained students of Turin prison, in co-operation with the Faculty of Political Science. She's the co-ordinator of the National Observatory about Prison Conditions carried out by *Associazione Antigone* and she's member of the editorial committee of the Italian Review "Antigone. Quadrimestrale di critica del sistema penale e penitenziario".

**Sandra Sicurella** has a bachelor's degree in Sociology, obtained at the faculty of Sociology at the University of Urbino "Carlo Bo" (Italy), on the 2.07.2003. Thesis in cultural anthropology: "Outside the borders. The foreigner' s role in setting–up social identities". She has M.A in applied Criminology for investigations and security (Capis), obtained at the Faculty of Political Sciences "Roberto Ruffilli" in Forlì (Italy), on the 20.09.2005. Thesis in applied criminology a: "Proximity police and centres for victims' assistance: case study of the situation in Forlì". She has finished her 3rd year of Ph.D. in Criminology at the University "Alma Mater Studiorum" in Bologna (thesis in criminology: "Victimization and walk of life: a challenge for the institutions") and she has obtained one year contract research at the University of Bologna "Alma Mater Studiorum", Department of Sociology.

**Christina Zarafonitou** is Professor of Criminology at the Panteion University in Athens (Greece).

She is the author of five monographies, and of many criminological articles published in Greek and European Journals of Criminology and Collective books. Editor of five collective books and scientific responsible of several research studies. She is a member of the International Society of Criminology, the European Society of Criminology, the International Society of Criminologist of French Language, the Hellenic Society of Criminology (Scientific Committee). Her main research interests are in urban criminology, fear of crime/insecurity, victimisation's surveys, local crime prevention, empirical Criminology, punitiveness, social representations about crime and criminal justice, police-public relationships, drugs.

**Diana Ziegleder** has a Diploma in Sociology (LMU Munich, Germany) and a Master in the Sociology of Law (IISL Onati, Spain). Since 2007 she is research associate and lecturer at the Ruhr-University Bochum (Germany) working in research, organisation (M.A. program) and teaching. Before she worked as research assistant at the MLU Halle-Wittenberg (Germany) in a project on economic crime. She has several years of empirical research experience and published on topics around criminology, police science and sociology of law.

# Index